Recasting the Ruhr, 1945–1958

Mark Roseman

In 1945 Ruhr pits faced enormous gaps in the workforce as a result of wartime losses and pre-war difficulties in recruiting young labour. Regenerating the workforce was the key to reviving Ruhr coal production and thus to German and Western European economic recovery. Using archival materials, private papers, contemporary printed sources and interviews. Recasting the Ruhr analyses the measures undertaken to win new labour for the Ruhr and the attempts to turn the newcomers into productive and settled miners. In so doing the book contributes to our understanding of a number of different features of the reconstruction, notably the origins and limitations of the 'economic miracle', the impact of and response to the enormous population mobility after the war and the nature of post-war industrial relations.

Mark Roseman is Lecturer in History at the University of Keele.

Recasting the Ruhr, 1945–1958

Manpower, Economic Recovery and Labour Relations

Mark Roseman

BERG

New York / Oxford

Distributed exclusively in the US and Canada by
St Martin's Press, New York

First published in 1992 by
Berg Publishers Limited
Editorial offices:
165 Taber Avenue, Providence, RI 02906, USA
150 Cowley Road, Oxford, OX4 1JJ, UK

Library of Congress Cataloging-in-Publication Data
Roseman, Mark.
    Recasting the Ruhr, 1945–1958 : manpower, economic recovery,
and labour relations / Mark Roseman.
        p.   cm.
    Includes bibliographical references (p.   ) and index.
    ISBN 0–85496–608–4
    1. Manpower policy—Germany—Ruhr Region.   2. Industrial
relations—Germany—Ruhr Region.   3. Ruhr Region—Economic
conditions.   I. Title.
HD5780.R82R67   1992
331'.0943'55—dc20   91–37299
                                                                              CIP

British Library Cataloguing in Publication Data
Roseman, Mark
    Recasting the Ruhr, 1945–1958: Manpower, economic
    recovery and labour relations.
    I. Title
    338.20943

    ISBN 0–85496–606–4

Printed in Great Britain by
Billing and Sons Ltd, Worcester

Contents

Contents

List of Tables and Figures

Tables

Figures

List of Tables and Figures

Acknowledgements

So many people and institutions have helped me in the course of writing this book that I would like to have produced the acknowledgements as a separate volume, divided into chapters. I know that my publishers, indulgent and helpful though they have been, would have balked at this. So let me begin by thanking all those who could not be named individually here, but who know how much they have helped me.

Among those who must be named are the patrons of the book, notably the then SSRC, which financed my initial two years as a research student, the Deutscher Akademischer Austauschdienst, the Leverhulme Trust and the German Historical Institute, London, all of whom gave me generous grants to study in Germany. Special thanks go to Jane Bennett of the Leverhulme Trust and Dr Bernd Weisbrod and Dr Gerhard Hirschfeld of the GHIL for their kindness and support.

Alongside the state and municipal archives who made papers available, I would particularly like to thank the representatives of the private bodies which gave me access to their collections: Dr Evelyn Kroker for the Bergbau-Archiv, Professor Dascha for the Westfälisches Wirtschaftsarchiv, the Bischöflicher Generalvikar of Münster and Dr Löffler for the Bistumsarchiv, Münster, Manfred Waarda and Norbert Ranft for the Industriegewerkschaft Bergbau und Energie, Herr Ganzen for the Landesoberbergamt, Dortmund, Dr Gierhardt for the Gesamtverband des deutschen Steinkohlenbergbaus, Herr Schroeder and Herr Bonhoeffer for permission to use papers at the Gneisenau colliery, Herr Fronz and Herr Kriener for the Westfälische Berggewerkschaftskasse, Dr Uli Borsdorf and Dr Dieter Schuster for the Deutscher Gewerkschaftsbund, Herr Franz for the Sozialforschungsstelle, Dortmund and Dr Werner Krause for the Friedrich-Ebert-Stiftung. Henry Collins CBE, Wolfgang Gottschalk,

Dr Ernst Schmidt and Dr Heinz Steffen kindly allowed me to see papers in their private possession. Special thanks go to Herr Marcus of the Statistik der Kohlenwirtschaft eV, Norbert Ranft of the IGBE, Dr Romeyk of the Hauptstadtsarchiv, Düsseldorf, and Dr Unverferth of the Westfälisches Wirtschaftsarchiv, all of whom put their considerable knowledge at my disposal, and to the staff of the Bergbau-Bücherei, Essen-Kray.

In addition, the study benefited substantially from interviews with a number of present and former officials, managers, trade unionists, works councillors and miners. I cannot name all of them here but special thanks must be given to Henry Collins CBE, the former head of the North German Coal Control and later NCB director who as well as supplying many invaluable insights also commented on an early draft of the manuscript, and the late Dr Heinz Steffen, who as former personnel director at the Hamborner Bergwerks AG gave me a great deal of valuable information about the industry. To supplement my own interviews, the LUSIR ('Lebensgeschichte und Sozialkultur im Ruhrgebiet zwischen 1930 und 1960') group in Essen and Michael Zimmermann kindly gave me access to their interview transcripts. I am grateful also to Dr Gierhardt and Herr Arndt for organising a tour of the Friedrich Heinrich colliery.

Research in a foreign country is always difficult initially, but in my case the support received from colleagues at the Ruhr universities took a lot of the pain out of the process. Professor Lutz Niethammer deserves special thanks for his hospitality and for introducing me to the members of the Essen-based LUSIR group, from whom I profited greatly. Professor Werner Abelshauser played the same role in Bochum and has consistently given a great deal of support, encouragement and generous hospitality over the years. The influence of his work is apparent in many sections of the book. Professor Dietmar Petzina, Professor Karl Rohe and Professor Klaus Tenfelde also deserve thanks. To my colleagues Werner Milert, Dr Detlev Peukert (who has since tragically died), Dr Falk Wiesemann and Dr Michael Zimmermann I am greatly indebted. Thanks too, for reasons they all know best, to Heidi Endler, Heike Hogreve, Theo and Gabi Horstmann, Gabi Musebrink, Eva-Maria Peine and Benno and Aron Reicher.

Closer to home, I am indebted to Professor Ian Kershaw, Dr Anthony Nicholls, Professor Willy Patterson and Dr Ian

Turner for comments on various versions of the manuscript and to Dr Christian Kunz, David Laven and my mother, Joan Roseman, for valuable stylistic advice. In addition, I would like to thank Dr Graham Cooper and Dr John Gaffney for their help and advice.

My biggest debt is to Professor Volker Berghahn, the supervisor of the thesis on which this book is based. It is hard to conceive of a supervisor more supportive than he. If I can be one tenth as helpful to my students as he has been to me, they will be doing very well.

This book is dedicated to the most interesting new minors of all, Jacob, Abigail and Kate, and to Sarah, in continuing love and friendship.

M.R.

List of Abbreviations

AA/AÄ	Arbeitsamt/Arbeitsämter
AA Do	Arbeitsamt Dortmund
AAA	Arbeitseinsatz- und Ausbildungsausschuß der DKBL [later UVR]
Arb.aus.f.A	Arbeitsausschuß für Ausbildungsfragen
ABB	Außenstelle Bergbau des Landesarbeitsamtes NRW
ASD-FESt	Archiv der Sozialdemokratie-Friedrich-Ebert-Stiftung, Bonn
AZG	Archive of the Zeche Gneisenau, Dortmund
BA	Bergamt
BAK	Bundesarchiv, Koblenz
BAM	Bundesarbeitsministerium
BAVAV	Bundesanstalt für Arbeitsvermittlung und Arbeitslosenversicherung
BAWBG	Gesetz zur Förderung des Bergarbeiterwohnungsbaues im Kohlenbergbau
BBA	Bergbau Archiv, Bochum
BECG	Bipartite Economic Control Group
BFM	Bundesfinanzministerium
BGBL	*Bundesgesetzblatt*
BICO	Bipartite Control Office
BM	Bistumsarchiv, Münster
BWiM	Bundeswirtschaftsministerium
BWoM	Bundesministerium für Wohnungsbau
CCCG	Combined Coal Control Group [successor to UK/USCCG]
CCG(BE)	Control Commission for Germany (British Element)

CDU	Christlich-Demokratische Union
CO	Control Office
COCOM	Coal Committee of the Bipartite Control Office
COPROD	Coal Production Committee [precursor of COCOM]
DGB/DGBA	Deutscher Gewerkschaftsbund/Archive of the DGB, Düsseldorf
DHS	Deutsche Hauptstelle für die Bekämpfung der Suchtgefahren
DKBL	Deutsche Kohlenbergbauleitung
d.u.	dwelling unit
ECA	European Co-operation Administration [later MSA]
ECOSC	Economic Subcommission
EGKS	European Coal and Steel Community
EIPS	Economic and Industrial Planning Staff
ERP	European Recovery Programme
FO	Foreign Office
GBAG	Gelsenkirchener Bergwerks AG
Ges.Verb.	Archive of the Gesamtverband des deutschen Steinkohlenbergbaus, Essen
GHH	Gutehoffnungshütte
GMSO	German Mines Supplies Organisation
HAfSH	Hauptamt für Sofort-Hilfe
HStAD	Hauptstaatsarchiv Düsseldorf
HStAD Kalkum	Hauptstaatsarchiv Düsseldorf, Zweigstelle Kalkum
IGB/IGBEA	Industriegewerkschaft Bergbau/Archive of the Industriegewerkschaft Bergbau und Energie, Bochum
IHG	Investitions-Hilfegesetz
IVB	Industrieverband Bergbau [later IGB]
JHStW PV	Jugendheimstättenwerk Pestalozzi-Vereinigung eV
KAB	Katholische Arbeiterbewegung
KfSA	Kommission für Soziale Aufgaben
KPD	Kommunistische Partei Deutschlands
LAA	Landesarbeitsamt
MBl-NRW	Ministerialblatt für das Land Nordrhein-Westfalen

MIC	Mines Inspection Control
MSA	Mutual Security Agency
NBB	Bestimmungen über die Förderung des Wohnungsneubaues (Kleinwohnungen und Kleinsiedlungen) im Lande Nordrhein-Westfalen
NGCC	North German Coal Control
NRW	Nordrhein-Westfalen
OBAD/	Oberbergamt Dortmund/Archive of the
OBADA	Landesobergergamt, Dortmund
OMGUS	Office of Military Government US
PA	Parlamentsarchiv, Bonn
PORO	Public Opinion Research Organisation, Political Division, CCG(BE)
PRO	Public Record Office, Kew
RAG	Revierarbeitsgemeinschaft für die kulturelle Bergmannsbetreuung
RCD	Ruhr Coal District
RWKS	Rheinisch-Westfälisches Kohlensyndikat
SBZ	Sovietische Besatzungszone
SoFoSt/	Sozialforschungsstelle, Dortmund/
SoFoStA	Archive of the SoFoSt
Soz.Min.	Sozialministerium NRW
SPD	Sozialdemokratische Partei Deutschlands
StAM	Staatsarchiv Münster
StdKW	Statistik der Kohlenwirtschaft eV
SVR	Siedlungsverband Ruhrkohlenbezirk
UK/USCCG	UK/US Coal Control Group
UVR	Unternehmensverband Ruhrbergbau
VfF	Verwaltung für Finanzen
VfW	Verwaltung für Wirtschaft
VfZ	*Vierteljahreshefte für Zeitgeschichte*
VOB	Verein oberer Bergbeamten
VSt	Vereinigte Stahlwerke
VWG	Vereinigtes Wirtschaftsgebiet
WAM	Wiederaufbauministerium NRW
WAZ	*Westdeutsche Allgemeine Zeitung*
WBK/WBKA	Westfälische Berggewerkschaftskasse/ Archive of the WBK, Bochum
WBSR	Wohnungsbezirksstelle Ruhr of the WAM

WWA	Westfälisches Wirtschaftsarchiv, Dortmund
ZAA	Zentralamt für Arbeit
ZdKW	*Zahlen der Kohlenwirtschaft* (DKBL)
ZfW	Zentralamt für Wirtschaft

Introduction

At the end of the Second World War, when the Allies liberated
the foreign conscripts with whom the Germans had maintained
their war effort, the Ruhr pits faced enormous gaps in their
workforces. Intense competition for labour in the overheated
economy of the 1930s, military call-up in wartime and losses on
the battlefield had all taken their toll. Many of the miners
remaining in 1945 were old or in poor health or both. The result
was a pressing need to recruit and integrate new labour. Between the end of the war in 1945 and the onset of the coal crisis
in 1958 the Ruhr mines were to hire over a million men. This
book is about rebuilding the colliery workforces, about the
measures undertaken to win new labour for the Ruhr and the
attempt to turn the newcomers into productive and settled
miners.

Manpower, Economic Strategy and German Recovery

It is barely an exaggeration to say that in 1945 the key, not just to
German recovery, but to the prosperity of Western Europe, lay
in getting manpower to the Ruhr mines. In the scarcities of the
post-war era, Ruhr coal was the lifeblood of the West European
economies. And the key to producing more coal was finding
new faces for the coalface. For ten years or more, the struggle to
meet the mines' manpower needs was to exert a profound
influence on German economic life. True, in 1947/8, coal lost its
claim to be *the* overriding obstacle to economic progress; and
within the mining industry, progress in output and efficiency
ceased to rest so exclusively on the shoulders of new labour as
mechanisation became a priority. Yet in 1950, when coal shortages again put the lights out all over Germany, this was in no

1

small part due to a failure to enlarge and stabilise the workforce. Even in 1955, economic observers were concerned that growth might be imperilled by the shortfall of underground labour in the Ruhr.

Rebuilding the workforce thus proved to be not only a vital task but also an immensely challenging one. It was a measure of British difficulties in the Ruhr during 1946 that Ernest Bevin personally received a weekly update of the mines' labour situation. Ten years later, the cabinets in Düsseldorf and Bonn were *still* debating how best to secure a stable workforce for the mines. The challenges thrown up by coal exposed important weaknesses and contradictions in the economic strategy both of the Allies and later of the German government. Governments and administrations were forced to think again and to revise basic tenets of their recovery programmes.

At no point were the urgency and difficulty of finding new labour for the Ruhr mines more in evidence than in the years of direct British control, 1945–6. The British, in whose Zone the Ruhr coalfield fell, were under a three-fold pressure to increase Ruhr coal production. To prevent starvation of the Germans in their Zone, it was vital to get the zonal economy working again and that meant producing more coal. Similarly, the pressure to reduce the burden of occupation costs on the British taxpayer meant that the German economy had to be made more self-sufficient. That, too, was predicated on producing more coal. Finally, the UK was under immense pressure from its Allies to export Ruhr coal, which was seen as a European resource under British custodianship. In August 1945, the UK government acceded to a request that it export 25 million tons of coal by April 1946. Getting more coal out of the Ruhr was therefore the British top priority.

Yet what this study, in particular chapter 1, will reveal is the military government's astonishing inability to meet the demand for coal. Between January and October 1946, despite the most strenuous efforts, workforce and output barely grew. Not only did military government fail to increase the number of miners, it allowed the productivity of the established workforce to fall disastrously. The problem of rebuilding the workforce thus became inextricably intertwined with the additional problem of reviving the established workforce's efficiency. The implications of all this for the German economy, for West European recovery

and for Britain's standing in relation to both the Germans and
the Allies were extremely grave and, in the end, were to contribute to forcing major changes in British policy.

How does this work relate to the existing historiography on
the British Occupation? Though many writers have made clear
the importance of Ruhr coal in British thinking and in its dealing
with the other Allies, there has not been a study of Britain's
management of coal production. A lot of the analysis here is
therefore covering new ground. It does, however, connect with
two broader debates about the character of the British Occupation.

The first concerns Britain's commitment to German recovery
and its efficiency as an administrator. In both popular perception and academic writing, Britain's role as an occupying power
has often been seen rather negatively in West Germany. From
early on in the post-war period, West German public opinion
tended, in so far as it attributed German revival to outside
influences at all, to see the Americans, not the British, as the
main sources of positive initiatives towards reconstruction. The
British were felt to be decent individuals, but muddled and
incompetent. Within the mining industry itself, there were
plenty of managers who saw the British in this light; given the
results outlined above, this is perhaps hardly surprising.
Another view widely held both at the popular level and among
German academics is that considerations of commercial self-
interest constrained Britain's commitment to German recovery,
and indeed were often more influential in determining British
policy generally than the higher principles to which the British
professed to adhere.[1] In so far as it has received serious analysis,
Britain's coal policy itself has been seen as an example of this
tendency. Werner Milert has argued that the shortcomings of
Britain's approach derived in part from a fear of future competition from the mines. Falk Pingel takes a slightly different line.
His argument is not that coal production was held back by

1. A contemporary and contemptuous view of the British from within the
mining industry can be found in the chapters on the occupation period in Paul
Breder, *Geschichten vor Ort. Erinnerungen eines Bergmanns*, Essen, 1979. On
German attitudes generally, see Barbara Marshall, 'German attitudes to British
Military Government 1945–1947', *Journal of Contemporary History*, vol. 15, no. 4,
1980, pp. 655–84; Josef Foschepoth, 'Zur deutschen Reaktion auf Niederlage und
Besatzung', in Ludolf Herbst (ed.), *Westdeutschland 1945–1955*, Munich, 1986,
pp. 151ff.; Christoph Buchheim, *Die Wiedereingliederung Westdeutschlands in die
Weltwirtschaft 1945–1958*, Munich, 1990, pp. 23–4.

Introduction

commercial fears, but rather that mining was allowed to grow faster than other German industries because it was in Britain's self-interest (in this case diplomatic, rather than commercial) that it should do so.[2] More recently this view has been challenged, as a growing number of British scholars have alighted on the subject of the British Occupation. They have been able to benefit from recently released British Control Commission files which make clear the distinctiveness of British as against US policy in the early post-war period. As a result some scholars, most notably Ian Turner, have argued that of all the Western occupying powers, Britain initially was the one most favourably disposed towards some sort of German economic recovery.[3]

In line with this recent work, the present book takes a somewhat more generous view of British intentions and ability. First, Britain's problems in the mines had little to do with fears of future competition from German coal. From the start of the occupation, British coal policy took for granted that the long-term recovery of Germany's mining industry should be encouraged. Secondly, while Pingel's analysis is not wrong it misses a crucial point: that despite Britain's enormous interest in getting the coal, it very largely failed to do so, at least until towards the end of 1946. Thirdly, it will be argued that the reason for Britain's failure was not incompetence, unless incompetence is extended to mean unwillingness at a high level to make some extremely painful choices. Britain found itself in a complex web of conflicting diplomatic, political and economic priorities which prevented it from providing the control or the resources required. As chapter 2 will demonstrate, the British government

2. Werner Milert, 'Die verschenkte Kontrolle. Bestimmungsgründe und Grundzüge der britischen Kohlenpolitik im Ruhrbergbau 1945–1948', in Dietmar Petzina and Walter Euchner (eds), *Wirtschaftspolitik im britischen Besatzungsgebiet 1945–1949*, Düsseldorf, 1984, pp. 105–120; Falk Pingel, 'Der aufhaltsame Aufschwung. Die Wirtschaftsplanung für die britische Zone im Rahmen der außenpolitischen Interessen der Besatzungsmacht', in Petzina and Euchner (eds), *Wirtschaftspolitik*, pp. 41–64.
3. Ian Turner, 'British Policy towards German Industry 1945–9: Reconstruction, Restriction or Exploitation?', in Ian Turner (ed.), *Reconstruction in Post-war Germany: British Occupation Policy and the Western Zones 1945–1955*, Oxford, 1989, pp. 67–92; Ian Turner, '"Being beastly to the Germans?" British Policy on Direct Imports of German Goods from the British Zone of Occupation to the UK 1946–1948', *Journal of European Economic History*, forthcoming; Buchheim, *Wiedereingliederung*, pp. 21ff.

4

was able to disentangle itself from this web only once fundamental changes in its overall foreign policy had been made.

This reference to a change of overall policy brings us to a second debate about the British Occupation. Whatever their views on Britain's priorities or abilities, most historians agree that the British Zone ran into a profound economic and financial crisis in the spring and summer of 1946. Most also agree that in the course of 1946 British officials sought some sort of major diplomatic realignment and a new course on Germany, a search which found its most tangible result in the decision to create UK/US bizonal agencies in September 1946 and to fuse the US and UK zones in 1947.[4] There is less agreement on the precise timing, nature and causes of this realignment. While it is obvious that the zonal economic crisis played a major role, some authors, most recently Anne Deighton, argue that the search for a new policy was prompted above all by fear of the Soviets. To combat the Soviets required a healthy Germany and a strong Western coalition and thus a break from the restrictive quadripartite framework of Potsdam. Indeed, some writers see the British as the first cold warriors, trying to wake the US up to the threat from the East.[5] On the other hand, historians such as Donald Watt and John Farquharson perceive such ideological and security issues as secondary and argue that the drain on British resources and the threat of total economic collapse in the British Zone were the prime stimuli to finding a new policy.[6]

Though it makes no attempt directly to analyse British

---

4. See the collection of essays edited by Turner, *Reconstruction in Post-war Germany.*; Buchheim, *Wiedereingliederung*, pp. 21–4; Anne Deighton, *The Impossible Peace: Britain, the Division of Germany and the Origins of the Cold War*, Oxford, 1990, p. 56.

5. Deighton, *The Impossible Peace*; Falk Pingel, '"Die Russen am Rhein"? Zur Wende der britischen Besatzungspolitik im Frühjahr 1946', *VfZ*, vol. 30, no. 1, 1982, pp. 98–116; Rolf Steininger, 'Westdeutschland ein "Bollwerk gegen den Kommunismus"? Grossbritannien und die deutsche Frage im Frühjahr 1946', *Militärgeschichtliche Mitteilungen*, vol. 35, no. 2, 1985, pp. 163–207; Sean Greenwood, 'Bevin, the Ruhr and the Division of Germany: August 1945–December 1946', *Historical Journal*, vol. 29, no. 1, 1986, pp. 203–12.

6. Donald C. Watt, 'Hauptprobleme der britischen Deutschlandpolitik 1945–1949', in Claus Scharf and Hans Jürgen Schröder (eds), *Die Deutschlandpolitik Großbritanniens und die britische Zone 1945–1949*, Wiesbaden, 1979, pp. 15–28; Robert W. Carden, 'Before Bizonia: Britain's Economic Dilemma in Germany 1945–1946', *Journal of Contemporary History*, vol. 14, no. 3, 1979, pp. 535–55; John E. Farquharson, *The Western Allies and the Politics of Food: Agrarian Management in Post-war Germany*, Leamington Spa/New York, 1985.

diplomacy, this book aims to contribute to the debate on a number of levels. By uncovering both the dimensions and the causes of the coal failure, it helps to identify the nature of the crisis in which the British found themselves in 1946. The failure to produce more Ruhr coal was so serious, and the causes of that failure so far-reaching, as of themselves to warrant major changes in Occupation policy. In other words, the book suggests that economic issues may well have been at least as influential as ideological ones in forcing the diplomats and policy-makers into action in 1946. Yet coal was not just an economic problem. This book will try to show that Britain's difficulties in the Ruhr were closely linked to its diplomatic commitments towards France. Britain, unsure of the US position, wary of the Soviets, was keen to remain in close alliance with the French. The glue that held this alliance together was ample exports of Ruhr coal to France. Yet the British came to recognise that Ruhr coal production could be increased, and Germany made more self-sufficient, only if exports were reduced and more coal ploughed back into the German economy. Thus Britain faced the agonising choice of imperilling German recovery or alienating its neighbour across the Channel. By moving into a closer alliance with the United States, Britain freed itself from dependence on France and thus gave itself the diplomatic freedom of manoeuvre to cut coal exports – a decision it took in September 1946. The evidence provided here, therefore, suggests that Britain's new policy was directed as much at Paris as at Moscow.

It is already evident that the British difficulties in the Ruhr, and their eventual partial resolution, bear on our understanding not just of British Occupation policy, but also of Germany's economic recovery. The importance of the progress made in the Ruhr in autumn and winter 1946 was first identified by Werner Abelshauser in his seminal 1975 study of German economic recovery.[7] Abelshauser overturned orthodoxies unchallenged in West Germany since Ludwig Erhard first propagated them at

---

7. Werner Abelshauser, *Wirtschaft in Westdeutschland 1945–1948. Rekonstruktion und Wachstumsbedingungen in der amerikanischen und britischen Zone*, Stuttgart, 1975. See also, by the same author, 'Probleme des Wiederaufbaus der westdeutschen Wirtschaft 1945–1953', in Heinrich August Winkler (ed.), *Politische Weichenstellungen in Nachkriegsdeutschland 1945–1953*, Göttingen, 1979, pp. 208–53 and *Wirtschaftsgeschichte der Bundesrepublik Deutschland 1945–1980*, Frankfurt, 1983.

the end of the 1940s. The orthodox view was that the recovery began in summer 1948 with the reinstatement of a largely liberalised market economy, the creation of a new currency and the adoption of a bundle of tax measures designed to encourage entrepreneurial initiative. The pre-currency-reform period was generally portrayed as a period of restrictive Allied policy, inefficiency and shortages. By contrast, Abelshauser suggested that the seeds of economic recovery were sown long before the currency reform and indeed that the first fruits of growth were reaped as early as autumn 1947. The conventional contrast between ineffective controlled economy and successful market economy was thus presented with a serious challenge. After a lengthy delay, Abelshauser's view has triggered a counter-reaction and there is now considerable debate about the degree to which growth and effective economic management were possible in the pre-currency-reform era.[8]

In the present study, an attempt has been made to reach some sort of synthesis. On the one hand, Abelshauser's analysis of the important progress made in coal in autumn 1946 is fully borne out here; yet on the other, chapters 2 and 3 aim to swing the pendulum back a little and reintroduce a little chaos into the historiography of the pre-currency-reform period! In particular they show just how fragile were the results achieved in the mines and how inefficient and wasteful the policies adopted. In many respects, the economy of the Occupation years could be termed an *un*controlled economy, with the conventional short-comings of controls and planning being exacerbated by the tensions and problems of an occupied country.[9]

Where I fully concur with the analysis of Abelshauser and also

8. For a critical response to Abelshauser's work, see Albert Ritschl, 'Die Währungsreform von 1948 und der Wiederaufstieg der deutschen Wirtschaft', in *VfZ*, vol. 33, no. 1, 1985, pp. 136–65; Werner Abelshauser, 'Schopenhauer's Gesetz und die Währungsreform', *VfZ*, vol. 33, no. 1, 1985, pp. 214–18; Bernd Klemm and Günter Trittel, 'Vor dem "Wirtschaftswunder": Durchbruch zum Wachstum oder Lähmungskrise? Eine Auseinandersetzung mit Werner Abelshausers Interpretation der Wirtschaftsentwicklung 1945–1948', *VfZ*, vol. 35, no. 4, 1987, pp. 571–624; Christoph Buchheim, 'Die Währungsreform 1948 in Westdeutschland', *VfZ*, vol. 36, no. 2, 1988, pp. 189–231; Wendy Carlin, 'Economic Reconstruction in Western Germany, 1945–55: The Displacement of "vegetative control"', in Turner, *Reconstruction in Post-war Germany*, pp. 37–66.
9. Apart from Abelshauser, other authors who have emphasised the successes achieved in coal include Pingel, 'Der aufhaltsame Aufschwung', p. 46.

of Adamsen, however, is in arguing that the currency reform, though it eliminated many of the difficulties noted above, was far from solving the industry's problems. Erhard's social market economy was not quite what it seemed. For a start it was by no means a full market economy. A number of key prices – transport, energy, housing, to name but a few – remained subject to official controls. Yet Erhard was loath to accept the implications of this fact for national policy. His distaste for planning and state investment meant that for years heavy industry faced serious capital shortages – shortages so severe that for a while they threatened to undermine the whole recovery programme.[10]

Chapter 4 shows that the expansion and stabilisation of the Ruhr labour force were critically retarded by a lack of finance for house-building. Despite being repeatedly reminded of the problems in the Ruhr, the Federal government resolutely refused to abandon its non-interventionism. In the end, however, it was forced to do so, above all because the outbreak of the Korean war led to an intensification of American pressure for a new policy. But even after the capital shortages had been overcome, the mines' growing inability to retain labour and compete on the labour market continued to expose the shortcomings of Erhard's approach to coal. Coal-mining found itself consigned to an increasingly cinderella-like role in the German economy and in the labour market, with the rotund Erhard unwilling to be cast in the figure of the handsome prince.

New Labour, Social Engineering and Labour Relations

As well as being a question of resource management, regenerating the workforce was also very much an issue for social policy and labour relations. These aspects are the focus of the second half of the book (chapters 5–9). Particularly after 1948, when the demand for coal abated somewhat and the Allies relinquished a lot of their direct control, colliery managements were faced with

10. See Abelshauser, *Wirtschaftsgeschichte*, pp. 65ff, and 'Ansätze "korporativer Marktwirtschaft" in der Korea-Krise der frühen fünfziger Jahre. Ein Briefwechsel zwischen dem Hohen Kommissar John McCloy und Bundeskanzler Konrad Adenauer', *VfZ*, vol. 30, no. 4, 1982, pp. 715–56; Heiner R. Adamsen, *Investitionshilfe für die Ruhr. Wiederaufbau, Verbände und soziale Marktwirtschaft 1948–1952*, Wuppertal, 1981.

the challenge of creating a new, stable and productive work-force. Other organisations, too, had an interest in influencing the way in which new labour was drawn and integrated into the mining community. For the mining union, an influx of labour on this scale could not but raise vital issues of payment, job se-curity, workforce cohesion, the political affiliation of the new-comers and much more.

Chapters 5–7 reveal the sometimes quite dramatic ways in which employers and other organisations tried to settle new labour and influence its outlook. A new apprenticeship scheme was promoted and expanded, not to impart valuable technical skills but to fashion out of new young recruits a stable and co-operative workforce. Housing projects and cultural welfare schemes were adopted, less to provide a simple incentive than in the hope of moulding the personalities of the recipients. In short, ambitious schemes of social engineering were under way in the Ruhr. At the same time, as chapter 8 reveals, these measures contrasted markedly with the approach to the induc-tion and management of new labour in the production process.

The great efforts made to integrate and settle the newcomers were a sign that the post-war situation represented not only a challenge to the mines but also a special opportunity. For, grievous though the costs of war had been, mining's labour problems had a longer pedigree. The collieries had long experi-enced difficulties in attracting and retaining labour. Well before the war, the mines had accordingly begun to give thought about how to enhance mining's status, expand recruitment and create a loyal workforce. The post-war situation provided a unique opportunity to take advantage of a huge pool of mobile labour. Millions had been uprooted from their former jobs, among them refugees and expellees from the lost territories who had been cut off from their former homes, former soldiers, Nazis and em-ployees of war-related industries for whom there was no job to return to and the millions more who found that their established profession did not earn them enough to live on in the tough climate of the post-war years. The mining industry was thus given a special chance not just to make good its wartime losses, but to undo the ill effects of years of poor recruitment.

The effort and ingenuity expended on integrating the new-comers reveal also that employers and other groups came to see in new labour many issues of far wider significance. After all, for

West Germany's bourgeoisie, entering the post-war era after the collapse of the Third Reich was a very threatening and unnerving experience. To create a stable society, and to restore its inner tranquility, Germany's bourgeoisie faced three major social 'questions'. First, there was the classical *'soziale Frage'* itself, the class question, and many elements of Germany's bourgeoisie were aware that they had to find some new *modus vivendi* with labour. Secondly, there was the refugee question, the challenge of integrating and defusing the radical potential of the millions of homeless and dispossessed. Thirdly, there was the generational problem, of re-establishing the older generation's authority *vis-a-vis* a younger generation whose political attitudes were uncertain after the Nazi era. As a large group of young people, many of them dispossessed and uprooted, entering a profession, mining, whose members were often seen as the arch-embodiment of the proletariat, the new miners seemed to embody all three threats and invited consequently a broad and revealing array of attempts to integrate them.

Were the measures taken in the mines typical of Germany's response to new labour generally? Or, indeed, typical of German industry's labour and social policies as a whole? The difficulty in answering this question is that there have been virtually no historical studies of workforce rebuilding.[11] Industrial social policy in general during the 1940s and 1950s is almost virgin territory for the historian. German industrialists, too, remain in many cases shadowy figures. Volker Berghahn's pioneering study has not yet been followed by other analyses of Germany's industrial leaders.[12] Looking beyond the factory gates, there are

11. During the 1950s new labour did receive some attention from sociologists, particularly in Carl Jantke, *Bergmann und Zeche. Die sozialen Arbeitsverhältnisse einer Schachtanlage des nördlichen Ruhrgebietes in der Sicht der Bergleute*, Tübingen, 1953 and in Theo Pirker, S. Braun and B. Lutz, *Arbeiter, Management, Mitbestimmung, eine industriesoziologische Untersuchung der Struktur, der Organisation und des Verhaltens der Arbeiterbelegschaft in Werken der deutschen Eisen- und Stahlindustrie, für die das Mitbestimmungsgesetz gilt*, Stuttgart Düsseldorf 1955. The only historical study to deal with new labour is a short *Examensarbeit* at the University of Essen based on interviews with new miners: Ingrid Grundmann, 'Erfahrungen Essener Neubergleute. Untersuchungen zur Problematik Vertriebener im Ruhrgebiet nach dem Zweiten Weltkrieg', Hausarbeit für die erste Staatsprüfung für das Lehramt, Essen University, 1981.

12. Volker Berghahn, *The Americanization of German Industry 1945–1973*, Leamington Spa/New York, 1986. See also Kurt Pritzkoleit, *Männer, Mächte, Metropole. Hinter den Türen der westdeutschen Wirtschaft*, Düsseldorf, 1953; Karl H. Herchenroeder, *Neue Männer an der Ruhr*, Düsseldorf, 1958.

many aspects of regional and national social policy that are similarly unresearched.[13] Youth policy for instance, has still to find its chronicler.[14]

One closely related area of policy which has admittedly recently received a great deal of attention is the response to the expellees and refugees.[15] The many excellent studies in this area have provided valuable information and insights about the experiences, mentality, legal status and other characteristics of the large minority of the new miners (probably around a third of them) who were refugees.[16] However, they did not produce hypotheses pertinent to this study. This is partly because those

---

13. H.-V. Sons, *Gesundheitspolitik während der Besatzungszeit*, Wuppertal, 1983 and Hans Günter Hockerts, *Sozialpolitische Entscheidungen in Nachkriegsdeutschland. Alliierte und deutsche Sozialversicherungspolitik 1945 bis 1947*, Stuttgart, 1980 remain the pioneering works in the field.

14. See Ian Turner. 'Research on the British Occupation of Germany', in Turner, *Reconstruction in Post-war Germany*, pp. 327–58 at 356–7.

15. 'Expellees' were the former citizens of Germany's lost eastern territories, deprived of their former homeland; 'refugees' were Germans who fled from the Soviet Zone of Occupation, later the GDR. For the sake of convenience, 'refugee' is frequently used in the present study as a generic term for both groups; where the narrower definition is meant, this is made clear in the text.

16. A useful survey of contemporary refugee studies can be found in Peter Waldmann, 'Die Eingliederung der Vertriebenen in die westdeutsche Gesellschaft', in Josef Becker, Theo Stammen and Peter Waldmann (eds), *Vorgeschichte der BRD. Zwischen Kapitulation und Grundgesetz*, Munich, 1979, pp. 163–92 esp. 163–4. Among the most important of contemporary studies was the three-volume collection by Eugen Lemberg and Friedrich Edding (eds), *Die Vertriebenen in Westdeutschland. Ihre Eingliederung und Ihr Einfluß auf Gesellschaft, Wirtschaft, Politik und Geistesleben*, Kiel, 1959. See also Elisabeth Pfeil's studies, *Der Flüchtling: Gestalt einer Zeitwende*, Hamburg, 1948 and *Fünf Jahre später. Die Eingliederung der Heimatvertriebenen in Bayern bis 1950*, Frankfurt/Main, 1951. Of interest for the Ruhr region is Gertrud Stahlberg, *Die Vertriebenen in Nordrhein-Westfalen*, Berlin, 1957. A review of *historical* research on the refugee question can be found in Hellmuth Auerbach, 'Literatur zum Thema. Ein kritischer Überblick', in Wolfgang Benz (ed.), *Die Vertreibung der Deutschen aus dem Osten. Ursachen, Ereignisse, Folgen*, Frankfurt/Main, 1985, pp. 219–31. For collections of the most recent research, see Rainer Schulze, Doris von der Brelie-Lewin and Helga Grebing (eds), *Flüchtlinge und Vertriebene in der westdeutschen Nachkriegsgeschichte. Bilanzierung der Forschung und Perspektiven für die künftige Forschungsarbeit*, Hildesheim, 1987, and Klaus J. Bade (ed.), *Neue Heimat im Westen. Vertriebene, Flüchtlinge, Aussiedler*, Münster, 1990. Of particular interest for the Ruhr are Falk Wiesemann, 'Flüchtlingspolitik in Nordrhein-Westfalen', in Benz, *Die Vertreibung*, pp. 173–82; Falk Wiesemann and Uwe Kleinert, 'Flüchtlinge und wirtschaftlicher Wiederaufbau in der britischen Besatzungszone', in Petzina and Euchner, *Wirtschaftspolitik*, pp. 297–326; Uwe Kleinert, *Flüchtlinge und Wirtschaft in Nordrhein-Westfalen 1945–1961. Arbeitsmarkt–Gewerbe–Staat*, Düsseldorf, 1988; and Uwe Kleinert, 'Die Flüchtlinge als Arbeitskräfte – zur Eingliederung der Flüchtlinge in Nordrhein-Westfalen nach 1945', in Bade, *Neue Heimat*, pp. 37–60.

aspects of refugee policy which most overlap with issues raised by the new miners tend to be the ones least well researched by historians.[17] But the main point is that refugee policy tended to leave off where industrial new labour policy began. Once the refugee had been secured employment and a place to stay, the primary task of those who were responsible for refugee integration had been solved; the task of the employers to mould and integrate the newcomer, on the other hand, had only just begun.

In at least one respect, looking at new labour is a valuable complement to refugee analyses. Because the refugees constituted the overwhelming majority of newcomers entering Western Germany, studies on refugee policy often assume, or convey the impression, that the refugees were the only significant mobile group *within* Western Germany. Yet, as even a cursory survey of the origins of the mining industry's post-war intake indicates, the refugees were joined by a great many other groups displaced from their former homes or occupations or both. For the North-Rhine-Westphalian economy as a whole, refugees accounted for only half the growth in employment in the period 1946–9 and somewhat less in the subsequent years up to 1953. Certainly in areas like the Ruhr, the response to and impact of the refugees can not be understood without looking at the other movement going on around them.[18]

Another limitation to many refugee studies which the present book has tried to remedy is that they have taken too little account of social change. In the first place, they have seen the refugees as objects of policy rather than agents of change. They have operated with a static model of integration, whereby the host society is seen as a fixed unchanging quantity. Only rarely, and over the last couple of years, has there been a recognition in the historiography that both the new arrivals *and* the established community had to adapt to each other. Secondly, they have failed to take account of the fact that almost all the institutions which responded to the new arrivals were themselves in a state of flux. In the case of mining, new labour entered an industry where, for example, the industry's structure – the legal relation-

17. It is only now, for example, that the social components of the official conception of 'integration' are coming under scrutiny. See Volker Ackermann, 'Integration: Begriff, Leitbilder, Probleme', in Bade, *Neue Heimat*, pp. 14–36.
18. Kleinert, *Flüchtlinge und Wirtschaft*, p. 25, table 2, and p. 32.

ship between mining companies, the form of the union movement, the nature and programmes of the political parties, the legal standing of the works councils – all these and many more institutional parameters were being reshaped and renegotiated.[19] The importance of these points becomes particularly apparent when we turn to the relationship between new labour and the labour movement and look at the newcomers' overall impact on the relations between capital and labour.

In some respects, the re-emergence of the labour movement has been the most exhaustively researched of all elements of West German reconstruction. It was one of the first topics West German historians looked at when post-war history began to be studied seriously in the late 1960s. Influenced by the critical reappraisal of the Federal Republic under way since the student revolt of the 1960s, many left-wing historians wanted to know why the German labour movement had been unable to prevent the restoration of a capitalist system. Many writers argued that the Social Democratic Party and the union leaders had betrayed the democratic ideal and the revolutionary potential of the rank and file. Though other authors have stressed the difficulties which labour leaders faced in the immediate post-war-years, such as the constraints imposed on them by the Allies, the notion that the labour movement was conservative and hesitant and failed to exploit the chances to create a democratic socialist society has continually recurred in the historiography.[20]

---

19. For a recent discussion, see Ackermann, 'Integration', pp. 23ff; Alexander von Plato, 'Fremde Heimat. Zur Integration von Flüchtlingen und Einheimischen in die Neue Zeit', in Lutz Niethammer and Alexander von Plato (eds), *"Wir kriegen jetzt andere Zeiten." Auf der Suche nach der Erfahrung des Volkes in nachfaschistischen Ländern*, Berlin, 1985, pp. 172–219.

20. For a powerful early expression of such a view, see Theo Pirker, *Die blinde Macht. Die Gewerkschaftsbewegung in Westdeutschland*, 2 vols, Munich 1960. For radical statements of the restoration thesis from the post-1968 generation, see Eberhard Schmidt, *Die verhinderte Neuordnung*, Frankfurt, 1970; U. Schmidt and T. Fichter, *Der erzwungene Kapitalismus*, Berlin, 1971; Autorenkollektiv (Ernst-Ulrich Huster, Gerhard Kraiker et al.), *Determinanten der westdeutschen Restauration 1945–1949*, Frankfurt/Main, 1972; Ernst-Ulrich Huster, *Die Politik der SPD 1945–1950*, Frankfurt/Main, 1978. The standard GDR work for many years was Gerhard Mannschatz and J. Seider, *Zum Kampf der KPD im Ruhrgebiet für die Einigung der Arbeiterklasse und die Entmachtung der Monopolherren 1945–1947*, Berlin GDR, 1962. For more recent works which continue to be highly critical of the union movement, this time in relation to the co-determination issue, see Horst Thum, *Mitbestimmung in der Montanindustrie. Der Mythos vom Sieg der Gewerkschaften*, Stuttgart, 1982; Gabriele Müller List, 'Die Entstehung der

13

This type of argument often depends on assumptions about the actual or potential radicalism of the mass of ordinary workers. Yet such assumptions have rarely been backed up by analysis of the real conditions facing the unions, of the behaviour and attitude of their members, the impact of labour market conditions and so forth. Only in the case of the early protest strikes and hunger marches has there been an attempt to link analysis of union behaviour with a more realistic appraisal of the rank and file.[21] Moreover, a great many studies of the labour movement have remained at the level of high politics, looking either at the political parties, or at the early struggles over institutional arrangements – for example over co-determination, the structure of the union movement or the fight to democratise the chambers of industry and commerce.[22] Aside from the great institutional battles, there have been few studies of individual unions or of day-to-day union activity. This is generally true for mining too, although a small number of excellent works have opened up the field.[23]

Montanmitbestimmung', in Walter Först (ed.), *Zwischen Ruhrkontrolle und Mitbestimmung*, Cologne, 1982, pp. 121–44.

21. Christoph Kleßmann and Peter Friedemann, *Streiks und Hungermärsche im Ruhrgebiet 1946–1948*, Frankfurt, 1977; Ulrich Borsdorf, 'Speck oder Sozialisierung. Produktionssteigerungskampagnen im Ruhrbergbau 1945–1947', in Hans Mommsen and Ulrich Borsdorf (eds), *Glückauf Kameraden! Die Bergarbeiter und ihre Organisationen in Deutschland*, Cologne, 1979, pp. 345–66.

22. In addition to the titles in note 20, see Ulrich Borsdorf, 'Der Weg zur Einheitsgewerkschaft', in Jürgen Reulecke (ed.), *Arbeiterbewegung an Rhein und Ruhr. Beiträge zur Geschichte der Arbeiterbewegung in Rheinland-Westfalen*, Wuppertal, 1974, pp. 385–414; Diethelm Prowe, 'Unternehmer, Gewerkschaften und Staat in der Kammerneuordnung in der britischen Besatzungszone bis 1950', in Petzina and Euchner, *Wirtschaftspolitik*, pp. 235–54; Werner Plumpe, 'Vom Plan zum Markt.' *Wirtschaftsverwaltung und Unternehmerverbände in der britischen Zone*, Düsseldorf, 1987; Rainer Schulze, *Unternehmerische Selbstverwaltung und Politik. Die Rolle der Industrie- und Handelskammern in Niedersachsen und Bremen als Vertretungen der Unternehmerinteressen nach dem Ende des Zweiten Weltkrieges*, Hildesheim, 1987; Rolf Steininger, 'England und die deutsche Gewerkschaftsbewegung 1945/1946', *Archiv für Sozialgeschichte*, vol. 18, 1978, pp. 41–118. For early union organisation in mining, see Norbert Brozio, *Gewerkschaftlicher Wiederaufbau im nördlichen Ruhrgebiet 1945–1947*, Münster, 1980.

23. Werner Abelshauser, *Der Ruhrkohlenbergbau seit 1945. Wiederaufbau, Krise, Anpassung*, Munich, 1984; Norbert Ranft, *Vom Objekt zum Subjekt. Montanmitbestimmung, Sozialklima und Strukturwandel im Bergbau seit 1945*, Cologne, 1988; Hans Eckbert Treu, *Stabilität und Wandel in der organisatorischen Entwicklung der Industriegewerkschaft Bergbau und Energie*, Frankfurt, 1979; Michael Clarke, 'Die Gewerkschaftpolitik der KPD 1945–1951, dargestellt am Beispiel des "Industrieverbandes Bergbau/Industriegewerkschaft Bergbau" im Ruhrgebiet', unpub-

One indication of the lack of empirical research on industrial relations is the fact that, while labour historians have frequently argued that a potentially radical rank and file was betrayed by the leadership, economic historians studying the economic miracle continue to assume the opposite: namely, that post-war Germany's huge population of migrant labour, particularly the refugees, acted as a 'reserve army', depressing wages and generally weakening organised labour's bargaining position![24] The point is not that these two interpretations of post-war labour history would be impossible to reconcile, but rather that the work has not been done which could establish to what degree either or both assumptions are true.

In this context, the mining industry is an interesting example to study. First, the pattern of industrial relations within mining had long exerted a powerful influence on the whole of Germany. It was heavy industrialists in the 1920s, for example, who effectively torpedoed the employers' hesitant *rapprochement* with the young republic. For the post-war era, we already know that the strikes and protests in the mining industry in 1946–7 were at the cutting edge of conflict between labour, the employers and the occupying powers. Thus the new miners might well be expected to have exerted an influence, not just on the mining union, but on the tone of industrial relations throughout West Germany. Secondly, mining was one of only two industries (iron and steel being the other) to be granted comprehensive co-determination, with parity between labour and capital in the supervisory boards and a special new labour director on the executive. Looking at the response to new labour and the approach to workforce rebuilding provides a test case with which to observe the impact of codetermination in action.

Against this background, then, the present study, in particular chapter 9, examines the new miners' impact on the politics of

---

lished dissertation, University of Bochum, 1982; Astrid Föllmer-Edling 'Die Politik des IVB im Ruhrgebiet 1945–1948. Die Anstrengung um die Erhöhung der Kohlenförderung im Ruhrbergbau', unpublished dissertation, University of Bochum, 1977.

24. See, for example, Christopher Huhne, reviewing Alec Cairncross's study of British post-war economic policy in the *Guardian*, Friday 2 August 1985. Huhne writes that 'Britain had no reserve army of labour, like the refugees who flooded into West Germany or the farmers sucked from France's land, so there was [in Britain] a relative lack of "labour discipline" and a willingness to maintain time-honoured demarcations'.

organised labour and the pattern of industrial relations in the mining industry. As well as looking at the new labour actually employed in the pits, the book also considers the impact of labour supply conditions more generally. In other words, it assesses the impact on the union's bargaining position not only of the new miners already hired, but also of the queues at the factory gates. It is, however, worth stressing that the book is *not* meant to be a general history of industrial relations in the mining industry. The focus remains firmly on the management and impact of rebuilding the workforce.

Ultimately this second half of the book is concerned with the great underlying question about the reconstruction of post-war German society: was it restoration, continuity or a new beginning?[25] 'Recasting' seemed an appropriately ambiguous word to use in this context. It could be taken as a metaphor from the theatre, describing a process whereby mining industry and Ruhr society received a new cast of players. In this metaphor, the stage and drama are taken as given; only the players on the stage are new. That would be to emphasise the continuity. But recasting also conjures up, appropriately enough, an image from heavy industry, of a fluid mass given new form (or re-stored to a former one) in a fiery process. The question, there-fore, is how far, in the act of replenishing the workforce, the mining industry, the labour movement and Ruhr society were forced to change.

From the Cabinet to the Coalface: Methods and Sources

Like many books, this one began life as something else. The original intention, more years ago than I, my former supervisor or my publisher would care to remember, was to write a social history of the reconstruction from below. In seeking the social

25. The best introductions to this question are Jürgen Kocka, '1945: Neube-ginn oder Restauration?', in Carola Stern und Heinrich A. Winkler (eds), *Wendepunkte deutscher Geschichte 1848–1945*, Frankfurt/Main, 1979, pp. 141–68; M. Rainer Lepsius, 'Die Bundesrepublik Deutschland in der Kontinuität und Diskontinuität historischer Entwicklungen: Einige methodische Überlegungen', in Werner Conze and M. R. Lepsius (eds), *Sozialgeschichte der Bundesrepublik. Beiträge zum Kontinuitätsproblem*, Stuttgart, 1983.

roots of post-war politics, I was inspired by David Crew's seminal study of nineteenth-century Bochum and resolved to adopt a similar strategy, viewing Germany's social reconstruction from the perspective of a small Ruhr town and particularly its working-class community.[26] The idea of grass-roots history or everyday history was then very much in vogue in Germany. Yet, as noted above, few of the labour histories on the post-1945 years had actually looked at policy below the leadership level.

Fairly soon, however, the local or grass-roots focus proved both problematic and very limiting. Germany's social reconstruction turned out to be a highly planned, heavily administered affair. Military government, national and regional authorities, powerful industrial planning staffs and heavily centralised union organisations, churches and voluntary organisations – in short, the whole panoply of a highly organised industrial society – were all busy working to influence the course of reconstruction. This activity lay at the very heart of Germany's road to recovery; yet at the everyday level much of it was invisible.

This is not to argue that everything happened according to some planner's blueprint. Nor is it to deny the power of individual Germans to shape their own destiny. But it rapidly became obvious that, far more than in the nineteenth century, and also probably far more than in post-war Britain, the local arena was more a repository of countless attempts to organise, control, channel and reshape social reality than an active source of policy and politics. Nothing brings this out more clearly than the documentation available for the reconstruction era. Because of the lack of local institutional clout, sources, even on local issues, are usually far poorer in the municipal archives than at the Land or industry-wide level. The amount of effort required to make even a modest statistical compilation for a particular municipality stands in marked contrast to the ease with which quite detailed and sophisticated collections of data can be found for the Ruhr as a whole, say, or for the mining industry. The historian of the period is forced to accept an only apparently paradoxical truth: the further away from the 'ground' one moves, certainly up to the level of the Land ministries, the more

---

26. David Crew, *Town in the Ruhr: A Social History of Bochum 1860–1914*, New York, 1979.

clearly can one make out the detail of what was going on.

Thus I was drawn away from grass-roots history towards a social history of the reconstruction that concentrated more on the higher organisational levels. At the same time, however, a history which never left the committee room, which always looked at the blueprint and never at the constituencies it was addressing, would not only be sterile, it would also fail to understand the interaction which determined the course of Germany's economic and social reconstruction. Consequently, the attempt has been made here to cover the full continuum, from the cabinet room down to the coalface and back, from formal protocols and minutes to newspaper clippings and oral history, in an effort to capture something of that interaction between policy-makers and population, between ministers, management and miners, that recast the Ruhr.

Definitions

Most of the specialist terms employed in the thesis are either self-explanatory or elucidated in the text, but it may be as well to define at the outset the way in which the terms 'new labour' and 'new miner' are employed. In the parlance of the 1940s and 1950s, *Neubergleute*, or 'new miners', was a term used to describe men who, with other working experience behind them, came to the mines as adults to retrain as miners. A more precise term for the same group was *Umschüler*, or 'adult trainees'. Both terms are used interchangeably in the present text. The term 'new labour', by contrast, denotes all new recruits, irrespective of their age or previous working experience. In the early chapters, 'new labour' and 'new miners' are used as virtual equivalent since the vast majority of recruits were in fact adult trainees.

Youngsters of 17 or under, who entered the industry straight from school as apprentices (*Berglehrlinge*) or juvenile trainees (*Bergjungleute*), were not normally classed as 'new miners'. The logic behind reserving the term *Neubergleute* for the adults was that youngsters were regarded as the industry's traditional source of intake, whereas the adult trainees were a special product of the post-war era. In fact, since many of the mining apprentices in the post-war period came from other regions and social backgrounds, they were just as much a new source of labour as the 'new miners' proper. Where the study wishes to deal with all such new groups together, this is made clear in the text.

PART I
Resourcing the Ruhr

1

Coercion and Constraint: Military Government, Manpower and the Mines, 1945–1946

Coal and the Manpower Problem

As the war drew to a close, there was no doubt in the Allies' minds about the importance of Ruhr coal and from the start there was agreement that Ruhr coal production should be maximised in the short term. When the US 9th Army advanced into the Ruhr in March 1945, the solid fuels section, G4, of SHAEF (Supreme Headquarters Allied Expeditionary Force) moved in directly behind it and, even before all the cities had been occupied, began to establish control over the mines in the area. The urgency of increasing coal production was underlined in June when the findings of the Potter–Hyndley report were submitted. The report, the outcome of a joint Anglo-American mission to countries in north-western Europe, argued that economic collapse and serious disorder would result throughout the area unless it received immediate and sizeable injections of German coal. In July and August, American and British commanders in Germany received directives to the effect that Germany should export 10 million tons of coal up to December 1945 and a further 15 million tons in the first four months of 1946.[1]

This urgency notwithstanding, the first few confused weeks of Occupation saw little coal being moved from the mines, largely through lack of transport facilities. The SHAEF team concentrated on setting up an administrative body, the Ruhr

1. PRO FO 942, 179, Combined Production and Resources Board. London Coal Committee, 'The coal situation in North West Europe. Report by the Potter/Hyndley Mission to North West Europe' (henceforth Potter-Hyndley Report), June 1945; WWA S22 (OMGUS) AG 45–46/103/1, Joint Chiefs of Staff to US Forces Berlin, 26.7.1945 and Robertson to Clay, 21.9.1945.

Coal Control, to supervise the mines, on restarting production and on collecting statistical data to determine the levels of manpower and material necessary for increased production. This interregnum continued until the British took over in July, and absorbed the Ruhr Coal Control into their own organisation, the North German Coal Control (NGCC).[2]

The NGCC could not help but recognise that improving the manpower situation was the key to increasing coal production. During the war, the Germans had had increasing recourse to foreign conscript labour as ever more German miners were called up to the armed forces. By the beginning of 1945, 43 per cent of the underground workforce had consisted of foreigners, most of them Russian prisoners of war. When, between February and April 1945, these men were removed or liberated from the mines, the underground workforce fell to 127,525 men, little more than half the size of 1938.[3]

The workforce was also over-aged. The ageing process had started in the 1920s, when as part of its rationalisation programme the industry had made little attempt to recruit new labour. In the 1930s, competition from the Wehrmacht and the metal industries had drawn potential recruits away from the mines and in 1939 the collieries had received only a quarter of the desired number of apprentices. During the war, the problem had been exacerbated by military call-up. By 1944 less than 9 per cent of the workforce was under 30 years of age, while almost two-thirds were over 40. Thus in 1945 many of the miners left in the Ruhr were due to retire or at least to leave the underground workforce. Clearly, a major regeneration programme was required.[4]

Accordingly, measures were begun immediately to replenish the depleted workforce. The NGCC's manpower target was 320,000 miners (above and below ground), roughly equivalent

2. WWA S22 BICO BISEC 11/103/2/22, report by William Strang and William Thorpe to the governments of the US and UK, September 1947, appendix: 'Review of Hard Coal Production in the Ruhr area since the capitulation'.

3. *ZdKW*, 1, p. 20.

4. See table 'Altersgliederung der Bergarbeiter im Ruhrbergbau. Prozent der Belegschaft', in OBAD (ed.), *Jahresbericht für den Oberbergamtsbezirk Dortmund 1958*, Dortmund, 1959; Hans Heinrich Bischoff, 'Die Altersgliederung der Arbeiter im Steinkohlenbergbau', *Glückauf*, vol. 88, nos. 40/41, 1952, pp. 1009–12 at p. 1012, table 5.

to the pre-war figure, and designed to attain the 1938 production level of around 400,000 tons a day.[5]

Initially the NGCC devoted its energies to returning former
miners to the industry. This meant, among other things, combating widespread absenteeism. In the first weeks after the war,
large numbers of miners had failed to report for work, prefer-
ring to concentrate on repairing their homes or make foraging
trips for food. By mid-July over a third of the available workforce
was not attending work. From the beginning of August onwards the NGCC therefore issued 'Orders to attend work' and
by November absenteeism had dropped from 36 to 17.2 per
cent.[6]

In addition to these measures, the manpower authorities
screened German prisoners of war in the British Zone for former
miners and these were rapidly released. By the end of August,
'Operation Coal-scuttle', as it was called, had returned 35,000
POW miners to the pits. Furthermore the workforce registers of
the collieries, the labour exchanges and the Ruhr Knappschaft
(the Miners' Insurance Association) were used to trace men with
mining experience who had taken on other employment.
Labour Supply Directive No. 2 ruled that all former miners,
without exception, were to be returned to the pits. In one week
in August alone, over 1,100 ex-miners were directed back to the
industry. The result of these measures was a steady rise in both
employment and output. Between April and October, underground employment increased from 127,525 to 157,415, while
monthly coal production jumped from 268,000 tons to 3,607,000
tons.[7]

Until September 1945, the majority of the men brought back to
the mines were Ruhr miners happy – or, at least, not too
unwilling – to return to their former employment. Neither
British administrative abilities nor the coherence of British recruiting policy had been put to the test. As the flow of former

5. PRO FO 1005, 345, NGCC Monthly Progress Report no. 2 (September 1945).

6. PRO FO 1005, 345, NGCC Monthly Progress Reports nos. 2–4; PRO FO
1005, 1819, Manpower Division, CCG(BE), 'Report on Labour, Housing and
Working Conditions in the Ruhr', Lübbecke 25.9.1945 (henceforth 'Manpower
Report 1945').

7. PRO FO 942, 183 (EIPS/97/146B), Economic Sub-Commission (ECOSC),
CCG(BE), 'Brief for the Chancellor of the Duchy of Lancaster. Part 1: Hard Coal
Production in the British Occupied Zone of Germany', 8.4.1946 (henceforth
'Hard Coal 1946'); *ZdKW*, 1, pp. 20, 3; 'Manpower Report 1945'.

Ruhr miners began appreciably to slow down towards the end of August 1945, the British authorities were under pressure to find a new source of manpower.

This would not be a simple task. Despite the huge migrations of refugees and expellees, there was no obvious and immediately accessible reservoir of suitable labour for the mines. Above all, the supply of experienced men was drying up, so that recourse would have to be had to inexperienced men, or 'green labour' in official parlance. In addition a significant proportion of the population in working age was unfit for heavy labour by virtue of age, exhaustion or injury. According to one estimate, three-quarters of male workers aged between 18 and 45 were underweight or in poor physical condition. When a census was taken in 1947, it was established that only a third of those available for work in the British Zone were fit for heavy labour.[8]

Then there was the problem that, despite the depressed economy, few workers were coming on to the labour market because the Reichsmark's loss of value encouraged a lot of economically meaningless employment. Normal relationships between wages and production figures did not apply. Many employers bartered much of their produce for foodstuffs and other commodities and reimbursed their workforce in kind. Not being under financial pressure to streamline the workforce, big industrial companies were 'hoarding' their workers in the hope of being able to resume normal operations before too long. Exact figures are not available but in mid-1947, when a similar labour market situation still prevailed, unemployment lay at 274,000 for the British Zone, or just 3 per cent of the employed workforce, despite the fact that industrial production in the same geographical area was barely more than one-third of the 1936 level. Therefore, the authorities might well be forced to screen workers in other employment and to transfer those who were engaged in inessential activity to the mines. Although an apparatus was being developed to do this in the form of Labour Priority Boards, it would be a complex and time-consuming task.[9]

8. PRO FO 1005, 1947, 'Minutes of the Committee to Investigate Coal Production 1946. Visit of Russian, French and US Experts to the Ruhr', August 1946. See especially minutes of meeting held on Tuesday 6 August 1946, remarks by August Halbfell; BAK Z40, 308, ZAA, 'Das Arbeitspotential in der britischen Zone', October 1947.

9. 'Manpower Report 1945'; ZAA, 'Das Arbeitspotential in der britischen

A further difficulty was that the bulk of the usable and inessentially employed labour was not in the mining locality but in rural areas. This was the result of a combination of wartime evacuations, the official direction of refugees and expellees to rural areas of intact housing and the voluntary migration of many city dwellers. Obtaining this labour would pose transportation problems and the housing difficulties would be almost insuperable, since the authorities were in any case engaged in a 'race against time' to provide accommodation for the existing Ruhr population before winter set in.[10]

The most serious problem, however, was that mining work, unattractive at the best of times, offered very little at the end of 1945. During the Third Reich miners' wages had dropped badly relative to other important industrial groups and the decline in the miners' position was not made up after the end of the war. Indeed, with the termination soon after German capitulation of the Goering decree (originally introduced in 1939), the miners suffered a 10 per cent cut in their monthly pay. Another blow in 1945 was the cut in pensions. During the war, the state had helped the industry by funding a major part of the contributions to the miners' health and old-age insurance organisation, the Knappschaft. The British did not feel in a position to continue this support and as a result the Knappschaft was forced to make large cuts in the levels of miners' pensions, eliminating one, the *Bergmannssold*, altogether. It was true that miners, like other workers engaged in heavy labour, still received higher rations than most groups, but in practice they suffered from the food shortages that affected most urban areas. Many miners or their families were compelled to go on foraging trips into the country to obtain food. It would take a major improvement in working conditions and incentives to induce new recruits to sign on at the Ruhr mines.[11]

Zone'; Wendy Carlin, 'Economic Reconstruction in Western Germany 1945–55: The Displacement of "Vegetative Control"', in Ian Turner (ed.), *Reconstruction in Post-war Germany: British Occupation Policy and the Western Zones 1945–1955*, Oxford, 1989, p. 51.

10. 'Manpower Report 1945'.

11. Klaus Wisotzky, *Der Ruhrbergbau im Dritten Reich. Studien zur Sozialpolitik im Ruhrbergbau und zum sozialen Verhalten der Bergleute in den Jahren 1933 bis 1939*, Düsseldorf, 1983, pp. 146, 244ff.; Werner Milert, 'Die verschenkte Kontrolle. Bestimmungsgründe der britischen Kohlenpolitik im Ruhrbergbau 1945–1947',

These were difficult problems, yet they were surely not insuperable. There was no true scarcity of labour but rather a maldistribution of human and other resources. To correct this maldistribution, the British had two options at their disposal. They could channel towards the mining community the resources (foodstuffs, consumer goods and building materials) that would ensure a plentiful supply of volunteers to the mines; or they could compel men to enter the pits. The British chose the second solution and in the autumn of 1945, the British Control Commission's Manpower Division, on whom the job of finding new labour devolved, set the administrative wheels in motion to detect usable labour and to direct – that is, coerce – it to the mines.

Losing Direction

Since a task of this size could not be undertaken by the British alone, the Division's main role was to co-ordinate, direct and monitor the activity of German officials. The actual detection and directions were largely carried out by the German labour exchanges which, as one of the very first elements of post-war German administration, had been revived soon after the British took control of the Zone. A huge amount of the labour exchanges' time and energy was expended on the miners' programme: according to a reliable estimate, at the beginning of 1946 up to 50 per cent of the total activity of German labour exchanges was devoted to finding new miners.[12]

Given this concentration of effort, it was not surprising that a steady stream of men began to arrive at the mines. In the fourth quarter of 1945 new labour outnumbered returning ex-prisoners of war by almost three to one and by March 1946 99 per cent of recruits were gained by directions to work. The unemployed who registered with labour exchanges were given a medical

---

in Dietmar Petzina and Walter Euchner (eds), *Wirtschaftspolitik im britischen Besatzungsgebiet 1945–1949*, Düsseldorf, 1984, p. 112; *Hochlarmarker Lesebuch. Kohle war nicht alles. 100 Jahre Ruhrgebietsgeschichte*, Oberhausen, 1981, pp. 200ff.

12. 'Manpower Report 1945'; 'Sechs Jahre Außenstelle Bergbau des Landesarbeitsamtes Nordrhein-Westfalen', unpublished MS, 1952, p. 4. I would like to thank Herr Naßkrent of the Landesarbeitsamt Nordrhein-Westfalen for lending me this manuscript.

examination and, if fit, sent off to the mines; discharged prisoners of war were checked for suitability for mine work; German labour officials and British military police carried out spot checks on street and cinema queues to flush out likely labour; and a series of labour supply directives established the overriding manpower priority of hard coal mining. By March 1946, the labour exchanges had directed 60,000 men to the pits.[13]

There was no doubt, however, that these results stood in no proportion to the amount of time and energy expended on producing them. Overall, the attempt to conscript unskilled miners required, in the words of a German observer, 'schließlich einen Umfang an Verwaltungskräften, an Leerlauf, an Zeit und unproduktiver Arbeit, die in keinem Verhältnis zum Erfolg standen'.[14] An even bigger problem was making sure the directed labour stayed and worked in the mines. This the British failed to achieve; indeed, they failed so completely and disastrously as to put the whole coal recovery programme in jeopardy. The directed labour often fled in the first week of employment and frequently absconded with work clothing that was hard to replace. Of 60,000 workers sent to the mines by labour exchanges up to March 1946, only 18,000 were still there by the end of March. Between January and the end of September 1946 almost 50,000 men were forced into the pits, yet over the same period the number of workers underground increased by less than 10,000 men. This meant that at any given moment, a large proportion of the newcomers in the mine had only just arrived – having been drafted in to replace those who had escaped the week before. The lack of skill of the newcomers coupled with their lack of motivation had a disastrous effect on productivity. In November 1945 the trend towards more normal coal production began to slow down and by the end of the year daily output per man/shift had fallen (from 2.76 tons for the week ending 26 November to 2.23 tons for the week ending 31 December). Production ceased to climb in January 1946, dropped sharply in March and did not significantly surpass the January level until October (see table 1). It was not just that the newcomers themselves were underproducing. The continued

13. 'Hard Coal 1946'; OBADA, I8010/723/47, OBAD, Lagebericht, February 1947, attached (DKBL) table; August Niehues, 'Ruhrbergbau und Arbeitsvermittlung', *Arbeitsblatt für die britische Zone*, vol. 1, no. 3, 1947, pp. 88–90.
14. 'Sechs Jahre Außenstelle Bergbau', p. 3.

Table 1.1 Workforce and production, 1945–6

Year/ month	Workforce underground (at month's end)	as % of 1938[a]	Coal produced (t)	as % of 1938
1938				
average[b]	228,813	100.0	10,607,000	100.0
1945				
October	157,415	68.7	3,607,000	34.0
November	166,958	73.0	3,844,000	36.2
December	174,740	76.4	3,909,000	36.9
1946				
January	177,756	77.6	4,394,000	41.4
February	179,295	78.4	4,088,000	38.5
March	180,790	79.0	3,875,000	36.5
April	181,148	79.2	3,629,000	34.2
May	180,728	79.0	3,927,000	37.0
June	180,410	78.8	3,794,000	35.8
July	181,573	79.4	4,493,000	42.4
August	182,986	80.0	4,485,000	42.2
September	184,250	80.6	4,197,000	39.6
October	186,421	81.5	4,618,000	43.6

(a) Workforce and production percentages are the author's calculation.
(b) Production figure for 1938 is average/month.

Source: ZdKW, vol. 1, pp. 3, 20.

influx of unmotivated men also lowered the general level of morale in the mines and in this way reduced the output of the experienced men as well. Thus at the very same time as it was proving impossible to meet the NGCC's manpower targets, those targets had to revised *upwards* to take account of the unexpectedly low productivity.[15]

Against the backcloth of the urgent European demand for

15. 'Minutes of the Committee to Investigate Coal Production 1946'; OBADA I8010/723/47, OBAD, Lagebericht, February 1947, attached (DKBL) table; 'Hard Coal 1946', esp. note 13. The output figures per man/shift for November are for face workers only.

coal, these results were striking indeed. How can they be explained? At the best of times, conscription is a makeshift measure, not designed to enhance workforce productivity or morale. Yet during the war production had held up well despite the growing proportion of conscript workers. Once a decision had been made to give them adequate food, Soviet prisoners of war and workers from Eastern Europe attained between 60 and 80 per cent of their German counterparts' productivity.[16] So why was the post-war experience so disastrous?

In June 1946, the labour exchange in Arnsberg gave an account of a recent recruitment action. Sixty-eight men had been given a preliminary medical examination and issued with directions to work in the mines. Three directions were for one reason or another withdrawn, leaving sixty-five men to be given a more thorough medical examination. Before this could be carried out thirty-one of the draftees had disappeared. The remaining men were then duly examined; thirteen were found to be unfit for mining work. The lorry to take those who passed the examination to the mines was supposed to arrive at 11 a.m. but in fact did not turn up till 1.15 p.m. By then seven more of the 'recruits' had slipped away, so only fourteen men were actually driven over to their destination at the Dortmund mines. A subsequent examination established that only eleven out of the fourteen men actually reported to the mine. By registration that evening the number had dropped to seven. On the following day, only two were still present. Later, some of those who left the mine made representations to the labour exchange in Arnsberg, complaining that the accommodation had been infested. For its part the labour exchange complained to the regional labour office that ever since the men returned to the area, recruitment for mining had become even more difficult than before.[17]

A similar pattern emerges in a report drawn up a month or two earlier by the works' council of the Gneisenau pit. The

---

16. See Ulrich Herbert, *Fremdarbeiter. Politik und Praxis des 'Ausländer-Einsatzes' in der Kriegswirtschaft des Dritten Reiches*, Berlin/Bonn, 1985, p. 282 and Christian Streit, *Keine Kameraden. Die Wehrmacht und die sowjetischen Kriegsgefangenen 1941–1945*, Stuttgart, 1978, p. 283.
17. StAM Arbeitsamt Dortmund, 47, AA Arnsberg to Präsident des LAA, Westfalen-Lippe, 28.6.1946 and enclosure: 'Niederschrift 26.6.1946, gez. Wenzel Plodek'; AA Dortmund to Präsident des LAA, Westfalen-Lippe, Bergbau Abteilung, 11.7.1946.

report dealt with fifty conscripts sent by train from Holstein, of whom thirty-eight arrived at Dortmund station. On their arrival the conscripts complained of having been sent against their will and of being treated like slaves. The majority declared themselves unwilling to work ('eine Aufnahme der Arbeit [käme] überhaupt nicht in Frage'). The response of the works council, already aggrieved by newcomers absconding with good work clothing when the established workforce received nothing, was to suggest that if they were going to leave they should do it now before they were kitted out. By the following day only three of the conscripts remained – and two of those departed shortly afterwards.[18]

Every works council and labour exchange could tell a similar story. The value of these particular accounts is that they convey concisely many of the conditions which undermined the labour directions. First, they were not properly policed. There were no guards at the hostel, no police at the labour exchange. Men were drafted from Holstein against their will and yet no guards accompanied them on the train. Secondly, the directions were not supported or accepted either by the draftees themselves or by those who should be enforcing them. Works council and management made no effort to restrain the newcomers. The works councillors actually invited the unwilling recruits to return home and no one lifted a finger to stop them. Even those who made the directions, the labour exchanges, seem to have given them so little support that the draftees were prepared to surface again at the labour exchange to make a complaint. The response of the labour exchange was not to send the men back to the mines but to pass on their criticisms to the regional labour exchange. Thirdly, the men evidently had very little anxiety about what would happen to them if they fled. They made no secret of their intention and did not go into hiding, simply returned home.

The recruits' lack of anxiety revealed that the established system of tracing labour was remarkably ineffective. In theory, it should have been possible sooner or later to trace all those who had disobeyed an order to work in the mines. Their names

18. AZG File 'I 126 Zuweisung von Arbeitskräften aus anderen Bezirken 1.11.45–31.10.56', 'Declaration of Miners' Representatives at Mine Gneisenau about the Last Transport of Workmen', 3.5.1946.

would be recorded in the labour exchanges' files. To obtain new employment they would have to re-register with a labour exchange and at that point the authorities ought to have been able to catch up with them. Yet this does not seem to have happened. The NGCC claimed that a large number of deserters from the Schleswig-Holstein action had been sent back to the Ruhr at their own expense but this did not tally with the mines' experience and was probably a bluff. The labour exchanges admitted in confidence that they were in no position to trace men who had absconded. In March 1946, it is true, three men were sentenced to six months' imprisonment for refusing to go the mines and another two were given three-month sentences for leaving the Ruhr without due cause. Yet, considering that in March alone 5,000 miners left the pits, this was no great achievement. Evidently by registering in a different district or by other means it was easy to avoid detection.[19]

Even when the newcomers stayed in the mines, it proved impossible to get much work out of them. In September 1946, the Oberbergamt Dortmund (OBAD) was investigating a complaint against a pit deputy who had refused to allow a young haulier to leave the mines. The deputy's defence provided an indication of the problems which the conscripts presented to mine managements. The haulier in question had been on the mine's books for about a month. Yet during that time, he had barely worked a complete shift. Either he had been absent altogether, or had arrived late or wanted to leave early:

> Wenn das Arbeitsamt glaubt, wir hätten hier eine Irrenanstalt, dann laß es auch die nötigen Wärter dazu stellen. Ich lehne jede Verantwortung für Z ab und bitte, ihn dem Arbeitsamt zur Verfügung zu stellen . . . Der Ton, den sich die im letzten Jahr eingestellten jungen Männer zum größten Teil angeeignet haben, geht entschieden zu weit. Sagen wir ihnen etwas, bekommen wir immer freche Antworten.[20]

The Mines' Inspectorate noted frequent complaints that the newcomers were not only refusing to do their share but were

19. WWA F26, 380, Concordia to HQ 1. Ruhr Coal District, 7.2.1946 and HQ NGCC to RCDs, 26.2.1946.
20. OBADA I 3850/2263/46, 'Nicht Herauslassen des Schleppers Z vom Revier 25, Prosper I', Bericht des Fahrsteigers Göbbelsmann, 30.9.1946.

also intimidating the established workforce and preventing it from working properly. Although the NGCC repeatedly demanded tougher measures, management seemed unable to assert its authority over the workforce.[21]

These failures revealed that the administrative system as a whole was simply not geared up to coerce labour on a large scale. During the war, directions had been carried out within the framework of a police state. A centralised, efficient and ruthless network of security forces had backed up the system of labour controls and had intimidated the labour force into compliance. By contrast, the authorities in the post-war period were from the start hampered by the lack of police. The British did not create a security administration to match the Nazi police apparatus. This was doubtless a good thing; but it made it very difficult to enforce the directions or to trace those who fled the mines and it meant that new labour was not deterred from quitting the mines.

The classic example here was Operation Clobber. At the beginning of December 1945, the German Mines Supplies Organisation (GMSO) informed the collieries that a large number of soldiers were to be released from prisoner of war camps in the near future and that these would be scrutinised for potential recruits for the mines. Thirty thousand new miners were expected from the action and, in view of this, recruitment of civilians was to be discontinued. A military government manpower report at the end of December was forced to reduce this estimate. It appeared likely that only about 40 per cent of the soldiers released registered with the labour exchanges. Civilian recruitment was therefore to be resumed. A further report on 12 January 1946 had to make the unhappy admission that of the 30,000 miners promised from the operation, 384 had been delivered.[22]

As well as making it more difficult to trace likely recruits or recalcitrants, the absence of an efficient and ruthless police force weakened the managers' ability to discipline the conscripts. During the war, the threat of bringing in the Gestapo, a step

21. OBADA I8010/28/47, OBAD to HQ NGCC, 'Kurzbericht über die Lage im Ruhrkohlenbergbau für November 1946', 10.1.1947.

22. WWA F35, 3495, GMSO Circular 161, 7.12.1945; PRO FO 1005, 1822, Manpower Division Fortnightly Technical Reports for fortnight ending 29.12.1945 and 12.1.1946.

which managements had not hesitated to take even in minor disciplinary matters, had been a major factor in sustaining the pressure to work.

It could be argued that the British might still have posted troops to the mines, guarding the new recruits' barracks and so on. Indeed this is what the French, concerned at the failure of the Ruhr's export programme and themselves inclined to a tougher approach, continually demanded. Yet the British were loath to adopt a more obvious military presence. Their unwillingness stemmed in part from their recognition that, no matter how many troops they posted in the Ruhr, they would not be able to create a watertight system. The labour might simply flee into other Zones. More significant was their fear of arousing the opposition of the established workforce and thus depressing rather than increasing production. The British had not forgotten the lesson of 1923 when the French occupation had resulted in a policy of passive resistance, the miners reporting for work and then idly sitting in the pits. It was not that the established workforce was particularly ill-disposed towards the British. Indeed, labour was the only group initially to have high expectations of the occupying powers. But it could not be expected to endorse a coercive policy which appeared to maintain the methods of the Nazis and was directed at their own countrymen. The unions continually protested against the directions and it was clear that the reaction of the workforce to an increased military presence, to guards and barbed wire at the conscripts' barracks and so on, would be very negative. Such a policy would not only offend against the loyalties of the miners, it might also seem to them the first step towards placing the whole workforce under coercion. So the British ended up trying to conduct a coercive policy in a non-coercive manner, hoping that new labour would knuckle down to mining the coal and doing very little in response when it turned out that it would not do so.[23]

Even given the limitations to the security system and the understandable reluctance to create a police state, the ineffectiveness of the directions was striking. Many of the problems

23. 'Minutes of the Committee to Investigate Coal Production 1946'; PRO FO 943, 185, 'Brief on Special Points Arising from Coal Experts' Report for Use in Foreign Secretary's Discussion with the French', October 1946; FO 943, 186, 'Informal Meeting with Mr H. E. Collins . . . at Norfolk House', 6.5.1947.

stemmed from the fact that most of the enforcement was actually being carried out by German officials. The British felt constrained in the amount of pressure they could put on the German administration because they saw themselves as being dependent on its co-operation. Military government apparatus was small. The size of the Manpower Division, for example, and even more so that of NGCC, bore no relation to the tasks involved unless they were to delegate large areas of their responsibility to German officials. The question as to why they were not larger goes beyond the limits of this study since it applied to all sections of the military government. Part of the answer is probably that the British felt they had no choice, since money was short and a British administration would have been expensive. On the other hand, at least some of the costs might have been borne by the Zone, so that financial pressures cannot be the sole explanation. The British seem to have believed that a system of indirect rule, in which German administrations carried out the bulk of the work, would be less likely to arouse resistance and so, ultimately, more efficient. There was much to support this view, but it meant that policies could be implemented only with the co-operation or at least on the sufferance of the German authorities. As a leading representative of the Manpower Division's Labour Supplies Branch put it, 'I do not think it is merely a matter of checking a sample here and inspecting there because on many sides of the work we have not sufficient Allied officials to carry out the detailed checks required if the German officials we are checking are in the overwhelming majority in complete opposition to our policy.' He went on, '. . . we have to consider facts, we have to see how far we can drive the human machine'.[24]

Many German officials gave the directions only half-hearted support. This was true, for example, of the German labour administration. The then president of the Westphalian regional labour exchange, August Halbfell, noted that both German and military government inspectors carried out controls in cinema and street queues but that only the military government's checks were effective. This may well have been a problem of

24. 'Minutes of the Committee to Investigate Coal Production 1946'; WWA S22 (OMGUS) CO HIST BR 3/406–1/22, undated notes by NGCC towards an official history of the NGCC.

legitimacy – that in the crucial moment of encounter, a rueful smile or a pleading look could deflect the German official not quite certain of his cause from pursuing his control too forcefully. It is true that the labour administration engaged in little open opposition to British policy. Yet senior officials did protest against coercion and, in private, repeatedly spoke against compulsory placings. The German authorities made such little attempt to place conscripts under guard or to prevent them from fleeing that it is evident they deliberately avoided bringing the full panoply of coercion to bear. Another piece of evidence for covert resistance to the directions was the low number of juvenile recruits to the mines, a fact which suggested that many careers advisers in the exchanges refused to obey the order to direct youngsters to the mines.[25]

Moreover, the negative or uncertain attitude of the labour exchange officials very probably transmitted itself to the recruits. Certainly, the willingness of the Arnsberg recruits to complain in person at the labour exchange suggests that they knew the officials to be of one mind with themselves. That the labour officials were uncertain of their cause is not surprising. For a start, the German officials probably found it very uncomfortable to issue labour directions in the name of the former enemy. Secondly, it was well known that most of the coal produced was going for export and at prices well below the market rate. It was generally felt that the British had no overall commitment to reconstruction as a whole, only where it suited their interests. Everyone knew of the Morgenthau plan, and the level of coal exports seemed to prove that German recovery was a low priority. Thus few Germans could see the coal recruitment programme as a contribution to German recovery.

The half-hearted approach to enforcing the directions was even more marked amongst the colliery managers. For them, recognition that the production drive was not serving national recovery was joined by a second concern: namely, that it contributed little to the recovery of the industry either. The mines were running on a loss and subsidy basis which covered operational costs but not depreciation, let alone making a profit. In

25. OBADA I8000/1147/46, President of LAA Hannover to Military Government, Hannover, 22 February 1946; 'Manpower Report 1945', appendix A, section 'Provision of Training'.

any case, the devalued Reichsmarks were a poor reward for an industry that desperately needed supplies, equipment and new preparatory and development work. In effect, every ton of coal mined was using up the reserves of the industry without putting anything back. American observers believed that under existing price and subsidy policies the managers' logical policy was to keep 'production at the lowest possible level consistent with its members continuing in office'. Given this situation, the employers could not be expected to exert themselves in extracting production from unwilling recruits. In addition, the influx of unskilled labour of all ages, often in poor condition, would in the long term intensify the industry's labour problems and costs.[26]

Thus, the managers tended not to share the British sense of urgency. They gave longer-term interests a greater priority to the detriment of maximising coal production in the short term. Halbfell complained to the British that a number of employers were paying no attention to the realities of the labour market and were setting unreasonable standards for new recruits. Large numbers of men were passed as fit by the labour exchanges, sent to the mines and then rejected by the doctors of the Knappschaft, the industry's health insurance body. Some of these rejections were understandable. The labour exchanges, mindful of the manpower quotas imposed by the British authorities, were remarkably unselective in the health standards they applied to possible adult recruits. Quite a number of the conscripts would have been 'useless in any industry'.[27] Nevertheless, there was clear evidence that the Knappschaft was more concerned about the possible future burden on its resources of large numbers of medically substandard recruits than about the urgency of the situation. It was therefore prepared to maintain a rigour in its standards which the British officials regarded as excessive. The Chief Medical Officer of the British Ministry for Fuel and Power estimated that at least 10 per cent more candi-

26. WWA S22 (OMGUS), BICO BISEC 11/104–1/39, Special Intelligence Report, 'Some German Views of the Political, Economic and Sociological Aspects of Ruhr Coal Mining', 19.6.1948 (henceforth 'Special Intelligence Report 1948').

27. PRO FO 1005, 1738, GPRB, Intelligence Division, CCG(BE), Social Survey Report no. 5: 'The Life and Working Conditions of the Mining Trainee', 31.12.1946, (henceforth Social Survey Report no. 5), p. 8.

dates could be accepted than had been passed by the Knapp-schaft.[28]

An even more important factor restraining management from imposing its will on the workforce was not opposition to British goals but uncertainty about its own position. A point often missed in historical accounts emphasising the swift return of German employers to power is that, in the early years, employers and managers in mining and in other industries were in a very peculiar and uncertain position. In some cases the top directors were in prison; in others the parent company was no longer able to control colliery policy. The chain of command had been broken and colliery managers often had to decide whose interests they should be serving. They had to weigh up the possibility that the British would be in charge for years to come against loyalty to their former bosses. Furthermore, at the end of 1945, the British expropriated the mine owners and it seemed as if the pits would be socialised or nationalised on the British model. The trade unions were in the ascendant and the managers had every reason to be cautious in their dealings with the men. Another, more direct and personal, threat to mine mangers was that of denazification. At the end of 1945, Bergamt Dinslaken reported that discipline generally was very lax and an improvement could not be expected, 'bis die Aufsichtsbeamten 100%ig sicher sind, daß ihnen keine Unannehmlichkeiten durch Anschwärzereien und Anzeigen entstehen'.[29] Managers feared that the workforce would make accusations to a denazification panel about their behaviour in the Nazi era. Despite repeated efforts on the part of the NGCC, denazification continued into 1947.[30]

As a result of their insecurity *vis-à-vis* the workforce, the employers were unable to apply much pressure to the new recruits. Bergamt Krefeld complained in July 1946 that the instructions of the overmen were continually being disregarded, even violently opposed. If the overmen tried to punish the offenders, the works council overturned the punishment. The industry's medical staff, who during the war had been extremely

28. 'Minutes of the Committee to Investigate Coal Production 1946', minutes of the 2nd meeting.
29. OBADA I 8010/1415/45, BA Dinslaken to OBAD, Lagebericht für November 1945, 2.12.1945.
30. 'Special Intelligence Report 1948'.

39

niggardly in allowing miners sick leave, suddenly became extremely lenient since 'bei eingetretenen [gesundheitlichen] Komplikationen wohl keine der Stellen, die darauf drängen, daß diese Leute möglichst weiterarbeiten sollen, den entscheidenden Arzt decken wird,' as the management of one colliery noted. Absenteeism in general was treated with great laxity.[31]

Given the difficulties in enforcing discipline, it is not surprising that managers adopted a resigned and passive attitude to the conscripts. Rather than forcing the recruits to work, managers favoured dismissing those who would not do so. Yet dismissals were clearly a measure of desperation in a situation where the men wanted to leave the industry. Managers must have been aware that they were thereby encouraging other recruits to behave badly on the off-chance of being sent home, thus undermining the whole coercive approach. Again and again, the Ruhr coal controllers had to warn the mines that they could not dismiss when they wanted to, which suggests that the warnings had little effect.[32]

The weakness and insecurity of management and deputies contrasted sharply with the wartime situation, a fact which helps to explain why production stayed so high during the war despite the ever larger proportion of conscript labour in the workforce. During the war 'tätliche Übergriffe' had been 'an der Tagesordnung', as miners subsequently recalled. For example, a foreman entrusted with the job of supervising Ukrainian forced labourers is recorded as having advised German miners working alongside them that the only way to get a Ukrainian to work was to beat him. So bad was the treatment meted out by the mines (and sometimes by the miners) that the Wehrmacht sections responsible for Soviet POWs felt obliged to warn the industry that the conscripts were being treated too badly.[33]

If management insecurity was a key problem in the post-war period, the question then arises why the British were under-

31. OBADA I 8010/1824/46, BA Krefeld, Lagebericht für Juli 1946; I3874/281/48, BA Lothringen, 'Gutachten über die Kranken- und Unfallzahlen', 31.5.1948; 'Hard Coal 1946'.

32. Paul Breder, *Geschichten vor Ort. Erinnerungen eines Bergmanns*, Essen, 1979, ch. 'Neubergleute', *passim*; OBADA I 5207/1275/46, BA Dinslaken to OBAD, 7.6.1946; WWA F26, 379, RCD1 to Concordia, 17.1.1946 and subsequent communications in 380, 782 and 783.

33. Herbert, *Fremdarbeiter*, pp. 225–6.

mining the authority of the very officials on whom their production drive depended. There are two points here. The first is
that different goals were in conflict. The moral and political
imperative of denazification was at odds with the drive for
economic recovery. Though the NGCC itself was hostile to
denazification and its officers frequently assured German managers that they looked at mining 'nicht aus politischen sondern
aus technischen Gesichtspunkten',[34] pressure came from higher
up to continue. Here in miniature was a problem that was to
confront the military government on a large scale in the following years – as we shall see in chapter 2.

Secondly, the British were playing an uneasy balancing act
between capital and labour. They needed management's help
but were unwilling to antagonise labour. The military government's nervousness was exacerbated by the fact that it felt
unable to offer the miners any special material gratification for
their work. There was therefore a readiness to make other
concessions. The expropriation of the mines, for instance, was,
carried out at least in part as a sop to labour demands. Even the
decision to continue denazification in the mining industry was a
concession to labour. In spring 1946, the NGCC had successfully
requested that all denazification be brought to an end because of
its impact on production. In July, however, union representations led to the establishment of a new denazification
committee.[35]

On a much smaller scale, a telling example of military government unwillingness to back management too strongly came in
an exchange between an NGCC district officer and the mining
directors in his area. The NGCC representative, Colonel Ritchie,
requested the directors to stop works councillors from coming to
his office to discuss matters which should be settled within the
colliery. The directors responded that they gave works councillors plenty of opportunity to air their grievances and suggested
that Ritchie might like to inform them himself. This Ritchie was
not prepared to do. He could hardly throw them out, he said,

34. WWA F26, 381, minutes of a discussion with RCD1 on 21.11.1946,
21.11.1946.
35. Henry Collins, *Mining Memories and Musings: Autobiography of a Mining
Engineer*, London, 1985, pp. 42ff.; PRO FO 1005, 379, COPROD/P(46)12, 'Denazification of the Coal Industry', 5.10.1946; Milert, 'Die verschenkte Kontrolle',
p. 110.

and hoped that management's influence would be sufficient to solve the problem. No one wanted to be seen wielding the big stick.[36]

Apart from opposition to British policy or insecurity, one thing that applied to all German participants was that early failures undermined the conscription programme's credibility and started a vicious circle in which lack of commitment and failure only served to strengthen each other. What so inflamed the works councillors of Gneisenau, in the example given above, was not the notion of conscripting labour itself but the inefficiency of an operation in which the newcomers were given the only supplies of work clothing and then allowed to disappear. Thus disposed against an inefficient system, the works councillors ensured that it failed to work.

The costs of British policy were felt not just in terms of coal production but also in human terms, particularly in the mines' appalling safety record in 1945 and 1946. The approach to training revealed that, despite initial good intentions, a coherent and safety-conscious approach to inducting the newcomers was impossible within a programme of unenforced directions. In the first place, the failure to hold on to recruits meant that the NGCC was under ever greater pressure to achieve results, and consequently to sacrifice even the minimum training programme envisaged by the collieries. Again and again the mines were ordered to get all possible men to the face. Even more decisive was that the trainees' own attitude meant in most cases that a measured training scheme was useless. For many conscripts, the main priority was to get out of the mines as soon as possible. Even if they were nervous of fleeing the mines without permission, they wanted to avoid becoming qualified, fearing that this might make it harder to leave in the future. This was manifest in the strikingly low attendance figures at training classes (particularly, though not only, when the instruction was held outside working hours). There was a self-perpetuating cycle, in which the conscripts' recalcitrance and uncontrolled behaviour strengthened management's indifference, unresponsiveness and even hostility to the recruits, while management's attitudes confirmed the unhappy conscripts' view that they had

36. WWA F26, 381, memo concerning directors' conference on 2.7.1947, 2.7.1947.

landed in a nightmare situation from which the only recourse was to escape.[37] The result was a catastrophic rise in accidents. During the war, the worst accident figure had come in 1943, with sixty-five reported accidents per 100,000 shifts. For 1945 as a whole the figure lay slightly higher at sixty-nine. In the first quarter of 1946 the figure reached 116 (and this excludes the disastrous accident at Grimberg 3/4 in which several hundred miners died) and rose further in the second quarter to 138 per 100,000 shifts, or over double the wartime record.[38]

On top of the economic and social costs, the mining programme also lost the British a lot of their prestige, not only because it was contradictory and ineffectual but also because it was so blatantly undemocratic. It appeared that the British regarded the new miners purely as a factor of production, as inert as capital equipment, without needs or inclinations. Men were coerced to the mines in Nazi fashion and the goal of democratisation seemed to have gone out of the window. Even those Germans reasonably well disposed to the British will have echoed Konrad Adenauer's sentiments when he said that Britain, with its democratic traditions, could afford to introduce the Bevan boys, but Germany needed a taste of freedom.[39]

Why had the British opted for coercion? To a certain extent the decision does seem to have reflected a rather utilitarian approach to German labour on the part of the military government. A Manpower Division report from September 1945, for example, concluded on the question of compulsory directions for the mines that 'management interviewed were reasonably confident of success in the light of their war experience and in spite of the reluctant attitude of the recruits'.[40] It comes as something of a surprise to see how readily this and other reports speak of reintroducing the German 'machinery', i.e. the Nazi

37. E.g. BBA 8, 401, note from the directors, ref.: D/Di 1. to sections B11/B21, 'Betr.: Einsatz Umschüler', 25.7.1947. See also Mark Roseman, 'New Miners in the Ruhr: Rebuilding the Workforce in the Ruhr Mines, 1945–1958', Ph.D dissertation, Warwick University, 1987, pp. 80ff.

38. OBADA I 3050/1499/46, OBAD to the Oberpräsident of Westphalia, 27.8.1946. This is not to suggest that the increase in accident *reporting* was due solely to an increase in the actual number of accidents, nor to attribute the increase exclusively to new labour.

39. PRO FO 1005, 379, COPROD paper P(46)18, 'Report on Conversation with Dr Adenauer by the Assistant Director ISC Branch', 5.12.1946.

40. 'Manpower report 1945'.

apparatus for controlling labour, of compelling youngsters to work in the mines against their will and of benefiting from the proven ability of German mine managements to squeeze production out of undernourished and poorly housed modern slave labour. Hostility towards the Germans on the one hand, and long immersion in the climate of total war on the other, had no doubt prepared the ground for these measures.

But it has already become clear that the attempt to rebuild the labour force by compulsion was more the result of constraint than of conviction. In a moment of wry humour, the Oberpräsident of the North Rhine Province, Robert Lehr, caught perfectly the dilemma of the British. Lehr had just advocated a sort of National Service in the mines for all young Germans as a means of solving the labour problem (see below) and was now defending himself against criticism from some German colleagues that such a policy was undemocratic. Dr Lehr, as the minutes record, 'betont die Pflicht als Regierungschef, die Jugend zur Demokratie zu erziehen und erklärt aber, daß er abends nach Beendigung seiner Dienstgeschäfte nicht ganz den Eindruck habe, daß er tagsüber ein guter Demokrat gewesen sei, aber er glaubt auf der anderen Seite, daß die Militärregierung ebenso wenig gute Demokraten gewesen sind'.[41] 'Dieses Bon-Mot', note the minutes, 'wurde von englischer Seite sehr gut und humorvoll aufgenommen.'

The British authorities' lack of conviction was manifest in the fact that they were neither able nor willing to introduce the measures necessary to make the directions work. On the positive side, the military government was neither ruthless nor immoral enough to wish to re-create the Nazi state. Its goals of democratisation and denazification undermined attempts to mount a coercive labour policy. On the negative side, it did not have the legitimacy, the resources or the nerve to be able to enforce its decisions. Military government's hold was doubly tentative: not only was its authority insecurely anchored in the general population, but its control over the German administration was equally tenuous. The result was not only a failure to produce coal but also a dangerous and scrappy approach to new labour's integration.

41. HSTAD NW53, 272, 'Notizen von der Konferenz im britischen HQ in Lübbecke am 9.5.1946', 13.5.1946.

So why did the British persist with directions? The alternative would have been to offer the sort of incentive which would have ensured a steady supply of voluntary and motivated workers. Given that mining enjoyed such a clear priority, one would not have thought this an insuperable task. Once achieved, it would allow the conscript to work without too much pressure or perhaps even enable the British to dispense with the whole sorry apparatus of coercion. Yet it is clear that this did not happen. The question is why.

The Missing Incentives

Conditions in the Ruhr, even when measured against the low standards of post-war Germany, were generally unattractive and indeed growing worse. In March 1946 miners' rations were cut from 3,400 calories per day to 2,864. According to British nutritional calculations, miners were receiving little more than half the calories necessary to do very heavy work. Some workers actually found themselves taking a wage cut by going into the mines. Small wonder that few recruits felt inclined to stay.[42]

Housing conditions were very miserable. Most of those new miners who came from outside the Ruhr were housed in barracks, many of them originally constructed for forced labour during the war. Many were little more than wooden huts; in some cases barbed wire was still around them when the first new miners arrived. Facilities were extremely limited. A British survey reported of such barracks that 'the buildings and surroundings are squalid. They bear the stigma of their former use and the atmosphere of the prison still remains.'[43] In many cases there were no partitions between rooms, just rows and rows of double or treble bunks. Some of the camps were infested with lice. Another British survey of six mines, carried out in autumn 1946, gave a graphic description of conditions in one of the worst hostels. It was an inn, half of which was occupied by thirty-four miners. Light and ventilation were poor and a small stove was all that was available for heating, cooking and drying

42. PRO FO 943, 186 (EIPS 147A), memo, 'The Coal Industry in the British Zone' (April 1947); IGBEA Nachlaß Heinrich Weeke I, 'Besprechungen mit den Arbeitervertretern der Zeche Julia und Recklinghausen am 21.1.1946', 21.1.1946.
43. Social Survey Report no. 5, p. 4.

clothes. The furniture consisted of beds, lockers, two tables and some benches. 'There was no other furniture and the whole place was sordid in the extreme . . . The beds had straw filled palliasses made of sacking. One or two beds had a single dirty sheet and all had either one or two ragged blankets, some of them torn into ribbons and crudely pieced together again with thread.' In common with many hostels there were practically no cooking utensils or crockery and any equipment was apt to be stolen immediately by those who absconded. Yet for lack of clothes, energy and money, the miners spent practically all their non-working time in the room.[44]

Poor conditions were not restricted to the new miners, of course, and the lack of incentives was also progressively sapping the established workforce's willingness to produce. It is true that other aspects of British policy were also responsible for alienating the miners – the slow pace at which the British allowed unions to develop, for instance, and their apparent unwillingness to democratise control over the mining industry. Another irritant was the high level of coal exports at below market prices; resentment at what were seen as covert reparations was to prove a continuing hurdle to getting the miners to commit themselves to greater production.[45] But by far the most important factor was the deterioration in the miners' standard of living, particularly the ration cut made in March. The cut undoubtedly had a physical impact on the miners, particularly on married men, since they did not consume their full ration anyway: miners' families received only the meagre civilian rations (as little as 900 calories a day in some cases) so that the men often shared their food with them. Clear evidence of the physical costs of lower rations was provided by a progressive decline in miners' weight. The British had, in effect, not only not regenerated the workforce but actually reduced its productive capacity. However, the biggest impact of the ration cuts was probably psychological. Productivity dropped sharply *before* the

44. PRO FO 1005, 1738, PRO FO 1005, 1738, Intelligence Division CCG(BE), GPRB, Social Survey Report no. 4, 'The Coal-miner and his Family – A Study in Incentives', December 1946; Social Survey Report no. 5.

45. Ulrich Borsdorf, 'Speck oder Sozialisierung. Produktionssteigerungskampagnen im Ruhrbergbau 1945–1947', in Hans Mommsen and Ulrich Borsdorf (eds), *Glückauf Kamaraden! Die Bergarbeiter und ihre Organisationen in Deutschland*, Cologne, 1979, pp. 345–66, esp. pp. 354ff.

cuts had even been introduced but *after* they had been announced. Periodical pronouncements about miners' weight loss hit morale harder than the loss of weight itself. To the miners, the food cuts symbolised the unwillingness of the British to put something into the industry in return for what they were demanding from it.[46]

So, why were the British unwilling to offer more to the miners? Let us dispose at the outset of the idea that the British did not want to build up the industry too far because of a fear of competition. It is true that attempts *before* the Occupation to develop a more constructive policy had at times been hampered by British fears of future competition from Germany. A policy document from 1944 concluded that 'it is unthinkable that the circumstances which may preserve the German coal industry intact to meet a vital short-term European coal deficiency should be allowed to give that industry any undue initial advantage when normal supply conditions again prevail'.[47] It was not then clear how long that deficiency would last and consequently there was no initial willingness to spend money on the miners. Yet this mood was short-lived. At no time after the end of the war was coal policy hampered by fears of building up the German industry too far. It is, for example, noteworthy that both the Manpower Division and North German Coal Control tried from the outset to recruit apprentices to the industry, a move clearly not orientated to purely short-term production requirements. In addition, the NGCC's Deputy Controller General, Henry Collins, gave permission for preparatory work in the new Walsum mine to go ahead, even though the mine would not be viable for many years to come.[48]

Clearly, then, the British did not feel any inhibitions in reviving the Ruhr pits. On the other hand, they were clearly inhibited from offering special incentives. Why? One factor which undoubtedly initially played a role in influencing policy was an understandable hostility towards the Germans. It was true that

46. OBADA I6305/609/46, Sammelberichte. Report from BA Gelsenkirchen, April 1946; I 3874/281/48, Bergbau AG Lothringen, 'Gutachten über die Kranken- und Unfallziffern', 31.5.1948; Collins, *Mining Memories*, p. 34.

47. PRO FO 942, 178, EIPS, 'The German Coal Industry. Report of the Working Party' (September 1944).

48. OBADA I6301/1339/45, circular from LAA Westfalen-Lippe to labour exchanges, 28.10.1945; interview with Henry Collins, 20.7.1990.

British Occupation policy was characterised by the view that harsh coercive policies were not enforceable and jeopardised that minimum of consensus necessary between rulers and subjects, but there remained in the hearts of military government officials a considerable degree of anger and distrust towards the Germans. This fostered coercive solutions to the labour problem and made it initially hard to accept that German workers should be allowed to call the tune and determine the conditions that were to be offered to them. Ernest Bevin himself opposed making extra rations available with the argument that German miners should not be better fed than Welsh miners. This was the voice of anger not of reason since, as American experts pointed out, there was at that time neither bread nor potato rationing in the United Kingdom and thus no limit on the calorie intake of the miner. But at all levels of the British administration there was the feeling that the Germans could jolly well take what they had been dishing out and that they should put their shoulders to the wheel and help rebuild Europe without worrying over much about their own comfort. Even in 1947, when attitudes had changed a great deal, the GMSO claimed that British authorities had forbidden it from ordering sheets for the hostels with the argument that English soldiers did not receive any sheets either.[49]

When German organisations, particularly the unions and the labour exchanges, called for an improvement, the British accused them of having a double standard. What had been tolerable for forced labour during the war was now apparently intolerable for German workers. This criticism was certainly justified. Far worse conditions *had* been accepted in wartime and racist thinking often lay behind the different standards now being applied. For example, a fact-sheet produced for labour exchanges and potential recruits contained, after an acknowledgement that most of the accommodation for outsiders was in barrack-style building, the undertaking that, 'Von Seiten der Zechen . . . [alles] geschieht, um die Gemeinschaftsunterkünfte in einen zumutbaren und angemessenen Zustand für deutsche Arbeitskräfte zu versetzen.'[50] Clearly, the sheet was trying to

49. WWA S22 (OMGUS), AG 45–46/103/2, J. K. Galbraith and W. W. Rostow to General Clay, 31.5.1946; HStAD NW9, 55, minutes of meeting on 22.2.1947 in the Mannesmannhaus, 22.2.1947.
50. AZG File 'I 126 Zuweisung von Arbeitskräften aus anderen Bezirken

allay anxieties that the accommodation for new miners resembled wartime conditions, and it was perfectly understandable that it should do so; but the language used revealed that the employers were operating with a mental distinction not between peacetime and wartime but between conditions appropriate for foreign workers and those appropriate for Germans. British, indeed Allied, impatience with this attitude was expressed forcibly in the bitter exchanges between British and French manpower experts visiting the Ruhr in summer 1946 and German labour and housing officials. Allied officials wanted to know why accommodation was not available for recruits, given that many men had been housed in the Ruhr during the war; by dint of angry and repeated questioning they forced the German representative, Dr Rappaport, to admit that the camps used during the war had, in many cases, by normal standards never been fit to live in.[51]

The initial reluctance to use incentives was reinforced by the NGCC's view that if the miners were overprivileged they would simply become more intractable and work less. On a number of occasions, Collins expressed the view that it would be 'unwise to give [the miner: MR] an exaggerated idea of his own importance'[52] and that 'whilst I am in favour of making the mining industry attractive to labour, this aspect can be overdone and the labour may tend to get out of hand'.[53]

It is therefore readily understandable that the British initially made no extra provision for the Ruhr miners beyond maintaining their status as recipients of the ration cards for very heavy labour (*Schwerstarbeiter*). A major report by the Manpower Division in September 1945, which dwelt at length on the manpower requirements of the Ruhr and on the need to direct labour to the mines, contained no discussion of incentives, suggesting that they were simply not on the agenda at that time.[54]

1.11.45–31.10.56', GMSO, 'Merkblatt für die Anwerbungsaktion in Holstein', no date.

51. 'Minutes of the Committee to Investigate Coal Production 1946', esp. minutes of Working Party on Manpower, Housing and Related Subjects, 7.8.1946.

52. PRO FO 1039, 693, Deputy Director General, NGCC, memo, 'Coal Production Prospects for 1946', December 1945.

53. PRO FO 1029, 51, Collins, memo on coal industry, 31.12.1945.

54. 'Manpower Report 1945'.

However, it was not long before both the Manpower Division and the NGCC realised that a different approach was needed. The NGCC in particular could not fail to recognise that the regeneration and above all the rejuvenation of the mining workforce required major and long-term improvements in the status and relative and absolute material position of coal miners. At a meeting with French representatives in spring 1946, the NGCC concurred wholeheartedly with the French opinion that more food should be available for the miners but regretted that this did not lie within the competence of the coal authorities. When the Deputy Controller General was asked in February 1946 what effect a small ration drop would have on the miners he predicted accurately the disastrous consequences which then ensued. Yet his words were not heeded and the ration cuts were implemented.[55]

Why, in view of the priority accorded to coal production, were the British unable to improve – indeed, even maintain – the miners' living and working conditions? There were, understandably enough, limits to what the British could be expected to offer from their own resources. The British budget was overburdened and the British population was in any case making increasing sacrifices to sustain occupied Germany. Yet if the British were not prepared to invest their own resources in Ruhr mining, they still had the option of using those of the Germans. To a certain extent this was done: the mining industry received sizeable subsidies from the British zonal budget to cover operating losses. However, taking German marks of little value from the zonal budget was comparatively easy. To obtain the resources that really mattered more serious steps were required.

Before looking in more detail at the options open to the British, it should be borne in mind that foodstuffs, consumer goods, building materials and so on were extremely thin on the ground throughout the British Zone. Above all, food was be-

55. NGCC, 'Interim Report on the General and Financial Situation of the Ruhr Mining Industry', in Astrid Föllmer-Edling, 'Die Politik des Industrieverbands Bergbau im Ruhrgebiet 1945–1948. Die Anstrengungen um die Erhöhung der Kohlenförderung im Ruhrbergbau', unpublished dissertation, University of Bochum, 1977, pp. 6–7; PRO FO 943, 183, 'Conversations with M. Parisot, Directeur des Mines, 13–15 May 1946', May 1946; Collins, *Mining Memories*, p. 34; conversation with Henry Collins, 20.7.1990.

coming desperately short. Even *before* the influx of several million refugees the area encompassed by the Zone had not been self-sufficient in terms of food production, and well before the cessation of hostilities it had already been clear that the future British Zone would be dependent on outside sources of food. Apart from the objective limits to agricultural production within the area, shortages of fertiliser and equipment had reduced agricultural yields. Furthermore, the controlled prices of the wartime and post-war economies gave farmers little incentive to sell their goods, so that a substantial proportion of agricultural produce never found its way into official distribution channels. Shortages of manufactured goods were no less acute than the shortfall in food. The closing stages of the war had brought production in most sectors to a virtual halt and coal and food shortages had prevented all but the most essential industries from making much of a recovery.[56]

One of the Zone's biggest problems was that a very considerable proportion of its coal was being exported. By the end of 1947 the three western Zones had exported 25 million tons of coal, primarily to France, the Low Countries and Scandinavia. As a proportion of overall production this was not dramatically above pre-war peacetime levels, but in the context of post-war conditions it represented a very serious drain on German resources.[57] Coal exports would not have had such a negative impact if the Zone had been properly recompensed for them. The Germans made much play of the fact that coal was being exported at $10.50 a ton while the market price lay between $25 and $30. Had Germany actually received the full price, it was argued, there would have been no difficulty in boosting ration calories and hence the level of coal production. This was an oversimplification which overstated the price differential between German and other coal: however, there was no doubt that the low price paid made the coal exports an almost intolerable burden for the British Zone's war-torn economy.[58] A

56. John E. Farquharson, *The Western Allies and the Politics of Food: Agrarian Management in Post-war Germany*, Leamington Spa/New York, 1985, pp. 28, 61ff.
57. Werner Abelshauser, *Wirtschaftsgeschichte der Bundesrepublik Deutschland 1945–1980*, Frankfurt, 1983, p. 31.
58. Friedrich Jerchow, cited in Falk Pingel, 'Der aufhaltsame Aufschwung. Die Wirtschaftsplanung für die britische Zone im Rahmen der außenpolitischen Interessen der Besatzungsmacht', in Petzina and Euchner, *Wirtschaftspolitik*,

reduction in coal exports would have had an enormously beneficial impact on the economy as a whole and on Ruhr coal production in particular. The extra coal available for internal consumption could have been channelled back to the miners via the production of consumer goods, for instance. Even more productive would have been to use the coal to produce fertiliser. This would rapidly have led to better food supplies for the Ruhr. Another option would have been to produce finished goods for export, the proceeds of which could have been employed for food imports and so on.

The argument for retaining coal in Germany was not restricted to providing incentives. Mining supplies, building supplies for the mines and miners' housing, transport to move the coal and many other areas vital for coal production were suffering as a result of the lack of coal. Indeed, as British Commission officials had long been aware, the whole strategy of boosting just one industry, while allowing others to vegetate or revive only very slowly, was being called into question. To build up coal production effectively required a whole infrastructure and that, in turn, would require coal to put it in order. As one key official put it, 'we need extra coal to manufacture railway and mining supplies. It is useless to buck the political issue and pretend we can make up the difference in economies.'[59]

Why, then, did Britain not reduce the level of coal exports? It was not as if these 'reparations' benefited Britain's economy; they went largely to other countries and in effect actually cost Britain large amounts of money. After all, if the Zone had been properly recompensed for its coal it could itself have afforded to pay for the large-scale food imports into Germany which became such a severe burden on British finances. These are not just abstract arguments. At least by March 1946, if not earlier, *all* levels of the Control Commission in Germany were convinced that more coal must be retained in Germany. In March, General Robertson, the Deputy Military Governor of the British Zone, wrote to Sir Arthur Street, the Permanent Secretary at the Control Office, a letter of the utmost gravity: 'I feel it so import-

p. 48; Farquharson, *The Western Allies*, p. 124; Till Geiger, 'British Policy on the Allocations, the Distribution and the Prices of Ruhr Coal Exports 1945–1947', MSc dissertation, London School of Economics, 1987, pp. 67ff.

59. PRO FO 1039, 693, Economic Division, Econ. 2 (Plans), to E. A. Seal, 13.10.1945.

ant that the main features of the coal problem in Germany should be clearly realised that I am venturing to put them before you briefly in this letter . . . I want to make it clear, and this is the chief object of this letter, that the allocations which we are making to the British Zone are too low.'[60] Yet, Robertson went on, evidently well aware of constraints on Street's freedom of action, 'I am not writing this letter in order that you should take any particular action on it.' What, then, were the constraints in London that prevented the government from acting on this advice?

The British government's policy can be explained almost in one word: France. France was the nation most dependent upon and most acutely interested in Ruhr coal and Britain had good reasons for keeping France happy. For a start, the British government was far from seeing the Americans as its natural allies at that stage. It wanted to ensure that it had some influence on the European continent independently of the Americans, particularly since senior British officials believed the US might return to isolationism in the near future, as after the First World War. Moreover, France was one of the four powers in Berlin. If the French did not get the coal they wanted, they could makes things very unpleasant for the British in the Control Council. One must bear in mind that in 1945 and early 1946 the British felt very vulnerable on the Ruhr issue. They were extremely keen to hold on to the region as an important bargaining counter in any future negotiations over Germany; yet they were well aware of the pressures from the other Allies to introduce quadripartite control over the region.[61]

As it was, the French were growing ever more critical of Britain's policy in the Ruhr and challenging its ability to control the area. As early as November 1945 they were already voicing dissatisfaction to the British. More worrying still, the French tried to enlist the support of the other Allied powers. In March 1946, the French complained to the US State Department that they were being deprived of Ruhr coal to benefit the German steel industry. French pressure came to a head in April because

60. PRO FO 1030, 303, General Robertson to Sir Authur Street, 26.3.1946.
61. PRO FO 942, 182, Economics and Reparations Working Party, agenda for meeting 19.11.1945, November 1945; Turner, 'British policy towards German industry 1945–9: Reconstruction, Restriction or Exploitation?', in *Reconstruction in Post-war Germany*, p. 73; Pingel, 'Der aufhaltsame Aufschwung', p. 48.

in that month the export directive based on the Potter–Hyndley report terminated and a new policy would have to be formulated. General Koenig presented to the quadripartite Allied Control Authority in Berlin a formal complaint about the supplies of coal from the British Zone and at the same time demanded international control over the Ruhr.[62] Given that the Russians certainly had an interest in extending their control over the Ruhr and that the British could not count on American loyalty either, the situation was now extremely worrying. The Americans themselves were urging the British to maximise coal exports to France. The US was very frightened that if economic chaos came to France it would lead to a communist victory.[63]

Clear confirmation of the intimate relationship between British policy on coal exports and its attitude towards France came in May 1946 at a conference between British experts and the German Zonal Advisory Council to discuss ways of improving German coal production. The Germans called for a moratorium on exports to allow them to produce finished goods for export. Over lunch the Deputy Chief of Staff, Major General Bishop, confided to Robert Lehr, Oberpräsident of the North Rhine Province, that a cessation of exports to France would not be in the British interest, because France might interpret a moratorium as an unfriendly act, particularly as elections were pending there. Thus, though no one in London doubted Germany's difficulties, the government remained too nervous about alienating the French to respond to them. In April 1946, when the original coal directive expired, export levels to France were not cut back and, indeed, a series of other measures was undertaken to try to placate the French government further.[64]

One option remained. The British could still have used German stocks of food and consumer goods, or the existing

62. PRO FO 942, 182, Economic and Reparations Working Party, agenda for meeting on 19 November 1945, November 1945; FO 942, 183, Paper, 'Ruhr Coal', no date [April–May 1946]; PRO FO 942, 183, Duff Cooper to Bevin, 8.4.1946; WWA S22 (OMGUS), AG 45–46/103/2 AGWar to OMGUS, 24.3.1946; AG 45–46/103/2, Echols, AGWar, to Clay, April 1946 (exact date illegible), ref: W–85224.

63. Farquharson, *The Western Allies*, p. 122; Pingel, 'Der aufhaltsame Aufschwung', p. 48.

64. HStaD NW 53, 272, 'Notizen von der Konferenz im britischen HQ in Lübbecke am 9.5.1946', Düsseldorf 13.5.1946; PRO FO 942, 183, EIPS/97/150, letter to Duff Cooper, April 1946; FO 942, 500, EIPS File 1330, 'Coal: Technical Advisors', *passim*.

scanty allocation of coal to German civilian uses, to give the miners favoured treatment. The French continually urged the adoption of this policy. A rigorous transfer of the meagre German resources to the Ruhr might well have ensured a flow of manpower to the mines, but this was just the type of ruthless occupation policy that the British were not prepared to undertake. From the start of the Occupation there was a great sensitivity on the part of military government to the dangers of mass unrest that might result if too few resources were allowed for general consumption. In August 1945, for example, Montgomery had protested against the Potter–Hyndley recommendations that coal consumption in Germany be kept to an absolute minimum with the argument that 'I consider that unless an adequate interpretation is placed upon the extent of civil and military requirements . . . grave consequences to the German people can be expected and a measure of trouble arising therefrom which would result in the necessity of increasing our military commitments.'[65] As the food situation in the British Zone became increasingly critical, as morale and public health worsened and productivity declined, the British saw their freedom of manoeuvre grow ever smaller. So strong was their fear of public unrest that they refused to countenance giving extra rations to the miners even when these were offered by other countries and would not have been at the expense of the normal consumer. It is this anxiety that explains why the miners suffered a ration cut in March 1946 like everyone else. When, in July, the British re-established the miners' pre-March rations, they did not make the move public. The US suggested that the increases should be given publicity, but General Robertson replied that he would do so only when he was in a position to give an all-round increase in rations. The restoration remained secret and the impact on recruitment was therefore very limited.[66]

The British probably felt that the German general public

65. WWA S22 (OMGUS), AG 45–46/103/1, Clay to Warcad for Joint Chiefs of Staff, 20.8.1945.
66. WWA S22 (OMGUS), AG 45–46/103/2, J. K. Galbraith and W. W. Rostow to General Clay, 31.5.1946; AG 45–46/103/2, Robertson to Draper, 11.7.1946; PRO FO 943, 183, record of a conversation between Mr Blaisdell, Mr Galbraith and Mr Mark Turner, 11.6.1946; FO 943, 183, Council of Foreign Ministers. Conversations between British, French and American experts about German coal. First meeting, 4 July 1946.

would react particularly sensitively on the issue of priority for the miners precisely because so much of the coal was being exported. Had the production drive been more clearly orientated towards German recovery it seems likely that the British would have been less nervous of giving the miners special status. It is true that, no matter what policy was being adopted towards exports, the severe food shortage in spring 1946 would have disposed the general population against special rations for miners. But the problem of absolute shortages was compounded by the problem of legitimacy and it was above all the level of coal exports which ensured that this was so.

It was in some ways ironic that the British should have fallen foul of this problem. For, as Ian Turner has shown, more than any other of the Occupation administrations, the British Control Commission was committed from the start to a German recovery. They were not out to exploit their Zones as the French or the Russians were. They did not arrive with such a strongly punitive attitude as the Americans. They had tried from the outset to modify the coal directive so as to allow more coal to stay in Germany. But because of foreign pressure their room for manoeuvre was small. The British *did* plough extra amounts of coal into the Zone but were forced to keep this secret for fear of antagonising the Allies (though the Americans at least suspected this was going on). Military government officials continually found themselves in the position of being unable to tell their German counterparts what they were doing for the Zone. Brigadier Marley of the NGCC noted rather ruefully one such encounter with Dr Lehr, Oberpräsident of the Rhine Province. Lehr had come to ask for more coal for the building industries. 'I did not tell him', noted Marley, 'that Building industries get more coal than was allocated . . . the colliery brickyards are producing to the maximum.'[67]

The British thus found themselves in a desperately difficult position. There was no constituency in Germany or in Europe which was prepared to make a sacrifice for the miners, to prime the pump, as it were, and begin a virtuous cycle whereby coal production fuelled other industries and economies which in

67. PRO FO 1030, 693, Brigadier Marley, HQ NGCC to Roberts, Economic Planning Committee, 22.2.1946; WWA S22 (OMGUS) AG 45–46/103/2, Echols, AGWAR, to Clay, April 1946 (exact date illegible), ref: W–85224.

turn would contribute to further growth in mining. The other victorious powers were unwilling to see a reduction in coal exports and yet at the same time were not prepared to provide the Zone with more food or to pay more for its coal. The German population, for its part, would bear no further sacrifice for the sake of an export-oriented coal production programme and the British were not powerful, respected or ruthless enough to demand that sacrifice of them. When the Potter–Hyndley mission had made its report in June 1945 it had recognised the enormous sacrifices that would be necessary to reach production targets. It had argued that 'if acute unrest is to take place somewhere, as would seem inevitable unless coal is made available, it would surely be better for this to occur in Germany than elsewhere. Should it become necessary to preserve order by shooting this would best occur in Germany.'[68] Yet the military government, though it had bowed to international pressure and accepted the Potter–Hyndley targets, was in fact not prepared to shoot.

What could the British do? Unable and unwilling to force production out of the workforce, they were equally unwilling to demand the sacrifices in or outside Germany that would be necessary to offer the miners a viable incentive. And if they did plump for incentives, who should bear the cost? The choice between neglecting their European allies' urgent need for coal or risking a catastrophe in the British Zone was almost unbearable. Symptomatic of the conflicting pressures was that in Germany the British found themselves under pressure to suspend or at least reduce coal exports, while at the same time the European Coal Organisation, on behalf of the liberated countries, continually urged the British government to reduce German coal consumption and increase exports to European countries.[69]

Yet, ultimately, the British would have to make a clear choice because their failure to get the coal was retarding recovery in Germany and the liberated countries alike. Coal was 'the life blood of German economy' and almost as important for Western

68. Potter/Hyndley Report.
69. HStaD NW 53, 272, 'Notizen von der Konferenz im britischen HQ in Lübbecke am 9.5.1945', Düsseldorf 13.5.1948. PRO FO 942, 183, Eaton Griffiths, ECO to Bercomb for Econ Coal, Berlin – several letters, April 1946; PRO FO 943, 183, memo, 'Informal Discussions on German Problems', July 1946.

Europe.[70] In a memorandum on measures to improve the coal position, the American economists J. K. Galbraith and W. W. Rostow wrote of the 'utter seriousness' of the British responsibility.[71] It is barely an exaggeration to say that the fate of European reconstruction depended on whether the British would be able to regenerate the labour force in the Ruhr mines.

It was therefore inevitable that British policy towards the Ruhr mines would change. Politically, economically and financially, the British could not afford to continue failing to get the coal. The only question was how quickly the pressure would reach a point where the British were forced to burst through the constraints and adopt a more consistent and successful approach.

70. Quotation from General Balfour, British Deputy Chief of Staff, at a conference on coal held in May 1946. HStaD NW 53, 272, 'Conference held at Main HQ CCG(BE) on 10 May on the Subject of "Methods of Increasing the Coal Output in the British Zone"', official minutes, May 1946; Werner Abelshauser, *Wirtschaft in Westdeutschland 1945–1948. Rekonstruktion und Wachstumsbedingungen in der amerikanischen und britischen Zone*, Stuttgart, 1975, p. 140.

71. WWA S22 (OMGUS), AG 45–46/103/2, J. K. Galbraith, W. W. Rostow to Clay, 31.5.1946.

2
Bringing Home the Bacon: Manpower, Incentives and Coal Production, 1946–1948

Turning the Tide

As 1946 wore on, the pressure for a new approach to coal mounted both inside and outside Germany. One prod in this direction came in April, when senior German economic experts, with the backing of industrial and trade union leaders, formulated an alternative to the coercion policy. Hitherto the German opposition to directions had lacked clear exponents. With the creation of the German Economic Advisory Board/Zentralamt für Wirtschaft (ZfW) in March 1946, a platform emerged for a more forthright German contribution. At a conference held in Düsseldorf at the beginning of April, ZfW experts, trade unionists and industrialists thrashed out their recommendations. Recognising that the problem of labour motivation had to be solved, they called for rations of 3,800 calories for underground workers, special entitlements to consumer goods, productivity bonuses in the form of tobacco allocations, wage and pension increases and a shortening of the working day for miners above ground.[1]

British military government itself became increasingly insistent in its calls for more incentives. On one demand, that the miners should have more food than other groups, opinion within the Control Commission remained somewhat divided. But even here there was a burgeoning consensus that the miners should be privileged. In April 1946, for example, the Food and Agriculture Division for the first time endorsed the suggestion

1. BAK Z1, 361, 'Bericht zur Kohlenfrage' and 'Gutachten des deutschen Wirtschaftsrats zur Kohlenfrage', 10.4.1946; PRO FO 942, 183, 'German Economic Advisory Board Coal Report', 10.4.1946.

that they should receive additional rations. And in the Control Office in London, too, the view was making headway that at 'one stage or another we have to put our trust in the miner and permitting him to have the disposal of the extra food allowance, in view of past events, appears a sound way to start the rehabilitation process'.[2] On the other key demand, that Germany should retain more coal, the military government was, as we have already noted, unanimous. 'The French cannot have any more coal, indeed will have to accept an overall reduction,' as General Robertson told the Control Office in March.[3] But Robertson himself made clear that he was arguing solely on the basis of the problems confronting him in Germany. He could not decide London's priorities for it. It was to be the repeated and exasperating experience of French and American officials in Germany that whoever they talked to agreed to the need for incentives but did not have the authority to implement the policy.[4]

By June, the message coming out of the British administration in Germany was even starker. The Military Governor, Sir Sholto Douglas, himself wrote to the Control Office on the issue: 'It may be very important to placate the French at this time, of that I am not the right judge, but I am sure that in the long run they and the other European countries would be worse off by reason of the failure of German industry to maintain the mines or to contribute anything to their needs.'[5] Douglas argued that a four months' moratorium on exports was essential if the Zone was ever to extricate itself from the vicious cycle of coal deprivation and economic stagnation.[6] The Control Office and the Chancellor of the Duchy of Lancaster accepted the desirability of a moratorium and, at a meeting of the Overseas Reconstruction Committee on 21 June, so did the Ministry of Fuel and Power.

2. PRO FO 943, 183, 'German Economic Advisory Board Coal Report', cover note from J. Simpson, 25.4.1946; and see FO 1005, 379, COPROD P(46) 5.

3. PRO FO 1030, 303, General Robertson to Sir Arthur Street, 26.3.1946.

4. PRO FO 943, 183, Conversations with M. Parisot, 'Directeur des Mines, 13–15 May 1946', May 1946; WWA S22 (OMGUS), AG 45–46/103/2, Leo Werts to Chief of Staff, 2.7.1946.

5. PRO FO 1030, 156, Douglas to Duchy of Lancaster, 21.6.1946.

6. Ibid. and PRO FO 371,58402, telegram from Douglas to Turner and Street, 4 June 1946, cited in Till Geiger, 'British Policy on the Allocations, the Distribution and the Prices of Ruhr Coal Exports 1945–1947', MSc dissertation, London School of Economics, 1987.

The government's problem, however, of which the Foreign Office was particularly aware, was that it continued to feel internationally very isolated on the Ruhr issue. On 25 June, the Control Office therefore indicated to Douglas that an export moratorium might be acceptable but only if American support were forthcoming.[7]

Over the next few weeks, the British tested the waters of international opinion on the issue. To show willing, they agreed to the formation of a quadripartite experts' committee to investigate coal production in all four Zones of Germany, but primarily in the Ruhr. As the committee was being set up, General Robertson met with American and French representatives in Paris to canvass their views on an exports moratorium. At the time, the American response was favourable, but in Washington US State Department officials supported French opposition to the idea. Worries about communist successes in France had evidently outweighed the State Department's undoubted understanding of the Ruhr's problems.[8]

The British government therefore did not make any cuts. In an informal meeting, Bevin promised his French counterpart, Bidault, every possible assistance. And a couple of weeks later a statement was made to the House of Commons to the effect that the Foreign Office could not accept any reduction in exports of coal to liberated countries. This, in turn, brought the fiercest retort yet from Sir Sholto Douglas and an apologetic reply from Sir Gilmore Jenkins, a senior civil servant in the Control Office. In view of the sensitivity of international opinion, he wrote, the Cabinet had resolved not to make any decision in advance of the findings of the Experts Committee. 'This is not the view of the Control Office nor of the Chancellor [of the Duchy of Lancaster], but we failed to get our way.'[9]

7. PRO FO 943, 183, Sir Mark Turner to Chancellor of Duchy of Lancaster, 20 June 1946 and 'Extract from the Conclusions of the 9th Meeting of the Overseas Reconstruction Committee held on Friday 21 June 1946', 3: Sitn of German Coal Industry; FO 1039, 652, telegram CONFOLK to BERCOMB, Chancellor of the Duchy of Lancaster to Sir Sholto Douglas, 25.6.1946; John E. Farquharson, *The Western Allies and the Politics of Food: Agrarian Management in Post-war Germany*, Leamington Spa/New York, 1985, p. 121.

8. PRO FO 943, 183, Council of Foreign Ministers. Conversations between British, French and American experts about German coal, First meeting 4.7.1946; and PRO FO 943, 183, 'Informal Discussions on German Coal Problems', July 1946; Farquharson, *The Western Allies*, pp. 122–3.

9. PRO FO 1030, 156 secret letter from Sir Gilmore Jenkins to Sir Sholto

By the end of August, however, there were signs of greater movement. Once again, it was Sir Sholto Douglas who took up the cudgels. It was clear, he argued, that the rancorous and divided Experts Committee would not come to a decision on the question of exports. In any case, its deliberations were dragging on longer than expected. The British therefore could not afford to wait: 'I feel so strongly about this that I propose to come to London on Monday 2 September to discuss the question of [sic] the highest level. I should like to have an interview with the Prime Minister about it.'[10] Given that an exports moratorium was said to be politically impossible, Douglas proposed significant cuts in coal exports over the next three months, giving the Western Zones between 300,000 and 400,000 tons a month more than they were at present receiving.[11]

This time, Douglas's exhortations did not go unheeded. Exports from the British and American Zones were reduced by 150,000 tons a month for October and November and further monthly reductions of 200,000 tons approved for the period December–March. What had finally induced the government to act? Certainly not any softening of French opposition. When Sir Mark Turner told the French Ministry of Foreign Affairs on 4 September that coal exports might have to fall, the French representatives, 'speaking very earnestly', as the British minutes note, 'emphasised the harm for French reconstruction and Anglo-French relations'.[12]

The real reason for the government's new stance lay in the progressive and interrelated changes in American reconstruction policy and Britain's overall international orientation which took place during the spring and summer of 1946. Above all, by proposing a fusion of the Zones, the US effectively agreed to

---

Douglas, 1.8.1946; telegram CONFOLK to BERCOMB, 1.8.1946; telegram BER-COMB to CONFOLK, signed Douglas, 31.7.1946; FO 1028, 51, HQ NGCC, Collins to DE(Exec), T&I Division, 17.6.1946, annex: 'Control of the German Coal Industry . . .'; Geiger, 'British Policy and Ruhr Coal Exports', p. 74.

10. PRO FO 1030, 156, telegram BERCOMB to CONFOLK, personal from Sir Sholto Douglas, 29.8.1946.

11. PRO FO 1030, 156, telegram BERCOMB to CONFOLK, 30.8.1946.

12. PRO FO 1028, 52, BIP board paper BIB/P(46)30, 31.12.1946.; FO 1030, 326, minutes of meeting with the (French) Ministry of Foreign Affairs on 4 September, signed H. Ashley Clarke, 4.9.1946. The end to the US coal strike had, however, improved the supply situation for France a little; Geiger, 'British Policy and Ruhr Coal Exports', p. 85.

carry some of Britain's burdens. Moreover, because the Americans now had to shoulder some of the responsibility for the Ruhr they too came out in favour of export reductions. Indeed, they demanded more swingeing cuts than the British government had done. So the British were no longer isolated. Freed from some of their dependence on French goodwill, they were able to give Germany's own need for coal a higher priority in their general economic strategy. By the autumn, in fact, they were refusing to engage in any formal bilateral talks with France on coal matters.[13]

At the same time as the exports question was being resolved, the British were also taking steps to increase the miners' privileges with respect to food and consumer goods. For one thing, the general food situation had improved. Sizeable grain imports had done much to ease the shortages. In addition, the Americans' new commitment to rapid recovery, as proclaimed in the Byrnes speech of 6 September 1946, brought with it the offer of more help for the British Zone, which would make an incentive strategy for the miners financially less burdensome to introduce. Another key point about Byrnes's public statement was that it made it easier for the Germans to see the coal drive as part of a general recovery programme and thereby gave the military government the legitimacy to favour the miners with incentives. Thus, in September 1946, the British announced an increase in miners' rations to 3,800 calories. In October, the face workers' ration was raised to 4,000 calories and further rises were to follow. Finally, by quadripartite agreement, miners' wages were increased by 20 per cent in November.[14]

Whilst debating whether to commit these resources to the Ruhr, the British had also been experimenting with yet another option: universal conscription. In June 1946, the Manpower Division began to make preparations for the scheme and in a secret directive to the labour exchanges ordered them to form a separate 'coal-mining register' of all men born in 1926, 1927 and 1928.[15] Here, as on the incentives question, the British

---

13. Gieger, 'British Policy and Ruhr Coal Exports', pp. 90–1; PRO FO 1028, BIP paper 'Policy about Coal Exports' see also FO 943, 185, 'Brief on Special Points Arising from Coal Experts Report for Use in Foreign Secretary's Discussion with the French', October 1946 and docs E 1/7/4 106ff.
14. PRO FO 943, 186, paper, 'The Coal Industry in the British Zone', April 1947.
15. PRO FO 1005, 776 Manpower Directorate Committee of Labour Supply

proceeded extremely cautiously. Trade union leaders were consulted, a formal request for views was made to the Zonal
Advisory Council (ZAC), the top German body in the Zone, and
a major public opinion poll was carried out. Since both general
public and unions proved hostile to the idea, it was never
implemented, although the fact that the British did not allow the
special coal-mining register to be dissolved until May 1947
suggests that they were keeping their options open.[16]

In any case, the plan for universal conscription rapidly became redundant as the new incentives improved labour supply
and motivation. The effect of higher rations on production was,
in fact, pretty well instantaneous: hard coal output averaged
180,000 tons per day in September and by 8 November had risen
to 193,500 tons, the highest daily output since the end of the
war. In March 1946, 99 per cent of newcomers to the mines had
been conscripted, but, by December, 85 per cent were volunteers. The overall number of recruits rose steadily. More important, observers in the Ruhr commented on the willingness to
work of the volunteers, in marked contrast to the conscripts.
Almost one-and-a-half years after submission of the Potter–
Hyndley report, the tide had begun to turn.[17]

The Points System

It is hard to say what would have happened to the flow of new
labour had no further incentives been introduced. It is probable
that the mines would have continued to attract workers away
from other Ruhr industries, at least for a while, but that the
rations on their own would not have been enough to draw large
numbers from areas further afield. Since essential industries in

and Manpower Allocation. Minutes of 30th and 31st meetings, April/May 1946;
FO 943, 190, Manpower Division, 'Labour Supply for Coal Mining', 29.6.1946;
FO 1005, 1824, Labour Supply Branch Directive 17, 19.6.1946.

16. PA, File 1, 203, ZAC P(46) 93; PA 1, 203, 'Stellungnahme der Gewerkschaft IV Bergbau, 15.11.1946; PRO FO 1005, 1738, German Personnel Research
Branch, Intelligence Division, Social Survey no.1, 'Attitudes of Germans to Coal
Mining'; StAM AA Dortmund, 47, LAA NRW Außenstelle Westfalen-Lippe,
circular to directors of labour exchanges, 2.5.1947.

17. PRO FO 943, 185, ECOSC/P(46)45, November 1946; August Niehues,
'Ruhrbergbau und Arbeitsvermittlung', *Arbeitsblatt für die britische Zone*, vol. 1,
no. 3, 1947, pp. 88–90.

the Ruhr, and hence the economy as a whole, would begin to suffer if mining recruits continued to come almost exclusively from the immediate vicinity of the mines, it was vital to offer something more.

This was one reason why the British considered introducing a coupon system to enable the miners to obtain scarce consumer goods. In August 1946, the Americans had introduced such a scheme for (the admittedly small number of) miners in their Zone and they offered the British help in supplying goods to develop a similar programme. At the beginning of November, members of the Economic Sub Commission (ECOSC), the NGCC, the Manpower Division and other sections of the military government met to discuss the issue and outlined a provisional solution. Discussions began with the GMSO and the miners' union, the Industrieverband Bergbau (IVB), and in mid-November the GMSO submitted a more detailed proposal for a coupon system. In December, the head of ECOSC, Cecil Weir, invited the German coal working party (Arbeitsgruppe Kohle), an organisation founded by the new bizonal Executive Committee for Economics (Verwaltungsrat für Wirtschaft), to help finalise proposals and in January the introduction of the Points System was announced, making headlines in almost every country in the western world.[18]

The basic outline of the system was very simple: it consisted of special coupons and points with which the miners were able to buy goods otherwise virtually unobtainable in Germany, except on the black market. The coupons for spirits and tobacco were graded according to the type of job, face workers naturally receiving the biggest allowance. Points were given in relation to wages, although there was a guaranteed minimum as long as a worker did not miss shifts.[19]

The Points System attracted much attention abroad because it was the first time that a major reward for success had been offered to the Germans and because it appeared to be the most overt indication hitherto of Allied commitment to rapid German

18. PRO FO 943, 185, Doc 121A, Bevin to Byrnes, 11.11.1946; DGBA, File 'Gewerkschaftliches Zonensekretariat, Britische Zone, 1947, 1', VfW to Economics Ministry, NRW and others, 25.3.1947. Appendices 3 and 7; OBADA I8000/294/47, 'Bericht der Arbeitsgruppe Kohle . . .', Düsseldorf 14.1.1947.
19. PRO FO 943, 185, NGCC Production Branch, memorandum, 'Points System', 14.1.1947.

recovery. Yet at least some of this attention was misplaced. As the account above has made clear, the scheme was in many ways merely the logical extension of policies already tried and tested. Moreover, it represented far less of an Allied commitment than appeared at first sight. In the first place, the resources given to the miners were obtained at the cost of other German consumers and not of the foreign recipients of German coal. No extra coal was made available to produce the miners' consumer goods: they were simply withdrawn from the general civilian stocks. In spring 1947, 20 per cent of all textiles available to the Germans went to the miners – or, in other words, one-sixtieth of the population received one-fifth of the goods. While in April 1947 civilian rations fell to a low of 900 calories per day in some parts of the Ruhr, the miners were receiving 3,000 calories.[20]

Secondly, this degree of favouritism was not really what the Allies had wanted. The original British proposal had been to limit the miners to four times the normal civilian allocation; in fact, as the above figures show, in textiles and other supplies the miners received eight to ten times the general rate. What had happened was that the scheme subsequently worked out between GMSO, IVB and NGCC linked the amount of incentives not to the total volume of available supplies but instead to the miners' wages. The original ceiling of four times the average civilian allocation was thus removed. Under the new proposal the top limit to incentives was governed solely by the wages earned. The GMSO and the IVB hoped that a share of the extra coal produced could be used to pay for imports of food and consumer goods and also to provide fuel for Germany's consumer goods industry; thus the miners would 'pay for' their own privileges and the special allocations would not be at the cost of the ordinary consumer.[21] Then, in December 1946, it became clear that other parts of military government and the Control Office were hostile to the idea of a guaranteed coal contingent for Points System goods. In view of their foreign commitments, the British were not prepared to make any

20. PRO FO 1030, 345, telegrams BERCOMB to CONFOLK, refs QUPEE 296 and 297, both 15.3.1947; FO 943, 185, 'Miners' Points Scheme', extract from BIB/M (47) 3, 3.3.1947.
21. PA 2, 558, VfW, memorandum, 'betr.: Anteil des Bergarbeiter-Punktsystems an der Gesamtversorgung des Vereinigten Wirtschaftsgebietes', 23.2.1948; VfW to Economics Ministry, NRW and others, 25.3.1947, appendix 7.

guarantee as to the amount of coal that could be made available to pay for imports nor to give a firm undertaking that extra coal would be injected in to the German consumer goods industries.[22]

The scheme might well have been dropped at that point since it suited neither the Germans nor the British administration. The Germans were hesitant to endorse a programme which could end up being supplied exclusively from existing German stocks at the expense of other consumers, while many British officials regarded as dangerous and immoral such heavy favouritism as might well ensue. The deputy Military Governor himself considered the scheme 'opportunist'.[23] Both sides recognised, however, that non-implementation might have a serious impact on production because news of the scheme had already been leaked to the miners. Indeed, as early as August 1946, August Halbfell had been suggesting to senior mining officials that a points system would soon be introduced in the British Zone. In an attempt to counteract the dangerous assumption that all was settled, the NGCC temporarily forbade public discussion of the matter. This was to no avail; it was then deemed too dangerous to disappoint the miners' expectations after so much publicity. With a heavy heart, the German authorities endorsed the Points System and agreed, if necessary, to allocate all available consumer goods to it alone.[24]

In other words, the scheme actually came into being as the result of political pressures, perhaps even of a little political brinkmanship from GMSO and IVB, who may well have deliberately raised miners' expectations in order to put pressure on the authorities: it was not the result of the careful cost–benefit analysis of diverting so many resources to the miners. This

22. 'Bericht der Arbeitsgruppe Kohle'; DGBA, File 'Gewerkschaftliches Zonensekretariat, Britische Zone, 1947, 1', VfW, 'Protokoll der Sitzung über die Durchführung des Punktsystems am 27.1.1947', Minden 28.1.1947; OBADA I 8000/ 542/47, Wirtschaftsminister Nölting to the executive of the IVB, 13.2.1947 (copy); PRO FO 943, 187, telegram from FO, German Section, to CO, Berlin, 25.7.1947.
23. PRO FO 943, 185, Extract from BIB/M(47)3, 3.3.1947. Clay concurred in this judgement.
24. WWA F35, 493, report of a talk by LAA President Halbfell in Herne, 9.8.1946; OBADA I 8000/2624/46, GMSO to OBAD, 2.12.1946; DGBA, File 'Gewerkschaftliches Zonensekretariat, Britische Zone, 1947, 1', report of a meeting of the Sonderausschuss at the VfW in Minden, 27.1.1947.

process seems to have been a characteristic feature of the post-war controlled economy (see chapter 3). It meant in this case that the scheme went into operation without any proof that the necessary stores were available and, over the following months, supply problems continually threatened to undermine the programme's credibility.

Labour, Incentives and Output, 1947

Despite this uncertain beginning, the Points System transformed the labour supply position in the mines. Small wonder, when according to the estimate of a top bank official in Düsseldorf, a miner's real income was equivalent to a gross annual salary of RM 300,000. Within weeks of the critical shortage of labour in the collieries, other industries were complaining about labour losses to the pits. Whereas 61,988 men had been taken on in 1946, the number rose to 87,235 in 1947. More important, these new miners did not disappear within the first few days. Fewer men left the pits in 1947 than in 1946, despite the higher intake. Even during the spring food crisis, the monthly level of recruitment remained above and the monthly labour losses below the average figures for the previous year. The new measures called forth not only the labour reserves in the British Zone but also thousands of young men in the Soviet Zone, many of them seeking to evade Russian registration of labour.[25]

To attain its zonal production goal of 400,000 tons a day by 1949, the NGCC had calculated that 300,000 underground workers would be needed in the Ruhr. Workforce growth in 1947 was well in line with this manpower target. By the end of the year the underground workforce had increased to 240,101, compared with 193,069 at the end of 1946, and it would have risen even more swiftly if shortages of housing and other supplies had not limited the mines' capacity to absorb newcomers. If 1948 was just as good as 1947, the 300,000 figure would be attained. The

25. See figures in OBADA I 8010 vols 2–5 OBAD Lageberichte; WWA S22 (OMGUS), BICO BISEC 11/104–1/39, Special Intelligence Report, 'Some German Views of the Political, Economic and Sociological Aspects of Ruhr Coal Mining', 19.6.1948. Ges.Verb., StdKW, unpublished table: 'Belegschaftswechsel. Arbeiter Untertage. Ruhr'; OBADA I8010/2189/47, OBAD Lagebericht for July 1947.

growth of 1947 was probably the biggest single year's increase in the history of Ruhr mining, without parallel even in the explosive growth phase at the end of the nineteenth century, and a sign of just how irresistible were the twin sirens of extra rations and scarce consumer goods.[26]

The influx of new labour overcame the worst of the coal shortage. As early as autumn 1947, experts involved in the distribution and allocation of coal observed that output was beginning to ease coal's stranglehold on the economy.[27] In a congratulatory speech to the NRW Landtag, General Robertson confirmed the connection between labour supply and production when he noted that 'Die Steigerung der Kohlenförderung ist größtenteils auf einen erhöhten Arbeitseinsatz in den Bergwerken zurückzuführen.'[28]

Nevertheless, the story of coal from autumn 1946 onwards is not the success story it seems. Undeniable though the Points System's effectiveness was in expanding the workforce, production and productivity lagged far behind expectations. The British had, not unreasonably, expected the underground miner's efficiency to rise by 15–20 per cent in the course of 1947. This would have brought shift output up to between 1.4 and 1.5 tons a head by the end of the year, a figure equivalent to around three-quarters of 1938 productivity. In fact, average output per man/shift in 1947 showed virtually no improvement over the previous year's level and was actually somewhat *below* the figures attained at the end of 1946 (see table 2.1)! Despite the Points System and other incentives, the underground workforce was operating at barely more than 60 per cent of pre-war efficiency.

As a result, production failed to meet its target. By the end of the year, the mines in the British Zone were supposed to be

26. PRO FO 943, 185, F. H. Harrison, Fuel and Power Division. 'The Forward Planning of Coal Production and Distribution', 3.3.1947; *ZdKW*, vol. 1, p. 20, vol. 7, p. 32. The nineteenth-century statistics do not distinguish between the arrival of newcomers to the *industry* and movement from colliery to colliery, so it is impossible to say how many genuine newcomers arrived in any one year. What is clear is that actual workforce *growth* never reached the 1947 level. Frans-Josef Brüggemeier, *Leben vor Ort. Ruhrbergleute und Ruhrbergbau 1889–1919*, Munich, 1983, pp. 271–2, 277.

27. BAK Z40, 2, Deutsches Kohlenstatistisches Amt, 'Die Kohlenwirtschaft zu Beginn des Winters 1947/1948', Essen, November 1947.

28. Außenstelle Bergbau (ed.), 'Sechs Jahre Außenstelle Bergbau des Landesarbeitamtes NRW', unpublished MS, no place, no date [1952].

Table 2.1 Workforce, production and productivity, 1946–7

Year/ month	Workforce size at end of month (underground)	Average daily production (metric tons)	O.m.s. (underground) (t)	Ration period begin[b]	Calories rec'd[a]
(1938 =	228,813	416,300	1.970)		
1946					
October	186,421		1.227	14.10.46	3,672
November	189,812		1.221	10.11.46	3,373
December	193,069		1.231	9.12.46	3,834
1947					
January	198,877	198,000	1.234	6.1.47	3,586
February	203,288	212,800	1.253	3.2.47	3,823
March	205,394	218,500	1.258	3.3.47	3,645
April	207,391	204,300	1.199	31.3.47	3,628
May	209,461	201,100	1.176	28.4.47	3,643
June	212,599	203,400	1.181	26.5.47	3,570
July	217,940	208,900	1.192	23.6.47	3,767
August	223,700	220,800	1.214	21.7.47	3,795
September	227,577	224,800	1.229	18.8.47	3,837
				15.9.47	3,929
October	232,627	229,400	1.198	13.10.47	3,855
November	238,267	260,700	1.212	10.11.47	3,833
December	240,101	244,600	1.230	8.12.47	3,780
1948					
January	240,755	237,100	1.196	5.1.48	3,637
March	242,916	269,600	1.307		
June	244,916	265,800	1.307		

(a) Rations for underground workers.
(b) Ration periods were exactly 28 days. They are aligned in the table with the month in which most of the ration period fell.

Source: *ZdKW*, vol. 1, pp. 20, 28; vol. 4, p. 2; vol. 7, pp. 32, 44; WWA S22 (OMGUS) CO HIST BR 3/404–1/8, telegram from Wright to Adcock, 26.2.1948.

producing 300,000 tons a day, yet for the period October 1947–March 1948, average daily production was only about 266,000 tons;[29] in other words the increase since the end of 1946 had been little over half that hoped for. In the period up to the currency reform, the gap between target and reality widened. In spring 1948, the coal shortage became, briefly, as pressing as it had ever been. By June 1948, daily production had not gone much beyond 265,000 tons, when it should have been well on its way to 400,000 tons.[30] Once again, the enormous priority given to coal had not produced the desired results. At first sight this is even more inexplicable than in the early period, for the miners had now been offered the incentives that had previously been so sorely lacking. On closer inspection, however, the production drive exposed fundamental weaknesses in the political and economic system of the occupation period. The characteristic deficiencies of a fixed-price economy were joined and exacerbated by the tensions arising from the relationship between occupying power and subject people. In the ostensibly 'controlled' economy, resources, management and labour proved, as this and the following chapter will demonstrate, to be largely beyond control.

How much more could the British have achieved? One thing not in doubt is that their general strategy of recruiting as many men as possible was the best way to achieve a rapid increase in production. Equally certain was, as the Ruhr mines had several times been reminded in the course of the twentieth century, that the effect of rapid recruitment was to depress or at least retard the progress of individual output.[31] The rationale of mass recruitment was that the costs to average individual output would be outweighed by the gains in workforce size. The highest production possible under the circumstances would be obtained, but at the cost of some inefficiency.

Quite a lot of the inefficiency of the post-war period falls into this category of the unavoidable and economically justifiable

29. Calculated from the monthly averages in *ZdKW*, vol. 4, p. 3. Production figures for British Zone.
30. Ibid.
31. E.g. after the First World War and again in the second half of the 1930s. See Rudolf Tschirbs, *Tarifpolitik im Ruhrbergbau 1918–1933*, Berlin, 1986, p. 251; Klaus Wisotzky, *Der Ruhrbergbau im Dritten Reich. Studien zur Sozialpolitik im Ruhrbergbau und zum sozialen Verhalten der Bergleute in den Jahren 1933 bis 1939*, Düsseldorf, 1983, pp. 231ff.

consequence of a mass recruitment strategy. For example, to obtain so much labour so swiftly, the selection criteria had to be fairly lax. At the behest of the military government, the mines continued to take 'alles, was Arm und Bein hatte'. Indeed, in the course of 1946 the British had raised the upper age limit to 45. Clearly, the recruitment of unskilled men over 40 was not likely to improve productivity.[32] Thus, the high rate of recruitment necessarily resulted in less than optimum individual productivity and this was perfectly acceptable. Given the objective value of coal to the German and wider European economies, a certain amount of labour inefficiency was more than justified. Not quite so easy to justify were the high human costs of the strategy. The minimal training levels resulted in an accident rate in 1947 almost as disastrous as the previous year's. Yet so much depended on getting the coal that possibly even these costs could be excused.

The point is, however, that a lot of the inefficiency in the 1946–8 period does *not* fall into this category of the unavoidable consequence of mass recruitment. To prove this we need only contrast the output of new and experienced men. We cannot do this directly, since the normal statistical returns do not distinguish between the experienced *Hauer* and the other face workers.[33] What we can say is that during 1947 productivity at the face rose by 10 per cent, attaining a level equivalent to 80 per cent of 1938 output per man/shift. Since we already know that for the underground workforce *as a whole* output per man stagnated, it is clear that results at the face were very much more successful than elsewhere in the mine.[34] From other sources we know that new recruits were concentrated at the face. In the two collieries belonging to the Gute Hoffnungshütte, for example, statistics show that new miners made up 42 per cent of the face

32. PRO FO 943, 185, British Monthly Report on Implementation of Agreed Recommendations of Part II of Coal Experts' Report, 28.10.1946.

33. Abelshauser offers some figures contrasting the output of the experienced *Hauer* and the rest of the workforce but in fact this is an understandable confusion based on misleading terminology in the OMGUS statistics which were his source (Werner Abelshauser, *Wirtschaft in Westdeutschland 1945–1948. Rekonstruktion und Wachstumsbedingungen in der amerikanischen und britischen Zone,* Stuttgart, 1975, pp. 140–1). The English-language term 'hewer' was in fact being used to denote all face workers, whether experienced or new. See H. E. Collins, 'Progress in Rebuilding the Coal-mining Industry in Western Germany', *Transactions of the Institution of Mining Engineers,* vol. 107, no. 8, 1947–8, p. 19, which properly refers to the same figures as face worker o.m.s.

34. Collins, 'Progress', p. 19.

workers in one case and 65.9 per cent in the other, but only 18.7 per cent and 40 per cent respectively of the underground work-force as a whole. In the Hibernia mines, at the end of 1948, three-quarters of all new miners were concentrated at the face. From the following year's statistics we can see that about 40 per cent of all face workers and over 50 per cent of those directly involved in coal getting itself were newcomers.[35] In other words, the concentration of newcomers was highest at the very point which was achieving the best results – suggesting that their inexperience was not the only, indeed not the major, factor depressing productivity.[36] In fact, what we will find is that the difficulties associated with the productive deployment of new labour had become inextricably interwoven with the problem of restoring the established workforce's efficiency.

Food, Authority and Coal

Why was it that a group so immensely privileged as the miners could not be induced to higher output? As a senior US official complained, 'Large proportions of raw materials [have] been diverted from the German economy to an exclusive set of workers, who [have] not in return delivered the coal.'[37] The results achieved were so poor that some sections of the military government considered removing the Points System altogether.

One key problem was that, despite the incentives programme, food was periodically in short supply. In 1947 there were two food crises in the Ruhr, one in spring and another one in December. To a certain extent the miners' rations were directly affected. The fluctuations in calorific content, though relatively small, could still make considerable impact and, in addition, the figures masked more serious drops in the quality of the ration. In January–February 1948, for example, the heavy worker's ration was adequate in terms of calories (3,875 per day) yet very poor in quality terms. There was no meat at all, the fat

35. I.e. adults who had been in the mining industry for under three years.

36. BBA 30, 34, GHH mines' annual report for period 1948–9; 32, 1509, 'Bergmännische Zahlenberichte' 1948 and 1949, table 'Umschülerbewegung'.

37. WWA S22 (OMGUS), BICO BISEC 11/103–2/16, minutes of meeting of Working Party on the Miners' Points Scheme, 21.8.1947; see also meeting on 11.9.1947.

ration was not fully met and a good deal of the calories came in the form of cereals and sugar.[38] In general however, the miners' ration held up reasonably well. In flat contrast to this, the rations allocated to miners' families and to other Ruhr 'civilians' (i.e. those not in special labour categories) fell to absolutely catastrophic depths, far below the subsistence level. The official civilian ration in 1947 was around 1550 calories a day, itself insufficient to maintain body-weight. In April 1947, the actual ration in a number of Ruhr towns averaged 970 calories. In May, citizens in Bochum were treated to just 629 calories. By July the Ruhr average was still only 1,260.[39]

These crises were accompanied by major reversals in the upward trend of production (see table 2.1). Until March 1947, productivity had risen rapidly but in April and May the trend was reversed abruptly and productivity fell well below the levels it had attained before the introduction of the Points System. Production was hit not just by a general fall in productivity and attendance but also by sporadic strikes from February 1947 onwards, often led by miners' wives. In April the Oberbergamt noted 'eine wachsende Unruhe und Gereiztheit unter den Belegschaften'.[40] Protests and strikes grew in number, culminating in a 24-hour protest strike on 4 April in which 300,000 miners took part. At the end of April, the NGCC reported that coal production estimates had had to be reduced dramatically. Instead of the original prediction of 292,193 tons a day by September, the expectation now was only 260,000 tons. It was not until August that daily production attained the performance of March. A renewed drop occurred in the December–January period, forcing a further revision of military government estimates.[41]

It is evident from all this that the Points Scheme and the extra

38. WWA S22 (OMGUS), CO HIST BR 3/404–1/7, UK/US Coal Control Group (UK/USCCG), report to the Bipartite Control Office for February 1948.
39. WWA S22 (OMGUS), CO HIST BR 3/406–1/22, NGCC, notes on NGCC; Werner Abelshauser, *Der Ruhrkohlenbergbau seit 1945. Wiederaufbau, Krise, Anpassung*, Munich, 1984, p. 40.
40. OBADA I8010/1343/47, OBAD Lagebericht for April.
41. Michael Clarke, 'Die Gewerkschaftspolitik der KPD 1945–1951, dargestellt am Beispiel des IVB/IGB im Ruhrgebiet', unpublished dissertation, Bochum University, 1982, p. 35; OBADA I 8010/723/47, OBAD Lageberichte for February and March 1947, PRO FO 1005, 380, COPROD P(47)23, NGCC, 'Forward Estimates of Coal Production', 29.4.1947.

rations for miners had not solved the problem of incentives. It was a striking indication of the scale of the food shortages in post-war Germany that rations in the Ruhr, the crucible of German recovery, should fall to such devastatingly low levels. Of course, the authorities could have introduced even more rigorous prioritisation within the Ruhr or within the British Zone than they did and have increased the disparity between miners and the rest of the population. This might have maintained coal production at a higher level. Yet the option of greater inequality and particularly the introduction of special privileges for the Ruhr area as a whole was rejected by the military governors, who felt that the limit of what was morally justifiable and politically advisable had been reached. The only concession made was to declare the Ruhr a special priority area with respect to any supplementary imports of food that would be made in future, a move which eventually had some impact on ration levels in the area.[42]

In the minds of the many anxious observers in the Ruhr, there was no doubt that the fall in the civilian ration was the primary cause of the drop in production. They could point to the fact that married men, who felt obliged to give an ever-increasing portion of their extra rations to their undernourished families, were directly physically hit by the ration cuts. Yet, though the food shortages were undoubtedly the trigger for the deterioration in productivity, the real causes were more complex. As in the earlier period, the cuts' psychological impact was probably more decisive than their direct physical implications. Productivity was hit harder and for longer than the mere calorie deficiency would warrant.[43]

Part of the background to this disappointing performance was the accumulated hostility and suspicion which the British had aroused amongst the miners during 1945–6. The delicacy of relations between NGCC and miners was graphically illustrated in September 1946. Henry Collins approached the IVB leader, August Schmidt, with the proposal that the miners would receive extra rations and the population some coal for domestic

42. WWA S22 (OMGUS), AG 1947/178/1–2, telegram from Clay to Draper, 10.8.1947; WWA S22 (OMGUS), BICO BIECO 17/8203/12, BIECO/M(47)13: 15th meeting of the Bipartite Economic Panel (BIECO), 19.5.1947; Farquharson, *The Western Allies*, pp. 188ff.
43. PRO FO 1005, 380, COPROD P(47)22, NGCC Progress Report, 3.5.1947.

use (which until then had not been the case) if the miners would agree to working one Sunday a month. Such extra shifts had been common during the war and the proposal was quite a clever one since it recognised both the material and the psychological causes of miners' discontent. Schmidt provisionally agreed, although the exact details of the incentives remained to be worked out. However, when the extra shifts were announced on 24 September, the miners greeted the news with considerable dissatisfaction. The fact that the extra rations were not yet on the table and, in addition, the continuing high level of exports at 'reparations' prices, served to dispose the miners against the shifts.[44]

This discontent was articulated and mobilised by the communist element in the union and works councils, led by the IVB deputy president Willy Agatz. The communists were keen to take a high profile on the issue after disappointing municipal election results in the Ruhr. They demanded better rations for miners without conditions, arguing that the beneficial effects would render Sunday working unnecessary. In effect this was a call for the miners to be given a more privileged status at the cost of the rest of the population. As Willy Agatz put it: 'Die 238.000 Bergarbeiter unseres Gebietes machen ein Prozent der gesamten Bevölkerung der britischen Zone aus. Von diesem einen Prozent hängt Leben und Gedeih der übrigen 99 per cent der Bevölkerung der britischen Zone ab. Sollte es nicht möglich sein, die 99 per cent der Bevölkerung zu einer genügend starken Hilfeleistung für die Bergarbeiter heranzuziehen?'[45] They also reiterated their call for socialisation of the industry, a demand which enjoyed considerable support amongst the men. As a result, Schmidt was outvoted and a delegate conference rejected the Sunday shifts.[46]

The miners' reaction in the early months of 1947 now becomes more intelligible. Even before the spring food crisis, the goodwill and commitment that the Points System might have earned

---

44. Ulrich Borsdorf, 'Speck oder Sozialisierung. Produktionssteigerungskampagnen im Ruhrgebau 1945–1947', in Hans Mommsen and Ulrich Borsdorf (eds), *Gluckauf Kameraden! Die Bergarbeiter und ihre Organisationen in Deutschland*, Cologne, 1979, pp. 355ff.

45. Ibid. and Clarke, 'Die Gewerkschaftspolitik der KPD', p. 24.

46. Christoph Kleßmann and Peter Friedemann, *Streiks und Hungermärsche im Ruhrgebiet 1946–1948*, Frankfurt, 1977, p. 42.

under more favourable circumstances was jeopardised by problems in supplying the goods for purchase. Some goods failed to
materialise altogether; others did not meet the miners' quality
expectations. These supply problems reinforced the miners'
scepticism towards the British recovery programme. Then came
the food shortages. It is easy to imagine the general mood in
spring 1947; hunger protests fused with political demands, an
amalgam skilfully mobilised by the Communist Party (KPD).
The socialisation movement reached its apogee.[47]

Hostility towards the authorities was probably strengthened
by the miners' acute awareness that they were regarded with
envy by the rest of the population. The combination of being the
butt of so much anger and at the same time not getting what
they felt had been promised was difficult for the miners to bear.
This undoubtedly contributed to the psychological impact of the
food crisis.[48]

This description of the miners' mood is a necessary but not yet
a sufficient explanation for the productivity problems in 1947.
Certainly the miners were disappointed with the goods they
received. Nevertheless, Points System goods, particularly the
cigarettes and spirits with their enormous black market value,
were still well worth working for. What remains to be established is why they did not stimulate higher output.

Part of the explanation lies in inherent features of the Points
System itself; and to understand these it is necessary to return to
1946, to the point at which the scheme was being designed.
After the débâcle over the Sunday shifts it was evident to the
British authorities that there was still a credibility gap between
themselves and the miners. The miners had shown they were
not prepared to commit themselves for uncertain future rewards. Any future scheme would have to ensure that enough
extra supplies were 'up front' to win support; and in addition,
the whole incentives question having now become highly politi-
cised, it would have to be introduced cautiously and full union
support would need to be secured in advance. Conscious of

47. Borsdorf, 'Speck oder Sozialisierung', pp. 354ff; Clarke, 'Die Gewerkschaftspolitik der KPD', pp. 35ff.
48. PORO (ed.), *The Ruhr Miner and his Family 1947: A Social Survey*, Bielefeld,
1948, p. 3; *Hochlarmarker Lesebuch. Kohle war nicht alles: 100 Jahre Ruhrgebietsgeschichte*, Oberhausen, 1981, p. 204; OBADA I8010/2189/47, Lagebericht for July
1947.

their own limited authority and of the continued weakness of German management, the British authorities were now more nervous than ever of pushing the miners too hard and risking a negative reaction which might actually bring production down further.[49] Therefore, when it came to discuss the Points System, the NGCC was very concerned to enlist the full support of all sections of the union. The German economic administration, too, regarded union endorsement – in particular, support from the union left wing – as the absolute precondition for success. As a result, the IVB was able to extract a number of important concessions from the British, which had a general effect of weakening the link between incentives and output and putting goods on the table *before* any great increases in production had been achieved. General Clay himself declared with some exaggeration that the 'incentive goes to the miner just because he is there. If he shouldn't get the incentives until he got up to 1.4t or 1.5t he would have been there a long time ago.'[50]

Two provisions exemplified this tendency most strongly. First, the scheme applied to virtually all wage-earners in the mines, including workers above ground and white-collar employees. Secondly, since the points were linked directly to earnings, all workers on fixed earnings (i.e. not piece-rates) received the same number of points no matter how hard they worked or how well their pit produced; there was no output-related component in the number of points they received. Thus a significant proportion of the points goods was being dispensed simply as a reward for good attendance.[51] As far as contract workers were concerned,[52] the number of points earned increased with the wage, and the wage in turn was

49. WWA S22 (OMGUS), CO HIST. Br. 3/404–1/8, memo, 'Re: German Coal Production. Summary Notes of Conference 13.10.1947'. Comments by Harrison.
50. WWA S22 (OMGUS), BICO BISEC 11/104–1/38, verbatim draft of meeting of General Clay with BICO staff, 14.5.1948; Astrid Föllmer–Edling, 'Die Politik des IVB im Ruhrgebiet 1945–1948. Die Anstrengungen um die Erhöhung der Kohlenförderung im Ruhrbergbau', unpublished dissertation, Bochum University, 1977, pp. 41ff; HSTAD NW73, 458, VfW, Arbeitsgruppe Kohle, to Reconstruction Minister Paul, 26.4.1947.
51. DGBA, File 'Gewerkschaftliches Zonensekretariat, Britische Zone, 1947, 1', VfW to Economics Ministry, NRW and others, 25.3.1947, appendix 8; Mark Roseman, 'New Miners in the Ruhr: Rebuilding the Workforce in the Ruhr Mines, 1945–1958', PhD dissertation, University of Warwick, 1987, pp. 130–1.
52. Contract wages (*Gedingelohn*) are the mining equivalent of piece-rates. See below for details.

related to output, so that there *was* an incentive to put in more effort. It is true that the union did manage to ensure that there was an upper limit to the amount of points that could be earned, thus limiting the pressure on the workers and the potentially divisive effects of the scheme. Furthermore, a guaranteed minimum of points, plus the coupons for cigarettes and spirits, were obtainable as long as the miner worked his shifts, no matter what the output.[53] Yet the contract workers' earnings tended to remain well above the guaranteed minimum wage – and thus their points earnings well above the minimum points allocation – indicating that they were not relying on the guaranteed wage and point allocation.[54] Conversely, average earnings were well below the point at which maximum points would have been earned. The miners could have produced a lot more than they did before reaching the point where the scheme deterred them from working any harder.[55] The upward progress of productivity in February and March 1947 testified to the miners' willingness to increase shift earnings, as the Oberbergamt observed in March. The Points System therefore was capable of stimulating higher productivity, if conditions were favourable.[56]

The guaranteed minimum points allocation and the supply of cigarettes and spirits that could be bought with it did reduce the stimulus to higher output, however, when it became apparent that nothing could be obtained with the extra points. In April, the Oberbergamt noted that not only was there a widespread fear that the entire system of food rationing was about to collapse but in addition textiles and shoes were almost impossible to obtain. It was only then, in the atmosphere of resentment and mistrust engendered by the shortages, that the Scheme became 'mehr und mehr eine Anwesenheitsprämie'.[57] The

53. There was no clause in the Points System specifically to this effect, but it was the logical consequence of the minimum-wage clause in the wage regulations.

54. *ZdKW*, vol. 23, p. 63. The table shows that average *Hauer* earnings in 1947 were well above the guaranteed minimum.

55. Miners received ten points for every Mark earned. Their average shift wage in the previous month was taken as the guide. Since the experienced men's average shift wages hovered around the 11 Mark level, average points earnings were around 110. The maximum earnings were 150 points. See *ZdKW*, vol. 23, p. 63 and *The Ruhr Miner*, p. 9.

56. OBADA I8010/1021/47, OBAD Lagebericht for March 1947.

57. OBADA I8010/1902/47, OBAD Lagebericht for June 1947; and see also report for April 1947.

problem lay therefore in a combination of factors: the problems of supply, the less than stringent terms of the incentive scheme and the existence of a black market which made it hard to maintain any rigorous link between incentives and output.

Just as important in limiting the pressure on the miners to increase productivity was the pattern of wage negotiations, for on the outcome of the negotiations hung not only the cash earned but also the number of points granted. Here some explanation is required of the wage system prevailing in the mines. Some 60 per cent of underground miners were contract workers whose wage, like piece-workers in other industries, depended on their actual output rather than on a fixed hourly rate.[58] In most German industries, piece-work rates were negotiated for the whole industry or for a whole region and remained in force until the next round of pay negotiations. They were (and are) rarely the subject of shop-floor bargaining. This is because the job specification could be standardised and defined in a national or regional contract. In mining, on the other hand, each face is unique and the conditions in each face are constantly in flux. Standardised regional piece-work rates for face workers were impossible. All that the regional pay settlements did was to establish the wage which the miner, at normal effort, could be expected to reach (*Hauerdurchschnittslohn*). It was then up to the monthly (sometimes less frequent) contract negotiations in each face to establish how much coal the miners could be expected to mine, how many props to recover, or how many cubic metres of packing to carry out in order to reach this standard wage. These negotiations, which took place between the pit deputy (*Steiger*) and a representative of the face workers (*Ortsältester*), therefore involved difficult judgements as to the severity of conditions. In reality they were a test of the *Steiger's* authority against the resolution of the men, a conflict in which a whole range of factors such as the demand for coal, the labour market, the degree of unionisation, the nature of the personalities involved and so on could influence the outcome.

Thus, more than in any other industry, mining wages were a test of authority and power, a continuous battle between management and men. Moreover, in the post-war period, the degree

58. H. H. Bischoff, 'Arbeiterzahl und Förderanstieg', *Gluckauf*, vol. 87, nos 23/4, 1951, pp. 563–7 at 566.

to which shifts in power could influence the outcome of the negotiations or, put another way, the openness of interpretation as to what output could be expected under the given conditions, was greater than ever. This was because there was general agreement that 'normal' output, by pre-war standards (*Friedens-leistung*), was not a realistic goal. Undernourishment, shortage of supplies and other factors meant that, with the best will in the world, the productivity of 1938 was unlikely to be attained. In September 1945, the NGCC formally laid down that, though the standard of 1938 was the ultimate objective, at present '80 per cent of this estimated output per man/shift will be taken as the normal'.[59] At the same time, the NGCC acknowledged that there would be cases where even 80 per cent of pre-war output could not realistically be anticipated and a procedure for vetting such special cases was established. In other words, the contract bargaining now had to determine not one but two intangibles: the ease of working at the face and the degree to which general living and working conditions allowed normal working.

The miners were in a good position to exploit this situation because management continued to feel insecure. Despite repeated attempts to halt it, denazification dragged on. As long as denazification was in the air, deputies could not be expected to be firm disciplinarians. A secret report by the Hibernia management noted that 'Bei den Angestellten ist es bekannt, daß ein gutes Zeugnis des zuständigen Betriebsrates vor den Entnazifierungsausschüssen besonders hoch gewertet wird.'[60]

The uncertain ownership situation and the threat of socialisation was another factor that continued to trouble management. Even after a five-year moratorium on socialisation was introduced at American insistence in the summer of 1947, the managers' position remained uncertain. Most regarded themselves as trustees for their former owners, yet in matters such as dismissing or disciplining lax deputies and foremen they lacked 'the protection of boards of directors' and had 'all the pressure

59. AZG, File 'I 1 13, Gedinge Regelung, 1.1.45–31.12.1945', directive from ADMG Production, no. 5, Ruhr Coal District, NGCC to Mining Companies, 29.9.1945.
60. BBA 32, 882, Hibernia, memo, 'Ernährungsverhältnisse', with additional heading in pencil: '*Geheim*. Bericht an Mr. Hughes 2RCD. 23.5.1947'; Henry E. Collins, *Mining Memories and Musings: The Autobiography of a Mining Engineer*, London, 1985, pp. 42ff.

in the world from below' not to take a tough line, as a senior figure in the industry remarked. The same source commented, with some exaggeration, that 'to secure the measure of discipline which is actually prevailing, managers are depending on trade unions and would never take a serious stand against them'.[61]

The continuing fragility of authority had direct and important implications for the wage negotiations. 'Bei der Vereinbarung der Gedinge haben die Aufsichtspersonen . . . meist keinen leichten Stand,' noted the Oberbergamt.[62] The introduction of the Points System served only to intensify the miners' interest in a favourable contract, since, as already noted, the number of points received was determined by the cash earnings and thus both money and points were dependent on the negotiations' outcome. The *Steiger* found themselves continually confronted with the demand for more lenient contract rates, often accompanied by the argument that the food shortages and the ill health of the men prevented any greater output. In general the *Steiger* – and behind them senior management – put up only limited resistance to these demands.[63]

In sum, it was not food shortages alone but instead a crisis of legitimacy and authority, exposed and exacerbated by food and other supply shortages, that was the real cause of low productivity. This was, quite clearly, a crisis involving not just new labour, but the workforce as a whole. Even so, management often found particular problems with the newcomers. A management survey produced in 1948 suggested that if it had not been for considerable efforts on the part of the skilled men, output would have fallen far more sharply than was the case.[64] True, we know that output at the face, where the newcomers were concentrated, recovered better than productivity elsewhere in the mine (see above, p. 72). Nevertheless, it does seem to have been particularly difficult to get substantial sections of the new intake to work properly. Newcomers seem to have been

---

61. 'Special Intelligence Report 1948'.
62. OBADA I8010/433/47, Lagebericht for January 1947.
63. OBADA I8010/1021/47, Lagebericht for March 1947; comments of the VfW, cited in Abelshauser, *Der Ruhrkohlenbergbau*, p. 41.
64. WWA F35, 3511, DKBL, circular no. I 11, 7.2.1948, appendix: Gerhard Rauer, 'Die Entwicklung der Leistung unter Tage und der individuellen Leistung des Bergmannes im Ruhrbergbau in den Jahren 1946–1947'.

more likely than their skilled counterparts to exploit the generous clauses in the incentive schemes. Many were young and single and were therefore less attracted by the consumer goods, particularly textiles and furniture, which might otherwise have given them an incentive to maximise their points earnings. Such men relied on black-marketeering of coupon and Care Packet goods (see below) to make up their income: so much so, that some mines went over to paying new miners less than the minimum wage in cases where it was felt that the men had deliberately underperformed. The *Bergämter* also reported that young trainees would not heed deputies' instructions, frequently left work early and did not take safety regulations seriously enough.[65] Even more serious were the high levels of wastage. Many newcomers departed after working only a few shifts. For example, over 30 per cent of all new miners hired by the GBAG's Gruppe Hamborn in the first half of 1947 disappeared within a few weeks of being laid on. In 1947 as a whole, the Ruhr mines hired 87,235 men and lost 42,346, of which three-quarters were voluntary losses.[66]

Most of these problems could not be laid at the feet of the newcomers. They were confronted not only by unfamiliar and unattractive working conditions, but also by an indifferent or hostile management and, in the case of outsiders to the Ruhr, by hostels which remained in many cases very miserable places. Even in 1947, some hostels were still surrounded by barbed wire and concrete pillarboxes, 'a grim reminder' of their former function.[67] The shortage of resources and the lack of managerial authority allowed a vicious circle to be perpetuated in which managerial neglect and the newcomers' recalcitrance reinforced each other.

In summer 1947 the British and particularly the Americans

65. BBA 32, 741, minutes of directors' meeting, 4.6.1948; 30, 268,minutes of meeting with mine officials on 18 August, 20.8.1947; OBADA I 8010/433/47, OBAD Lagebericht for January 1947, and also reports for March, April, May and June.
66. WWA F35, 493, 'Erfahrungsbericht der Zeche Prosper I/II, Betriebsabteilung 1', July 1947; F35, 494, copy of report from Abteilung U (GBAG Gruppe Hamborn) to Vorstand, 'betrifft.: Erfahrungsbericht über Neubergleute', 14.7.1948; unpublished figures of the Ges.Verb.StdKW, tables 'Belegschaftswechsel – Arbeiter unter Tage. Ruhr' and 'Aufteilung des Abganges nach Gründen – Arbeiter unter Tage. Ruhr'.
67. PORO (ed.), *A Social Survey: The Mining Trainee 1947*, Bielefeld, 1948, p. 18.

made considerable efforts to increase the pressures and incentives to extra production. Within the organs of the Bipartite Control Office (BICO) the Americans worked with their British counterparts to revise the incentives schemes. The Points System was tightened up in a number of ways. A supplementary three-phase programme of incentives was introduced. In Phase 1, mines were given a four-week production target which, if met, entitled the miners to so-called '10-in-1' or 'CARE' packets of luxury goods, foodstuffs, textiles and so on. There were three such Care Packet actions. The new philosophy manifested itself not only in the direct linking of the incentives to a specific production target but also in the fact that, in the first action, only underground workers were to receive the Packet. Phase III, which began in January, was also linked to output and provided the miners with a variety of imported food and consumer goods. The miner received a certain number of coupons or *Import-Kaufmarken* on the basis of individual performance and that of the mine. The intervening Phase II, on the other hand, had no such productivity link and was designed simply to protect the miner from fluctuations in the food supply in the period between the first and second Care Packets.[68]

These additions made some contribution to productivity but the weakness of the Care Packet actions was that they produced a great deal of effort in the target month itself and a relapse as soon as the Packet ceased to be in operation. In addition, it proved not to be possible to protect the miners or their families from the renewed food shortages at the end of the year. Moreover, none of these measures filled the 'authority vacuum'. The revised Points System regulations contained the clause that contracts should be periodically reviewed to ensure 'daß sie einer normalen Leistung entsprechen'.[69] Yet this instruction, introduced in September 1947, could have little impact until the mining officials believed their situation to be more secure.

68. Föllmer-Edling, 'Die Politik des IVB', pp. 68 ff., 74; WWA S22 (OMGUS), CO HIST BR 3/404–1/8, Bipartite Board memo, BISEC M(47) 25, 'Incentive Scheme for Coal Miners', 27.8.1947. The acronym CARE stood for Cooperative for American Remittances to Europe.

69. Abelshauser, *Der Ruhrkohlenbergbau*, p. 41.

The Bergassessoren Fight Back: Management's Return to Power, 1947–8

Both British and Americans increasingly believed that the key to raising output was to strengthen management's confidence and control. As early as the beginning of 1947, the British and Americans had decided that the time was opportune to give the Germans control over the mining industry. However, for a number of reasons the idea proved more difficult to implement than expected and the transfer of power was therefore shelved for the time being, the NGCC remaining in control.

In many ways, the August 1947 Washington conference, organised by the US to discuss coal matters, was a turning-point. The Americans persuaded the British to put a five-year moratorium on the question of socialisation in the Ruhr. This removed a lot of management anxiety, particularly since denazification was gradually coming to an end. Following the conference, the bipartite[70] authorities decided to create a German organisation to run the mines. The outcome was the Deutsche Kohlenbergbauleitung (DKBL), a body consisting largely of industrial representatives, though with some trade union representation, which came into existence in November 1947. The NGCC was wound up and replaced by a smaller bipartite organisation, the UK/US Coal Control Group, whose job it was to supervise the DKBL and report directly to the Bipartite Board. The British interdepartmental coal production committee COPROD was replaced by a bipartite committee in Frankfurt, COCOM, charged with advising the Bipartite Board on coal matters and ensuring that the recommendations of the Washington conference were implemented. The military government's influence continued to make itself felt in the mining industry for several years, but the creation of the DKBL undoubtedly represented a considerable transfer of authority back to German management and reduced the scope for outside control.

Under these circumstances, managers began to regain their lost confidence. Despite General Robertson's declaration to the North Rhine-Westphalia parliament in April 1948 that the industry would never be returned to its former owners, the possibility

70. In line with contemporary usage, 'bipartite' always refers to the British and Americans, while the 'bizonal' administration was the German counterpart.

of socialisation ever being introduced was looking increasingly remote. As the US chairman of the UK/USCCG, Bob Estill, prepared to leave for the US, he organised a special luncheon with senior DKBL figures at which, as the minutes record,: 'he desired to point out that he definitely did not agree to any plan of nationalisation or socialisation of the coal industry and specifically referred to the bad results that England had experienced in the nationalisation of their coal recently'.[71] True, there were still examples of management nervousness; the Control Group criticised the fact that works councils were still sometimes being consulted on the appointment of senior management personnel. Yet there were many other signs that management was beginning to assert itself in relation to both labour and labour exchanges. There was a greater willingness to carry out dismissals. In February 1948 the IVB's Bochum district complained about colliery managers' 'increasing aggressiveness' and in March the union noted a disturbing increase in the number of pits refusing to keep to the minimum wage agreement.[72]

These conditions and a more favourable food situation, in which most ordinary consumers in the mining areas kept above hunger rations throughout the spring, combined to push productivity (output per man/shift) up from 2.473 tons in January to 2.627 tons in March. That it did not go higher was evidence of the many continuing constraints, such as the inherent limitations of the incentive schemes and the unremitting and increasingly severe shortage of mine supplies.[73] In addition, there was one constraint on mining output whose impact was actually strengthened by the DKBL's formation, namely that existing coal prices and supply conditions offered management no incentive to maximise production. Members of the Coal Control Group soon became aware that neither management nor its spokesmen in the DKBL shared the Allies' interest in boosting coal production irrespective of the cost. The Group reported that it 'was evident that the DKBL had no real policy with regard to

71. WWA S22 (OMGUS), BICO BISEC, 11/104–1/38, report on 'Luncheon Meeting of Hard Coal District Production Directors As Guests of A. F. Marshall, Member (US)', 2.8.1948; 'Speicial Intelligence Report 1948'.

72. DGBA File 'Industrieverband Bergbau 1946–1948. Tätigkeitsberichte', reports for February and March 1948; BBA 10, 594, minutes of meeting of colliery directors in the DKBL's Bochum district 25.5.1948.

73. *ZdKW*, vol. 7, p. 45; WWA S22 (OMGUS), BICO BISEC 11/104–38, verbatim draft – Meeting of General Clay with BICO Staff, 14.5.1948.

immediate production . . . The Directors are taking a long-term view and would appear indifferent to the necessity of immediately maximising coal production.'[74] In confidential discussions with the Americans, a senior management representative admitted that the employers were not doing their very best to secure maximum output. He also revealed the reason for this. How could they be expected to maximise production, he asked, 'when we are only allowed to include 1.50 RM for the depreciation of our equipment per ton of coal mined for subsidy purposes, while our capital goods depreciate at the rate of from 2.00 RM to 2.20 RM or more per ton of coal extracted'?[75] The Americans concluded that 'under existing price and subsidy policies the board of managers should keep production at the lowest possible level consistent with its members continuing in office'.[76] Not only were the subsidies currently provided insufficient to meet depreciation, in some cases insufficient even to meet operating costs, but in addition there was anxiety that the subsidies might soon cease, indeed that the industry might have to pay the subsidies back in the future. In other words, controlled coal prices meant that the financial interest of the collieries was out of step with the economic needs of the nation. There was no material incentive to respond to the urgent need for coal.

There was an inherent contradiction in the Allied policy of giving management greater freedom and authority on the one hand but on the other not restoring the economic incentives that made production worthwhile. It would be inappropriate here to dwell on all the circumstances governing the Allies' policy towards the domestic (i.e. non-export) coal price. Until summer 1947, Britain's attempts to increase coal prices had been overridden by the other occupying powers in Berlin because of the latters' interests as coal consumers. In summer 1947, the Americans acknowledged the need to raise coal prices and a modest increase was implemented but there was much resistance to further rises from within the German economic administration, where it was felt that the inflationary consequences would destabilise the rickety price structure in the two Zones. This fear of cost-push inflation was to be of fundamental importance in

74. WWA S22 (OMGUS), BICO BISEC 11/104–2/3, UK/USCCG report, 'Review of Hard Coal Production in the Ruhr', 10.6.1948.
75. 'Special Intelligence Report 1948'.
76. Ibid.

determining future German policy towards the industry.[77]

The divergence between Allied and management interests was to make itself swiftly apparent in the approach to workforce rebuilding. In January 1948, the new Director General of the DKBL, Heinrich Kost, proposed to the UK/USCCG that recruitment in future be restricted to covering wastage and that increases in production be obtained only by improving productivity. The Control Group was unimpressed by Kost's proposals which in its view contained overly optimistic estimates of future developments in both individual output and absenteeism. Recruitment was therefore to go on as before, except that the Group agreed, in the interest of other industries, to limit recruitment from the Ruhr area to 500 men a week.[78] Nevertheless, as table 2.2 shows, recruitment in the first half of 1948 was 20–25 per cent below 1947 levels. The effect of the drop was particularly marked because wastage did not decline, despite the smaller number of newcomers entering the industry. Taking the underground workforce on its own, the period July–December 1947 had seen an increase of over 27,000 men; between January and June 1948, on the other hand, the workforce grew by less than 5,000. As far as the underground workforce is concerned; recruitment did indeed do little more than cover wastage.[79]

In its reports to the Control Group, the DKBL argued that this low increase was the result of mining supply shortages which were severely limiting the collieries' ability to absorb new labour. Whilst there was no doubting the seriousness of supply shortages, there is plenty of evidence that they were not the prime factor inhibiting recruitment. At a meeting between senior colliery representatives and the DKBL's manpower experts it became apparent that both mines and DKBL were ill-disposed to any great increases in workforce size. Indeed, the mines wanted to close down the central reception camp in Hiltrop altogether; but the DKBL advised caution, because it accurately predicted that wastage would rise, thus necessitating continued recruitment to preserve current workforce levels. Over the following months, suspicions hardened at the UK/

77. Collins, *Mining Memories*, p. 47.
78. PRO FO 1005, 1624, minutes of 5th meeting of UK/USCCG, 16.1.1948.
79. *ZdKW*, vol. 7, p. 32.

Table 2.2 Recruitment, wastage and workforce growth, 1947–8

Month	Men hired	Wastage	Workforce growth
1947			
July	12,400	5,700	6,700
August	13,300	6,400	6,900
September	10,000	5,500	4,500
October	12,000	5,800	6,200
November	11,000	4,800	6,200
December	6,500	3,900	2,600
1948			
January	8,274	6,908	1,366
February	8,820	6,551	1,569
March	8,129	5,203	2,926
April	12,931[a]	6,385	6,546
May	7,200	6,100	1,100
June	8,200	7,600	600

(a) High figure reflects apprentice recruitment.

Source: OBAD Lageberichte in OBADA I 8010, vols 2–4. Figures have been rounded up and include all labour below and above ground and in ancillary works.

USCCG that no attempt was being made to maximise the number of men underground. However, the Control Group was reluctant to intervene since it wanted to give the DKBL a chance to prove its effectiveness.[80]

Not only was recruitment down on the previous period but, in addition, the influx of newcomers was not being used to build up the workforce at the face. The figures in table 2.3 show that throughout the post-war period a far smaller proportion of the underground workforce was at the face than before the war. At first sight this is the very reverse of what one would expect. Throughout 1945 and 1946, the NGCC gave out continual

80. WWA S22 (OMGUS), BICO BISEC 11/104–1/39, 'Extract from the March 1948 Report by German Coal Mine Management', March 1948; BBA 32,741, minutes of directors' meeting, 30.1.1948; PRO FO 1005/1624, UK/USCCG, minutes of 8th and 10th meetings, February –April, 1948; remarks of H. E. Collins in WWA S22 (OMGUS), BICO BISEC 11/104–2/6, 'DKBL. Verbatim Minutes of the Meeting of the Military Governors with Bizonal Officials, 14 June 1948'.

Table 2.3 Face productivity and face size, 1938 and 1946–8

| Year | Output/man shift | | Shifts at face as % |
	Face	All underground	of all shifts underground[a]
1938	3.10	1.970	63.5
1946	2.19	1.208	55.2
1947	2.41	1.215	50.41
1948	2.51	1.286	51.2

(a) My calculation using the simple formula: underground productivity/face productivity = face shifts/underground workforce shifts.

Source: Abelshauser, *Wirtschaft in Westdeutschland*, pp. 140–1; *ZdKW*, vol. 12, p. 54.

instructions that all possible labour was to be concentrated at the face and that developmental and preparatory work (*Aus-* and *Vorrichtung*) was to be cut down to a minimum. This should have led to a higher proportion of face workers than before the war, when the mines had been engaged in a considerable amount of development.[81] A partial explanation is that during the war the proportion of the German labour force who were face workers had declined sharply. Many had become too old for contract wage work and moved into the gentler shift-wage jobs away from the face.[82] In 1938, for example, there were 156,908 German *Gedingearbeiter*, making up some 68 per cent of the underground workforce. By 1943 this figure had fallen to 129,661 or 61 per cent and in 1946 it was down to 106,697 or 59 per cent.[83] This explains why, as the war came to an end, the face was disproportionately undermanned. However, the influx of new miners rapidly brought the number of contract workers up to the pre-war level and by mid-1948 154,000 men, or 63 per cent of the workforce, were earning a contract wage.[84] So why,

81. WWa S22 (OMGUS), CO HIST BR 3/406–1/22, undated notes by NGCC towards an official history of the NGCC, section 2: 'History of Coal Production since the Occupation'.
82. Virtually all workers employed at the face were on contract wage. Away from the face, there was some contract work, particularly in developing and preparing new seams and ways, and also a considerable amount of shift-wage employment in maintenance, repair and haulage.
83. Bischoff, 'Arbeiterzahl und Förderanstieg', table 7.
84. Ibid.

in 1948, was the face still so underrepresented in relation to pre-war manning levels and why had the face workforce in fact grown more slowly than the rest of the mining population in the 1946–8 period?[85]

There are a number of reasons. First, the mines were in much poorer shape than they had been in the 1930s and so a fair amount of repair work was unavoidable. Secondly, because of the way the incentive schemes worked, face workers were working nearer to pre-war output norms than the shift-wage earners away from the face.[86] However, a major part of the answer seems to be that German employers were disregarding British instructions and were secretly devoting a considerable proportion of their manpower to rebuilding and extending the mines' capacity – to compensating, in other words, for the lack of development work carried out during the war. Managers were evidently not trying to maximise output by redistributing the workforce. Over the 1946–8 period, the number of contract workers as a whole grew by almost 50 per cent – faster than the growth in the workforce as a whole;[87] in other words, contract workers *away from the face* must have shown a disproportionate increase. This can only have been in development work.[88] Furthermore, the available statistics indicate, as we know, that German management concentrated the newcomers at the face. In other words, the growth in the proportion of contract workers away from the face must have been achieved by moving *experienced* men to development and other work, while allowing newcomers to fill up the face. If more of the experienced men

85. As proven by the fact that the face's share of shifts worked fell.

86. It might appear that this is not a matter of conjecture but a proven fact based on the o.m.s. statistics in table 2.3. However, the way the statistics are derived means that they are not necessarily an indication of how efficiently the men are working. The o.m.s. is calculated by dividing the mines' output by the number of shifts worked. If, for instance, the mines introduce many new workers to do development work, then these shifts will not immediately contribute to production. The number of shifts worked will go up and the productivity statistics will fall, even though the men may be working just as hard and effectively as before. In other words the o.m.s. figures say nothing directly about the efficiency of the individual miners and may merely reflect the deployment of labour within the mine.

87. Calculated from Bischoff, 'Arbeiterzahl und Förderanstieg'.

88. For the Duisburg area see HStaD, Kalkum, Bergamt Duisburg, 236, Lagebericht for February 1947, which openly linked the slow progress of production with the amount of development and preparatory work, claiming that the planned production increases made these necessary.

had been kept there, not only would the size of the face work-force have gone up but face productivity might have increased as well, because the balance between experienced and inexperienced men would have been more favourable.

The Coal Control Group was well aware of this problem. In April, in a stormy meeting with the DKBL, the US representative argued that 14,000 men had entered the industry over the last few months yet the number of face workers had actually declined. In June 1948, at a conference with US officials, Collins argued that, when left to their own devices, German managers were not restricting development work and were taking the long view: 'It is a perhaps a good thing in normal times, but it has always been our point of view that the immediate production of coal is rather more important than the long-term policy.'[89] Yet with its limited staff, there was little the Coal Control Group could do. As Collins himself argued, over 'such a large industry it has not been possible to exert a very profound control'.[90] This fact, as well as the Group's general reluctance to undermine the DKBL, allowed the colliery managers to continue pursuing their own labour policy.

The only exception to the UK/USCCG's unwillingness to intervene more forcefully was a short period in April and May, when the positive trend in production was reversed. Daily production fell badly and the Allies began to put on the pressure. At the beginning of May, General Clay wrote to the UK/USCCG to stress that European recovery was dependent on more coal. The April performance, he wrote, might turn out to have disastrous consequences.[91] At a meeting with BICO staff, Clay spelt out the position even more clearly: 'The fact remains that we have all these raw materials coming in . . . If we don't get more coal, it is not one bit of use to bring any of it in . . . The whole German economy is in a position for a rapid recovery if we can get more coal. Without it, it is not going to go anywhere.'[92] This crisis indicated just how wide the gap had be-

---

89. WWA S22 (OMGUS), BICO BISEC 11/104–2/6, verbatim minutes of the meeting of the military governors with bizonal officials, 14.6.1948. See also Collins, 'Progress' p. 19.

90. Ibid., p. 6.

91. WWA S22 (OMGUS), AG 1948/163/5, Clay to Coalco, 5.5.1948.

92. WWA S22 (OMGUS), BICO BISEC 11/104–1/38, verbatim draft of meeting of General Clay with BICO staff, 14.5.1948.

come between the needs of the economy and the mines' own financial interests.

The DKBL's response was a series of short-term measures such as temporary halts to preparatory and development work and the introduction of a new incentive drive, the *Fettaktion*, whereby the miners received meat and fats for production increases attained in the May–June period. These were not without their success and the DKBL was thus spared from having to revise its recruitment strategy. In any case, the currency reform in June so radically altered the mines' economic and financial situation that the Allies, too, were forced to change their whole approach to coal. A new economic era had begun.

The Missing Supplies

One key question about workforce regeneration in the controlled economy remains. The factors which hindered efficient deployment of human and material resources in the pits have been analysed in detail. Yet just as symptomatic of the controlled economy as these problems of resource deployment were problems of resource *procurement*. As we have seen, almost every aspect of labour policy was bedevilled by the shortage of supplies. Why did it remain so difficult to furnish the mining industry with even the bare minimum of pit supplies, building materials, hostel furnishings, consumer goods and so on? It is to this question which the following chapter is addressed.

3
Supplies in Demand: Housing New Labour in the Pre-Currency-reform Economy

Supplies, Supplies!

Towards the end of 1946, men from all over Germany were flocking to the pits, seeing in mining a way of keeping themselves above water, if not above ground. They key problem of the early era had been solved. Welcome as it was, this new influx nevertheless presented the authorities with new tasks and challenges, above all the problems of housing, equipping and feeding the newcomers. Beyond the need to provide that minimum standard of equipment and accomodation without which it would be impossible to set the men to work, it was well recognised that morale and productivity of both established and new miners would benefit if the quality of existing housing and supplies could be improved.[1]

Over the following period an enormous amount of energy was spent on procuring resources. Yet the drive for coal was continually put in jeopardy by missing or poor-quality supplies. The industry lived from hand to mouth and some of the materials necessary to increase coal production never arrived. As chapter 2 has already shown, the incentive schemes were dogged by problems of delivery and quality. Food was periodically in very short supply.[2] Work clothing was sufficient only to kit out new recruits to the meanest of standards and American experts reckoned that the miners were getting less than half the

1. See comments of August Schmidt in PRO FO 1005, 947, 'Minutes of the Committee to Investigate Coal Production 1946. Visit of Russian, French and US experts to the Ruhr', August 1946.
2. DGBA File, 'Gewerkschaftliches Zonensekretariat, Britische Zone, 1947, 1', VfW to Economics Ministry NRW and others, 25.3.1947, appendix 11.

clothing supplies that production demanded. Many recruits found that they had to wait for up to a month for their gear, during which time they could not work and were required to pay for lodging and food. In summer 1947 shortages became so acute that recruitment had temporarily to be restricted. The lack of pit supplies became increasingly desperate. In 1946, 1947 and 1948 the collieries received less than half the steel required. The quality of the lubricating oils, electrical installations, conveyor belts and air hose delivered was so bad that many items lasted only a couple of days. This in turn had a deleterious effect on morale. In many cases, it was not to be until the currency reform that the quantity and quality of deliveries began appreciably to improve.[3]

Rather than attempt to analyse the progress and problems in procuring all these different commodities, some of which bore only peripherally on rebuilding the labour force, the following account focuses on one of the most complex supply problems of all: miners' housing. A number of the challenges thrown up by housing were unique, but in many respects the transfer, allocation and deployment of housing and building supplies in the miners' housing programme offer a model of the problems of resource control in the pre-currency-reform economy.

Housing Policy in the Pre-incentives Era, 1945–6

No one entering the Ruhr in 1945 could fail to be struck, even moved, by the sheer scale of housing destruction. Henry Collins recalled: 'In my early travels around the coalfield I saw just vast areas of rubble and yet, at night, pin points of light appeared in the ruins over wide areas. The miners and their families were living in the cellars beneath the ruins.'[4] Before the war, there had been 1,217,000 dwellings in the greater Ruhr area (SVR – Siedlungsverband Ruhrkohlenbezirk – territory). The war had destroyed 456,000 of them and left only 196,000 undamaged. Of the quarter of a million miners' houses standing before the war, only a fifth remained undamaged while over a quarter were

3. Mark Roseman, 'New Miners in the Ruhr: Rebuilding the Workforce in the Ruhr Mines, 1945–1958', PhD dissertation, Warwick University, 1987, pp. 160ff.
4. Henry E. Collins, *Mining Memories and Musings: The Autobiography of a Mining Engineer*, London, 1985, p. 28.

totally destroyed. Even in 1947, after considerable repairs, there were still only half the inhabitable rooms in the Ruhr that there had been in 1939. Thus, a swift programme of repair was doubly necessary: first, to house the new labour entering the Ruhr, and secondly, to improve morale and productivity in the workforce generally.[5]

By December 1945, a fair number of houses had been repaired, a fact which owed as much to the miners' private initiative and the collieries' willingness to allow part of their pit supplies to be illegally hived off to housing repairs as it did to any concerted action by the authorities. However, over the following months progress dropped substantially. What seems to have happened is that the failure to retain labour was tacitly used as an excuse to avoid finding ways of building additional miners' accomodation. Although new and better billets and hostels might have altered the situation, the slow growth in the workforce took the immediate pressure off the housing authorities. In May 1946, for example, so many of the former inhabitants had fled that there was room for 20,000 new recruits in the camps. Moreover, most new arrivals did not require housing because the manpower authorities concentrated more than ever on recruiting local labour. Between 1 April and 2 August 1946, for example, 18,000 of the 23,000 men directed to the mines came from the Ruhr.[6]

When in late autumn the accelerating pace of workforce growth put the Ruhr housing stock under renewed pressure, the region was thus just as unprepared to receive this influx as it had been in 1945. The only major difference between the situation in autumn 1945 and that of a year later was that in the meantime a number of important bodies had been created which were to play a key role in the miners' housing programme. The Beratungsstelle für Arbeit, Siedlungs- und Wohnungswesen, a zonal organisation charged with assisting military government in housing and manpower questions, was brought into the miners' housing question some time around

5. HStAD NW9, 54, Wohnungsbezirksstelle Ruhr (WBSR) to WAM, 3.11.1947, appendix.
6. PRO FO 1005, 379, COPROD P(46) 6; 'Minutes of the Committee to Investigate Coal Production 1946. Visit of Russian, French and US experts to the Ruhr'; BAK Z40, 451, Lt-Col. Fielder to Housing Branch, Manpower Division, 14.5.1946; HQ NGCC, memo, 'Building Material for the Repair of Miners' Housing', Essen, 1947.

June and July. Philip Rappaport, the head of the Beratungs-
telle's housing section, was to be doubly influential because he
was also director of the re-established SVR, an organisation that
was to be more closely involved with miners' housing than any
other in the coming years. Another important development in
the summer of 1946 was the Manpower Division's creation of a
Ruhr Housing Office (RHO) to institute a more coherent and
co-ordinated approach to miners' housing. RHO and SVR were
to work closely together. Finally, in August 1946 the ministries
of the newly created Land Nordrhein-Westfalen (NRW) began
to take shape, including the Reconstruction Ministry (WAM)
under the communist Hugo Paul. By military government decree, housing became the responsibility of the individual Land
governments, and thus the Reconstruction Ministry was to exert
a decisive influence in the Ruhr.[7]

Housing in Crisis, September 1946–February 1947

As we know, August and September 1946 saw a change of gear
in the coal drive. Naturally enough, the new responsiveness to
the needs of German coal production led also to recognition of
the importance of miners' housing. In September the quadripartite Committee of Experts' report contained the recommen-
dation that miners' housing conditions should be given the
'highest priority in any scheme for increasing coal production'
and that a programme of 'substantial repair and reconstruction
including temporary houses and hutments' be commenced immediately.[8]

In response, the British authorities raised the amount of coal
allocated to production of building materials by 50,000 tons a
month or about 50 per cent. At the same time, the priority accord
ed to mining was strengthened on a number of different levels.
The Manpower Division developed a new five-year programme

7. BAK Z40, 345, Rappaport, Deutsche Beratungsstelle für Siedlungs- u.
Wohnwesen to Dr Weißer, 20.7.1946; PRO FO 1005, 1821, Manpower Interim
Report for month ending 9 July 1946; HStAD NW10, 91, RGO HQ Military
Government NRW to Ministerpräsident NRW, 10.4.1947, annex (translation).
8. PRO FO 943, 184, Doc. 74, A.C.A. committee of coal experts, special
minutes of 22nd meeting, 6.9.1946, appendices; FO 1005, 379, COPROD P(46)2,
16.9.1946.

for miners' housing which foresaw 20 per cent of all housing repairs in the British Zone going to the miners. At a lower level, the building officers of the Ruhr municipalities were directed to give mining greater priority.[9]

Even had these decisions been implemented, it is unlikely that they would have prevented a housing bottleneck from developing in the Ruhr. But in fact, the amount of coal actually allocated to building materials did not amount to a fraction of the planned levels. Indeed, in the first quarter of 1947 the allocation was actually well below what it had been *before* the 50,000 ton increase had been announced. This was partly because less coal was available for allocation than had originally been assumed, but in fact the cut in the share going to building supplies was even bigger than the shortfall in available coal. It was clear the authorities were not even attempting to honour the priority decisions of September and October. Sooner or later, though, military government would have to accept the fact that unless it put more coal into secondary industries, the primary industries, above all mining, would suffer.[10]

The crunch came at the end of January. On the thirty-first, the NRW Manpower Department learned that there was no barrack or hostel accommodation left. Suitable billets had run out and other types of building could not be converted for miners' use because of the dearth of accommodation stores – beds, cupboards, tables, chairs and blankets. For the previous four days, all new non-local recruits had had to be transferred to Aachen coalfield because there was nowhere to house them in the Ruhr. This was a major blow to the whole recruitment programme.[11]

Whatever impact the crisis was to have on the repairs and reconstruction programme, in the short term the only measure swift enough was the commandeering of existing living space

9. BAK Z2, 53, 7, Sitzung des Zonenbeirates, 174: Antrag Reimann/ Hoffmann, annex 38: memo from the Co-ordinating Office of the ZAC (Britischer Verbindungsstab), Ref: HQ/14107/1/ZAC, 'betr.: Wohnungslage im Bergbau', 16.9.1946; Z40, 451, DCOS (Policy), CCG(BE), Berlin to Standard Distribution List G Ref AHQ/8400/Sec. G., Subject Miners' Housing, November 1946; PRO FO 1005, 379, COPROD P(46)6.

10. Werner Abelshauser, *Wirtschaft in Westdeutschland 1945–1948. Rekonstruktion und Wachstumsbedingungen in der amerikanischen und britischen Zone*, Stuttgart, 1975, p. 144, table 43; Collins Papers, Report on Miners' Housing, AGC/22, Gen/16, 14 August 1947, Enclosure 'B', appendices A and B.

11. HStAD NW9, 55, Land Mp. Dept. NRW to WAM, 3.2.1947; WBSR to WAM, Abt. VI, 3.2.1947.

and supplies of bedding and furniture. On 1 February a crisis meeting was held at Villa Hügel, the former Krupp villa where the NGCC had its headquarters. Represented were the NGCC, the NRW Manpower Department, the Ruhr Housing Office, the GMSO and the Reconstruction Ministry. A whole battery of measures to achieve more effective utilisation of available room were proposed. Private accommodation should be more rigorously requisitioned and proven workers should be transferred from the camps into the accommodation. Miners were to be given absolute priority in the allocation of living space ahead of all other housing programmes. Housing inspection to identify inadequately used living space was to be intensified and buildings at present not classified as dwelling space were to be reviewed for possible use as temporary lodgings. The voluntary evacuation of non-miners was to be considered. Finally, the new miners themselves were initially to be given only temporary residence permits which could be revoked if they left the mines.[12]

Most of the policies implemented over the following months were those suggested at this meeting. The WAM, for example, demanded a more vigorous housing inspection and instructed the municipalities that all rooms discovered by the inspection were to be made available to the mining programme. A steady stream of instructions strengthening and clarifying the miners' priority followed throughout this and the following year. At the same time, intensive efforts were undertaken to improve the supply of furniture and, after repeated representations from the manpower authorities, miners were placed very high on the priority list for furniture allocation, preceded only by the Occupation forces and certain other mandatory customers.[13]

A key development was the creation in March of a 'Co-ordinating Committee', founded and chaired by the head of the NRW Manpower Department, Phillip Bate. This Committee brought British and German manpower, housing and mining officials together on a fortnightly basis to co-ordinate supplies

12. HStAD NW9, 55, WBSR to WAM, Abt. VI, 3.2.1947; WBSR to Oberstadtdirektoren, 1.2.1947; WAM to Bate, 6.2.1947; NW 53, 465, Chief Manpower Officer, Mil Govt., NRW to WAM, 3.2.1947 (translation).
13. HStAD NW9, 55, WAM (Wohnraumbewirtschaftung) to Oberstadt/Kreisdirektoren, 20.2.1947; WAM (Wohnraumbewirtschaftung), Referat Bergarbeiterkunft, Essen, to Dept. IVC, 1.7.1948.

and information. The municipal housing departments, for example, were instructed to phone through weekly reports on available living space to the WAM's Ruhr office and these were co-ordinated with information about labour demand and availability.[14]

These measures were rewarded with considerable success. Over the year as a whole 23,000 billets for miners were found in private lodgings. An additional number were created in temporary accommodation, such as the halls of public houses and so on. As the chairman of the Co-ordinating Committee observed, 'any suggestion that the Ruhr could not accommodate the men had been disproved immediately the committee had been established'.[15]

In part, success was due to inherent features of the housing market. Unlike other goods which might slip out of the official channels on to the black market, houses could not easily be concealed and still less be transported out of reach of prying officials. But the scale of requisitioning showed also that in the new political climate of a public and demonstrable commitment to speedy reconstruction, the British authorities now had the nerve to take steps involving considerable costs and distress to other members of the population. Even so, there were still limits to the public resentment which the authorities were prepared to contemplate. No forced evacuations were made and even voluntary evacuations were approached so cautiously that very few appear to have taken place.[16]

Building Castles in the Air: The Miners' Housing Programme 'Ruhr 47/48'

Even had all the 23,000 billets gone to new miners, they alone could not have met new labour's requirements. The manpower target at the beginning of 1947 was to bring in 1,700 workers from outside the Ruhr each week, of whom only 500 were to replace wastage, the remaining 1,200 representing a genuine

14. HStAD NW9, 55, Bate, Land Manpower Dept to NGCC, 14.3.1947; WBSR to Oberstadtdirektoren, 17.2.1947.

15. HStAD NW9, 55, Co-ordinating Committee, minutes of 7th meeting, 2.5.1947.

16. Roseman, 'New Miners', pp. 177–8.

new requirement for accommodation.[17] In any case, the housing programme had to respond to the established workforce's needs as well. This might well improve productivity: even if it did not, there was little doubt that concentrating all supplies on the newcomers would have caused resentment among the established men and risked falls in output.

Short of mass evictions, little more could be expected through inspection and requisitioning of existing property. The only answer was to expand the building programme. Yet in the first quarter of 1947, the allocation of building materials to miners' housing had fallen to an all-time low, amounting to only a fraction of even the Manpower Division programme's modest requirements. As before, coal was the missing ingredient. The severe winter of 1946–7 led to more coal being allocated for domestic heating, hospitals, schools and so on. It also exacerbated Bizonia's transportation problems with the result that, despite the acute need for fuel, pithead stockpiles of coal doubled between January and February 1947.[18]

In March 1947 further cuts in the coal allotted to building materials production appeared imminent. On top of the problems noted above, additional pressure came from the Anglo-American desire to maintain at least a moderate level of exports to the French, despite the lower than expected coal output. Bevin, in particular, remained acutely conscious of the need to be as accommodating towards the French as possible. But Britain's diplomatic gain was Germany's loss. Manpower officials and the NGCC made repeated and vigorous protests at the declining construction rates, yet with little effect. 'In the anxiety to increase exports this year,' a British manpower official said to one of his American counterparts, the allocations were 'in effect establishing limits which would operate for years to come'.[19]

More to identify the dimensions of the housing shortage than with any great hope that the resources would be forthcoming, the British manpower authorities invited the NRW Reconstruc-

17. WWA S22 (OMGUS), Manpower 7/43–1/47, OMGUS Public Relations Office, statement for joint Anglo-American release at 1900 hours, 31.3.1947.

18. HStAD NW73, 481, Der Verbandsdirektor des SVR, Programm für den Bergarbeiterwohnungsbau 'Ruhr 1947/1948', 28.3.1947.

19. WWA S22 (OMGUS), Manpower 7/43–1/47, George S. Wheeler to Director, Manpower Division, 24.3.1947; Abelshauser, *Wirtschaft in Westdeutschland*, p. 144, table 44; PRO FO 1005, 380, NGCC progress report, 15.2.1947; FO 1030, 345, Secretary of State to Robertson, 14.1.1947 and 3.3.1947.

tion Ministry to outline the requirements for housing the mines' present and projected labour force. The British brief was very general and did not stipulate a limit to the material or financial costs involved, specifying only that, in order to encourage the newcomers to stay, camps and hostels were to be avoided as far as possible. Philip Rappaport drew up a plan which was given a cautious welcome by Manpower Division officials towards the end of March. One would be hard placed to find a more luke-warm statement than the following: 'In principle, the British officers are of the opinion that it may be correct to set up such an extensive programme, even if they have considerable doubts regarding its execution (as have the German agencies also).'[20] Both the WAM's initial remit and the British response indicate that this was very much a theoretical exercise. For, as manpower officials were all too aware, the Bipartite Economic Panel was still actively considering reducing the amount of coal allocated for building supplies (among other secondary industries) in order to boost exports. The Rappaport plan seemed destined to end up on that great unused pile of Worthy Memos on the Ruhr housing question. Fate decreed otherwise, however, in the form of a piece of political brinkmanship by the Office of Military Government US (OMGUS) manpower administration. In effect, the miners' housing programme, like the Points System, was set in motion not by a carefully considered decision about resource allocation but by short-term political pressures which resulted in a complete reorientation of the established system of priorities.[21]

What happened in this case was that ever since Clay had agreed in January to supply 55,000 US Zone workers to the Ruhr, the OMGUS Manpower Division had been growing in-creasingly restive at the Ruhr housing situation. Finally, in exasperation at what he saw as lack of acknowledgement of the housing problem, George Wheeler, chief of the Labour Allo-cation Branch, authorised a press release stating that recruit-ment 'has had to be curtailed, despite the continued coal

20. BAK Z40, 451, translation no. 285, 'Discussion Regarding the Housing Programme "Ruhr 1947/1948" on 24th March 1947'; HStAD NW53, 465, Bate to WAM, 24.2.1947 (translation); BAK Z40, 451, minutes of meeting in Essen on 13.3.1947, 13.3.1947.
21. WWA S22 (OMGUS), Manpower 7/43–1/47, OMGUS Public Relations Office, Communiqué for joint Anglo-American release, 31.3.1974.

shortage, because of shortage of housing materials'.[22]

This press release had an immediate effect. As soon as he learned of it, the director of the US Economics Division contacted his British counterparts to apologise for any damage to the recruitment drive. General Clay, at that point attending the four-power conference in Moscow, sent an angry telegram pointing out that Wheeler's communiqué was 'absolutely inconsistent with our drive; it is a unilateral action completely at variance with our Bizonal Economic Agreement'.[23] Clay instructed staff to take 'immediate steps in every possible way to correct damage and to put new vigour in the recruiting programme'.[24] The deputy director of Manpower Division noted after Clay's telegram that 'things have been pretty hot round here ever since'.[25] A meeting was hurriedly organised in the Ruhr between the Americans Leo Werts (director of OMGUS Manpower Division), M. S. Szymczak and R. C. Henry and their British counterparts. Suddenly the SVR programme (dubbed 'Ruhr 47/48'), from being little more than a theoretical exercise, became the object of serious discussion.[26]

Rappaport's programme presented a complete solution to the Ruhr miners' housing problem. Within two years, according to the plan, 130,000 members of the established workforce were to be rehoused or have their accommodation repaired while housing was to be found for 100,000 new miners. Through repairs and new construction, a total of 5,243,000 square metres additional living space was to be created, almost four times the figure envisaged by the Manpower Division's five-year programme. During the first year, the new plan would require more than three times as many building materials as the five-year programme; in the second year almost five times as many. The programme had not attempted to make the difficult choice

22. Ibid.; WWA S22 (OMGUS), Manpower 7/43–1/47, OMGUS Public Relations Office, for information of correspondents, Berlin 21.3.1974; R. G. Wheatley for Chief Manpower Officer, CCG(BE) to RGO, 28.3.1947.

23. WWA S22 (OMGUS), 7/43–1/47 telegram US Military Attaché Moscow, from Clay to Keating 31.3.1947.

24. Ibid.

25. WWA S22 (OMGUS), 7/43–1/47, V. C. Stevens, Acting Director Manpower Division, OMGUS, memo for Mr Werts, 1.4.1947.

26. WWA S22 (OMGUS), 7/43–1/47, OMGUS Public Relations Office Communiqué for Joint Anglo-American release, 31.3.1947; OMGUS Public Relations Office Communiqué for Joint Anglo-American release, 3.4.1947.

between improving the housing quality of the established men or making space for newcomers: it did both. Apart from the prefabricated houses rather unwillingly introduced on American advice, there were no provisional solutions. Neither Nissen huts nor temporary accommodation were envisaged and, an even more radical departure, all married men amongst the new miners (there seems to have been the assumption that two-thirds of the new men would be married) were to receive family accommodation within the two-year period. The space allocation allowed per miner – 9 square metres for a single miner and 45 square metres for a miners' family (including hall and kitchen) – was, while certainly not overgenerous, acceptable by normal standards.[27] Thus all Ruhr interests would be satisfied: the housing authorities would not be forced to approve substandard dwellings; the established miners would not resentfully look on while newcomers absorbed all the available supplies; and the newcomers would not only be found a place to live but would be offered a standard of accommodation which they could not find anywhere else, encouraging them to put down permanent roots in the Ruhr.[28]

The other side to the programme, of course, was that it would create large inequalities and involve very heavy social and economic costs at a time of general scarcity. At the current level of coal allocation, for instance, the miners' housing programme would absorb half of all building materials in the British Zone. It would place enormous demands on the available supply of timber. The Bavarians had still not fulfilled their 1946 timber commitment of just 28,000 cubic metres and yet the new plan cheerfully required 112,375 cubic metres of timber in the first year for repair and reconstruction and a further 180,000 cubic metres for the first nine months of the prefabricated housing programme! Over three-quarters of construction workers in the Ruhr would have to be directed to miners' housing. It was far from certain whether this degree of resource concentration could be economically or socially justified.[29]

27. Hostels for single miners would have a combined dwelling space of around 300,000 m² or room for approx. 35,000 new miners.
28. HStAD NW73, 282, Director SVR, 'Programme for the Erection of Miners' Dwellings "Ruhr 47/48"' (henceforth 'Ruhr 47/48'), p. 4.
29. HStAD NW73, 282, minutes of 2nd meeting of the Working Party on Miners' Housing to the Bipartite Economic Control Group, 14.5.1947; NW73,481, Rappaport to WAM, 22.9.1947.

Nevertheless, the plan received a series of endorsements from the bipartite economic authorities. On 28 March the final plan was submitted and three days later, COPROD called on the Bipartite Economic Control Group (BECG) to set up a working party to investigate its feasibility. On 18 April, the working party submitted an interim report to the BECG, supporting the plan and suggesting that the coal allocation of 28,000 tons be made mandatory. The BECG and its senior sister in the bipartite administration, the Bipartite Economic Panel, both endorsed the report. Though it hesitated to introduce a mandatory coal requirement (in order not to reduce unnecessarily the flexibility of the coal allocation machinery), the Bipartite Economic Panel nevertheless called for 'strong pressure' to be exerted on the Executive Committee for Economics (Verwaltungsamt für Wirtschaft), the bizonal German body now responsible for coal allocation, to ensure that the housing programme received the necessary coal and also preferential treatment in respect of timber and glass.[30]

It might be expected that endorsement from the highest economic authorities within the military government would suffice to ensure the plan's implementation. There was, however, strong resistance to the recommendations from the Verwaltungsamt and its successor, the Verwaltung für Wirtschaft (VfW), with the result that, until July, monthly coal allocations to the building programme were only about half the recommended levels. In addition, the VfW was very reluctant to allot wood to miners' housing in anything like the amounts required, so that in June the BECG working party felt obliged once again to stress that the miners' housing wood contingent should be given top priority.[31]

It would go beyond the limits of this study to attempt a national cost – benefit analysis and establish whether the VfW's resistance was justified. But when it is borne in mind that for the whole of the bizonal area, only 160,000 tons of coal a month were available for building requirements, and that this had to

30. HStAD NW73, 282, minutes of 2nd meeting of the Working Party on Miners' Housing to the Bipartite Economic Control Group, 14.5.1947; PRO FO 1005, 380, COPROD P(47)21, 18.4.1947; WWA S22 (OMGUS), BICO BIECO Series 17/8203/12–1947, BIECO/M(47)12, 14.5.1947.

31. HStAD NW53, 465, HQNGCC, Mines Supplies Department, translation of minutes of 3rd meeting of BECG working party, 4.6.1947; NW10, 91, President of the ZAA to WAM, 30.9.1947.

cover all industrial reconstruction, transport repairs and private building, it is easy to understand why the VfW was very hesitant to provide the mines with a quota of 28,000 tons.[32]

What distinguished 'Ruhr 47/48' from the Points System was that the former impinged far more directly on established economic priorities, whereas the Points System could be met largely at the cost of private consumption. The social cost of the Points System was high, but the impact on economic reconstruction was limited mainly to the loss of workers' productivity caused by their actual or relative deprivation in terms of foodstuffs and consumer goods. Housing was different. Even those VfW officials who were advocates of special measures for the miners argued that it was virtually impossible with the available coal to provide for a special miners' building programme. As far as wood is concerned it was apparent to the VfW that many recognised priority consumers would have to be neglected if the 'Ruhr 47/48' plan was to be honoured in full.[33]

The VfW's resistance to this level of favouritism would have been strengthened by the knowledge that 'Ruhr 47/48' went far beyond the minimum requirements necessary for housing new labour and was an optimum plan, in which few corners had been cut. The VfW might well argue that it made no economic sense to treat mining as though supply conditions had normalised, while the rest of the economy was desperately short of coal and wood. Under these circumstances, the 13,300 tons allocated by the VfW was probably much nearer an appropriate figure than the 28,000 tons of Rappaport's plan.

Why were the perceptions of the VfW and the bipartite economic authorities so divergent? One reason must be that the latter were continually under pressure to increase coal exports, whereas the VfW regarded the high level of underpriced coal transfer to overseas countries as a major hindrance to reconstruction. The VfW had no interest in delaying the rest of the reconstruction in order to maximise coal output that would only partly benefit the nation's economy.[34] To a certain extent, then, both sides were making rational economic decisions within their

32. Collins Papers, Report on Miners' Housing, enclosure 'B', appendices 'A' and 'B'.

33. HStAD NW73, 458, VfW, Arbeitsgruppe Kohle, to WAM, 26.4.1947, signed Deissmann; NW10, 91, President of the ZAA to WAM, 30.9.1947.

34. Abelshauser, *Wirtschaft in Westdeutschland*, p. 143.

own different frames of reference. Yet it is doubtful whether the
bipartite bodies had fully considered the implications of the
allocations they demanded. Under pressure to do something
fast for miners' housing, it had taken only a couple of meetings
for Rappaport's policy to be approved. Somehow, perhaps
because of a communication gap between the German administration that had produced the housing plan and the Allied
administration that approved it, the Allies lost sight of the fact
that Rappaport's plan was a rather theoretical exercise. It had
simply set out to show what would be required, were satisfactory housing for all miners within two years to be accepted as a
general target. It had *not* tried to show what quantities of
resources could reasonably and feasibly be devoted to miners'
housing.[35]

It might be countered that, given the bureaucratic inertia of a
controlled economy, it made sense for military government to
demand the impossible in order to attain the possible. Yet there
is ample evidence that the bipartite agencies remained for many
months under the impression that the full plan could be
achieved. In addition, the exaggerated demands proved counter-
productive because in the long term they strengthened the
resistance to giving miners' housing priority and because the
battles over the allocation diverted attention from ensuring
the efficient deployment of those resources that were allocated.[36]

The importance of the latter point becomes apparent if the
repair figures for the first half of 1947 are considered. As already
noted, the first three months of 1947 had seen building supplies
for miners' housing fall to an all-time low. Repairs fell to between 1,450 and 1,850 dwelling units (d.u.) a month. In the
second quarter of 1947, the VfW increased the coal contingent
by almost thirteen times[37] over the levels actually received in the
first quarter. Yet the repairs completion rate rose only to 7,700
for the quarter or around 2,550 d.u. a month. That this did not
manifest simply a delay between making a coal allocation and

35. HStAD NW73, 481, Rappaport to WAM, 'Betr.: Bergarbeiterwohnungsbau', 22.9.1947.
36. HStAD NW73, 481, Rappaport to WAM, 22.9.1947; Collins Papers, loose
paper, Report on Miners' Housing, Enclosure 'A'.
37. 13,300 tons is of course *more* than thirteen times 1,000 tons but the former
figure included the allocation for the small Cologne and Aachen coalfields as
well.

seeing its impact on repairs was proven when in July and August repairs progressed even more slowly; in August, normally the peak building month of the year, the completion rate was virtually as low as it had been at any time since the capitulation.[38]

This strikingly weak performance initially went unnoticed by the Allied authorities, who were more concerned at the VfW's unwillingness to implement the full agreed allocations. That concern increased when it appeared that the successful room-requisitioning programme was beginning to exhaust the available supplies of private dwelling space. Just as significant was the growing seriousness of the labour supply situation in North-Rhine Westphalia, where the Ruhr mining industry's reliance on local recruits was denuding other key industries of able-bodied men. In June, the Chiefs of the British and US Manpower Divisions visited the Ruhr and subsequently requested that the bipartite economic authorities make the 28,000 tons of coal a mandatory requirement. The BECG acceded to this request and the VfW was thus at last obliged to comply. Top-level endorsement of this mandatory top priority was given by the Washington Coal Conference. The conference also called for the BECG working party on miners' housing to be made into a permanent committee, in order to ensure that the programme was carried out.[39]

The full 28,000 tons allocation of coal was given to miners' housing for the first time in August and continued to be awarded more or less in full until December. According to British experts, 60 per cent of available building materials in the British Zone was being injected into miners' housing. Yet the amazing fact is that the progress of repairs actually fell (see table 3.1). Even more disastrous was the failure of the prefabricated and new housing programme. In the first year, according to the plan, 15,000 prefabs were to be delivered. By January 1948, just twenty-two had been delivered and six more called forward. Overall, the first year of the programme created 200,000 square

38. HStAD NW9, 112, SVR, First Aid Housing Repairs Ruhr area, reports for North-Rhine and Westphalia, February–March 1947; WAM, Ref. 01/314 – Bo/N., memo, 'Bergarbeiterwohnungsbau – Wohnraumzugang', 21.1.1948.

39. PRO FO 1005, 380, COPROD P(47)34; WWA S22 (OMGUS), BICO BISEC 11/103–2/22, COCOM, minutes of the 1st meeting of the Coal Committee, 15.12.1947, annex: BIB/P(47) 112/1.

Table 3.1 Repairs to Ruhr miners' housing, 1947

Month	Repairs
June	2,561
July	2,044
August	1,661
September	1,816
October	1,502
November	2,097
December	2,088

Source: HStAD NW9, 112, WAM, Ref. 01/314–Bo/N., memo, 21.1.1948, re 'Bergarbeiterwohnungsbau – Wohnraumzugang.

metres of dwelling space, or less than 4 per cent of the two-year target.[40]

How were these figures possible? Though the coal contingent had been made mandatory, this was not true of timber or other ancillary materials. As a result, the VfW simply maintained its resistance to the 'Ruhr 47/48' programme in these allocations and refused to give miners' housing any greater priority 'wegen der berechtigten Anträge anderer Bedarfsträger'.[41] Indeed, as the importance of the coal bottleneck receded in comparison with other shortages (such as transport), the VfW's resolve only hardened. 'Wichtiger als neue Anlegungen zu forcieren,' wrote the VfW's Dr Keiser in November, 'scheint mir dafür zu sorgen, daß die Reichsbahn in der Lage ist, Kohle zu transportieren, und daß die Wirtschaft in den Stand gesetzt wird, sie entsprechend sinnvoll aufzunehmen.'[42] In consequence, Ruhr repairs and particularly the prefabs programme suffered from an acute shortage of wood and other supplementary materials.

Why was the VfW successful in preventing the introduction of a mandatory timber priority where it had failed on the coal contingent? For one thing the VfW's stance was strengthened by the resistance of the southern Länder that would be supplying most of the wood. Disinclined to do NRW favours at any time, they grew increasingly hostile to what they saw as the inordinate

40. HStAD NW53, 465, minutes of meeting held on 15.1.1948, January 1948; NW9, 56, Land Manpower Department, NRW to Ruhl, WAM, 29.1.1948.
41. HStAD NW73, 47, Dr Keiser, VfW, to ZAA, 9.12.1947.
42. HStAD NW73, 47, Dr Keiser, VfW, to Rappaport, 12.11.1947.

demands of the housing programme. It is hard to say whether it was the southern Länder that induced the VfW to reduce allocations to the Ruhr or whether the latter skilfully fanned the flames of southern opposition as a counterweight to the bipartite muscle backing up 'Ruhr 47/48'. There is evidence for both points of view.[43]

Even then, a clearer priority on wood and other materials might have emerged had not the Americans themselves supported the opposition to the programme. This was partly from doubts about the advisability of the plan, but more because of their more general federalism, which led them to support the Länder's autonomy against the encroachments of the bizonal agencies in Frankfurt. For example, the US building trades' chief and original proponent of the prefabs programme, R. C. Henry, backed the southern Länder's resistance to the VfW's demands. British experts were well aware of the Americans' role here. A Fuel and Power Division official wrote with heavy irony that 'the Americans, as you know, consider that all Lands [*sic*] should have equal treatment in all things,' concluding that the deliberate unco-ordinated activation of industries on a regional level was hampering reconstruction.[44]

Many projects for which bricks and stone were available were held up by the absence of ancillary materials. The SVR reported in September 1947 that electrical materials were in such short supply that not even the small supply of Nissen huts had been put in order. Only a fraction of the roof tiles needed had been supplied. In the financial year 1947 repairs and new construction (excluding the prefabs) required some 58,849 cubic metres of wood. Yet up till the beginning of October 1947, only 4,400 cubic metres had been delivered and over the year as a whole, only about one-sixth of wood ordered actually arrived. The British Manpower Department in NRW reported that 'We have now all around us partially completed jobs.'[45] 'Ideally,' continued the report, 'this job would be staged as a "major oper-

43. HStAD NW73, 282, WAM to VfW, 26.11.1947; NW10, 91, President of the ZAA to WAM, 20.9.1947; NW73, 47, WAM, Ref. IIIA–150/1, memo, 29.1.1948, signed Baerlecken.
44. HStAD NW10, 91, President of the ZAA to WAM, 20.9.1947; PRO FO 1030, 345, F. H. Harrison, Fuel and Power Division, to President, ECOSC, 2.7.1947.
45. WWA S22 (OMGUS) BICO BISEC 11/107–2/1–4, HQ NRW Land Manpower Dept to Joint Chairmen, UK/USCCG, 16.4.1948.

ation" and catered for as such in regard to every aspect.' As it was, every single item – coal, wood, labour, transport and so on – was covered by different priorities and conditions.[46]

One factor which strengthened the VfW's opposition to the miners' housing programme was the enormous wastage and inefficiency that characterised it from its inception. The fact that there were fewer repairs in August 1947 than there had been in February, though the coal allocation had in the meantime increased by a factor of at least ten, was evidence that a huge amount of coal earmarked for miners' housing was seeping into other building projects – and indeed other economic sectors in NRW. All observers in the Ruhr talked of an enormous black economy in the building sector. The British officer responsible for the administrative district of Arnsberg, into which fell a substantial portion of the eastern Ruhr area as well as some more rural parts of NRW, reported in May 1947 that 'the German administration seems to have completely failed to direct building materials to the places where they are wanted. Everywhere I go in this Regierungsbezirk I see building going on except in the Ruhr areas. Unless something is done to stop this tremendous leakage of building materials to the Black Market, I do not think we shall ever get enough houses built for the miners.'[47] By August 1947, the same observer noted that 'the lamentable failure of the German Administration to take adequate steps to house the miners in the Ruhr area becomes more obvious every day'. After estimating that 75 per cent of building materials were going on to the black market, he reported that '*All* mining Kreise say that repairs for miners' housing are practically at a standstill owing to lack of building material and labour,' a fact which he attributed to an 'incompetent and corrupt German administration', and to low fines for illegal building.[48]

The exasperation was genuine and understandable but the explanation was an oversimplification. Some of the problems had little to do with either corruption or incompetence and more with the inherent weakness of a controlled economy. For example,

46. HStAD NW73, 481, Rappaport to WAM, 22.9.1947; NW73, 47, copy of minutes of meeting in Frankfurt at the VfW on 22.1.1948, 26.1.1948.
47. PRO FO 1005, 1603, HQ Military Government, Regierungsbezirk Arnsberg, Monthly Report for May 1947.
48. Ibid., Monthly Report for August 1947, emphasis in original.

the firms responsible for transporting the building materials often demanded to be paid in kind, receiving sometimes as much as four-fifths of the contingent![49] An even more fundamental problem, as Werner Plumpe has shown recently, was the weakness of the regional administration. British authorities in NRW acknowledged that it was 'administratively impossible' for the Housing Ministry rigidly to control the Kreise. Such inspectorates as did exist were hampered by shortages of personnel, transport and paper. Even more important than objective resource shortages were the vested interests, particularly NRW industrialists and chambers of commerce, which had been able to prevent the Economics Ministry from setting up an effective administration. As a result, the authorities were simply not in a position to ensure that the allotted coal really did produce building supplies, that the supplies really did reach the miners' housing programme or that the programme's repairs really did benefit miners. When a special commission was set up to investigate the problems in the Ruhr, both German and British participants discovered that it was virtually impossible to obtain a clear picture of the size of coal transports to the building industry, of the level of building materials production or of the amount of materials made available to miners' housing projects. The Economics Ministry's reports were completely inadequate.[50]

Partly because of this weakness, there was a willingness from the WAM downwards to accept a considerable amount of losses to the black market. Though everyone knew of the miners' importance, few believed that the coal production programme was for German benefit alone, so that many officials were not completely persuaded of the housing programme's virtues. To add to their readiness to turn a blind eye, the seepage on to the black market benefited both general population and NRW economy. At the first meeting of the BECG's Standing Committee on

49. HStAD NW53, 465, minutes of meeting held on 15.1.1948 to discuss building materials for miners' housing, January 1948.
50. Werner Plumpe, 'Auf dem Weg in die Marktwirtschaft: Organisierte Industrieinteressen, Wirtschaftsverwaltung und Besatzungsmacht in Nordrhein-Westfalen 1945–1947', in G. Brunn (ed.), *Nordrhein-Westfalen und seine Anfänge nach 1945/1946*, Essen, 1986, pp. 67–84; WWA S22 (OMGUS) BICO BISEC 11/107–2/1–4, HQ NRW Land Manpower Dept to UK/USCCG, 16.4.1948; HStAD NW9, 55, WAM to HQ Military Government, NRW, 13.3.1947; NW73, 47, Baerlecken to Paul, 13.1.1948.

Ruhr Miners' Housing in August 1947, at which German officials were in attendance, the bipartite authorities stressed the need for vigorous action to eradicate illegal building. It was noteworthy that the NRW Reconstruction Minister pointed out not only that it was very difficult to combat such 'black building' but also defended it with the comment that it was not only the miners who needed housing. Not surprisingly, he received a very firm reminder of the economic reasons for giving the miners priority.[51]

It was at the municipal level that the resistance to giving the mines priority was clearest. Municipal housing offices frequently allotted houses constructed in the 'Ruhr 47/48' programme to non-miners. It is a plausible contention that a lot of the misallocations at municipal level were deliberate. A regional official charged with checking municipal housing allocation procedures noted with barely concealed disbelief that the Dortmund housing administration had 'bis August 1947 angeblich nicht gewußt, daß aus dem Bergarbeiterwohnungsbauprogramm nur für Bergarbeiter vorgesehene Wohnungen versorgt werden konnten'.[52] Yet, because of its lack of administrative clout, the NRW regional administration could do little about this even when it wanted to.[53]

The British were well aware of the problem; yet in housing as in other areas of resource control they proved unable to achieve the radical restructuring required. In July 1947, at a meeting of the BECG working party on miners' housing, questions from R. C. Henry about controlling coal allocations resulted in an embarrassed silence, presumably because the British did not feel in a position to introduce a more rigorous control of the German administration. In autumn 1947 the wastage was so catastrophic that the pressure for a thorough investigation could not be resisted. Yet despite a special Co-ordinating Committee investigation, lasting six weeks and involving some very tough talking, enormous losses continued.[54]

---

51. BAK Z40, 449, BECG, minutes of 1st meeting of the Standing Committee on Ruhr Miners' Housing, 25.8.1947.
52. HStAD NW9, 57, WAM, Dept IIIB 3–150/3–(12), 'Prüfungsbericht über die Durchführung des Bergarbeiterwohnungsbauprogramms in der Stadt Dortmund', 14.5.1948.
53. HStAD NW9, 56, WBSR to WAM, 5.2.1948 and annex.
54. Plumpe, 'Auf dem Weg', pp. 173ff; HStAD NW73, 259, WAM, Dept III B1, memo, 9.7.1947; NW9, 112, minutes of the 25th meeting of the

113

One other source of inefficiency worth noting is the low productivity of construction workers. Often poorly housed, underequipped and underfed, construction gangs were working at only a third of pre-war productivity. Consideration was given to the idea of an incentive scheme for the construction workers, but the idea was rejected because of the negative impact it would have on other sections of labour. In reality, this was a problem that could not be solved until more food was available and enough goods could be purchased to give wages real value.[55]

Alongside the enormous wastage, one other feature of the housing programme which raised hackles in Frankfurt was that the question of its financing was never resolved. At first sight it is strange that finance should have been a problem at all. In a planned economy, money could be expected to have little significance, serving merely as a sort of supplementary coupon establishing the right of the recipient to obtain goods. Yet in respect of finance, the economy in the Occupation period revealed itself to be not a planned economy at all. Finance had not been centralised in the same way as the allocation of material resources, and money led an independent existence.[56] In the case of the miners' housing programme, bizonal supplies were being allocated to the mines but no provision had been made for a flow of bizonal funds to go to the Ruhr in order that the supplies might be paid for. Coal and wood allocations were made at bizonal level but housing was generally a matter for the individual Länder and not normally a charge on the bizonal budget. Moreover, the Land's responsibility was not entirely clear-cut either. In particular, it was not certain what its obligations were *vis-à-vis* privately owned housing. In the British Zone, the Länder and municipalities were committed to provide money for repairs, yet at a rate which did not in fact cover the full cost. For new construction, on the other hand, there was no

Co-ordinating Committee, 27.11.1947; NW53, 465, minutes of meeting on 15.1.1948 to discuss building materials for miners' housing, January 1948.

55. HStAD NW53, 643, WAM to Minister President, 4.3.1948; BAK Z13, 198, VfW to Verwaltungsrat, 15.5.1948.

56. HStAD NW73, 458, translation, BECG, minutes of 3rd meeting of Standing Committee, 19.9.1947; Theo Horstmann, 'Die Angst vor dem finanziellen Kollaps. Banken- und Kreditpolitik in der britischen Zone zwischen 1945 und 1948', in Dietmar Petzina and Walter Euchner (eds), *Wirtschaftspolitik im britischen Besatzungsgebiet 1945–1949*, Düsseldorf, 1984, pp. 214–34 at 220.

firmly established financing arrangement.[57]

Even so, it is hard to see why finance should have been a problem when it is born in mind that goods were so much scarcer than money. In the pre-1948 economy, it rarely happened that consumers lucky enough to receive an allocation of supplies were not in a position to pay for them. So why was it that as early as September 1947 the whole issue of finance loomed so large that Rappaport saw it as 'die wichtigste aller Fragen im Bergarbeiterwohnungsbau'?[58] Surely NRW could have advanced enough money to keep the programme going for quite a while? Failing that, could the Länder not have put up the money?

Indeed they could. The finance question became critical long before cash reserves ran out. By March 1948, less than half the money set aside for miners' housing by the NRW Reconstruction Minister had been spent. In other words, the financial problem was not directly a question of lack of money.[59] The point was that no one wanted to set a precedent. The overall volume of miners' housing was so large that no one wanted to be saddled with the eventual bill. The cost of the envisaged new construction, for example, were it ever to be realised in its entirety, was getting on for ten times the entire NRW budget for new housing.[60] For the other Länder there was an additional fear. The Bavarian representative in the Exekutivrat wrote in December 1947 that: 'Die Leistung von Zuschüssen zum Bau von Bergarbeiterwohnungen im Ruhrgebiet durch die Bizone oder deren Länder müßte auch unter dem Gesichtspunkt Bedenken auslösen, daß sie wohl der erste Schritt zur Einbeziehung der süddeutschen Länder in die Subventionierung des Ruhrkohlenbergbaus wäre.'[61] Apart from the sheer size of the potential sums involved, the other source of anxiety was that, by contrast with material allocations, which were seen as

57. HStAD NW10, 91, President of the ZAA to WAM, 11.10.1947; BBA 32, 1064, Hibernia report, 'Bergarbeiterwohnungsbau 1945–1948', February 1949.

58. HStAD NW53, 643, WAM to personal assistant of the Minister President, 4.3.1948; HStAD NW73, 481, Rappaport to WAM, 22.9.1947.

59. HStAD NW53, 643, WAM to personal assistant of the Minister President, 4.3.1948.

60. HStAD NW10, 91, President of the ZAA to WAM, 11.10.1947 and WAM to ZAA, 17.10.1947.

61. *Akten zur Vorgeschichte der BRD 1945–1949*, vol. 4: *Januar–Dezember 1948*, Munich, 1983, p. 185.

short-term expedients, financial allocations were viewed as
having long-term implications. Conscious that a currency reform would at some point re-establish the real value of money,
every group wanted to ensure that it was not left holding the
baby. This explains, for example, the hostility of the NRW
Finance Minister to the idea of even a modest housing programme financed solely by NRW. The Land would not accept
sole responsibility for a task that was in the interest 'des gesamten deutschen Volkes' and it would not finance the rebuilding of
housing owned by the mines. Neither NRW nor the other
Länder were prepared to settle their differences for the sake of
the benefits to the national economy. Indeed Bavaria, the most
particularist of the all the Länder, went so far as to assert that
the advantages would accrue only to NRW![62]

Why did the military government not settle the issue? It could
either have forced the Germans at bizonal level to commit funds
or it could have provided money directly through its control of
the mines. Let us start with the second option, which seemed
not illogical since a large proportion of miners' housing was
colliery-owned. (Much of the rest belonged to *gemeinnützige
Wohnungsgesellschaften*, private housing associations, few of
whom had sufficient funds for new building in the immediate
post-war era.) During 1946, most building work in fact had been
financed by the mines, although on the understanding that at
least a proportion of their outlay would be reimbursed by the
state under the general zonal arrangements for financing repairs. In 1947, too, the financing of repairs looked relatively
secure. The real problem was the large volume of new construction envisaged by the housing programme, coupled with growing British anxieties about the zonal budget deficit.[63] In July
1947, the NGCC suddenly announced that it would not allow
the collieries to pay for any more housing. Indirectly, Hembry,
the NGCC's financial director, admitted the real reason for the
change, namely, that the financial experts in Berlin were growing increasingly anxious about the amount of subsidies that
were being pumped into the mines. Until June 1947, these

62. HStAD NW10, 91, WAM, 'Bericht über die Besprechungen betr. Finanzierung des Bergarbeiterwohnungsneubaues', 30.7.1947; *Akten zur Vorgeschichte*,
vol. 4, pp. 183ff.
63. HStAD NW10, 91, WAM, report on discussions concerning finance for
new construction of miners' housing, 30.7.1947.

subsidies had been given as credits by the Reichsbank, but they were deemed too large to continue in this way and became direct subsidies from the zonal budget. The zonal budget was heavily in debt and the British were very concerned about the financial instability that might ensue. As a result, Finance Division forbade Hembry from providing any funds for miners' housing.[64]

Initially, though somewhat reluctantly, NRW had agreed to put up RM 30 million towards new construction, on the understanding that the collieries would also make a substantial contribution. Now that the NGCC had withdrawn its support, all NRW's anxieties about admitting responsibility came to the fore. Though the NGCC stated that the Land should spend the RM 30 million and worry about the principles later, the NRW government argued that the fundamental question as to who was responsible for building had to be settled.[65] By the beginning of September the matter still had not been resolved. Unwillingly, the Reconstruction Ministry agreed to consider financing individual cases on their own merits and it was on this basis that the tiny consignment of prefabs reached the Ruhr. At the same time the Land applied to the bizonal administration for a tax on coal which could be used to finance the housing programme. Here the resistance of the other Länder made itself felt and the proposal made little progress.[66]

If the NGCC could not provide funds, why then did the Allies not put pressure on the bizonal administration to provide the requisite cash? It is possible that, if the NGCC's financial difficulties had emerged early enough, BICO would have made appropriate arrangements, yet the full extent of the problem became clear only towards the end of the summer. In October the BECG, on the advice of the Standing Committee on Miners' Housing, requested BICO to ensure that finance for the programme was made available. Yet BICO was slow in putting pressure on the German institutions to find a solution,

64. Horstmann, 'Die Angst vor dem finanziellen Kollaps', p. 222; Collins Papers, A2, Paper 5, letter from Hembry to Chief, Fuel and Power Division, CCG(BE), et al., 8.7.1947.
65. HStAD NW10, 91, WAM, 'Besprechungsnotiz', 19.9.1947.
66. HStAD NW10, 91, WAM to President of SVR, 2.9.1947; Finance Ministry to Hauptverwaltung für Finanzen beim Zwei-Zonen Wirtschaftsrat, 16.9.1947; WAM to Head of the Press Office, 14.6.1948.

probably, once again, because of American opposition to central controls.[67]

To add to the financial confusion, another difficulty emerged, namely, that a lot of the land on which the houses were to be built was owned by the mines and that meant that tenure was insecure. The future ownership of the mines was undecided and the NGCC was unwilling to agree to land leases (*Erbbauverträge*) that would have tied the hands of future owners. Without security of land tenure, the housing associations were unwilling to risk their money on building.[68]

The result of all these difficulties was that the new housing programme limped on at a pace slower even than that allowed by the VfW's modest allocation of wood. In fact, in January 1948 manufacturers' yards in the US zone were full of completed fabricated houses which could not be brought into the Ruhr because the property leases obtainable were too short and because payment from the Reconstruction Ministry still had not been settled. As late as summer 1948, virtually no new construction apart from a small number of prefabs had been funded.[69]

The point about a lot of these issues, with the exception of the property leases, was that though their impact was palpable enough, they were not genuine problems. It would not have hurt NRW to commit its RM 30 million in advance, any more than the Länder would have suffered by making an allocation of cash to help finance the new construction. It was the precedent that was at issue. The more imminent the prospect of a currency reform became, the less willing was any party to shoulder the burden.[70]

Tinkering with the System, 1947–8

Because of wastage and financial shortages, the VfW took the opportunity in September of provisionally cutting by a substan-

67. HStAD NW10, 91, BECG to BICO, 7.10.1947; NW73, 47, Director, SVR to SRMO, Essen, 30.1.1948 (translation).

68. HStAD NW10, 92, Treuhandstelle für Bergmannswohnstätten to Director, SVR, 20.2.1948; WAM, Memo for Ministerialdirektor, Rühl, 11.3.1948.

69. HStAD NW9, 56, Land Manpower Dept, HQ Land NRW to Rühl, WAM, 29.1.1948.

70. WWA S22 (OMGUS) AG 1948/163/4, A. J. Hillhouse, 'Report on the Rühr Coal Industry Field Trip', January 1948.

tial amount the programme's coal allocation for the first quarter of 1948.[71] An amusing incident followed which surely proved, if proof were needed, the impenetrability of the bureaucratic jungle surrounding the housing question. On 21 October, the German participants of the Standing Committee on Ruhr Miners' Housing met to agree on common ground before the full committee met on the thirtieth. It is evident from the minutes that the NRW representatives not only did not know of the VfW's decision but also had not realised that the chief source of opposition to the miners' housing plan was the VfW itself. Rappaport, thinking himself among friends, 'erklärte freimütig, daß das Programm nur zu 40 per cent erfüllt werden kann' and admitted that the Allied Standing Committee members were still unaware of this fact.[72] He declared himself to be against a revision of the programme to a more realistic target, because he felt it was important not to endanger the full coal contingent. This was grist to the VfW's mill and the NRW delegates were suddenly shocked to hear the VfW representative declare 'überraschenderweise und sehr bestimmt' that the coal allocation could under no circumstances be given in full. The absolute maximum was 20,000 tons a month.[73] A day later, the VfW sent the BECG and the other Länder a letter arguing that the 'Ruhr 47/48' programme could not be fulfilled, had never been properly thought through and indeed had never, with the exception of the coal allocation, been fully authorised by the military government.[74]

Now began a fight between the NRW representatives and the VfW over the allocations to the miners' housing programme. NRW was hampered in its demand for better allocations by the revelations emerging about the amount of wastage and uncontrolled building in the Ruhr. In January, the newly formed DKBL suggested that it and not the Reconstruction Ministry should handle the coal and materials contingents, a suggestion which only added force to the criticism of existing control and co-ordination of supplies in NRW.[75]

71. HStAD NW73, 47, President of the ZAA to WAM, 22.12.1947.
72. HStAD NW73, 282, 'Bericht über die Besprechung am 21.10.1947 über das Bergarbeiterwohnungsbauprogramm', 23.10.1947.
73. Ibid. and Roseman, 'New Miners', p. 205 fn. 1.
74. HStAD NW73, 282, copy of letter from VfW to BECG, 22.10.1947.
75. HStAD NW73, 282, WAM to VfW, 26.11.1947; NW73, 47, Director, SVR,

For its part the VfW came under increasing pressure from military government to give the miners' housing programme more support and in January 1948 a series of compromises were reached. The coal allocation was brought up to its old level again, and the allocation procedure ('*Endverbraucherkontingentierungsverfahren*' in German officialese!) was changed, allowing NRW greater flexibility. After tough negotiations, the transport facilities offered to the programme were improved. Yet Länder and VfW opposition continued. In April, the VfW cut the wood contingent for miners' housing by 75 per cent, despite the fact that there was still a large backlog from 1947. The Länder grew bolder and Bavaria openly declared itself unwilling to honour its commitments. Notwithstanding attempts by NRW to bypass the official allocation procedure and barter coal for timber, the volume of wood received in the first half of 1948 was actually lower than it had been in 1947.[76]

Thus little improvement was to be seen in the building programme. True, the pace of repairs was somewhat faster. Yet the improvement had been achieved only by increasing the proportion of lightly damaged buildings in the repairs programme. Such properties yielded little additional living space once repaired so that the nominally faster completion rate was not really a gain at all.[77]

Housing and Workforce Rebuilding

In April 1948, Rappaport felt called upon to defend the achievements of the housing programme against its critics (primarily against the DKBL). 'Immerhin dürfte es eine nicht unbeachtliche Leistung sein,' he wrote to the Reconstruction Minister, 'wenn trotz aller Schwierigkeiten im Jahre 1947 rd. 23,500 Instandset-

to Ministerialdirektor Dr Spiecker, Exekutivrat, 8.1.1948 and WAM to VfW, 12.1.1948; Dr Keiser, VfW, to ZAA, 9.12.1947; Director SVR to WAM, 5.1.1948; copy of minutes of a meeting at the VfW, Frankfurt on 22.1.1948, 26.1.1948.

76. BAK Z40, 500, ZAA, memo, Ref: Ve/3825/48, 1.2.1948; HStAD NW73, 457, WAM, 'Bericht über den Bergarbeiterwohnungsbau', 22.6.1948; NW73, 47, Bate to UK/USCCG (translation), 16.4.1948; NW81, 520, notes of a conversation with Mr Bate, signed Rappaport, 17.6.1948; WAM, memo concerning visit of Dr Dach on 28.5.1948, 1.6.1948.

77. HStAD NW73, 47, SVR, report for May, 11.6.1948; SVR Aufstellung (1949); HStAD NW73, 479, SVR, miners' housing progress report for May 1947.

zungen im Bergarbeiterwohnungsbau durchgeführt wurden.' 'Tatsächlich,' he continued, 'ist es bisher gelungen, den gesamten Zustrom an Bergarbeitern unterzubringen.'[78]

The latter assertion was rather misleading. It was true that no one brought into the Ruhr found himself without accommodation, but it was not true that labour supply had been unaffected by the housing shortage. It had limited the number of people from outside the Ruhr and, to some degree, the overall size of the recruiting programme. Between August and November 1947 first clothing and then accommodation shortages had curtailed recruiting outside the Ruhr. To a certain extent, this limited the pace at which men were taken on, but to a greater degree it induced the authorities to concentrate more than they wanted to on local recruits. It was true that by dint of great efforts and not least of the Co-ordinating Committee's services, 50 per cent of recruits in the second half of 1947 came from outside the Ruhr. This was a considerable achievement; but it fell far short of what was necessary to protect other Ruhr industries. In their manpower planning towards the end of 1947, British and German officials calculated that three-quarters of new recruits ought to come from outside the Ruhr. The costs were borne largely by the other Ruhr industries thereby deprived of labour, but sometimes by the mines themselves when, as not infrequently happened, the mines' own suppliers were hit by labour shortages.[79]

In any case a lot of the accommodation offered, probably more than half, was not the result of the building programme at all, but derived from the intensified use of available dwelling space in the Ruhr. In 1947, for example, some 23,192 miners were provided with living space in this way. By contrast the repairs programme over the same period produced at most 9,000 extra rooms in repaired housing with an additional few thousand in repaired or converted hostels, public halls and so forth.[80] A lot of the accommodation offered was temporary, either because of

78. HStAD NW73, Rappaport to WAM, 9.4.1948.
79. Außenstelle Bergbau (ed.), 'Sechs Jahre Außenstelle Bergbau des Landesarbeitantes NRW', unpublished MS, no place, no date [1952], p. 58; WWA F35, 494, DKBL, circular no. V 19, 1.3.1948.
80. HStAD NW9, 112, WAM, Dept IVC (WB), memo, 12.1.1948 and NW73, 480, Director, SVR, 'Ein Jahr Bergarbeiterwohnungsbau. Bericht über das erste Jahr des Bergarbeiterwohnungsbaus im Ruhrgebiet', 31.7.1948.

its quality or because the mines would not be able to use it indefinitely. Much of the private accommodation gained though room inspection and requisitioning, for instance, would eventually go back to the free disposal of its former owners. As the housing shortage became more acute, increasingly low-quality and provisional accommodation had to be used. The room requisitioning programme made increasing recourse to public halls and other emergency housing. Slow progress in housing repairs induced the authorities to begin a special action 'Lager und Herbergen' in the summer of 1947, the purpose of which was to convert existing unusable camps and other public buildings into emergency accommodation for new labour. By June 1948 some 6,600 single miners and 400 or so families had been housed in this way.[81]

The initial goal of offering good-quality accommodation had thus been abandoned. No new miners' families were given proper family accommodation and most married trainees from outside the Ruhr had to leave their families behind them. If they came with them, it was normally only because there were relatives in the Ruhr with whom they could stay, often in very cramped conditions. In addition, the mines offered a few hundred families emergency housing in camps and so forth. And for the single men, though some of the worst billets of 1946 had been removed, much of the accommodation on offer remained extremely primitive.[82]

Supply Problems in the Uncontrolled Economy

In conclusion, it is worth noting that the difficulty of obtaining resources was not confined to the housing programme. Providing the miners with other goods and materials proved to be just as challenging. Supplying food was the most critical problem, of course, and one which has already received detailed analysis from John Farquharson.[83] In food production, just as in building materials production, a coal-cycle was much in evidence, since coal shortages affected the production of fertiliser and farming

81. Ibid.
82. Ibid.
83. Farquharson, *The Western Allies.*

implements, while the shortage of food in turn affected coal production. The ineffectiveness of controls and the absence of incentives hit deliveries of agricultural produce just as they did the building trade. NRW proved to be if anything even more incapable of collecting grain and food than it had been of monitoring the construction industry. At bizonal level, Land opposition to central controls, particularism and the American tendency to side with the particularists all undermined collection and transfer of both types of resources; the Bavarians were just as protective about their grain as they were reluctant to hand over their timber. In other words, the problems generated by the miners' housing programme can be taken as potent illustrations of Germany's 'uncontrolled economy' in the years 1945–8.[84]

84. Ibid., pp. 45ff, 149, 157, 161ff, 191.

4

An Imperfect Market: Financing Workforce Regeneration in the Social Market Economy

Rebuilding the Workforce after the Currency Reform

In June 1948, currency reform and economic liberalisation consigned the ungainly machinery of the controlled economy to the scrap heap. The economic bureaucracies were rapidly dismantled and most prices freed from official controls. A new, hard currency replaced the devalued Reichsmark. Thus the basis for a functioning market economy was created. The question posed by the present chapter is whether these changes solved for good those problems of resource management which so bedevilled workforce rebuilding in the controlled economy.

In addressing this question, we need to bear in mind that the creation of a market economy was not the only major change taking place in the political and economic environment in which coal policy was formulated. In the first place, there was a major transfer of power back to the Germans. As a consequence of economic liberalisation, the bipartite economic agencies lost much of their ability to control the economy. The most important remaining governmental mechanism for directing the economy was the budget – and that lay in German hands. Moreover, as the creation of an independent West German state drew closer, the Allies became loath to intervene directly in policy-making (though at the highest level their influence remained substantial). Thus, German politicians and administrators, above all the VfW's new director, Ludwig Erhard, were increasingly able to set the tone of economic policy.

Secondly, there was a change in the significance of coal itself. Coal shortages, though still pressing, were no longer as acute as they had been a year earlier. While the coal supply situation eased, other areas of the German economy, hitherto neglected, clamoured for attention. No government could now afford to give the mines quite the same attention as they had been wont to receive. Beyond such objective economic realities, Erhard's own choice of strategy also ensured that mining would no longer bask in the limelight of official attention. After all, Erhard was no great believer in state intervention to benefit particular industries. In addition, his prime area of interest was not heavy industry but the consumer goods sector. The hope was that pent-up popular demand for consumer and household goods would act as a motor to drive economic growth.[1]

Yet Erhard's policy towards the mines was contradictory. Though left to their own devices, the mines were deprived of one of the essential elements of managerial independence: freedom to set the price of their product. Admittedly, Erhard could not have freed the export price for coal, even if he had wanted to: that still lay in Allied hands and was fixed by the International Authority of the Ruhr. But the domestic coal price *was* within his gift. The fact that it remained pegged at well below its real value was a sign that in the German Economics and Finance Departments the free market was not the only household god. It vied for devotion with an even more fickle and awe-inspiring master, namely, price stability. The German authorities felt that, because of the multiplier effect, the economy was especially vulnerable with respect to coal, and there was great reluctance to allow any price increases at all. Thus mining was effectively excluded from the market economy.[2]

These new political and economic realities forced the mining industry itself to re-evaluate its goals and strategy. There is little doubt that as part of this re-evaluation the task of workforce rebuilding moved several notches down the industry's agenda. It was clear that large-scale workforce expansion was no longer a viable strategy to achieve increased coal output. This was partly because the faces were nearing capacity. The underground

1. Werner Abelshauser, *Wirtschaftsgeschichte der Bundesrepublik Deutschland 1945–1980*, Frankfurt, 1983, pp. 52–3.
2. Werner Abelshauser, 'Kohle und Marktwirtschaft. Ludwig Erhards Konflikt mit dem Unternehmensverband Ruhrbergbau am Vorabend der Kohlenkrise', *VfZ*, vol. 33, no. 3, 1985, p. 504; comments by Adenauer, minutes of cabinet meeting on 28.9.1949, in Hans Booms (ed.), *Kabinettsprotokolle der Bundesregierung 1949*, Boppard/Rhein 1982, pp. 93ff.

Table 4.1 Average age of male workers in Ruhr mining

Year[a]	Hewers	All underground	Overall
1930			33.16
1946	42.64	40.21	40.61
1947	42.85	38.85	39.37
1948	42.82	37.83	38.54

(a) At 30 June each year.

Source: OBAD (ed.), *Jahresbericht 1957*.

workforce was already considerably larger than it had been before the war. But even more it was because in the market economy the employers had to think in terms of cost-effectiveness. The industry could no longer allow itself the luxury of counting coaltubs and ignoring the balance sheet. Thus the DKBL's 'Plan A', produced in February 1948, envisaged underground output per man/shift rising rapidly to 1,850 kg by 1953 but allowed for only modest workforce growth. The employers' top priority was to find the capital for mechanisation and sinking new pits. According to DKBL calculations, the mines would need to make over DM 1.5 billion capital investment over the next three years.[3]

Even so, the employers were well aware that the job of rebuilding the workforce was far from over. In the first place, rejuvenation was vital. For, despite the massive recruitment since 1945, the workforce was still very much over-aged. Indeed, the average age of the *Hauer* was actually higher in 1948 than it had been at the end of the war (see table 4.1). Secondly, there was the challenge of stabilising the workforce. Many key figures in the industry were aware that getting on for 40 per cent of the underground workforce was composed of newcomers, a large proportion of whom had come to the mines with no intention of staying for long. Despite the growing level of general unemployment, the mines' labour turnover continued to run at a disturbing level. It was clear that if and when

3. DKBL, *Voraussetzungen des Förderanstiegs im westdeutschen Steinkohlenbergbau*, Bonn, 1952, p. 4; DKBL (ed.), *Entwicklung des Kohlenbergbaus in den Vereinigten Zonen (Plan A)*, Essen, 1948; BAK (OMGUS) BICO COALCO 17/8186/30, DKBL to Joint Chairmen US/UKCCG, 2.11.1948 and attached Plan A figures; ZdKW, vol. 12, p. 54.

unemployment began to fall, wastage would increase while replacements would be harder to find. Thirdly, there was a strong feeling on the part of management that both the new recruits and the established workforce had been working in a slack environment with little managerial authority for far too long. Even more than the established men, the newcomers needed educating to be efficient workers. In sum, workforce regeneration continued to be a vital prerequisite for continued improvement in coal production and, indeed, for sustained economic recovery.[4]

Resources, Housing and the Currency Reform

In the pre-currency reform-era, the main difficulty in rebuilding the workforce had lain in procuring and deploying resources effectively. Had the currency reform and the restoration of a market economy now banished those problems for ever? There is no doubt that the market did eradicate many of the ills of the controlled economy. In an age of hard currency, the miners' wage regained its value as an incentive and, moreover, one that was far easier to link to output than the paper schemes of the earlier era. Because there were now no real scarcities in food-stuffs and household goods, it was soon possible to dispense with the Points Scheme and Import Kaufmarken – IK Marken – altogether. With respect to pit supplies and building materials, too, the authorities could soon report that there were no longer serious shortages.[5]

The mines' new problem, however, was that because of the artificially low coal price they were running out of that most valuable of commodities: the Deutschmark. They were liquid enough to cover the wage bill, but lacked the finance to make any serious investment. In the second half of 1948, the industry's cash crisis became so severe that anxious managing directors were forced to put even their most precious projects on ice. This affected manpower policy in a number of ways, but

4. WWA S22 (OMGUS) BICO ERP SEC 11/95–2/3–4, DKBL paper 'Plan A', Essen, 20.2.1948.
5. PA 2, 271, WAM to Dr Hartmann, 15.11.1948, annex; OBADA I8010/1238/49, OBAD Report for 1st Q. 1949.

nowhere was its effect felt more severely than in the sphere of miners' housing.[6]

In summer 1948, no one in the Ruhr doubted the importance of a rapid construction programme for the miners. According to an official survey, almost half the workforce were living in inadequate accommodation. At the end of the year, there were around 10,000 new miners whose wives and children were still in the former German territories in the east, in the Soviet Zone (SBZ) or in the Western Zones outside NRW; many more had families in other parts of NRW itself. In all, as a DKBL survey at the end of 1949 discovered, 61,000 miners were separated from their families. It was in recognition of the continuing pressing need for housing that the SVR's new version of its housing programme, produced in March 1948, confirmed the housing targets of the original. New in the plan was above all a more realistic timescale; completion was projected for October 1952 rather than the end of 1948 as before.[7]

In a number of respects the currency reform made house-building more urgent than ever. Miners separated from their families were hard hit by the reform which considerably increased the real cost of paying two rents. For a considerable proportion of newcomers the costs were too high and the DKBL survey noted above found that some 20 per cent of those leaving the mines did so because of accommodation problems. Even this figure understates the importance of housing, however. Many people for whom accommodation was a problem did not actually cite it as their reason for leaving because the housing situation was bad in all urban areas and the leavers could not expect to find better housing elsewhere – at least, not in areas where there was also employment. The point was that if good housing had been on offer, it was a reasonable assumption that many more than 20 per cent of the leavers would have stayed.[8]

6. Werner Abelshauser, *Der Ruhrkohlenbergbau seit 1945. Wiederaufbau, Krise, Anpassung*, Munich, 1984, p. 34.; WWA S22 (OMGUS) BICO BISEC 11/104–2/3, UK/USCCG, review of hard coal production, 10.6.1948.

7. HStAD NW9, 57, WAM, internal memo from Referat Bergarbeiterunter-kunft to Abteilung Wohnraumbewirtschaftung, 5.10.1948; NW9, 56, WAM to NRW Labour Ministry, 28.12.1948 and subsequent documents; NW9, 112, WAM I A3, Memo for Dr Fuchs, 28.2.1950; NW73, 47, Director, SVR, draft, 'Bergar-beiterwohnungsbauprogramm Ruhr 47/52' [the initial designation of the new programme], 30.3.1948.

8. HStAD NW9, 56, WAM, internal memo from Referat Bergarbeiterunter-

For refugee miners with families still in the SBZ, the creation of two different currencies in West and East Germany and the increasing problems in conducting financial transactions between the two made it almost impossible to give family and relatives financial support. It was no surprise therefore that August and September 1948 saw an influx of families from the SBZ. Often there was no suitable housing and squalid overcrowding resulted.[9]

There were thus plenty of good reasons for accelerating the pace of house construction. The problem, however, was finding the cash to build with. According to the DKBL, the investment required up to the end of 1951 would be DM523 million, a substantial sum equivalent to almost one-third of the parallel figure the industry wanted to spend on plant modernisation. Moreover, that DM523 million covered only the proportion of housing costs for which the DKBL had planning responsibility. The overall cost of the housing programme was estimated by the SVR at DM1.5 billion.[10] Yet so limited were the sums of money being made available that, despite the ready availability of building materials and labour, progress on the housing programme actually *slowed down* after the currency reform! As early as August 1948 the Coal Control Group noted that building had fallen 'very much in arrears' due to financial difficulties. Since the reform, lack of funds had led to the workforce employed on miners' housing being cut by about 30 per cent. In January 1949, despite good weather, completed repairs amounted to less than one-third of the SVR's target monthly figure and were far below the pre-currency-reform levels.[11]

The problem was not just that the collieries themselves had little cash to spare. A central characteristic of the post-war

kunft to Gruppe Wohnraumbewirtschaftung, 11.6.1949; WWA S22 (OMGUS), BICO BISEC 11/104–1/39, Combined Coal Control Group (CCCG) report to BICO for April 1949; BBA 8,384, Concordia to DKBL, Abt. Arbeitseinsatz, 25.2.1949.

9. HStAD NW73, 457, IVB to WAM, 18.8.1948.

10. WWA S22 (OMGUS) BICO ERP SEC 11/95–2/3–4, DKBL paper 'Plan A', Essen, 20.2.1948; calculation from DKBL, *Voraussetzungen*, p. 4; Horst Ewald Kirsch, 'Die Investition im Steinkohlenbergbau des Ruhrgebietes und deren Finanzierung', unpublished dissertation, Cologne University, 1956, pp. 46–8; WWA S22 (OMGUS), BICO BISEC 11/107–2/1–4, Joint Chairmen UK/USCCG to Joint Chairmen BICO, 9.12.1948, appendix F.

11. WWA S22 (OMGUS), Manpower, 7/51–1/3, UK/USCCG report to BICO, January 1949.

housing market was that rents were too low to make construction profitable. Rents had, for price and social policy reasons, been frozen since the 1930s. Yet because of costly raw materials and low labour productivity, construction costs were far higher than in the pre-war period. In June 1948, they were in fact double what they had been ten years earlier. So at existing rents, it was not profitable to build new houses and often not financially possible even to repair existing ones. Thus much of the finance required could not be raised on the capital market at commercial rates. Some sort of subsidy was necessary, be it from owners, employers, the state or some other source. Indeed, capital was so short that even the profitable part of house construction was hard to finance on the market. Public money had repeatedly to be substituted for missing market loans.[12] This discrepancy between rents and building costs was a general problem in post-war Germany, but applied particularly to mining, where rents were even lower than average. Low rents had long been a way in which mining employers had tried to hold on to their workforces. Between 1930 and 1949, the state had given house-owners several opportunities to make legal rent increases, yet the mines had availed themselves of none of them.[13]

In the pre-1948 period, housing subsidies had come from the Land and the mines. But now, neither felt in a position to continue. Until December, it is true, the UK/USCCG encouraged the mines to make some capital expenditure on the assumption that Marshall Plan funds would be made available through the Reconstruction Loan Corporation. But by the end of the year, the failure of the Corporation to take shape and the severity of the financial crisis forced the Control Group to take the extreme step of ordering the mines to desist from all further capital expenditure and even to discontinue inessential work in progress. In March 1949 the Group reported that 'every week the

12. Otto Lübcke, *Die Subventionierung des Wohnungsbaues insbes. seit 1945*, Münster, 1951, p. 54; *Ministerial-Blatt Nordrhein-Westfalens*, Ausgabe A, 6.4.1948, 1, 12, p. 121; HStAD NW53, 465, Land Manpower Dept., Housing and Building Branch to Chairman of Housing Reconstruction Committee, 5.5.1948; NW 10, 15, WAM, circular to Regierungspräsidenten, 18.6.1951.
13. BAK B102, 3304, Fehlemann to Hensel, 25.11.1949, annex; Julius Brecht, 'Die gemeinnützigen Wohnungsunternehmen in einer marktwirtschaftlichen Wohnversorgung', in *Deutsche Siedlungs- und Wohnpolitik. Gegenwarts problematik und Zukunftsaspekte*, Cologne, 1956, pp. 151–75 at 164.

financial situation gets tighter and tighter'.[14] Even the GBAG, the wealthiest of all the mining companies, was forced to bring its housing operation to a virtual standstill.[15]

For its part, the NRW government argued that the burden of financing miners' housing was such that the other Länder or the bizonal government should help. Unless there was outside support, the SVR's miners' housing plan 'Ruhr 48/52', with its total cost of around DM1.5 billion,[16] would mean that, even after allowing for modest contributions from the mining industry and for the share which could be raised on the market, *all* of NRW's DM200 million annual housing budget would go to the miners, leaving nothing for other sections of the population. The NRW government did not believe it could justify this. For the population of NRW as a whole, less than a third of war-damaged houses had been repaired; for the miners, on the other hand, three-quarters of damaged housing had now been put right.[17] Non-miners in NRW could reasonably expect a greater share of housing grants in the future: 'Innerhalb des Ruhrgebiets sind schon z.T. dieserhalb allerstärkste soziale Spannungen aufgetreten, die sich verstärken und bis zur Unerträglichkeit steigern müssen, wenn immer weitere Millionen nur einer Arbeiterklasse zukommen, während die übrigen notleidenden Bevölkerungskreise mehr oder minder leer ausgehen'.[18] It was to avoid this that, in the first months after the currency reform, NRW restricted itself to keeping existing projects going and would not fund new construction work for miners. Even then, mining still absorbed three times as much Land funds as the miners' share of the population would have entitled it to.[19]

14. WWA S22 (OMGUS), BICO BISEC 11/104–2/2, minutes of 3rd Meeting of the CCCG, 23.3.1949, appendix: report by W. E. Fourqurean.

15. WWA S22 (OMGUS), BICO BISEC 11/104–2/2, UK/USCCG report to BICO for December 1948; PA 2, 550, BIB/P(49)43, Bipartite Board, report on financial problems in the coal mining industry, 16.3.1949; BBA 55, 12200, no. 10, Bergausschuß-Sitzung, 23.9.1949.

16. WWA S22 (OMGUS), BICO BISEC 11/107–2/1–4, Joint Chairmen UK/USCCG to Joint Chairmen BICO, 9.12.1948, appendix F.

17. HStAD NW9, 112, WAM, memo, 25.1.1949.

18. HStAD NW73,259, 'Darlegungen des Verbandsdirektors Dr Ing. P. Rappaport, Essen, gelegentlich der Besichtigungsreise des bizonalen Bauwirtschaftsausschusses am 7.1.1949 im Ruhrgebiet', January 1949.

19. WWA S22 (OMGUS), Co Hist BR 3/404–1/7, minutes of the 13th meeting of the UK/USCCG, 21.5.1948; HStAD NW9, 112, WAM, memo, 25.1.1949, annex 1.

In the period following the First World War, when a similar problem had applied, a special coal tax had been introduced, the proceeds of which had gone to finance miners' housing. Both NRW and the DKBL advocated the reintroduction of such a coal tax and in July 1948, the NRW cabinet voted to apply to the bizonal authorities for the appropriate legislation. At the same time, NRW requested funds from the bizonal budget to provide interim cover until the coal levy was in operation. Concurrently with these efforts, BICO called upon the VfW to draw up proposals on how the mines' operating costs and investment needs, including miners' housing, might best be met.[20]

Though they accepted the importance of housing in mining's regenerative strategy, the bizonal authorities were loath to accede or respond to any of these initiatives. The key change from the post-1918 reconstruction era was that in that period little priority had been given to stemming inflation, indeed, inflation had consciously been preferred to the politically potentially explosive consequences of a post-war deflation. However, the experience of economic chaos in 1922–3 changed all that for succeeding generations and for the post-1945 policy-makers in particular. Thus, hostile to increases in the price of coal, the VfW would not entertain the idea of a sales tax. There was also hostility to other types of capital transfer towards heavy industry. Erhard was unwilling to tax growth in the consumer goods industries by charging a levy on these areas to help the mines.[21]

On the housing question itself, the authorities could take refuge behind the fact that housing was formally a responsibility of the individual Länder and this was indeed the argument used by the VfW when in September 1948 it turned down NRW's claim for bizonal funds. As later developments were to show, however, this argument was somewhat disingenuous, since the formal responsibility of the Länder did not preclude federal support. It was a mark of how bad relations between NRW and bizonal authorities were on the issue that in June 1948 two separate conferences on mining's problems and needs were

20. BAK Z13, 198, DKBL to VfW, 15.7.1948; HStAD NW53, 643, memo, 12.7.1948; Ministerpräsident NRW, 'Antrag . . . auf Bereitstellung von Mitteln zur Durchführung des Bergarbeiterwohnungsbauprogramms', 13.7.1948; Ministerpräsident NRW to VfF, 24.7.1948; BAK Z4, 59, BICO M(48)/52, 23.7.1948.
21. BAK Z13, 198, VfW to Direktorialkanzlei, 14.3.1949.

held in the Ruhr simultaneously, one chaired by NRW and one under the auspices of the VfW, the representatives of each organisation refusing to attend the other's conference.[22]

Because of the Allies' interest, and because not even Erhard could allow the mining industry to be totally starved of funds, the Economic Council did resolve in June 1948 (following the VfW's conference) to set up a special committee to investigate the financial problems of the industry with particular reference amongst other things to miners' housing. Yet it was noteworthy that the first meeting of the committee did not take place until November. The lack of interest of the VfW and Verwaltung für Finanzen (VfF) in the committee's proceedings was striking. In March 1949, for example, the committee invited Erhard and a senior representative of the VfF to take part in the discussions. Erhard notified the committee that he was elsewhere on business but that a *Ministerialdirektor* would appear in his place. In the event, the *Ministerialdirektor* did not appear either, but sent a subordinate. The behaviour of the VfF was even more offensive; they sent along a representative who had been in the department for only a few weeks and was unable to answer even those questions that had been agreed in advance. Under these circumstances it was not surprising that the committee's progress was slow, and the minutes show no evidence of the committee being under pressure from the German side to produce speedy conclusions.[23]

For their part, the Allies continued to apply pressure to the German authorities for a speedy solution to the mining industry's capital requirements. In August 1948, the Coal Control Group proposed to BICO a number of measures including price increases, payment of the full export value of coal to the mines and further subsidies from the bizonal budget. It also suggested using counterpart funds from the Marshall Plan to meet the

22. HStAD NW53, 643, VfF to Minister President NRW, 7.9.1948; HStAD NW53,736, *passim*; PA 2,549, President of the Economic Council to Minister President Karl Arnold, 2.6.1948.
23. PA 2, 549, WAM to the President of the Economic Council, 11.6.1948; 2, 223, minutes of the 1st meeting of the Sonderausschuß zur Behandlung von Fragen der Kohleförderung, 3.11.1948; 2, 271, Dr Georg Berger to the President of the Economic Council, 7.3.1949; BAK Z4, 58, Wirtschaftsrat des Vereinigten Wirtschaftsgebietes, Drucksache 19149 no. 1606: 'Zusammenfassender Bericht des Sonderausschusses zur Behandlung von Fragen der Kohlenförderung', 5.8.1949.

capital needs of the mines, including housing, and also to fund non-mine owned housing. Some of these measures could be implemented by the Allies directly or were carried out at their behest (on the question of exports, there was disagreement amongst the Allies themselves as to whether the mines should receive the full export price so that as an immediate measure only a limited export rebate was offered).[24] But the provision of a larger bizonal subsidy lay in German hands and continued to be opposed by the bizonal authorities, who tended to use delaying tactics, rather than outright opposition, as a means of defeating Allied intentions. By 1949, the Allies had become extremely impatient.[25] In March, a major paper from the Bipartite Board on the financial problems of the mining industry, the so-called Schumacher Report, began with the following statement:

> Military Government has had bold plans for the rehabilitation of the coal mining industry. The German mining technicians have proved enthusiastic co-planners and implementers. Bold physical planning and execution, however, has not been matched by equally bold financial measures. A Reconstruction Loan Corporation (with limited resources) was planned immediately prior to currency reform. After eight months, however, the corporation is not yet in complete operation. Nor have the Germans come forward with other effective means of providing much needed long-term credit resources.[26]

The problems were, as the report noted, not restricted to mining:

> The larger context of the problem is that what is happening in the coal mining industry is not peculiar to that industry. Military Government wants, and the ERP plans require, the stepping up of production. Yet since currency reform, only meagre long-term capital funds have been available even for the most essential capital development projects.[27]

Considerable investment had been made, but only by unortho-

---

24. WWA S22 (OMGUS), CO Hist Br 3/404–1/6, UK/USCCG paper, 'Financial Problems in the Coal Industry', 27.8.1948; UK/USCCG to Joint Chairmen BICO, 9.12.1948, appendix F; PA 2, 223, minutes of the 4th meeting of the Sonderausschuß zur Behandlung von Fragen der Kohleförderung, 3.3.1949; Volker Bahl, *Staatliche Politik am Beispiel der Kohle*, Frankfurt, 1977, p. 73.
25. See Mark Roseman, 'New Miners in the Ruhr: Rebuilding the Workforce in the Ruhr Mines, 1945–1958', PhD dissertation, Warwick University, 1987.
26. PA 2, 550, BIB/P(49)43.
27. Ibid.

dox short-term means and this could not continue. At the same time a BICO paper specifically on miners' housing urged that 'this is too important a problem to become snarled by some of the old conflicts, such as whether this is a German problem or an Allied problem; whether this is a problem for the British Zone Länder as opposed to the Southern Länder; whether this is a problem solely of welfare or morale versus a more business-like approach'.[28] The paper went on to argue that the poor progress of 1948 made it necessary now to build twice as fast as over the previous two years. The Allies believed that housing was absolutely essential if the workforce was to be expanded and productivity improved: 'Without adequate housing facilities, it is doubtful whether the present labor force and the required rate of recruitment can be maintained. The problem of housing is more than one of morals [sic: presumably "morale" was meant]; it is one of the most serious bottlenecks to increasing production and reaching target goals.'[29] On the basis of the Schumacher Report, BICO suggested that DM400 million be provided for Ruhr miners' housing, of which DM150 million should come from bizonal funds and DM160 million from the Reconstruction Corporation, alongside DM50 million from NRW and DM40 million from private sources. It had thus largely accepted the arguments of NRW.[30]

However, the German authorities were no better disposed than before. Unlike the Schumacher Report, which had advocated new taxes to finance the payment to the mines, they argued that such taxes appeared 'weder notwendig noch wirtschaftlich tragbar'.[31] They reiterated their suspicion that an increase in the coal price would trigger inflation. They suggested that DM300 million was the maximum that could reasonably be spent on miners' housing in all regions, given that no more than DM1.5 billion was being spent on housing as a whole. Once again, it was argued that housing was a Land matter. No doubt under the influence of the southern Länder, the authorities in Frankfurt suggested that the bulk of the money should come from NRW. The VfW proposed that NRW

28. WWA S22 (OMGUS), BICO BECG PA Br 11/122–3/3, BICO paper, 'Miners' Housing Programme', March 1949.
29. PA2, 550, BIB/P(49)43.
30. Ibid.
31. PA 2, 550, Hermann Pünder to BICO J. Sec, 30.5.1949.

should put up DM175 million, most of it in the financial year 1949–50; DM30 million should come from the other Länder while the remainder of the DM300 million could, it argued, be raised by normal financing methods. In order to avoid delays, however, it suggested that DM50 million of counterpart funds might be used as a bridging loan until the capital market had properly revived. Predictably enough, NRW declared itself unable to come up with DM175 million, a figure which, after all, corresponded to over 85 per cent of its housing budget, and repeated its demand for a coal tax.[32]

Though the 'memorandum war'[33] continued, the DM30 million proposed by the VfW was all the subsidy miners' housing was to receive from federal funds in 1949. In 1950, Bonn was even less forthcoming. Though the Cabinet finally agreed in December 1950 to make a repeat payment of DM30 million, the Finance Minister blocked the allocation and the funds were, in fact, never transferred. Since NRW had made further support contingent on a federal contribution, the Finance Ministry's decision dealt a heavy blow to housing activity in the Ruhr. By the end of 1950, NRW had put up only DM28 million or slightly more than one-third of its envisaged total commitment. It was clear that at this rate it would take years to satisfy the housing demands of even those miners who were already in the industry, let alone to provide decent housing for future recruits.[34]

Korea, Coercion, Construction

Though the industry had been unsuccessful in obtaining greater federal support, the discussions in Bonn during 1950 revealed that a different political climate was emerging. It was noteworthy, for example, that, in contrast with previous years, the Economics Ministry (BWiM) had consistently endorsed the industry's demands and had pleaded the industry's case in

32. WWA S22 (OMGUS), BICO BECG PABr 11/134–3/15, undated copy of memo from VfW, Abt. I A, 'Investition und Finanzierungsplan des Ver. Wirtschaftsgebiets für das Haushaltsjahr 1949/1950'; 'Zusammenfassender Bericht des Sonderausschusses', op.cit; PA 2, 550, Hermann Pünder to BICO J. Sec, 30.5.1949; BAK Z4, 58, 'Kurzprotokoll der 8. Sitzung des Sonderausschusses', 22.6.1949; Z13, 198, WAM to Sonderausschuß, 8.6.1949.

33. Abelshauser, *Wirtschaftsgeschichte*, p. 66.

34. For more detail on this period, see Roseman, 'New Miners', pp. 230–3.

discussions with other departments. In December 1950, the NRW Cabinet made a renewed application for a coal levy; though no more successful than its predecessors, this was the first to enjoy support from the Economics Minister. It was hostility from the BFM and the Länder representatives in the Bundesrat that had blocked it. A sign of this new mood was that when, in the Cabinet discussions about a possible coal levy, Finance Ministry representatives argued that it was up to the Länder to give aid to miners' housing, the Minister for Economics was joined by the Labour Ministry, the Minister for the Marshall Plan and the Minister for Justice in refuting this. In 1949, by contrast, none of the bizonal departmental directors had opposed the notion of Länder responsibility. As another sign of his support for miners' housing, Erhard wrote to the President of the Hauptamt für Sofort-Hilfe (HAfSH), the body responsible for allotting aid to refugees, asking if it was possible to make a contribution to the housing programme.[35]

In part, this new mood was the result of a growing awareness within the BWiM that the contradiction between the *laissez-faire* approach to capital movements, on the one hand, and the continued price controls in capital goods, on the other, meant that heavy industry and particularly mining was being starved of capital, thus undermining the entire economy's prospects for growth. Outside the Economics Ministry, too, Cabinet colleagues and senior Christian Democrats showed growing impatience with Erhard's failure to ensure sufficient capital flows to the capital goods sector.[36] However, much more important than such shifts in domestic opinion was, as Abelshauser and Adamsen have documented, the new pressure from the US. Throughout 1948 and 1949, the Allies had (as the example of miners' housing has shown) grown increasingly concerned about the failure to direct investment towards heavy industry, about the lack of response to the Federal Republic's growing unemployment and, in 1950–1 particularly, about West Germany's burgeoning trade deficit.[37]

35. BAK B134, 1365, BWoM, memos, 25.8.1950, 6.12.1950 and 11.12.1950; minutes of 115th Cabinet meeting on 5/6 December, Point 13, in Booms (ed.), *Kabinettsprotokolle der Bundesregierung 1950*, p. 871; HStAD NW10,83, copy of letter from Erhard to President, HAfSH, 27.2.1951.

36. Abelshauser, *Wirtschaftsgeschichte*, pp. 66ff.

37. Ibid., pp. 65ff, 76ff; Werner Abelshauser, 'Ansätze "korporativer Mark-

Nevertheless, until 1950, Erhard was largely able to keep his freedom of action. It was the outbreak of the Korean war in June 1950 that transformed the situation. Suddenly, America ceased to be the slightly overbearing uncle, concerned to see the investment in his nephew's education well spent, and became the stern father, set on steering an errant son in the right direction. In the view of the United States, Germany had to accept its responsibilities in the protection of the free world against communism; its role was to supply raw materials and capital goods to those Western economies now hard at work producing armaments and it was therefore vital for the American war effort that Germany use its resources effectively. Though American pressure reached its high point only in 1951, the last months of 1950 saw the West German government increasingly resigned to the necessity of a more active management of the economy.[38]

As well as heralding a new urgency in American representations, the Korean war also initiated a new phase of growth in the West German economy and this too exposed the weaknesses in coal-mining. In December 1950 the government was forced to initiate temporary power cuts in order to husband scarce coal supplies. The coal shortages increased public awareness of the mining industry's investment needs. 'Erst die seit Mai 1950 einsetzende Verknappung der Kohle,' noted Fehlemann, the DKBL's housing expert, 'hat in der breiten Öffentlichkeit den Bergarbeiter-Wohnungsbau als das Problem Nr.1. des Kohlenbergbaus und somit der deutschen Wirtschaft in den Vordergrund gerückt.'[39] Quite apart from the general goal of offering good-quality housing, the accelerated pace of recruitment meant that the mines began to run out of any dwelling space at all.[40]

---

twirtschaft" in der Korea-Krise der frühen fünfziger Jahre. Ein Briefwechsel zwischen dem Hohen Kommissar John McCloy und Bundeskanzler Konrad Adenauer', *VfZ*, vol. 30, no. 4, 1982, pp. 715–56 at 734–5.

38. Abelshauser, *Wirtschaftsgeschichte*, pp. 76ff; 'Ansätze "korporativer Marktwirtschaft"', pp. 722ff.

39. Ges.Verb File 'Wohnungswesen 4 Bergarbeiterwohnungsbauprogramm 41 Programme 1951–1953', paper from Fehlemann, 'Das Gesetz zur Förderung des Bergarbeiterwohnungsbaus im Kohlenbergbau und sein Einfluß auf den Bergarbeiterwohnungsbau', 12.11.1951.

40. See HStAD NW62,386, LAA NRW, report for December 1951 and NW45,207, report for October 1951.

In housing policy, the first direct response to the new situation came not from Bonn but from the American Economic Co-operation Administration (ECA, later MSA), the body which supervised the allocation of counterpart funds. Ever since Korea, noted the Federal Housing Ministry (BWoM), the Americans had shown 'stärkstes Interesse für den Bergarbeiterwohnungsbau'.[41] Hitherto, the limited ERP funds given to miners' housing had been offered at market rates, as a substitute for other types of market loan, and had therefore not been a genuine subsidy. Now, however, the ECA proposed more positive measures. The immediate stimulus here was a press release issued by the DKBL in October 1950 which conveyed the danger of the present slow pace of building. A few days later, the ECA organised a fact-finding mission to the Ruhr and in November, the DKBL was requested to outline a housing programme based on DM35 million, later revised to DM45 million, of ERP funds. Though the negotiations as to the form of the building programme were to prove very complex and involved, work on the building projects began in late spring 1951.[42]

On the German side, the pressure grew for a greater national commitment to miners' housing. In January, all the major parties in the NRW parliament united to pass a motion calling upon the Land government to undertake all possible steps to promote the building of miners' housing and to persuade the federal government of the necessity of further support. In February, the WAM wrote to the federal Housing Ministry expressing its dismay at Bonn's failure to endorse a miners' housing levy. The mining employers kept up the pressure too, with the federal Coal Commissar, Martin Sogemeier, declaring in June 1951 that an accelerated housing programme was the only way to prevent a dangerous drain of labour away from the mines.[43]

In addition, 1951 saw two major international commitments to improve the productivity of German coal. In August the Council of Ministers in the OEEC agreed on a broad programme of

41. BAK B134, 1365, BWoM, memo, 31.1.1951.
42. BAK B134, 1365, BWoM, memos, 28.9.1950, 13.10.1950, 7.11.1950, 31.1.1951; B134, 1367, SVR to WAM, 16.10.1950 (copy); HStAD NW10, 90, DKBL to WAM, 12.6.1951 and annex.
43. BAK B102, 4391, Hensel to Kattenstroth, 5.6.1951; B134, 1365, BWoM, memo, 25.10.1950; HStAD NW10, 83, Landtag NRW, '2. Wahlperiode, Bd. 1, Drucksache Nr. 142'; WAM to BWoM, 23.2.1951.

productivity increases in Western Europe with special emphasis on German coal production. At the same time, the ECA in Washington outlined a similar productivity programme – again with special emphasis on coal. The ECA reckoned that there was an annual shortfall of 30–50 million tons of coal in Europe. As a result of these initiatives, a special committee was set up in Germany, headed by the Minister for the Marshall Plan, to look into ways of increasing productivity in coal-mining.[44]

The combination of American pressure, regional and industrial lobbying and the coal shortages was irresistible. By summer 1951, both the majority of Bundestag delegates and the Cabinet acknowledged the need for major investment measures in the mining industry, including miners' housing. In the case of housing, it was clear that neither the mining industry nor the Länder in which the mines were situated were in a position to provide adequate funding. So, in October 1951 a Miners' Housing Law was passed in the Bundestag which finally, three-and-a-half years after the currency reform, introduced a coal levy to pay for housing.[45]

The law raised for a period of three years (extendable if necessary) a levy of DM1 on every ton of coal sold. The revenue was to flow into a central fund (*Bundestreuhandvermögen*), whence it would be allotted to the mining regions by the federal Housing Minister and then to individual building projects by special regional committees created by the law. The money was to be given in the form of low-interest loans, as a supplement to loans raised on the capital market, employer contributions and regional subsidies. In exceptional cases, non-repayable subsidies could be made. Though some of the other clauses of the Act were not to the liking of the NRW Reconstruction Ministry, its financial terms fulfilled all NRW's wishes. Henceforth, NRW was able to restrict mining's share of its housing budget to a level equivalent to the miners' share of the region's population.

44. IGBEA T4, Bundesminster für den Marshallplan to IGB and DGB, 2.10.1951.
45. BAK B102, 4391, 164. Sitzung des Deutschen Bundestags, 26.9.1951; B134, 1372, extract from the 'Kurzprotokoll über die 175. Kabinettsitzung der Bundesregierung am 26.9.1951'; Gesetz zur Förderung des Bergarbeiterwohnungsbaues im Kohlenbergbau, *BGBl*, no. 50, 1951, pp. 865ff.

Miners' Housing, Investment and Economic Recovery

Why had the mines had to wait so long for funding? Was it simply short-sightedness on the part of the government? The federal government wanted coal to grow with the rest of the economy without central help, yet at the same time it maintained tight price controls. Out of fear of inflation it shrank back from introducing a truly free market, without seeming to recognise that this in turn necessitated a break with free market principles of capital allocation.

Erhard's position was not quite as irrational as it appears. First, there was definitely a case for some sort of controls on the coal price. Erhard was a bitter critic of the 'Verkrüstung der Kohlenwirtschaft', pointing out that because of the semi-cartelised arrangements for selling coal, there was no genuine competition in the industry. Thus, the price which the industry could have extorted from its customers would have been a monopoly price, overstating coal's value to the economy. This does not, however, justify the degree to which the mines were being starved of revenue. It is very possible that Erhard was counting on more Marshall Plan aid being forthcoming than was actually the case. Moreover, Erhard's policy of favouring consumer industries at the cost of heavy industry was not simply a strategy for growth. It is a little-remembered fact that Erhard was quite prepared to accept some retardation of the growth process as the result of favouring the consumer industries if by doing so he could strengthen popular confidence in the economy. It was Erhard, after all, who announced before the currency reform that: 'Ich persönlich würde keinen Zweifel darüber lassen, daß man das bisherige Maß an Opferfähigkeit dem Volke einfach nicht mehr zumuten kann. Ich würde lieber ganz bewußt eine gewisse Rückständigkeit, einen längeren Nachholzeitraum innerhalb der Produktionssphäre hinnehmen, wenn wir durch eine Steigerung und Ausreicherung des Konsums eine Besserung der sozialen Lage erreichen könnten.'[46] Finally, it is worth bearing in mind that Erhard was far from being alone in his reluctance to raise the price of coal. In 1951, when Erhard responded to the Korean crisis by proposing a price increase,

46. Heiner R. Adamsen, *Investitionshilfe für die Ruhr. Wiederaufbau, Verbände und soziale Marktwirtschaft 1948–1952*, Wuppertal, 1981, p. 41.

there were many senior voices raised in protest, not least that of
the eminent banker, Herman J. Abs.[47]

It would go beyond the limits of this study to determine
whether, if there had been no Korea boom, Erhard would have
been able to continue neglecting heavy industry and mining in
particular. It seems unlikely. What is certain is that for miners'
housing, as will be seen, the change in policy came rather late.
Mining had partly wasted the best opportunity of the post-war
years to win a stable workforce.

Exactly what impact did the lack of central funding have on
the housing programme? The best figures available are the
monthly, later quarterly, reports from the SVR (most of which
have been preserved) on the progress of repairs, extensions,
reconstruction and new building throughout the period
1948–51.[48] The problem with these figures, however, is that
they were substantially revised halfway through 1949 as a result
of checks in the municipal building departments (which revealed that a lot of completed building had never been properly
reported).[49] As is evident from table 4.2, the revisions make it
seem as if there was a massive jump in the housing completion
rate for the second half of 1949.[50] Clearly this adjustment intro-
duces a measure of uncertainty into the statistics.[51] However, if,
as seems a reasonable assumption, the previously unreported
housing was evenly spread throughout the period February
1948–July 1949, then table 4.3 provides a fair guide to the
changing pace of house-building. The most important fact revealed by the table is that though, as we know, the miners'
housing programme had to wait until the end of 1951 for a major
central subsidy, it began recovering earlier from the depths to

47. I would like to express my gratitude to Professor Werner Abelshauser for
many of the insights offered here. See also Abelshauser, 'Kohle und Marktwirtschaft', p. 496 and minutes of Cabinet meeting on 6.3.1951 in *Kabinettsprotokolle
der Bundesregierung 1951*, p. 207.

48. Unless otherwise stated, all SVR monthly/quarterly reports can be found
in HStAD NW73, 120.

49. SVR reports for July 1949 and 4th quarter 1949. There was also political
pressure on the SVR to make revisions. See NW73,73, WAM IA304 (13) to
Director of SVR, 28.9.1949.

50. Cf. HStAD NW73,73, WAM IA304, table 'Bergarbeiterwohnungsbau. Soll
ab 1.1.50–30.9.52', 22.2.1950.

51. A reassuring point, however, is that the UVR evidently believed the
revised figures to be accurate. See the figures in UVR (ed.), *Jahresbericht
1953/1954*, Essen, 1954, pp. 32–3 which match those of the SVR very closely.

Table 4.2 Repairs and new construction, 1948–51, according to SVR reports

| Until end of | D.u.s completed from 1.2.1948 (cumulative) | | |
	Repairs	New and Reconstruction[a]	New/recon./subdiv. attic conversions
July 1948	12,544	775[b]	943
December 1948	18,280	1,569	1,895
June 1949	23,471	3,191	3,663
December 1949	47,247	11,184	15,421
June 1950	53,418	15,806	21,819
December 1950	58,991	n.a.	31,138
June 1951	63,876	29,722	37,157
December 1951	65,995	38,108	46,408

(a) Includes a small number of Nissen huts and prefabs.
(b) Mostly Nissen huts and prefabs.

Source: SVR monthly and quarterly reports in HStAD NW73, 120.

Table 4.3 Housing construction, 1948–51 (adjusted figures)

In half year ending	Repairs (d.u.s/month)	New/recon.[a] (d.u.s per month)
July 1948	2,990	383
December 1948[b]	2,040	393
June 1949	1,760	524
December 1949	1,440	613
June 1950	1,030	770
December 1950	930	n.a.
June 1951	810	1,160[c]
December 1951	350	1,398

(a) Excluding subdivisions and attic conversions.
(b) Five-month period.
(c) Twelve-month period.

Source: Up to June 1949: adjusted SVR cumulative figures; Dec. 1949: WAM figures in HStAD NW73, 73, WAM IA–304, table 'Bergarbeiterwohnungsbau. Soll ab 1.1.50–30.9.52', 22.2.1950; remaining figures calculated directly from SVR reports in HStAD NW73, 120.

Table 4.4 Expenditure on Ruhr miners' housing, 1948–53 (UVR figures)

Year	Expenditure (DM)	
	Overall miners' housing	Mine-owned housing alone
1948[a]	71,500,000	n.a.
1949	160,000,000	74,000,000
1950	160,000,000	61,000,000
1951	333,000,000	87,000,000
After intro. of Miners' Housing Levy:		
1952	500,000,000	79,000,000
1953	445,000,000	42,000,000

(a) Currency reform to end of year.

Source: UVR (ed.), *Jahresbericht 1953–4*, pp. 30, 41.

which it plummeted in the aftermath of the currency reform. True, the number of repairs continued to fall, but this reflected the dwindling number of properties available for restoration rather than a shortage of resources. New construction and total rebuilding ('reconstruction'), both of which involved far more resources than did repairs, increased substantially. Over the period June 1950–June 1951, for example, the monthly completion rate for new and rebuilt houses was almost three times as high as it had been at the end of 1948.

Where did the money for this building come from? Unfortunately there are no satisfactory, consistent compilations before 1952.[52] A UVR report notes total expenditure on miners' housing as shown in table 4.4, but does not give the source of the funding. With the aid of various Land and DKBL reports, however, it is possible to paint a more detailed picture. For 1948/9, we can make a comprehensive breakdown of all funding and, for the following years, of public subsidies (see figure 4.1 and table 4.5).

52. It is possible that the now available DKBL papers in the BBA, released too late to be included in this volume, contain some more consistent figures.

Figure 4.1 Sources of subsidy for miners' housing, 1948–9

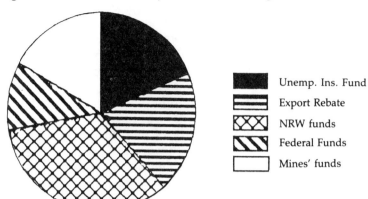

Unemp. Ins. Fund
Export Rebate
NRW funds
Federal Funds
Mines' funds

Total spending 247,476,000 DM

Source: WAM figures as table 4.5 and DKBL figures in BAK B134, 1367, table 'Bergarbeiterwohnungsbau', October 1949.

Table 4.5 Public subsidies for miners' housing in NRW, 1948–51

Year	Total expenditure on housing (UVR figures)	Land & federal grants	Unempl. insurance funds	Marshall Plan funds (ECA)
1948/9	231.5	111.4	45.0	–
1950	160.0	38.2[a]	–	23.1
1951	333.0	35.0[b]	38.0[c]	145.0[d]

(a) Figure taken from a different WAM table so as to include the funds reaching the mines via the refugee relocation plan (*Umsiedlungsprogramm*). Without the relocation funds, the figure would have been around 28 million. See HStAD NW10, 83, IIIB 3–348, 'Übersicht über die für den Bergarbeiterwohnungsbau durch NRW bereitgestellten Wohnungsbaumittel', 6.6.1951.
(b) As at 20.6.1951.
(c) Source as note (a).
(d) Source: BAK-ZwSt.H B102, 21258, BWiM III A 2, 'Zusammenstellung aller für den Kohlenbergbau seit der Währungsreform durchgeführten Kreditmaßnahmen', 19.8.1955.

Source: UVR (ed.), *Jahresbericht 1953–4*, pp. 30, 41 for figures in column 1 (Ruhr only); HStAD NW73, 136, WAM IA203, 'Übersicht über die Verteilung der Wohnungsbaumittel des Landes seit der Geldordnung' (NRW); see also notes above.

The first and most obvious point is that even before the levy was introduced, sizeable public subsidies were received. Public subsidy for house-building was an accepted part of the social market economy. Rents were controlled by law and the main brunt of housing expenditure fell on the Länder. The federal government gave assistance inasmuch as it provided funds to enable refugees build a new home or find accommodation near a place of work (*Aufbaudarlehen*). More unexpectedly, the labour insurance funds (*Arbeitslosenstockmittel*) turn out to have played an important role: in the early years after the currency reform, these funds formed one of the few sources of capital available at interest rates affordable for social housing projects.[53]

But perhaps the most striking aspect of housing expenditure is the way in which its composition changed from year to year. In 1948/9, aware that the housing programme would collapse without its support, NRW diverted a large part of its housing budget to the mines. In 1950, it reduced this contribution substantially. Nevertheless, overall spending did not fall and this was undoubtedly the result of the new income tax law introduced in April 1949. Section 7c of the new law introduced the notion of accelerated depreciation while allowing the employers to include spending on house construction as capital spending. For those mines making a profit this was, as the DKBL itself commented, 'eine außerordentliche Begünstigung' which provided a major incentive to proceed with new house-building. According to calculations made in the early 1950s by the Friedrich Krupp mines in Essen, the tax incentives meant that from the DM5,000 put up by employers for each new apartment, they had to pay effectively only DM1,500. (For the many mines which were only breaking even or running at a loss, however, section 7c was a poor substitute for the missing state subsidies.[54] Finally, in 1951 there was a change again, as the Americans' new drive for coal led to a large injection of re-

53. See for instance BBA 55, 12200, no. 10, minutes of Bergausschuß meeting on 23.9.1949.
54. HStAD NW10,83, WAM, memo, 3.4.1951; BAK B134, 1365, BWoM, memo, 19.3.1951; WWA F35, 3522, DKBL, circular no. Cj to 43 mining companies, 31.8.1949, annex; L. Falk and W. Blümich (eds), *Einkommenssteuergesetz. Kommentar*, Munich, 1982, introduction; Abelshauser, *Wirtschaftsgeschichte*, p. 74; BAK B102, 21574, 'Finanzielle Opfer der Fried. Krupp Bergwerke Essen im Wohnungsbau seit dem Währungsstichtag', 3.7.1953; B102, 4391, Kost to Erhard, 4.7.1951.

sources from the ECA, for which both NRW and the insurance funds provided additional capital. Thus, by dint of normal social housing support, a little refugee aid, tax relief and US help, mining had been enabled to make sizeable advances in its housing programme.

Housing and Workforce Rebuilding

The SVR plan 'Ruhr 48/52' had envisaged a total outlay of around DM1,400 million between the currency reform and the end of the plan in September 1952.[55] Although, for reasons explored below, the SVR plan had become increasingly notional, it does at least provide a useful yardstick with which to evaluate progress. By the end of 1951, i.e. nine months before the planned completion date, total expenditure lay at around DM720 million. This was more favourable in relation to the original plan than appears at first sight because building costs had fallen by over 10 per cent during the period 1948–51.[56]

If the SVR's building figures are taken as reasonably accurate, some 66,000 houses had been repaired and a further 46,000 rebuilt or newly built by the end of 1951. This was just under two-thirds of the 173,000 dwelling units planned to be completed by the end of summer 1952. In terms of new building and reconstruction, the plan had actually already been exceeded. Progress in repairs was less favourable than the statistics suggest because many more lightly damaged houses and far fewer heavily damaged properties had been repaired than was originally envisaged. The amount of dwelling space created through repairs was probably only about one-third of plan levels.[57] This was offset by the increasingly good progress of new building so that, all told, between one-half and two-thirds of the additional living space originally envisaged had been created.[58] This was far from being a disaster. In effect, the depreciation allowances

55. HStAD NW73, 47, Director, SVR, draft of 'Bergarbeiterwohnungsbauprogramm Ruhr 47/52', 30.3.1948.

56. Lübcke, *Die Subventionierung des Wohnungsbaues*, p. 54.

57. Author's estimate based on the original plan figures and statistics for the second quarter of 1951, showing the typical dwelling space gained through different categories of repairs. For source see HStAD NW73, 120.

58. As above and bearing in mind that a proportion of the new building was actually created through subdividing existing apartments.

of section 7c had at least partly compensated for the fact that public subsidies were lower than originally anticipated.

Nevertheless, achievements were not only well short of plan targets but even further short of the workforce's needs. The SVR plan itself proved an increasingly inadequate guide to the miners' true requirements. This was because of a discrepancy between the basis of the SVR's calculations and the way housing was actually allocated. The SVR had calculated its building targets by estimating not the number of apartments required but instead the amount of living space that needed to be rendered inhabitable.[59] It had set out a modest ratio of dwelling space to occupants as the basis for its calculations and had then worked out how much dwelling space would be needed to house the Ruhr workforce as a whole. Yet when it came to repairing houses in practice, these notional averages had little meaning. There is no record that, when houses were repaired, the existing occupants were then forced to take on lodgers or vacate rooms simply because, according to SVR norms, they were occupying too much living space. It was understandable that this was so, but it meant that the SVR plan was inadequate to meet the workforce's needs. At the end of 1949, therefore, the DKBL produced its own estimates of housing requirements and these were increasingly used as the basis of the housing programmes.[60]

We do not know how many miners were seeking accommodation at the time the SVR's plan was drawn up. But we do know that at the end of 1949 the DKBL believed there to be around 57,000 miners in the Ruhr who were separated from their families, a further 3,500 families in emergency accommodation and 10,000 more in cramped conditions.[61] In addition, extra housing was needed to compensate for the expected retirement of a fairly large number of miners (whose housing would thus be lost to the active labour force for a while), for general ageing and decay of part of the mines' housing stock and to meet the needs of married men who would be hired over the next couple of years as part of the mines' expansion programme.

59. HStAD NW73, 47, Director of SVR, draft paper, 'Bergarbeiterwohnungs-bau', 30.3.1948.
60. See DKBL (ed.), *Überblick über den Umfang, die bisherige Abwicklung und die weitere Durchführung des Bergarbeiterwohnungsbaues*, Essen, 1950.
61. Ibid.

In all, the demand at the beginning of 1950 was for 112,379 dwelling units over the next two years, relatively few of which could be supplied by repairs to partially damaged property.[62] Yet between then and the beginning of 1952, only 31,000 houses were newly constructed and a further 2,800 heavily damaged houses repaired. Again, a number of the former were rather temporary affairs, created by subdividing existing accommodation or by converting attic space. On this basis it can be estimated that the housing programme up to 1951 provided a permanent good-quality house or apartment to less than half those on the housing lists. Since the established miners tended to come first, it is not surprising that the reminiscences of former new miners suggest that only a small proportion of the newcomers had obtained decent apartments by the end of 1951.[63]

How important was the slow pace of building? Chapter 6 will look in more detail at the link between housing and workforce stability. There was no doubt that many of those who left the mines would not have done so had they been provided with decent accommodation. Workforce stability and productivity would therefore have benefited. Because of the housing shortages, the mines were unwilling to hire married men, and the single men they did take on proved to be a highly mobile population. The result was that many mines found themselves caught up in a vicious circle of recruitment and wastage from which they could not escape throughout the 1950s.[64]

In addition, there were a limited number of years after the currency reform when many people not normally inclined to occupational mobility, and certainly not inclined to making a sideways jump into the mines, were looking for an occupational and physical home and were prepared to settle somewhere unfamiliar for the sake of putting down roots.[65] These included

62. Ibid.
63. In the Hibernia mine Shamrock 3/4, for instance, 65 per cent of those who had received housing up to the end of 1951 were members of the established workforce, despite the fact that new miners made up 70 per cent of the workforce! See BBA 32, 3055, minutes of Belegschaftsausschuß meeting, 3.10.1951.
64. Institut für Sozialforschung, Frankfurt University, 'Die subjektiven und objektiven Abkehrgründe bei sieben Zechen des westdeutschen Steinkohlenbergbaues in ihrer Auswirkung auf die Sicherung des Belegschaftsstandes unter Tage', mimeo, Frankfurt, 1955, *passim* and esp. pp. 230–1.
65. For statistical proof of this, see chapter 8.

many married men who had come to the mines before 1948 for the Care Packets and were now wondering whether to stay. What made them willing to embrace a long-term career in the mines was the double legacy of the currency reform: on the one hand, economic conditions seemed at least to be normalising, so that one could think on a more long-term basis; on the other, unemployment was on the increase and it looked to many people as if they would not find employment in their chosen profession. Ullrich, the most senior official in the DKBL Manpower Department and a shrewd and realistic observer of the manpower situation, wrote in early 1949 that if good housing were not available to replace the Care Packets, the refugee new miners would quit the industry. 'Der Bergbau würde damit gerade den Teil seiner Neubergleute verlieren, bei dem sein Bestreben eine bodenständige Belegschaft zu gewinnen, die beste Aussicht auf Erfolg bietet.[66]

By the mid-1950s, when ample housing *was* finally available in the mines, many of the 'unwillingly mobile' had found their occupational home elsewhere. Those people who were coming on to the labour market in the 1950s did so in a climate of rapidly diminishing unemployment and expanding opportunities. By 1953, the mines' attempts to recruit refugees from the 'refugee Länder', for example, were running into difficulties for lack of willing candidates. Recruits tended to view mining work as a stopgap measure or as a stepping stone to something better.[67]

It is of course hard to say whether scarce capital would have been better employed in investment in miners' housing than it was elsewhere. It is, after all, possible that the productivity and other advantages accruing to the mining industry would have been outweighed by the opportunity costs to other sectors of the economy. What the previous remarks do suggest, however, is that it would have been a lot more profitable investing in a big housing programme in 1948 than it was to be in 1952. It was an expensive delay.

66. Ges.Verb. File 'SBZ Flüchtlinge Arb 130.30–132.15', Ulrich, memo, 4.3.1949 (copy).
67. See e.g. BAK B102, 21395, BWiM to Ehmke, BAM, 31.10.1952; HStAD NW10,32, WAM, memo, 15.9.52 [*sic*: it should be 1953].

Fixed Prices and Free Markets: The Coal Price, the Miners' Wage and the Labour Market in the 1950s

The capital transfers of 1951 and 1952[68] created all the investment capital the mines needed. It was true that the money was less effective than it would have been had it been made available in, say, 1948, but for all that, acute shortages of investment capital were now a thing of the past. What the gentlemen in the Economics Ministry had *not* banished for ever, however, was the discrepancy between the coal price and coal's true value. True, substantial price increases were granted during the period of the Korean crisis itself, but the coal price remained subject to government control and thus the mining industry had not been granted any greater powers to determine its own revenues than before.[69]

This position was not changed by the admission of the Federal Republic into the European Community for Coal and Steel (EGKS) in 1952. True, it was the EGKS's avowed policy to achieve gradual price normalisation and Germany's entry was preceded by a sizeable price increase for Ruhr coal. Moreover, the final say on the coal price moved from federal government to the Montan Union's High Authority, so that Bonn might have been expected to lose some of its influence. In fact, however, both the EGKS and in particular the BWiM remained committed to cheap energy and, in addition, Bonn was always closely consulted by the High Authority before any changes to the German coal price were introduced. As a result, German coal remained the cheapest in the Community.[70]

For a while, the industry was able to foot the wage bill with little difficulty. However, wastage grew progressively more serious and the industry found itself under pressure to make wage rises it was ill-placed to afford. There were pay increases in both 1953 and 1954 and in addition a steady growth in welfare

68. The pits' capital investment needs other than housing were met by the Investitionshilfegesetz (IHG), passed in 1952. See Abelshauser, *Wirtschafts- geschichte*, p. 75.

69. Indeed, in 1950 the Allies had actually lowered the export price, bringing it further than ever from its true value price. See Bahl, *Staatliche Politik*, p. 73.

70. Bahl, *Staatliche Politik*, pp. 73–4; UVR (ed.), *Jahresbericht 1955–1957*, p. 34; Abelshauser, *Der Ruhrkohlenbergbau*, p. 79.

expenditure of one sort or another. New inducements were offered to potential recruits. Charges for the first months' board and lodgings in mining hostels were now generally suspended and often waived altogether. Despite rising costs, hostel charges barely increased and became one of the biggest items in the mines' social budget.[71]

These inducements were unable to prevent the mines from falling behind the wage offers of the competition, particularly the iron and steel industry. For hard coal mining suffered from two key disadvantages. On the one hand, it enjoyed annual productivity increases of only 3 per cent, whereas its competitors saw their productivity go up in some cases by as much as 15 per cent a year. On the other hand, the share of total production value accounted for by wage costs (in German parlance, *Lohnquote*) was more than three times as high in mining as in iron and steel and indeed in most of mining's major industrial competitors on the labour market. In early 1952, average male earnings in iron and steel surpassed those in the pits and were to stay ahead for the following four years. This was by no means the only reason for the collieries' labour losses and a great many former miners actually chose to move to employment which offered lower pay. The fact remains, however, that wage offers in other sectors put the collieries under increasing pressure, to which price controls prevented them from responding.[72]

The crisis point came in 1955. The mines had been sparing in their recruitment during the previous year because demand for coal had been poor. During 1954 overall workforce size had fallen considerably (see table 4.6). Now, with demand for coal booming, the collieries were desperately trying to restore the number of face workers. Yet in the January–March period, despite a heavy frost which limited the building trade's competition on the labour market, despite thirty-seven special recruitment campaigns in three months and despite the employers' willingness to take on applicants who would previously not have got past the colliery gates, the mines obtained less than

71. EGKS (ed.), *Entwicklung der Löhne und die Lohnpolitik in den Industrien der Gemeinschaft 1945–1956*, Luxembourg, 1960, section on Germany, pp. 16ff. OBADA I8007/520/55, ABB, Annual Report 1954.
72. EGKS, *Entwicklung der Löhne*, pp. 26–7; UVR (ed.), *Jahresbericht 1955–1957*, pp. 53, 33 facing, 60 facing.

Table 4.6 Underground workforce size, intake and wastage, 1948–58[73]

Year	Workforce size (1 January)	Intake[a]	Labour loss[a]	Movement from pit to pit
1948	240,101	62,688	51,900	8,528
1949	253,531	62,189	43,503	10,970
1950	273,972	55,328	51,976	16,511
1951	278,306	61,779	56,514	22,041
1952	287,692	62,417	57,494	23,577
1953	299,099	59,320	59,181	24,297
1954	307,145	34,440	50,120	18,217
1955	300,308	43,834	53,224	23,478
1956	300,166	53,233	54,704	28,834
1957	308,162	51,602	57,886	25,591
1958	312,185	28,316	52,073	19,494

(a) Excluding movement from pit to pit.

Source: Ges.Verb., StdKW., table: 'Belegschaftswechsel – Arbeiter untertage. Ruhr'.

half the men they required.[74] Seizing the initiative, the IGB demanded a large wage increase to reduce wastage and improve recruitment. To underline the point, it balloted its members for strike action. The employers' response was that they simply could not afford the increase. On top of mining's general inability to keep up with iron and steel, the minor recession of 1953–4 meant that in 1955 the mines were looking to improve their margins. In other words, the IGB's demands could be financed only by a substantial price increase – something that did not lie within the employers' control. The onus lay on the federal government and the EGKS.[75]

Mining thus found itself in a similar position to that of 1948–51. Then as now, the controlled coal price deprived it of the resources it needed. Whereas prior to 1951 the major problem had been finding capital for investment, mining's main difficulty now was footing the wage bill. And in 1955, just as five

73. Note that workforce *growth* cannot be directly calculated from the net effect of intake and wastage because the transfers from above ground to below ground (and vice versa) have to be taken into account. See chapter 6, note 52.

74. Calculated from OBADA I8007/1310/55, ABB quarterly report 1.1.–31.3.1955.

75. UVR (ed.), *Jahresbericht 1955–1957*, p. 34; EGKS, *Entwicklung der Löhne*, pp. 26–7.

years earlier, there was little doubt that the government would have to give support. If it did not, German industry would be forced to turn to imported coal or alternative energy sources, thus adding more to its energy bill than would the very coal price increase the government was trying to avoid. So, despite their reluctance, both the EGKS and the federal government agreed to modest increases in the price of German coal.[76]

Any illusions that the mines' problems might, even temporarily, have been solved by these modest measures were shattered within weeks. The 9.5 per cent wage rise that the employers felt able to offer should theoretically have brought mining to the top of the earnings scale, but in practice the iron and steel industry and the construction industry continued to outbid the mines. This was partly because the collieries did not pay out the full increase to contract wage-earners – the wage scissors effect was particularly noticeable this time round – and also because of steady increases in the wages of minings' competitors. In the April–June period, the colliery workforces actually fell by over 5,000 men. Daily production always dropped in the summer months, but the percentage fall in 1955 was the biggest since the currency reform.[77]

The pressure was on the state to offer more substantial relief. In March 1956 (though backdated to February), the NRW government introduced a temporary incentive scheme for miners, pending the conclusion of a federal scheme. The federal measure came into effect at the end of the year. Under the Miners' Bonus Scheme, as it was called, contract wage-earners received DM2.50 per shift, tax free, on top of their normal earnings. Shift workers received a bonus of DM1.25. Coupled with a number of other measures introduced at the same time, this was a major financial commitment on the part of the state. As a result, recruitment increased by almost one-quarter over the previous year, while wastage barely rose. By the end of 1956 the underground workforce had attained and narrowly surpassed the size it had reached before the 1954 recession.[78]

76. Ibid.
77. Workforce figure is underground only. *ZdKW*, vol. 34, p. 3; IGB (ed.), *Jahrbuch 1955*, pp. 78ff; OBADA I8007/2142/55, ABB quarterly report 1.4–30.6.1955
78. BAK B102, 33133, UVR, circular no. 29 to mining companies and collieries, 10.3.1956, annex; UVR (ed.), *Jahresbericht 1955–7*, p. 56; and see table 4.6.

One of the problems in assessing how far the controlled coal price deprived the mines of resources they could legitimately have expected is that it is hard to say at any time what coal's 'true' value was. Certainly, if there had been no price controls, the Ruhr could have sold its coal for more than it actually received. But under the existing monopolistic selling arrangements, the price which the industry could have extracted would have overstated coal's value. Another source of uncertainty in any calculation is that world energy prices fluctuated considerably. Thus it is hard to estimate how much potential (non-monopolistic) revenue was withheld from the mines.[79]

It seems reasonably certain, nevertheless, that in the years preceding the introduction of the Miners' Bonus Scheme the mines could have earned significantly more than they did, even if one discounts the monopoly profits to be earned through the absence of internal competition. Workforce regeneration suffered as a result and employers were, both in 1948–51 and 1953–5, hampered in their attempts to rebuild the workforce. Whether it was to the national advantage that this was so is a different question and one that cannot be answered here. Suffice it to say that the main argument for holding the price down was not very convincing since, by the 1950s, coal's inflationary potential was probably very limited. It may well be, therefore, that the government was being over-cautious and making the mines' life unnecessarily difficult.[80]

As a result of the Bonus Scheme and associated measures recruitment picked up and the mines found themselves for a while in 'einer befriedigenden Assiette', as the UVR itself acknowledged.[81] Yet within months, the industry found itself faced with labour problems again. Even in 1956, wastage was higher than adult intake and the workforce grew only because of the large number of apprentices being transferred below ground. Since apprentice rolls were falling rapidly, these transfers would soon begin to diminish. In 1957, though earnings in mining continued to remain above those in iron and steel, wastage was more than 10 per cent higher than recruitment.

79. Bahl, *Staatliche Politik*, p. 78.

80. See, for instance, the comments of Walter Tengelmann and Heinrich Kost in Abelshauser, 'Kohle und Marktwirtschaft', pp. 517, 522.

81. Comment by Werner Söhngen at an extraordinary UVR meeting with Ludwig Erhard in ibid., p. 504.

Production actually fell. These were clear signs that, even allowing for heavier use of foreign labour in future, a major wage increase was needed.[82]

In one way, therefore, the situation in 1957 was merely a revival of the problems that had been temporarily alleviated by the Bonus Scheme. Once again, the mines found it impossible to generate the resources necessary to consolidate workforce growth. Once again, production targets were threatened by labour shortages. And, as before, the mines were prevented from increasing the coal price. In April 1956, it is true, the EGKS removed controls on coal prices but, through a sort of gentlemen's agreement between the UVR and Erhard, informal controls persisted in the FRG until October 1957.[83]

On another plane, however, the nature of the problem was gradually changing, although it is impossible to say exactly when this occurred. It was ceasing to be 'government-induced' and becoming a sign that coal was too expensive to mine. The gap between the Ruhr's tariffs and those of its competitors began to decrease as a result of underlying changes in world energy supply. Between 1956 and 1960, mineral oil prices fell by 50 per cent, as the international oil companies struggled to increase their market share in Europe. American coal, which during the Suez crisis had been expensive to ship, fell in price by around 14 per cent over 1957–60. At the same time, the Ruhr's own production costs were rising and it was clear in 1957 that wages would soon have to rise even further. In other words, the Ruhr's long-term competitiveness problem – apparent in the 1920s but then suppressed by the autarky drive, war and reconstruction – was beginning to re-emerge.[84]

The point was not that the mines had in 1957 lost their market. On the contrary, controlled prices ensured that they were still cheaper than the competition. But, had the mines charged a genuine price that would have given them a full profit margin and allowed them to pay an attractive wage, they would have found alternative sources of energy, making rapid inroads

82. See table 4.6 and UVR (ed.), *Jahresbericht 1955–1957*, p. 60 facing, 64–5; *ZdKW*, vol. 39, pp. 4–5.

83. Bahl, *Staatliche Politik*, p. 81; Abelshauser, 'Kohle und Marktwirtschaft', pp. 491ff.

84. UVR (ed.), *Jahresbericht 1958–1960*, pp. 18–20; Abelshauser, 'Kohle und Marktwirtschaft', pp. 491, 509.

into the German market. Germany's balance of payments could now comfortably absorb the costs of sizeable energy imports so that oil as well as coal from America, Russia and Poland would have been able to compete successfully against realistically priced German coal. The more efficient mines would have been able to cope with this, but not the Ruhr industry as a whole. Government pricing policy was therefore in a way protecting the mines. It reduced their revenue but shielded them from competition.[85]

The real cost of price controls in the period 1956–8 may well have been that they blinded the industry to the changing shape of the energy market. Because they could not charge a realistic price and were being forced to sell cheap, the employers were protected from the knowledge of their declining competitiveness. So output and workforce targets remained unchanged and no attempt was made to remove the marginal pits from production. The transformation from coal shortages to a coal glut at the beginning of 1958 came as a complete surprise (though not, interestingly enough, to the IGB).[86]

It was only in the early months of 1958 that the new realities of the energy market became apparent to all. So confident had the employers been of Ruhr coal's continuing competitiveness that in October 1957 they had broken from the gentlemen's agreement and imposed a hefty price increase. Within a few weeks, coal began stockpiling in the Ruhr. The effects on demand of the price rise itself had been exacerbated by a temporary downturn in iron and steel production and even more by the end of the Suez crisis. The Suez canal had become navigable again and the American coal industry was able for the first time to exploit recent cost improvements in shipping. Suddenly, American coal was on the German market at a price close to the home product. Another problem for the Ruhr producers was that many German coal consumers had committed themselves to long consumer agreements with American exporters. The Ruhr mines here suffered from the EGKS policy which had forced them to export a considerable proportion of their coal in the period 1955–7 even though the German market was undersupplied. Now that the domestic market's demands had fallen, the

85. See tables in UVR (ed.), *Jahresbericht 1955–1957*, pp. 8 and facing.
86. Bahl, *Staatliche Politik*, p. 82.

German coal producers found many potential customers con-
tractually tied to US suppliers.[87]

From spring 1958 onwards, mining's main problem was not
where to obtain new labour and how to retain it, but how to
reduce the workforce in response to the shrinking demand for
coal. The mining industry's 'reconstruction conjuncture' had,
almost overnight, come to an end.

Resources and Rebuilding, 1948–58

The essence of this chapter has been that in the years between
currency reform and coal crisis the mines were for the most part
faced by a tricky combination of high demand for coal on the
one hand and a shortage of resources on the other. Initially this
was because they were held back by the government. Towards
the end it became apparent that demand was being kept artificially high by low prices. Such a situation naturally made any
attempt to rebuild the workforce more difficult. Yet the lack of
funds was, for much of the time at least, not so pressing or
constraining as to preclude the formulation of a coherent regeneration strategy or to deny the mines any chance of building a
stable and productive workforce. It was simply the difficult and
sometimes confining framework within which managers and
other interested groups had to operate. How they responded to
these conditions is the subject of the following four chapters.

87. Ibid., p. 81; Abelshauser, 'Kohle und Marktwirtschaft', *passim*; Abelshauser, *Der Ruhrkohlenbergbau*, pp. 89ff.

PART II
Reshaping the Ruhr

5
Between Induction and Indoctrination: The Apprenticeship Programme, 1948–1958

In 1948, rebuilding and reshaping the workforce became in some respects more interesting than ever for the employers. True, as we know, it no longer dominated the industry's endeavours in the way it had, say, in the period 1946–7; as noted in chapter 4, obtaining capital for plant modernisation was now an even more pressing concern. Yet the point about manpower policy was that the employers were at last in control. Military government was no longer breathing down their necks, telling them what to do. The German agencies were giving them a relatively free hand. Moreover, the unions' influence was on the wane and the labour market situation was favourable. Indeed, at the end of 1948 the OBAD noted that there more men asking for work in the pits than there were jobs to be had. Thus, management could afford to be selective with regard to newcomers and firm towards the existing labour force.[1]

When we look at the employers' response to these opportunities, we discover that it was not just the problems of the immediate post-war period that they were trying to solve. Ever since the 1930s mine management had been discussing ways of regenerating the workforce and many of the policies brought to bear after the currency reform had, in fact, been conceived before the war. To understand the employers' behaviour, we must therefore first cast a glance back to the pre-war period.

1. Werner Abelshauser, *Wirtschaftsgeschichte der Bundesrepublik Deutschland 1945–1980*, Frankfurt, 1983, p. 64; OBADA I8010/386/49, quarterly report, 4th quarter 1948; I8010/1238/49, quarterly report, 1st quarter 1949.

Rationalisation in the Inter-war Period

During the 1920s the Ruhr mining industry embarked on a major rationalisation programme. Hand-cutting was replaced by the pneumatic pick (*Abbauhammer*) which after 1924 very rapidly established itself as the dominant means of cutting coal.[2] Then long-wall mining was introduced. Instead of a large number of small tunnels working into the coal, with faces just a few metres wide, now the face might extend across 400 metres. This allowed a dramatic reduction in the number of individual working-points. In conjunction with the introduction of long-wall mining, the use of shaker-conveyors to transport the coal away from the face increased significantly. Underground electrification was extended. Another important change was that the shafts were linked up and consolidated to form much larger mines.

These changes had in turn very significant implications for the character of the work, particularly at the face. In pre-rationalisation mining, the faces had been worked by small, isolated teams (Kameradschaften) performing the full range of jobs required at the face such as shotfiring, cutting coal, transporting it, erecting pit supports, packing the emptied field and so on. Within the individual *Kameradschaften*, there were sharp distinctions between the work performed by the skilled hewers, the trainee hewers (*Lehrhauer*) and the putters or hauliers (*Schlepper*). The putters' job was to fill coal-tubs and pull them to the loading point. Sometimes they were enlisted to help with the packing. The trainee hewers' work varied depending on the willingness of the hewers to offer genuine instruction and on the character of the particular face. The hewers themselves were called on to exercise a large variety of skills, ranging from handling explosives and laying rails for the coal-tubs to cutting and placing the pit props and using the right coal-cutting

2. For this and the following remarks on rationalisation in the inter-war period, the main sources were Franz-Josef Brüggemeier, *Leben vor Ort. Ruhrbergleute und Ruhrbergbau 1889–1919*, Munich, 1983; Stephen Hickey, *Workers in Imperial Germany: The Miners of the Ruhr*, Oxford, 1985; Helmuth Trischler, *Steiger im deutschen Bergbau. Zur Sozialgeschichte der technischen Angestellten 1815–1945*, Munich, 1988; Rudolf Tschirbs, *Tarifpolitik im Ruhrbergbau 1918–1933*, Berlin/New York 1986; and Michael Zimmermann, *Schachtanlage und Zechenkolonie. Leben, Arbeit und Politik in einer Arbeitersiedlung 1880–1980*, Essen, 1987, as well as GBAG records in the BBA.

techniques to exploit the geological pressures on the coal.

With the introduction of long-wall mining, the individual work teams grew vastly in size from a few men to fifty or more. They also became more specialised, with many mines moving on to a three-shift rhythm. One shift, usually the night shift, was used to shift the conveyor to catch up with the progress of coal-cutting the day before. The morning or midday shift would be the principal coal-getting shift, while the remaining shift would be used for a mixture of packing and coal-getting. As a result the work of the individual hewer became less varied. In addition, the teams lost a lot of their close-knit character. For one thing, many of the jobs that had been performed as a team were now dealt with by the individual miner. For another, the hierarchy of skills within the group was eroded. With a lot of the simple loading and haulage work removed, there was often little difference in the work performed by *Hauer*, *Lehrhauer* and such putters as were working at the face (the so-called *Gedingeschlepper*).

In general, the technical changes facilitated and required a lot more managerial control over the production process. Whereas the isolated work teams in pre-rationalised mining had worked alone for hours, sometimes for days, at their own pace with little interference, management was now able to maintain more consistent observation and monitoring. Previously, a deputy might have to monitor the activity of some sixty separate working-points. Now, the average deputy would control between two and ten faces. The spread of electrification made the faces easier to observe. With the long coalfaces, management now had to make sure that the whole group moved forward at the same pace, not least so that the conveyor remained in line. Even so, the nature of the working environment (and, after 1945, the shortage of lower management) continued to mean that miners had a great deal more freedom from managerial interference than in most factory environments. And it continued to be difficult for management to assert itself consistently on the work process.

The patterns of technology and working practice established in the 1920s and early 1930s were to last, with some wartime interruptions, until the late 1950s. True, experiments were made during the war with more advanced mechanisation; and in the post-1945 era, a small number of pits saw the introduction of mechanised coal-cutters, such as the coal plough, and of semi-mechanised hydraulic supports. Yet for most mines, shortage of cash, technical difficulties and the large number of faces on steep gradients meant that mechanisation was slow to be introduced.

Rationalisation involved not just new technology but also a new approach to management and new aspirations to mould and control the worker. The founding of the Deutsches Institut für technische Arbeitsschulung (DINTA) in 1925 was an important stimulus here. Not that the *Bergassessoren* readily adopted the doctrines of Taylor or the US human relations school. Particularly at the level of production management, there was little enthusiasm for experiments in new styles of man-management. Even the more authoritarian variant of Taylorism advocated by DINTA figures such as Carl Arnhold was regarded by mining engineers with suspicion. Instead, they set their faith on the traditional *Grubenmilitarismus* to maintain lower management's position with respect to the men. Yet alongside this hard and authoritarian approach in production management itself, the mines began to seek new ways of systematically shaping the workforce's outlook and behaviour. New training programmes were adopted, involving strong elements of character training. Works newspapers started appearing around this time, with their aim of enhancing company loyalty. Traditional elements of company welfare policy, the provision of housing, kindergarten, holiday homes and so on were also extended.

For our purposes, the most interesting developments were in the field of youth training, for it was here that the mines developed a strategy of social integration that was to be extremely influential on their post-war labour policy. Traditionally, the Ruhr mines had given miner's training very little attention. It had been up to the individual hewer to train the *Lehrhauer* as best he could. With the introduction of long-wall mining, however, the individual hewer's ability to demonstrate mining techniques was significantly reduced. The steady tempo demanded of each miner and the more rational approach to production saw to that. Thus some special training programme seemed desirable and during the 1920s a number of mines created their first training workshops.

Even so, as one of the leading post-war figures in the mines' training policy recalled in an interview, it was hard to get managements to give training much priority during these years.[3] The real change came during the 1930s. As the economy picked up after the depression, many mines came to realise that they faced a fundamental problem on the labour market. At the prices they were allowed to charge, they could not afford to pay the wages necessary to win adequate new labour and create a stable workforce. One reason was that rationalisation had not made mining much easier or safer. True, the spread of the shaker-conveyor and the pneumatic pick had removed some of the most laborious hammer-and-spade work; and improvements in lighting, communications and pit supports had reduced some common sources of accident. Yet the pneumatic pick was a taxing tool with deleterious long-term consequences for the miners' health. More serious still was the fact that widespread use of the pneumatic pick brought with it an increase in the amount of coal-dust in the atmosphere and thus in the incidence of silicosis.

Apart from the miserable working conditions, mining was seen in the Ruhr as a low-status occupation. To be seen as a miner was to be seen to have failed. Engineering, on the other hand, benefited from that fascination with technology that characterised young Germans in the 1930s.[4] Thus, to compensate for its poor image, mining's wages had to be well ahead of its competitors. Yet the low coal price made this impossible. As a result, mining employers began to give thought to ways in which they might improve the situation without requiring resources they did not possess. The main strategy adopted was to build on the training initiatives of the 1920s and create for the first time a formal, officially recognised apprenticeship, a goal finally realised in 1941. To a certain extent this proposal was advisable on purely technical grounds, but the real hope behind it was that it would restore mining's status, increase recruitment and create a new core of loyal, stable and highly qualified young workers. The more the industry faced recruitment and wastage problems in the 1930s, the more workforce stability became the employers' dominant consideration.

The idea was that apprenticeships would have a two-fold effect. On the one hand, they would convince parents and

3. Interview with Dr Steffen, later training director for the HBAG, December 1982.
4. Cited in Hanns W. Brose, 'Eine Gemeinschaftswerbung zur Gewinnung von Nachwuchs für den Bergbau', reprinted from *Die Werbung*, July 1950.

youngsters 'daß im Bergbau eine qualitativ ebenso wertvolle Ausbildung vermittelt wird wie in der übrigen Industrie'.[5] On the other hand they would enable the employers to bring to bear 'erziehliche Einflüsse . . . die auf die Schaffung einer verantwortungsbewußten Arbeiterschaft abgestellt sind'.[6] Ultimately, the influx of high-quality and closely supervised new recruits would transform what the employers regarded as the unstable and unreliable workforce of the 1920s into a permanent, responsible and cooperative one.[7] The mines hoped to win apprentices from groups previously unwilling to send their offspring to the mines and set about constructing special apprentice hostels to accommodate outsiders to the Ruhr. However, the needs of total war forced a halt to the construction programme and a number of the hostels were given over to housing forced labour. Nevertheless, the apprentice strategy was ready and waiting, as the speed with which it was revived after the war was to demonstrate.[8]

Apprenticeships after 1945

Almost from the first days after the British took over the industry, there were calls for apprentice recruitment to be revived and expanded. The NGCC itself was well aware of the mines' general need for rejuvenation and partially accepted the employers' arguments about the importance of status. However, since its main efforts had to lie in finding adult recruits who could make an immediate contribution to increasing coal production, juveniles remained but a small fraction of overall intake. By 1948, however, employers and unions were talking of adult recruit-

5. Archive of the Landesoberbergamt, Dortmund (OBADA) I6300, GMSO, circular no. 138, November 1945, annex 2.
6. Rudolf Schwenger, *Die betriebliche Sozialpolitik*, cited in ibid.
7. Cited in OBADA I6300, GMSO, circular no. 138, November 1945, annex 2. See also H. H. Büttchereit, 'Probleme des bergmännischen Bildungswesens', *Mitteilungen der WBK*, vol. 5, 1957, pp. 5–10.
8. Brose, 'Eine Gemeinschaftswerbung', *passim*; Michael Zimmermann, 'Ausbruchshoffnungen. Junge Bergleute in den dreißiger Jahren', in Lutz Niethammer (ed.), *'Die Jahre weiß man nicht, wo man die heute hinsetzen soll'. Faschismuserfahrungen im Ruhrgebiet*, Berlin/Bonn, 1983, pp. 97–132 at 114; Hans-Georg Erzmoneit, 'Was tut der Ruhrbergbau für seinen Nachwuchs?', *Bergbau*, vol. 7, 1956, pp. 168–75 at 172.

Table 5.1 Juvenile intake, 1946–58

Year	Overall	From outside mining area
1.7.46–30.6.47	11,740	2,130
1.7.47–30.6.48	10,911	1,725
1.7.48–30.6.49	5,207	1.328
1.7.49–30.6.50	11,832	2,539
1.7.–30.12.50	2,933	829
1951	14,467	3,933
1952	16,462	5,210
1953	17,430	6,176
1954	19,021	6,281
1955[a]	11,849	4,745
1956[a]	8,912	3,728
1957[a]	6,984	2,982

(a) Apprentices only.

Source: 1946–49: OBADA I6301/2448/49, DKBL to OBAD, 5.11.1949, annex: table, 'Einstellungen von Jugendlichen im Ruhrbergbau; 1949–57: OBADA I6303, vols 1 and 2, ABB monthly reports on juvenile hirings; I8006, vol. 2 and I8007, ABB annual reports.

ment as a temporary stopgap measure. True, expansion of juvenile intake was initially retarded by the lack of finance for apprentice hostels and by the small number of school-leavers in 1948–9. But an increasing number of mines devoted considerable ingenuity to their apprentice recruitment campaigns. After a test-run in 1949, the practice was begun of assigning each colliery *Patenbezirke*, or foster-areas, in which it was the only mine recruiting youngsters. Good relations with local schools and careers advisers were assiduously cultivated and the collieries encouraged frequent trips to the mines for officials from the *Patenbezirke*. All this effort and ingenuity soon began to pay handsome dividends. By 1954, there were some 35,000 apprentices in the pits, a healthy figure by any standards.[9]

What was the logic behind the call for more apprentices? Young labour was cheap, of course, and this was attractive to the mines on a number of counts. It meant that apprentices

9. OBADA I6300, GMSO, circular no. 138, November 1945, annex 2; Manfred Daberkow, 'Die Seßhaftmachung der vom westdeutschen Steinkohlenbergbau aus bergfremden Gebieten angeworbenen Berglehrlinge', unpublished dissertation, Sozialschule Gelsenkirchen, 1955, p. 63.

could be used to do menial jobs above ground, such as sorting coal at the picking-belt. And it meant that the mines could afford to give them good training. Yet the financial argument should not be given too much weight. It was cheaper to take on youngsters as juvenile trainees (*Bergjungleute*), with their lower wage and more rudimentary training programme, than as apprentices (*Berglehrlinge*). The fact that *apprentice* recruitment was given such priority proved that the wage costs were not the only, indeed not the main argument in their favour. In addition, apprentices in mining were extremely well paid in comparison with their counterparts in other industries, receiving two-and-a-half times as much as the average.[10] Nor can the undoubted need for rejuvenation explain the specific stress on apprentices as opposed to juvenile trainees or, indeed, to young adults. The latter would bring just as much youth and physical strength to the mines as the apprentices. Indeed, rejuvenation at the face would have proceeded far faster if juvenile trainees or young adults, with their shorter induction period, had been preferred to apprentices. Yet the preference given to apprentices over hiring young adults was virtually universal.[11]

A plausible explanation would seem to be that the apprentices' lengthy training made them more productive members of the workforce. Yet there was little evidence that this was so. It was true that the very inadequate training given to adult trainees made them more susceptible to accidents and less able to carry out difficult jobs like properly erecting supports after the coal had been mined. With their all-round training, apprentices were better placed to adapt to new conditions. But it was noteworthy that neither the mines nor the DKBL produced any statistics comparing the efficiency of former apprentices and adult trainees.[12]

10. IGBEA, Handakten Rudi Quast, File 'Arbeitskreis-Arbeitsdirektoren 1952–1956', minutes of meeting of Essen/Gelsenkirchen district, 13.5.1954; minutes of meeting of Recklinghausen district, 1.12.1954; OBADA I8006/36/53, DKBL (ed.), *Berglehrlingsheime zur Behebung von Berufsnot und Arbeitslosigkeit unter den Jugendlichen*, Essen, [1953], table 'Gegenüberstellung der Erziehungsbeihilfen der Berglehrlinge und der Handwerkslehrlinge'.

11. AZG File 'I 1 26 Zuweisung von Arbeitskräften aus anderen Bezirken', memo concerning meeting of the NRW mines' Tarifausschuß, 28.1.1949; Außenstelle Bergbau (ed.), 'Sechs Jahre Außenstelle Bergbau des Landesarbeitamtes NRW', unpublished MS, no place, no date [1952], p. 76.

12. The NCB, too, found no evidence that the apprenticeship enhanced

Clear evidence of the 'ideological' nature of the apprentice-ship programme was that a lot of training period involved training in name only. Most boys started at 14 and, for health and safety reasons, the state allowed them underground only at age 16. Thus two years of their apprenticeship were generally spent above ground. The mines created special training faces on the surface (*Lehrstollen*), but, even so, were hard put to it to occupy the youngsters for the full period. There were simply not enough formal skills to fill up the two years. Indeed, a number of mines tried (particularly in the early post-war period when training procedures were still rather in flux) to reduce the actual training period and to get the apprentices into production at a much earlier stage.[13] Of course, the mines could have taught more advanced work in the mechanical workshop or in electrics and so on, but they were understandably hesitant to impart skills that would not then be used in occupational life. It was bound to lead to dissatisfaction if skills were taught that were not then used. On the other hand, shortening the apprentice-ship would downgrade mining and undermine the attempt to improve its status.[14]

In short, the apprenticeship's real virtues must be sought elsewhere. They lay first of all, in what one might call its 'public relations' aspect and, secondly, in the potential for transforming the character of the workforce.

Status and Recruitment

There was no doubt that mining had a status problem. Many observers of the Ruhr from the 1920s onwards had commented on the low esteem in which the profession was held. During the 1930s, young miners from the Ruhr would go to elaborate lengths to conceal their occupation – because that was the only

productivity. See National Coal Board (NCB), *Training and Education in the Ruhr Coalmining Industry*, printed NCB paper, 1955, pp. 39–41. On accidents and training, see BBA 10, 135, Mine Friedrich der Große, memo for Herr Bergrat Heintzmann, 4.4.1955.

13. OBADA I6303/1004/46, Essener Steinkohlenbergwerke to BA Werden, 18.6.1946, cited in BA Werden to OBAD, 10.7.1946.

14. OBADA I6303/1004/46, Rheinische Stahlwerke, Essen to BA Bottrop, 4.7.1946; OBADA I6303/1004/46, BA Werden to OBAD, 10.7.1946.

way to get the girls. Heinrich Husmann too, in his ethnographical study of workers in Hamborn, noted the tendency to look down on the miner. And in a semi-autobiographical story in the collection *Streuselkuchen in Ickern*, novelist Hans Diether Baroth brilliantly captures the reverence of a 1950s mining family, the Woetkes, towards the one son who had managed to get a trade outside the pits.[15]

Thus one of the central tasks of the apprenticeship programme was to raise public perceptions of mining. Apprenticeship, so the theory ran, would give mining the status of a skilled profession and thus win over potential recruits (and their parents). Again and again, discussions about apprenticeship were dominated by its 'public relations' aspect; considerations of status, not productivity, prevailed.[16] In early post-war debates about the proper length of training, for example, the main difficulty was to find a balance between not overqualifying the apprentice, on the one hand, and on the other not giving rise to the impression 'daß die bergmännische Lehre im Vergleich mit anderen Lehrberufen minderwertig sei . . . .'.[17] It was to avoid such an impression that the OBAD strongly resisted any attempt to offer shorter training.[18]

The possibility of dramatically increasing labour intake by altering the profession's status seemed in 1947–8 greater than ever because in the next few years a very large number of youngsters would be leaving school for whom training opportunities would be limited. Indeed, until well into the 1950s, NRW was to be the only Land in the West Germany with a surplus of apprenticeship places. Refugees, in particular, found themselves in the position of neither having the contacts to obtain scarce apprenticeships for their children, nor the money to pay for their upkeep were a traineeship offered. If such

15. See Zimmermann, 'Ausbruchshoffnungen', p. 102; Hans Dieter Baroth, *Streuselkuchen in Ickern*, Cologne, 1980, p. 188; Heinrich Husmann, 'Lebensformen und ihr Wandel beim Arbeiter in Hamborn', unpublished dissertation, Mainz University, 1952, p. 14.
16. 'Das Nachwuchsproblem im Bergbau', *Bundesarbeitsblatt*, 1950, pp. 331–4; 'Zur Pflege bergmännischer berufsethischer Gesinnung', *Arbeitsblatt für die britische Zone*, vol. 1, 1947, pp. 259–62; 'Männer von Morgen', *Junior Magazin*, vol. 12, 1952, pp. 474–6; OBADA I6301/1339/45, LAA Westfalen-Lippe, circular to labour exchanges, no. 165/45, 28.10.1945.
17. OBADA I6303/1004/46, BA Werden to OBAD, 10.7.1946.
18. OBADA I6303/85/48, OBAD to AA Gelsenkirchen, 21.1.1948.

parents could be persuaded of the worth of mining training, they might well wish to avail themselves of the undoubtedly good earnings and possibilities for upward mobility in the mining industry. Thus the post-war situation presented the mines with a perhaps unique opportunity to achieve a large influx of new blood. It was a sign of the mines' determination to take advantage of the situation that by the end of November 1947 there were already twenty-five apprentice hostels in the Ruhr with 1,359 places.[19]

An additional, though related, virtue of the apprenticeship programme was that state officials found it morally reassuring and politically important to be able to offer young refugees an officially recognised training programme and a proper qualification, rather than just shoving them down the mines. Particularly outside mining areas, many labour exchange officials were reluctant to send youngsters to the pits. Yet they were well aware of mining's importance and aware too that other training opportunities were limited. The promise of a formal and supervised apprenticeship made it palatable to propose mining as a career. Similarly, it made it politically and psychologically easier for federal ministries, particularly the Refugee Ministry, to provide funds for the mines. This explains why it was that the NRW labour administration, and particularly the Außenstelle Bergbau (ABB), was such an enthusiastic proponent of apprenticeship. For it was this administration which faced the task of persuading officials elsewhere to provide the mines with a steady supply of good labour. The ABB's Dr Herwegen was a passionate advocate of the *Berglehre*. His circulars, written in a unique style of what one can only call *Bergarbeitervermittlerdichtung*, were full of poetic and romantic statements calling on the mines to build more hostels for apprentices or improve the ones they had already, and urging the labour exchanges' careers advisers to take mining seriously, recognise its advantages and send the mines top-quality youngsters.[20]

---

19. OBADA I6301/969/47, ABB, circular to colliery managements and labour exchanges, 17.3.1947; *Informations-Rundbrief zur sozialen Lage der Jugend*, vol. 4, no. 12, 1952, p. 12; OBADA I6301/927/46, LAA Westfalen-Lippe, circular, signed Dr Herwegen, 25.4.1946; OBADA I6303/3163/47, GMSO to OBAD, 28.11.1947.
20. OBADA I6303/568/47, ABB to OBAD, 25.2.1947.; I6301/969/47, ABB, circular to colliery managements and labour exchanges, 17.3.1947; I6301/927/46, LAA Westfalen-Lippe, circular, signed Dr Herwegen, 25.4.1946; I6301/628/47, ABB,

By 1948–9 it was already clear to the mines and the ABB that the federal Refugee Administration might provide considerable subsidies if it could be proven that the mines were offering refugees a sound training and a good educational environment. In 1949, the DKBL produced an impressive public relations booklet, entitled *Die Berglehrlingsheime des Steinkohlenbergbaus der Nordzone . . . im Dienste der Bekämpfung von Berufsnot und Arbeitslosigkeit unter den Jugendlichen*, the primary aim of which was to elicit state funding for hostel construction. Subsequently revised and reprinted many times, the booklet drew attention to the economic, social and pedagogical virtues of mining apprenticeships and the comparatively good opportunities for youngsters from poor families to rise up within the industry.[21]

At a fairly early stage, the drive to win apprentices from outside the Ruhr gained added impetus from the view that the outsiders, or at least a proportion of them, were of a particularly high quality. In part this was based on purely educational criteria. Within the Ruhr region, school-leavers with good results tended to avoid the mines and go into more desirable trades. But outside the Ruhr, the mines faced little competition on the juvenile labour market. In the period 1949–52, between one-third and two-fifths of interregional apprentice movements were accounted for by the mines. So it was not surprising that the collieries soon found they were able to obtain youngsters with very good school results. The outsiders' performance in the apprentice exams, particularly in the theoretical parts, was correspondingly better than the locals'. In a 1949 report to the OBAD about the general development of training since the war, the DKBL took pains to note the refugee apprentices'[22] 'besonders hervorstechende Beteiligung an der betrieblichen und schulischen Ausbildung'.[23]

However, the attraction of the outsiders went further than

---

circular, 22.2.1947; HStAD NW73, 458, Arbeitsminister NRW, Hauptabt. LAA, memo, 8.2.1949.

21. HStAD NW41, 769, report on an interministerial meeting at the BWiM, 6.6.1950; OBADA I6301/2448/49, DKBL (ed.), *Die Berglehrlingsheime des Steinkohlenbergbaus der Nordzone . . . im Dienste der Bekämpfung von Berufsnot und Arbeitslosigkeit unter den Jugendlichen*, Hamborn, 29.10.1949.

22. The majority of hostel occupants were refugees (see below).

23. *Informations-Rundbrief zur sozialen Lage der Jugend*, vol. 4, no. 1, 1952, pp. 1ff; Daberkow, 'Die Seßhaftmachung', p. 15; OBADA I6301/2448/49, DKBL to OBAD, 5.11.1949, annex.

this. At the IGB's first youth conference, which took place in 1950, a miner with the memorable name of Roman Mrug stood up and complained at what he saw as the favouritism being given to youngsters from outside the Ruhr. What the employers were arguing, Mrug moaned, was that it was better to recruit youngsters: 'Die aus ländlichen Gegenden kommen [i.e. from outside the Ruhr], weil diese im allgemeinen ein weit höheres Niveau an den Tag legen, eine andere Erziehung hätten, zum anderen seien sie schulisch mehr auf der Höhe und es sei deshalb weit mehr mit ihnen anzufangen.'[24] Often from non-working-class or small-town backgrounds, the outsiders were seen by the employers as bringing desirable values and attitudes to the mines. Above all, it was felt, they would remove the low behaviour and negative attitudes which the culturally and racially inferior Poles had brought in at the end of the nineteenth century. The ABB's Dr Herwegen, for instance, observed that because of 'die Anlegung der in den meisten Fällen kulturell tiefer stehenden Personen von außen, . . . hat sich im Bergbau-Milieu ein Umgangston entwickelt, der vielen Arbeitswilligen als untragbar erscheint'.[25] 'Geistig geeignete' outsiders could play a key role in introducing new standards of behaviour. There would thus be a virtuous circle whereby the status of a proper qualification would attract outsiders and the outsiders' standards and behaviour would, in turn, enhance mining's standing in the community.[26]

Creating a Stable and Contented Workforce

These last remarks indicate that the *raison d'être* of the apprenticeship programme was not solely to make mining more attractive to potential recruits – or to the officials involved in

24. DGBA Protokoll-Sammlung, 'Protokoll des 1.Verbandsjugendtags der IGB', Bochum, 1950.
25. HStAD NW41, 746, minutes of a meeting of the 'Ausschuß zur Ausarbeitung eines Lehrganges für Heimleiter' on 16 December 1948, 27.12.1948; see also 'Schmelztiegel Kohlenpott', in DKBL (ed.), *Ruhr-Almanach. Vom Bergmann und Bergbau*, Cologne, 1950, esp. pp. 95ff.
26. HStAD NW41, 768, Sozialwissenschaftliche Arbeitsgemeinschaft zur Erforschung von Jugendproblemen (ed.), 'Maßnahmen zur Behebung der Not der berufslosen und heimatlosen Jugend in NRW', unpublished MS, no date [1951]; Daberkow, 'Die Seßhaftmachung', pp. 50ff.

providing those recruits. The further goal of altering the workforce's behaviour and changing its attitude to the mining profession remained just as attractive to the employers as before the war – indeed, even more attractive, because management's feeling that the workforce needed to be licked into shape had been considerably strengthened by years of diminished managerial authority, a massive influx of outsiders in the shape of Soviet prisoners of war and then the new miners of the post-war years, and by high wastage rates.[27] The miner who had gone through the apprenticeship, so it was argued, would have a new self-esteem, be unlikely to leave the mine and also be better disposed to company and employers. At a major conference of colliery training directors in 1953, Heinrich Kost, the DKBL's general director and one of the individuals most closely associated with promoting apprenticeships since the early 1940s, listed what he saw as the most important virtues of the traineeship. In first place, according to Kost, was not training's contribution to productivity but its potential for creating a stable workforce.[28]

The hopes and expectations which the industry attached to the apprenticeship were frequently linked to a myth of the miner as he had once been. Indeed, they are fully explicable only once the power of that myth has been understood. In a 1948 article for the mining industry's journal, *Glückauf*, Karl Bax evoked this image when he wrote: 'Für die Berufe der Urproduktion reichen Kenntnisse und Fertigkeiten nicht aus. Bauer, Hochseefischer und Bergmann verdienen ein hartes Brot, und sie bedürfen einer besonderen Einstellung zum Leben: einer berufsständisch bestimmten Weltanschauung. Alle Urerzeugung ringt mit der Natur. Sie lauscht der Natur ihre Geheimnisse ab, wagt den Kampf mit ihren Gewalten.'[29] The miner of yore was thus bound to his profession by deep inner ties to the earth and an almost mystical desire to unlock its secrets and

27. 'Das Nachwuchsproblem im Bergbau', p. 331.

28. Ibid; HStAD NW41, 761, Senft, report on the conference of training directors at the DKV Haus Essen, 15.1.1953; Hansgerd Friedhoff, 'Die Bedeutung der beruflichen Bildung für die Fluktuation im Ruhrbergbau', *Bergbau-Rundschau*, vol. 9, no. 1, 1957, pp. 48–50.

29. Karl Bax, 'Die Nachwuchssorgen des Steinkohlenbergbaus. Gründe des Nachwuchsmangels und Versuche zu ihrer Behebung', *Glückauf*, vol. 85, nos 27/8, 1949, pp. 477–85 at 78.

bring its treasures to the surface. A perceptive correspondent from the *Neue Zeitung* noted in 1951 that both union and employers were trying to create out of the young miners members of 'eines Bergmannstandes mit ausgeprägtem Standesbewußtsein, wobei für viele die fast legendäre Gestalt des alten Bergmanns auftaucht, für den die Arbeit im Pütt nicht bloßes Mittel zum Geldverdienen war, sondern Glück und Abenteuer eines ständigen Ringens mit der Naturgewalt des Berges'.[30] The key word here was *Standesbewußtsein*. The miner of yore was seen as being secure in his social position. At peace with the world, he was characterised both by self-esteem and by loyalty and respect for his employers. By contrast, the high wastage rates and recruitment problems of more recent times and the militancy of the mining community seemed to the employers to denote a loss of self-respect and security. The works newspaper of the GBAG's Hamborn Group, for instance, bemoaned the passing of the 'in sich geschlossenen, harmonischen und von Berufsethos erfüllten Menschen' of past generations.[31]

As these remarks suggest, linked to the image of the miner of the past was a more general view of the problems of the modern age. Very often we find contemporaries juxtaposing two concepts, namely, *Persönlichkeit* and *Vermassung*. Indeed, this antithesis, between *Persönlichkeit* or *echte Persönlichkeit*[32] or *Personalkern des Individuums*,[33] on the one hand, and *Vermassung*[34] or *Kollektivierung*[35] on the other was so widespread that it became a sort of shorthand, which could be communicated and understood without the need for thought or explanation. Here, for example, is Jürgen Heuer, writing about the work in apprentice villages: 'Daß über allem letztlich das Moment der

30. 'Der "Lager Mensch" – Symptom einer Entwicklung', *Neue Zeitung*, 7.8.1951.
31. *Der Förderturm*, June 1948, pp. 1–2; 'Zur Berufsethik des Bergmanns', *Arbeitsblatt für die britische Zone*, vol. 1, 1941, p. 171.
32. 'Statt Kasernengeist die echte Persönlichkeit', *Rheinischer Merkur*, Koblenz, 5.2.1949.
33. HStAD NW17, 141, lecture from Sieburg, 'Ziele staatsbürgerlicher Willensbildung in der kulturellen Bergmannsbetreuung' in report on the RAG conference at Kronenburg 21–6.9.1953.
34. SoFoSta File 'Dr Jantke. Sozialausschüsse der evangelischen Kirche 4/11/1951.12', Pastor P. Arnold Dannenmann, *Das Jugendproblem heute*, reprint of lecture given on 22.1.1952 in Essen, no date [1952].
35. Report on speech from Heinrich Kost, in HStAD NW41, 761, Senft, Tagungsbericht von der Ausbildungstagung im DKV-Haus, Essen, 15.1.1953.

Persönlichkeitsbildung steht, entspricht nicht nur der Notwendigkeit, bereits in der Jugend das Gefühl des Kollektivismus einzudämmen, sondern auch dem Ziel, dem werdenden Bergmann mit den ersten Ansätzen der Ausbildung ein festes Berufsethos zu vermitteln, das der Tradition des Bergmannes entspricht.'[36] On the one hand, Heuer is talking about re-creating a mining tradition and establishing a strong commitment to mining. On the other hand, there is the more fundamental danger of collectivism. The notion of *Persönlichkeitsbildung* meant trying to prevent the individual personality from being swallowed up by mass society. For, whereas in an organic society the individual has firm roots, a clear social picture and strong values, in mass society, these are lost and the individual is open to the dangers of extremism and radicalisation.

In line with this view of modern society, many observers argued that the dissolution of the organic hierarchy had removed the miner's sense of self-worth and of the worth of his profession. Job-changing was seen as a sign of a lack of social roots and the consequent loss of a rounded personality. In his guidelines for constructing and running hostels for apprentices, Klaus von Bismarck attributed wastage primarily not to material causes but to 'Verlust von Heimat und Besitz, Auflösung der gesellschaftlichen Ordnung und Bindung, das Versanden aller standesmäßigen Gruppierung, die allgemeine Ungeborgenheit in einer sachlich und unpersönlich gewordenen Welt'.[37] Another churchman, this time the very influential Pastor Dannenmann, one of the leading figures in youth voluntary work in post-war Germany and a major voice in advising where and how federal funds should be allocated, also saw job-changing in these terms. In a speech to mining employers, Dannenmann talked of the wandering youngster, today mining coal in the Ruhr, tomorrow perhaps labouring in south Germany. Dannenmann argued that the fact that they did not stay in the best-paid jobs, by which he presumably meant mining, proved that it was a spiritual problem and not a material one. 'Es ist zuletzt die

36. Jürgen Heuer, 'Pestalozzidorf – Sozialleistung des Bergbaus. Aufbau und Probleme', in H. J. Seraphim (ed.), *Siedlungen und Wohungen von heute*, Münster, 1952, pp. 54–72 at 62.
37. HStAD NW41, 747, Sozialamt der evangelischen Kirche, 'Vorschläge zum Bau und zur Führung von Knappenheimen', 15.10.1951.

Frage nach dem Sinn des Lebens.'[38] The hope, therefore, was that apprenticeship, flanked by additional measures in the field of education and housing, could provide a stable social framework, an 'organic' way of life, in which the young miner could find pride and contentment.[39]

The Apprenticeship's Political and Moral Function

The proper integration of young miners came to be seen by many groups and individuals not just as a means to achieve workforce stability, but also as a sort of political and spiritual immunisation against the dangers of the modern age. That was why policy-makers took as their goal 'den Menschen von heute aus seiner Vermassung zu lösen und ihm den Übergang zu organischen Lebensformen der Ehe, der Familie, der Siedlung auf eigenem Grund und Boden zu ermöglichen'.[40] The firm guiding framework provided by the apprenticeship was intended to help re-create not only a stable workforce but also a stable society, an organic social hierarchy of settled individuals.

With these criticisms of mass society and aspirations to return to a vaguely defined 'organic' hierarchy, the Ruhr bourgeoisie was in many ways merely reviving a long-standing conservative tradition. But the frequency with which *Persönlichkeit* was invoked in the post-war era showed that there were new elements and a new urgency to the call for a reversal to *Vermassung*. It is clear, though it was seldom said at the time, that the explanatory and emotional power of the juxtaposition between mass and personality derived in part from the way many middle-class Germans were attempting to deal with the experience of fascism and war. It is evident that their attitude towards the fascist era was to reject its 'excesses', which they interpreted as the excesses of a 'mass age' in which conventional values had disappeared. No doubt there was something to this, but it also sanitised National Socialism and allowed its crimes to be referred to almost anonymously under the heading of 'problems of the modern age'. (It was noteworthy that the Nazi era was

38. Dannenmann, *Das Jugendproblem heute*.
39. HStAD NW41, 747, 'Vorschläge zum Bau und zur Führung von Knappenheimen'.
40. Ibid.

never referred to by name, only by the euphemism *jüngste Vergangenheit*.) Presenting Nazism as the product of mass man also buried the question of bourgeois complicity and involvement.

In a similar fashion, many bourgeois commentators interpreted the disruption caused by war and its aftermath as quintessentially modern experiences, intensifying the more general negative effects of the modern age, above all eroding roots and creating mass man. For example, in Klaus von Bismarck's comments about *Vermassung* and the origins of labour wastage, noted above, the writer moves effortlessly from specific features of the war and post-war period ('Verlust von Heimat und Besitz') to the more general lack of security and protection in the modern world ('die allgemeine Ungeborgenheit in einer sachlich und unpersönlich gewordenen Welt').[41] Many other contemporaries employed *Vermassung* in this way, and part of the term's appeal seems to have been precisely its ability to subsume Germany's recent experience under broader categories of modern social change.

Clearly, this analysis expressed a great deal of anxiety about the political dangers of the present. There was considerable concern about the ostensible propensity to extremism on the part of the younger generation – the generation which had been most strongly exposed to National Socialist ideas and a generation which had missed out on proper education in wartime and the immediate post-war years. In a draft paper for a conference of hostel wardens, Dr Herwegen jotted down as key words on the situation of youngsters in post-war society 'Vernachläßigung, Verelendung, Gefährdung, Verwahrlosung, Kriminalität'.[42] Refugees and other groups who had been swept away from their homeland or their former life by war and the consequences of war were also believed to be vulnerable to the call of the mass. One of the field-workers involved in cultural welfare policy observed that the refugees had a high educational level but had lost any sense of genuine morality and ethics as a result of brutal wartime and post-war experiences.[43]

41. Ibid.
42. HStAD NW41. 746, Dr Herwegen, 'Entwurf für die Tagesordnung einer Heimleiter-Tagung', no date [1948/9].
43. BBA 8, 191, copy of report from Fischer, 'Alkohol in Bergarbeiterwohnheimen', 27.4.1950.

There was felt to be a danger that radical organizations would exploit and intensify the negative consequences of this *Vermassung*. The solution, so it was hoped, lay in *Verwurzelung* through the apprenticeship. When Heinrich Kost, for instance, emphasised the importance of apprenticeship for creating a stable workforce, he went on to say that it had the vital additional function of protecting youngsters from the dangers of political extremism. Both state and church believed that by fostering the *Berufsethos*, they could remove the workers' *Berufsminderwertigkeitsgefühl* and thus a potential source of radicalism, and there were many spokesmen both in and outside the industry who emphasised the importance of apprenticeships for integrating young refugees.[44]

Did the employers' talk about combating 'radicalism' also imply a hope of weakening organised labour in general, i.e. of using the apprentices as a fifth column against the union and works councils? Certainly, there had been overtones of this in the discussions of the early 1920s and 1930s. Yet in the post-war situation it was extremely difficult for mining industrialists to make such statements. When it came to persuading outside agencies to offer help in promoting the apprenticeship, for example, management often found it expedient to enlist union support. On the other hand, when we look at the way the employers controlled the apprentice hostels (see chapter 7), it is clear that there continued to be strong but concealed ambitions to weaken the labour movement's influence.

The Apprenticeships and the State

Though it was, in the last analysis, the employers who had set in motion the drive to turn the miners into a qualified profession, it is evident that outside groups, and particularly the various state administrations, played a key role in encouraging and expanding the apprentice programme after the war. In

44. HStAD NW41, 761, Senft, report on the conference of training directors at the DKV Haus Essen, 15.1.1953; Heinrich Werth to Weber, 21.6.1951, annex; NW41, 769, report on an interministerial meeting at the BWiM, 6.6.1950; 'Objektive und subjektive Berufsnot der Jugend', *Informations-Rundbrief zur sozialen Lage der Jugend*, vol. 4, no. 4, 1952, pp. 1ff.; 'Maßnahmen zur Behebung der Not der berufslosen und heimatlosen Jugend in NRW', in ibid.

addition to the labour administration, whose role has already been examined, the Mining Inspectorate was one of its most enthusiastic proponents, partly for reasons of safety but also because of a strong commitment to improving the miners' status. But many other public agencies also played key parts. For some colliery managements not quite convinced of the need for apprenticeships, it may well have been the promise of state support for hostel building programmes, for example, that galvanised them to prefer apprentices to other types of labour.[45] The state was particularly influential when it came to increasing the importance attached in the mines' rhetoric and policy to the broader political, cultural and moral issues. It was vocational training officers in the labour administration, officials in the refugee ministries and parliamentarians who most frequently and forcefully expressed the deeper spiritual and political concerns of Germany's post-war bourgeoisie. Churchmen, often brought in by the state to help supervise voluntary-aided institutions and projects, also played a major role in getting the mines to take such questions more seriously.[46]

Since the mines could not do without state funding or administrative support, they made a point of stressing that they were not just trying to get workers for a job but were embarked on a high moral mission. That sort of thing went down well with the responsible officials. After a visit to the Ruhr in October 1952 by a parliamentary committee for youth welfare, the chairman reported to the Chancellor that they were very impressed by what they saw and above all 'von dem eindeutigen Bekenntnis des Herrn Generaldirektors Kost, daß die Bergbauunternehmer nicht gewillt seien, bei der Übernahme der Berufsausbildungspflichten auf die erzieherischen und ethischen Werte des Christentums zu verzichten'.[47] Apparently the Chancellor himself was very pleased and promised to praise Kost at the appropriate opportunity.[48] Of more significance than such praise, however, was that the mines were frequently reminded that

45. OBADA I6303/273/48, OBAD to AA Gelsenkirchen, 31.1.1948; I6301/969/47, ABB, circular to colliery managements and labour exchanges, 17.3.1947; Paul Breder, *Geschichten vor Ort. Erinnerungen eines Bergmanns*, Essen, 1979, chapter 'Neubergleute'.

46. See references in note 44.

47. BAK B102, 3306, Hensel to Ullrich, 23.10.1952.

48. Ibid.

funding was conditional on the right pedagogical measures being adopted.

The Union, Employers and Apprentices

The IGB, too, gave its unqualified support to the attempt to turn mining into a skilled profession and to increasing apprentice recruitment. As early as 1946, it had joined with employers' representatives and labour administration officials in working on a special committee designed to promote apprentice recruitment. At the big Ruhr coal conferences in 1948 organised by North-Rhine-Westphalian government and by the bizonal authorities in Frankfurt, union leaders, state officials and employers were unanimous in calling for rapid expansion of apprentice intake.[49]

The union shared the employers' preoccupation with the status of mining work and the miner. Indeed, the union was one of the strongest advocates of increasing mining's social standing and encouraging the public to see it as a skilled profession. 'Der bergmännische Berufsstolz verlange es, die öffentliche Meinung dahingehend zu beeinflussen, daß nicht jeder ohne weiteres Hauer werden könne.'[50] Other union figures were continually at pains to point out, as Johann Platte put it, that: 'Die bergmännische Tätigkeit setzt eine Reihe von Fertigkeiten und Kenntnissen voraus, die nur in einer systematischen Ausbildung und Schulung erworben werden können.'[51] Many union figures seem to have been as absorbed as their managerial counterparts by the image of the miner of the past. Certainly, the *Neue Zeitung* correspondent quoted earlier found this to be so.[52]

The other key reason for the union's support for apprenticeships was their unhappiness with the continued influx of adult new labour. The adult newcomers were seen as hard to organise,

49. DGBA File 'IV Bergbau 1946–1948', memo, 'Werbung für den Bergbau', 6.5.1947.
50. OBADA 118.10/4/56, memo concerning a meeting to discuss the draft directive on miners' training of 2.8.1956, 2.11.1956.
51. Johann Platte, 'Die Nachwuchsfrage im Kohlenbergbau', *Arbeitsblatt für die britische Zone*, vol. 2, no. 11, 1948, pp. 399–400 at 400.
52. 'Der "Lager Mensch" – Symptom einer Entwicklung', *Neue Zeitung*, 7.8.1951; Platte, 'Die Nachwuchsfrage'.

partly because of the high wastage rate and partly because of a lack of understanding for the union movement. Even more seriously (as chapter 9 will show in greater detail) the IGB became worried in 1948–9 that the employers were using continued recruitment of adult labour as a means of intimidating and undermining the existing labour force. In effect, the IGB wanted to construct a skill barrier, controlling and restricting access to the workforce through insisting on a lengthy training period.

There is a sense in which the close co-operation between employers and unions on the apprenticeship programme was paradoxical. Both appear to have been partially motivated by fears or attitudes towards the other which their very co-operation on apprenticeships might have allayed. Employers promoted the apprenticeship scheme because they were worried about the radicalism of the labour force; yet the unions' attachment to the scheme revealed the labour movement to be almost as 'romantically conservative' as the employers themselves. The union was worried about the employers using mass recruitment to weaken the labour movement, when in reality, as we have seen, there was nothing management would have liked more than to have done without adult recruitment altogether. The contradiction between the union's fears and management's behaviour became clear in negotiations over the trainees' wages at the beginning of 1949. Frightened that the employers were trying to weaken the workforce with large numbers of adult recruits, the unions entered the negotiations keen to reduce the privileges offered the adult trainees (*Umschüler*), and thus to reduce the supply of adult labour to the pits. What they discovered, however, was that the employers were equally desirous of removing these entitlements.[53]

The two sides give the impression of shadow-boxing, of fearing imaginary opponents. In part, this is to argue with hindsight, disregarding the uncertainties of the situation in 1948–9. The IGB could not yet be sure how the employers would behave. They could not know yet that European coal demand would remain reasonably firm and the mines' demand for labour reasonably strong. They remained, not unnaturally, worried by

53. AZG File '"61" [= I1 61], Bezahlung der Neubergleute bzw Umschüler', undated memo concerning meeting of the Tarifausschuß on 11.3.1949; and see below, note 63.

the precedents of the second half of the 1920s. For their part, the employers could see a power struggle between communists and social democrats taking place in the union and works councils. They could not yet be sure that the spirit of co-operativeness and conservatism would prevail within the IGB. At another level, however, the paradoxical nature of the co-operation on apprenticeship does reveal, particularly on the employers' side, a profound contradiction between, on the one hand, their ideal labour force and ideal model of labour relations, in neither of which the union figured, and on the other the day-to-day reality of the post-war situation in which they found themselves not only having to, but also easily able to, co-operate with union leaders. This is a point to which we shall return in chapter 9.

The Impact of the Apprenticeship

At the beginning of the 1950s it seemed as if the coal industry was well on its way to transforming perceptions of mining in the outside world. Above all, there were its achievements in recruiting good-quality youngsters for the apprenticeships. As well as mobilising reserves of young labour from far-flung regions, the mines appeared to have changed attitudes within the Ruhr too. In 1952, male school-leavers in Dortmund put down mining as their first choice more often than any other trade. In Rheinhausen in 1951, 20 per cent of male school leavers went to the mines and the proportion was even higher in the following year. An impressive community study carried out by the Sozialforschungsstelle Dortmund (SoFoSt) argued that general perceptions of the miner in the town were improving. Local girls, it was argued, no longer had any negative feelings about marrying miners.[54] Yet, in reality, the mines' achievements in this area fell far short of expectations. The employers' overall target of an apprentice population of around 35,000–40,000 could not be sustained (see figure 5.1). By the mid-1950s the apprentice population was already on the wane.

---

54. See e.g. 'Bergbau zieht auch Bergmannssöhne wieder an', *WAZ*, Moers edn, 25.10.1952; Helmuth Croon and K. Utermann, *Zeche und Gemeinde. Untersuchungen über den Strukturwandel einer Zechengemeinde im nördlichen Ruhrgebiet*, Tübingen, 1958, pp. 109ff.

Reshaping the Ruhr

Figure 5.1 Young workers in the Ruhr mines 1950–8

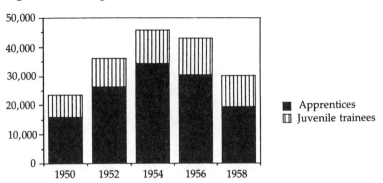

Source: UVR (ed.), *Jahresbericht fur die Jahre 1958–60*, p. 89 facing.

Part of the explanation was that school rolls were falling. In the school year 1953–4, 485,070 boys left school, whereas in the year 1957–8 there were only 360,244 male school-leavers, a drop of 25 per cent. Yet over the same period, the number of mining apprentices hired fell by almost 60 per cent, indicating that there were other problems too. It was evident that the growth of other opportunities on the labour market was drawing potential recruits away from the mines.[55] The collieries had never really succeeded in establishing mining as a desirable profession, despite appearances. The mines' ability to attract young labour, considerable though it was, was based on the temporary exigencies of the post-war period. This applied particularly to the substantial recruitment from outside the Ruhr. Between 60 and 70 per cent of hostel occupants were refugees, suggesting that acute material pressures were the main reason for sending youngsters to the mines. Few established citizens of West Germany were willing to send their sons into mining, even for a well-paid apprenticeship that offered good accommodation. It was clear from the start that once the expellees were more settled and more prosperous the same would apply to them. An even more revealing aspect of the apprentices' social background was that almost one-third of hostel occupants had lost at

55. 'Das Nachwuchsproblem im Bergbau', p. 331; BAK B102, 33189, BWiM, internal memo from Imhäuser to Classen, 30.5.1951; UVR, *Jahresbericht für die Jahre 1958 bis 1960*, p. 89 facing.

least one parent, in most cases the father. This was proof that the mines were benefiting from the acute but temporary financial difficulties in which a significant proportion of the population found itself after the war.[56] Within the Ruhr, too, the mines had never succeeded in transforming perceptions of mining. A lot of the references to change in the SoFoSt study, for instance, were exaggerated. The Dortmund team felt they had a mission to help the miner lose his proletarian status and this influenced their interpretation of the material.[57]

Apart from leaving public perceptions largely unchanged, the other major disappointment to the employers was that they failed to create out of the apprentices a new type of miner with greater stability and loyalty than his established or adult compatriot. Though the apprentices themselves normally stayed until the end of their training, the ex-apprentices or *Knappen* (i.e. those who had completed their training but had not yet had the further working experience necessary to take the *Hauer* exam[58]) were not much more likely to stay in the mines than other young adults. Indeed, a great many left soon after passing their exams.[59]

The Imaginary Elite

It is easy to see why the employers failed to convince the apprentices that they were part of a new elite. Almost every aspect of their working experience contradicted it. As Hans Diether Baroth's autobiographical reminiscences make clear, apprentices were well aware that for much of the apprenticeship period their training was almost a sham – all the more so,

56. 'Maßnahmen zur Behebung der Not'; Daberkow, 'Die Seßhaftmachung', pp. 50ff; 'Sechs Jahre Außenstelle Bergbau', p. 109.

57. Information from an interview with Professor Helmut Croon, 9.4.1984. For more detail, see Mark Roseman, 'New Miners in the Ruhr: Rebuilding the Workforce in the Ruhr Mines, 1945–1958', PhD dissertation, Warwick University, 1987, pp. 282ff.

58. Strictly speaking, they were *Knappen* only for the first year of employment after training and then became *Lehrhauer*. However, the term is used here as a blanket term in order to distinguish easily between former apprentices and former adult trainees.

59. See Hibernia Konzern (ed.), *Sozialbericht 1957*, p. 24; Ges.Verb. File 'Arbeitsausschuß 1948–1958', minutes of Arbeitsausschuß für Ausbildungsfragen (Arb.aus.f.A) meeting, 17.3.1955 and 5.4.1955.

because the mines' response to the problem of how usefully to employ the youngsters was invariably to put them at the picking-belt, sorting coal. Here was an unpleasant job that needed to be done and one not easily mechanised. As a comparatively low-paid group, the apprentices were a cheap source of labour. Of all the complaints raised about the apprenticeship, the one about lengthy stints at the picking-belt was the most common. For years, the labour directors tried to reduce the time spent there by apprentices and with time they seem to have had success. But as late as the mid-1950s it was still a frequent topic of complaint and discussion.[60]

The cost of this type of work was not that apprentices left in droves during their training. On the contrary, wastage during the apprenticeship was low.[61] But it was detrimental to the general goal of enhancing the industry's status. It was widely recognised both inside and outside the industry that the training offered by mining fell short of that offered by other trade apprenticeships. A confidential paper on training produced by one of the mining industry's leading experts concluded 'daß die Knappenprüfungen den handwerklichen Gesellenprüfungen, Industriefacharbeiterprüfungen und kaufmännischen Gehilfenprüfungen in ihren Anforderungen im allgemeinen nicht voll entsprechen'.[62] Nothing proved this more effectively than the fact that the *Knappen* did exactly the same work as the former adult trainees with their few months of training. This was one very obvious reason why the apprenticeship strategy could be only partially effective in enhancing mining's status.

Because they did the same work, it proved impossible to introduce anything more than a symbolic differential between the remuneration of adult trainee and skilled *Knappe*. This came out clearly in the 1949 pay negotiations, when both employers and unions sought to downgrade the position of the adult

60. BAK B102, 33091, minutes of AAA meeting on 10.4.1956, annex; IGBEA, Handakten Rudi Quast, File 'Arbeitskreis-Arbeitsdirektoren 1952–1956', minutes of meetings of Essen/Gelsenkirchen district, 13.5.1954 and Recklinghausen district, 1.12.1954.

61. Ges.Verb. File 'Arbeitsausschuß 1948–1958', minutes of (Arb.aus.f.A) meeting, 17.3.1955.

62. Ges.Verb. File 'Arbeitsausschuß 1948–1958', annex to minutes of meeting on 21.3.1957: Steffen, 'Grundsatzfragen der bergmännischen Berufsausbildung', Hamborn, no date.

trainees and enhance that of the qualified apprentices.[63] The regulations which emerged did remove some of the special contractual privileges the trainees had enjoyed. Yet they were noteworthy for the very limited way in which they favoured apprentices and *Knappen* at the cost of adult trainees. During their first year on contract wage, adult trainees received 90 per cent of the full wage, in the second year 92.5 per cent and thereafter until they became *Hauer* 95 per cent. Previously the *Knappen* had been on this scale too, but now they were made 2.5 per cent better off, beginning with a 7.5 per cent deduction and attaining the minimum 5 per cent deduction already in their second year. This small advantage was a sign that in practice the two groups did the same work and that neither the employers or the union could afford to alienate new trainees.[64]

In practice, there was often no difference at all between the two groups' earnings because the mines frequently did not make these deductions. The reason was the increasing number of men employed under the one-man contract-wage system. Under the older collective contract, the wage was divided up between the men, the *Hauer* receiving a full share each and the less experienced men receiving their share minus the appropriate percentage. A new trainee would thus receive a full share minus 10 per cent. In other words, the smaller wages for the newcomers had never benefited the employers and instead were designed to compensate the experienced men for the lower output of newer colleagues. In faces where the one-man contract wage was introduced and wages were paid individually, rather than to the group, the situation was quite different. Here the newcomer was entirely dependent on his own work rather than receiving his share of a wage achieved by group output. He enjoyed no benefit from the higher output of experienced colleagues and, equally, did not depress their wages either. There was thus no justification for taking a percentage off his wage –

63. AZG File 'I 1 26 Zuweisung . . .', GMSO, circular no. 41, 4.2.1947, annex: 'Merkblatt für die Anwerbung von Arbeitskräften für den rheinisch-westfälischen Steinkohlenbergbau', 10.1.1947; memo concerning meeting of the NRW mines Tarifausschuß, 28.1.1949; AZG File '"61" [= I1 61] Bezahlung der Neubergleute bzw Umschüler', minutes of meeting of Tarifausschuß on 11.3.1949.

64. AZG File 'I 1 26 Zuweisung . . .', minutes of meeting of Tarifausschuß on 11.3.1949; IGB (ed.) *Jahrbuch 1947*, p. 99; *Jahrbuch 1950/1*, p. 238.

his lower output and thus lower earnings themselves penalised him enough for his inexperience. Though some employers still made the deductions, many did not, and it became increasingly general practice to pay all men on one-man contract wage the same amount. Consequently, even the small status difference laid down in the wage regulations disappeared.[65]

The apprentices thus did not form an elite within the work-force, just as the miners no longer formed an elite within the industrial workforce as a whole. In their eulogies to the miner of yore, this was one fact the employers conveniently ignored. To see the mentality of past generations while ignoring the material context of that mentality was to misrepresent the past and misunderstand the present. The proud and loyal miner of Prussian tradition had undoubtedly existed; his sense of self-esteem had undoubtedly expressed considerable spiritual gratification at his occupation and his work. Yet that gratification at being a miner had developed and flourished against a background of very clear material and social privileges. Pay levels, the length of the working day, the existence of a social security system, the privilege of uniform and the special relationship to the monarch – these were but some of the very real benefits accruing to the miner before liberalisation in the mid-nineteenth century. In the meantime, *all* these benefits had disappeared or had been acquired by other groups of workers as well. It was nonsense to harken back to the mentality of the nineteenth century and yet ignore the vastly changed social and economic context.

Status and Stability

The failure of the apprenticeship programme to create work-force stability was not due solely to the discrepancy between the formal qualification and the reality of training, work and re-muneration in the mines. A second major point must be that the hopes placed in the scheme were based on a misunderstanding of workforce stability. The employers, as we have seen, chose to believe that there was a link between a rounded, secure person-

65. See Köker's complaint in BAK B102, 33091, minutes of AAA meeting, 14.12.1953; BWiM, memo, 17.12.1953; BBA 32, 741, minutes of Hibernia directors' meeting, 4.6.1948.

ality and a willingness to remain in the same job. The view that those leaving the mines in the post-1945 period were suffering from social anomie, as (for instance) Pastor Dannenmann claimed, while those who stayed were socially secure and well adjusted, was widely held. 'Es liegt nahe', wrote one observer, 'Arbeitsplatzmobilität mit einer Tendenz zur unsteten Lebensführung, zur Aversion gegen feste und ungeregelte Arbeit, zur Renitenz und alldem zusammenzubringen, was durch den Sammelnamen des Asozialen gedeckt wird.'[66] Consequently, countless lectures and works newspaper articles wallowed in mining's traditions or sought to revive a belief in stable, recognisable social hierarchies.

Yet, as a careful contemporary investigation of wastage in the mines revealed, if anything the reverse was true. Those leaving the mines were often precisely those who were secure, qualified and socially well-integrated enough not to worry about job changing and to be confident of finding employment elsewhere. By the mid-1950s, the employers were grudgingly accepting this. In 1956, the UVR's Manpower and Training Committee acknowledged that the 'Tendenz zur Verwandlung des Berufs in einen Job, die z.T. in der Veränderung der technischen Produktion selbst begründet ist' was spreading to the German economy.[67]

Apprentices and Adults

Whatever the intrinsic weaknesses of the apprenticeship programme, or the measures which accompanied it, it is a fact that few apprentices left before they qualified. True, large numbers left soon after completing their training and some planned this during the apprenticeship itself, indicating, at the very least, that the apprenticeship was not engendering any love of the mining profession. For many others, however, the decisive stimulus to leave the industry came with the experience of working on the adult faces after qualifying. It was the shock of transition from the relatively protected world of the apprentice

66. Institut für Sozialforschung, Frankfurt, 'Die subjektiven und objektiven Abkehrgründe ', p. 226.
67. See ibid. and BAK B102, 033092, minutes of AAA meeting, 12.12.1956.

to the harsher environment outside that stimulated their departure. Even after employers made greater efforts at easing the transition, for instance by creating special faces where output norms were set below those of the adult faces, it proved very difficult to square the two worlds of apprentice and adult miner.[68] Ultimately, the point was that the apprentice strategy could not be expected to achieve workforce stability on its own. It could succeed only if the mines managed, at least partially, to create a hospitable environment for their *adult* labour. The high levels of wastage among both adult trainees and qualified former apprentices suggests that the industry failed to do this.

The longer the collieries were forced by wastage to maintain high levels of unskilled adult recruitment, the more suspect appeared their claim that mining had become a skilled profession. The questions of wage and skill comparability would not have arisen with the same intensity if, as the mines had intended, the apprentices had indeed become the main source of new labour for the pits. Yet wastage remained such that the pits were forced to hire 50,000 or more new adult recruits each year.[69] This dwarfed the apprentice intake and, given the fact that adult recruits and apprentices did the same work and received the same pay, made nonsense of the notion that mining was a skilled profession. In many respects, therefore, the mines' response to adult new labour held the key to the success of the apprenticeships – much as the industry had hoped that the relationship would be the other way round. It is thus time to look at the industry's strategy for retaining and stabilising its adult workforce.

68. Ges.Verb. File 'Arbeitsausschuß 1948–1958', minutes of Arb.aus.f.A meeting, 5.4.1955.
69. Ges.Verb., StdKW., table 'Belegschaftswechsel – Arbeiter untertage. Ruhr'.

6
The Foundations of Stability?
Housing New Labour, 1948–1958

Housing and Integration

Dream though they might of a future in which there were no adult trainees and in which the growing number of former apprentices transformed the industry, the employers could not ignore the fact that it was vital to retain the 150,000 or so adults who had come to the industry since the war. Continuing high wastage rates in 1948 merely served to underline the urgency of doing so. The key to the problem was believed to be adequate provision of decent housing. 'Die Frage der Beständigkeit der Neu-Bergleute steht im ursächlichen Zusammenhang mit der Lösung der Wohnraumsfrage,' commented a manager from the Concordia mine in 1949.[1] And a major report on the mining industry concluded in 1951 that 'there is general agreement that miners' housing is the No. 1 requirement for stabilizing the workers and increasing efficiency'.[2]

There were some obvious reasons for extolling the virtues of housing development. The employers evidently felt they had more scope away from the work process to forge the right conditions for integration and regeneration. The mines themselves would be dirty and unhealthy places whatever the employers did; but a positive living environment might compensate for the negative aspects of the work. *Ausgleich*, compensation, is a word that crops up in almost every piece ever written about miners' housing; and it is a mark of the importance ascribed to creating the right living environment

---

1. BBA 8, 384, Concordia to DKBL, Abteilung Arbeitseinsatz, 25.2.1949.
2. BAK B102, 21258, Office of the US High Commissioner for Germany, PR Division, 'The West German Coal Industry since 1945', 14.11.1951, p. 6.

that there were a great many such pieces written.[3] Then, too, there was historical precedent. Ever since the nineteenth century, housing had been used to reduce workforce fluctuation. Given that in the post-1945 period, as in the nineteenth century, there was an acute scarcity of housing in the Ruhr, it seemed plausible that men would once again settle wherever they and their families could find a decent home. For the collieries, the idea of offering housing as an inducement was attractive also because of the financial assistance they expected (and, as we have seen, eventually received) from the state.[4]

Thus there were plenty of obvious reasons for believing that housing would act as a powerful and not too costly inducement to stay in the mines. Yet it would be a mistake to see in housing simply a material *incentive*, a financial inducement on top of wages and pensions. Policy discussions about house design and home ownership reveal that housing was seen as an important task of social engineering. In addition, there was implicit in the idea of making housing an incentive the difficult social–political issue, which generated considerable discussion in the post-war era, of whether it was legitimate to link tenancy agreement and job contract. Looking at these issues in more detail, we find, once again, the Ruhr bourgeoisie engaged in a modest but concerted attempt at reshaping post-war society.

Designing the Miner's House

What was the optimal living environment for satisfying the miner and settling the newcomer? A useful point of entry to the views of the policy-makers is a short paper written by Professor Franz Knipping, which exemplifies in concise form many of the demands, images and hopes that gave impetus and shape to the miners' housing programme.[5] Knipping was director of

---

3. Dr Fütterer, 'Bergmannswohnstätten im Ruhrgebiet', *Arbeitsblatt für die britische Zone*, vol. 1, 1947, pp. 450–1.

4. Otto Lübcke, *Die Subventionierung des Wohnungsbaues insbes. seit 1945*, Münster, 1951, p. 54; Ministerial-Blatt NRW, Ausgabe A, 6.4.1948, 1, 12, p. 121; HStAD NW53, 465, Land Manpower Dept, Housing and Building Branch to Chairman of Housing Reconstruction Committee, 5.5.1948.

5. HStAD NW73, 136, Professor Knipping to WAM, 30.10.1951, annex: Knipping, 'Der Bergarbeiterwohnungsbau', Essen, October 1952.

the Treuhandstelle für Bergmannswohnstätten,[6] the housing association set up in connection with the miners' housing levy of 1920 and, ever since then, a central participant in the construction of miners' dwellings. The paper was written in October 1951, when the Miners' Housing Act was becoming law and it was apparent that a major new building initiative was about to begin. Sent to the WAM, the paper's main purpose was to ensure that the NRW government's building policy took into account the Treuhandstelle's wishes.

The actual architectural and architectonic demands made in the paper are very simple and can be summarised in a couple of sentences. The ideal house, argues Knipping, should have plenty of light and a good-sized garden with a stall built into the house so that the miner can keep small animals. The need for light and a garden in turn calls for a semi-detatched, two-storey building style. Whilst this is more expensive than multi-storey flats, Knipping argues that the miners' house would not fulfil its function if the only criterion were to be low building costs. In any case, the higher costs of this design can be considerably offset by keeping the level of amenities fairly simple. As far as the internal structure of the house goes, the most important feature is the combined living room-kitchen (*Wohnküche*), a traditional feature of mining homes.[7]

More significant, for our purposes, than the actual design proposed were the reasons for choosing these specific features and the hopes and expectations attached to them and to the miner's house in general. The first thing that strikes the reader is the confidence with which Knipping speaks for the miner. The author has no hesitation in defining the miner's needs and without a trace of hesitation or embarassment describes the miner's daily rhythm, even the mental state with which he returns home from work. 'Nach getaner Arbeit kommt der Bergmann nach Hause, körperlich sehr ruhebedürftig, geistig aber mit dem Wunsch, sich zu unterhalten. Er will seine Frau und seine Kinder um sich haben.'[8] The author's assurance is all the more striking when it is borne in mind that, at the time

6. The Reconstruction Minister was in fact a member of the Treuhandstelle's controlling exective.
7. Knipping, 'Bergarbeiterwohnungsbau', *passim*.
8. Ibid., p. 3.

Knipping was writing, more than 50 per cent of those on the housing lists had been in mining for six years or less, and many had spent their formative years in other occupations. Yet this confidence was a pervasive feature of the housing establishment. There were hundreds of articles talking about the wants and needs of the miner, but until the Americans came and commissioned one, there was not a single survey of miners' wishes and preferences. The German housing officials were ostensibly privy even to the deep-seated wishes of the miner's wife. The ECA representatives in the Ruhr noted wrily that 'der Bergmann hat viele Sprecher, vom Zechendirektor bis zum Gewerkschaftsvertreter. Es sind dies natürlich alles Menschen [*sic*; it should be *Männer*], aber sie haben keine Hemmungen einem zu sagen, was die Bergmannsfrau haben möchte.'[9] It was evident that Knipping and many other writers were operating with a mental image of the miner so firm that it allowed them to utter apodictical truths without the need for market research.[10] Indeed, market research would be almost irrelevant, since the policy-makers were aiming to satisfy the miner's deep and unconscious needs rather than his mere subjective wishes.[11]

The most important of these perceived unconscious needs relate to the garden, to the soil. At one level the garden provides a necessary compensation to mining work. The noise, the poor air and the artificial light at work make it imperative that the miner receive fresh air and sunlight outside working hours. At a deeper spiritual level, garden work confirms and sustains that close relationship to nature and the earth which is the mark of

9. HStAD NW73, 55, translation (into German) of an MSA Housing Dept paper, dated 17.10.1952, German title 'Deutsches Kohlenbergarbeiter-Wohnungsbauprogramm. 2. Fortschrittsbericht', p. 14. It is striking that in this German translation, the English 'men' was mistranslated as 'Menschen'. It is evident that in the climate of the day, the idea of male officials making these decisions was so much part of the order of things that the translator did not even notice the point the text was trying to make.
10. Even the composite nouns used (*Bergmannswohnstätte* and *Bergmannssofa*), indicate the strength of the notion of a timeless *Ur-Bergmann*, transcending the vagaries of labour fluctuations and the changes of generations.
11. SoFoSt, 'Soziologische Erhebung zum Bergarbeiterwohnungsbauprogramm. Schlußbericht', unpublished MS, Dortmund, 1952, p. 5; Elizabeth Pfeil, *Die Wohnwünsche der Bergarbeiter. Soziologische Erhebung, Deutung und Kritik der Wohnvorstellungen eines Berufes*, Tübingen, 1954; Knipping, 'Bergarbeiterwohnungsbau', pp. 3, 1; Franz Knipping, 'Die Treuhandstelle für Bergmannswohnstätten im rheinisch-westfälischen Steinkohlenbezirk', *Glückauf*, vol. 85, nos. 31/2, 1949, pp. 570–3.

the true miner. An urban way of life and the concomitant disassociation from the soil (*Grund und Boden*) always bring the wish to change occupation and the miner does not remain a miner, or at least not one whose heart and soul are committed to mining. A little earlier in the text, another passage also conveys the importance of maintaining a close link with the soil. Knipping writes that it is particularly important that miners with children have this type of house 'in der die Kinder heranwachsen und dann auch mit der Gartenarbeit vertraut gemacht werden'.[12]

These images reoccur in countless other places. In 1948, when miners' housing was just beginning to move from repairs to new construction, the Reconstruction Minister, aware that this was the first major new housing project in the whole of North Rhine-Westphalia, commissioned a number of architects to come up with new housing designs. There were, however, several features deemed too important to be left to the whim of the architects and the ministry therefore specified them in advance. They were, almost without exception, precisely the points Knipping outlined above, again with special stress on low buildings, large gardens and the outhouse.[13]

The notion of the link between farmer and miner, of the symmetry between two different types of battle with nature, continually resurfaces. The miners, the Reconstruction Ministry's Dr Fütterer was glad to say to a group of foreign visitors, are not really *Städter* at all and 'haben noch ein gesundes, ein unmittelbares Verhältnis zum Boden, zum Gartenbau'.[14] Even the miners' union shared a similar vision. 'Wohnen ist mehr als bloßer Aufenthalt innerhalb vier Wänden,' wrote the IGB's housing specialists in a letter to the DGB in 1953; 'Wohnen ist für uns der Ausdruck einer Weltanschauung. Gerade unser Bergmann erstrebt das Eigenheim mit einem kleinen Garten, in dem er etwas Gemüse zieht, seine Hühner, Tauben und Kaninchen hält und nach der Arbeit sich entspannt . . .'[15]

Other planning proposals introduced an additional, though

12. Knipping, 'Bergarbeiterwohnungsbau', pp. 2–3.
13. HStAD NW73, 260, WAM, memo, 'Der Wohnungsneubau für die Bergarbeiterfamilie', 4.10.1948.
14. NW73, 55, WAM, copy of untitled speech dated 4.12.1952, signed Dr Fütterer, Abteilungsleiter I.
15. DGBA File 'IGBergbau (1949–1966)', IGB Hauptverwaltung to DGB Vorstand, 21.3.1953. See also chapter 9.

related, 'romantic' vision, namely the idea of 'rooting' (*verwurzeln*) the newcomer. The simple house, the semi-rural atmosphere and the large garden were seen as vital ingredients in settling the newcomers and tying them to mining and the Ruhr. When in 1948 the Reconstruction Minister laid down that every house should have a vegetable garden and an integral stall, he did so not only to meet the wishes of the established miners, but also explicitly to help root the newcomers in local soil.[16] Here, the image of the simple miner at peace with nature is fused with that of the newcomer 'growing roots' through work in the garden, a mixture also present in Knipping's own work, in his vision of the youngster being acquainted with garden work. Sometimes this image was linked to a belief that many newcomers had their own stable, rural qualities that needed to be protected. When Dr Fütterer argued that the miners were not really urban folk, he extended this praise to the newcomers too, and no doubt had in mind the many refugees from small-town and rural environments who numbered amongst the new miners.[17]

Of course, it would be wrong to underestimate the (perhaps unconsciously) tactical element in Knipping's lyricism and other similar broadsides. The housing societies in general and Treuhandstelle in particular were worried about a loss of influence. The specific problem for the Treuhandstelle was that it was already clear that the new Miners' Housing Act was not going to give it the same special function as had the earlier law of 1920. Knipping was trying to make sure his organisation was nevertheless closely involved in the building programme. Thus the notion that the miner had unconscious needs and that it was necessary for experienced experts to transform these into architectural reality was at the same time an argument for the continued involvement of the Treuhandstelle, which 'aufgrund ihres gesetzlichen Auftrages sich einzig und allein mit dem Bau und der Verwaltung von Bergarbeiterwohnungen befaßt hat'.[18]

All of the Ruhr housing societies were on the defensive in the early 1950s because the American ECA administration was

16. HStAD NW73, 260, WAM IA/300, memo, 4.10.1948; see also *Mitteilungen der KfSA 1952*, nos. 1/2, p. 3.
17. HStAD NW73, 55, WAM, copy of untitled speech dated 4.12.1952, signed Dr Fütterer, Abteilungsleiter I.
18. HStAD 73, 136, Knipping to WAM, 30.10.1951.

leading a concerted attack on traditional building practices. The housing associations were worried that the ECA's idea of an architects' competition would result in outsiders taking over Ruhr building, bring in new ideas and force the associations to make complicated and expensive revisions in their building methods in order to compete. To a certain extent, therefore, talk of the miners' needs was simply an attempt to legitimate existing practices. It was no accident that so many officials were agreed on the same housing design. It was precisely this type of house that the Treuhandstelle and many other housing societies, particularly those building outside the densest urban areas, had traditionally built. There was more than a little disingenuousness in Franz Knipping's lyrical ode to the *Wohnküche*; the point about the living-room/kitchen was that if the whole family congregated there, the cooking stove could double as the heating system and the rest of the house could remain unheated. In most miners' houses until then the *Wohnküche* was the only heated room.[19]

Nevertheless, there was clearly much more than tactics involved. The three related images – the simple miner with basic but modest needs, the miner reaffirmed through working the soil, and the newcomer rooted in the locality by the right house and especially the right garden – go a long way to explaining not only the strong commitment to established patterns of house construction, but also the hopes and expectations which the employers had of housing. 'Werden die vorher skizzierten Bedürfnisse des Bergmanns berücksichtigt,' Knipping assured the Minister, 'dann erfüllt seine Wohnung neben der Unterbringung noch einen anderen Zweck. Sie macht den Bergmann zufrieden, erfüllt seine von der Natur als Folge seiner beruflichen Tätigkeit gegebenen Notwendigkeiten, ihm selbst meist unbewußt[!], und läßt den Wunsch des Berufswechsels erst gar nicht aufkommen.' But if the wrong house were built, if the link to the land were broken, then the miner will be lost to his profession, 'er bleibt nicht mehr Bergmann, sicher nicht mit Lust und Liebe'.[20]

19. MSA, '2. Fortschrittsbericht'; Knipping, 'Bergarbeiterwohnungsbau', p. 3; HStAD NW73, 55, WAM, copy of untitled speech dated 4.12.1952, signed Dr Fütterer, Abteilungsleiter I.
20. Ibid.

'All mod cons': The Challenge to Romantic Conservatism in Housing Design

In addition to the romantic conservatives there were also, initially in small numbers, the 'modernisers', who believed that the miners should be given the chance to raise their standard of 'living-culture', as it was termed. Very often the 'modernisers', be they in the IGB or in the WAM, shared many assumptions with the romantic conservatives. But they challenged the image of the simple, rustic interior and called for such features as a separation of kitchen and living-room, the introduction, where possible, of modern equipment and so on.[21]

The strongest challenge to the romantic conservatives came from the Americans. The head of the ECAs (later MSA) department for industrial building, James Butler, organised a veritable crusade against what he saw as 'building by committee'. Butler believed that 'die bescheidenste deutsche Wohnung [ist] eine teuere, solide aussehende, aber unpraktische Angelegenheit' and that the conservatism of the German building administration and housing associations was hindering the development of more modern building methods and houses with more modern amenities. In 1951, in an initial programme costed at DM45 million, the ECA failed to get many of its proposals adopted, partly because the programme was co-financed with German money. It therefore resolved in 1952 to finance its own programme fully so that it would be able to control the conditions. Butler commissioned a major survey of miners' housing preferences, which at one stroke abolished a great many myths about the miners' supposed conservatism. The 1952 programme was also preceded by a fully open competition between architects, whereas in 1951 the ECA had only succeeded in achieving a very limited competition.[22]

Both the survey and the MSA housing project which followed it gave the 'modernisers' a decisive boost. The ECA buildings were mainly large estates composed of long rows of two-storey houses, each with a large garden. Apart from the generally

21. HStAD NW73, 260, WAM IA/300, memo, 4.10.1948; NW73, 10, WAM, internal memo from Ref. IA2 to Ministerialdirektor, 7.10.1952; IGB (ed.), *Jahrbuch 1953*, p. 740.

22. MSA, '2. Fortschrittsbericht', pp. 8–11; HStAD NW10, 90, DKBL to WAM 12.6.1951 and annex; NW73, 55, BWoM II56/51, memo, 20.12.1951.

unpopular long row, adopted for money-saving reasons, new aspects of the houses' design were the modern kitchen with built-in cooker and, in some cases, the unheard-of luxury of a fridge, central heating and modern bathrooms. Though there were a number of protests afterwards, the buildings were really a triumph for the MSA since they cost no more to build than the traditional miners' house. Within four years of the first MSA project, virtually all houses in the Miners' Housing Programme were being built with separate or semi-separated kitchens and most of them with built-in cookers.[23]

The Americans saw the strength of the opposition to the programme as a sign that vested interests were being undermined. Certainly, there was anxiety that provision of fridges, for example, would force other builders to do likewise. But at a deeper level, by challenging the myth of the simple miner with his simple unchanging tastes, the Americans were also challenging the myth of the house's power of integration. The Americans themselves saw housing purely in terms of a subjective incentive. As modernism spread during the 1950s, some of the initial hopes of miners' housing disappeared.[24] On the other hand, the acceptance of a modern interior did not necessarily mean acceptance of a purely functional attitude towards the house. There is considerable evidence that many of the German advocates of the new designs linked to their demands the hope that by raising the status and self-esteem of the miner they would create a settled and contented social class. This applied to the IGB, which, having previously been lined up with the romantic conservatives, became an enthusiastic adherent of housing 'durch die die Wohnkultur unseres Berufstandes gehoben wird'.[25] Yet, as this formulation implies, the union did not relinquish its belief in housing's socially integrative powers. Some of the new labour-directors[26] seem to have made it their

23. HStAD NW73, 10, WAM, internal memo from Group IA, IA2 to Ministerialdirektor, 7.10.1952; Group IIIA 4, memo, 18.12.1952; MSA, '2. Fortschrittsbericht', pp. 10ff; P. Christoffel, 'Bergarbeiterwohnungsbau im rheinischwestfälischen Steinkohlenbezirk' in *Deutsche Siedlungs- und Wohnungspolitik. Gegenwartsproblematik und Zukunftsaspekte*, Cologne, 1956, pp. 343–6 at 344.
24. HStAD NW73, 55, Minister für Arbeit, Soziales und Wohnungsbau VIA2 to MSA Housing Mission, 31.12.1953.
25. Quote is from IGB (ed.), *Jahrbuch 1953*, p. 740. See also Schulz's comments in MSA, '2. Fortschrittsbericht', p. 21 and IGB (ed.), *Jahrbuch 1954*, p. 662.
26. The *Arbeitsdirektoren* were the labour-nominated members of the management board (*Vorstand*). The directors were introduced by the 1951 Codetermina-

personal mission to raise the miners' social standing and self-esteem through better housing, as Walter Wille wrote in 1954: 'Ganz besonders wurde die Wohnkultur nach neuen Richtlinien durchgeführt. Es kam mir besonders darauf an, der Wohnung des einfachen Menschen die persönliche Note zu geben, vor allen Dingen ihn aus dem "Arme-Leute-Milieu" herauszurei-ßen.'[27] Amongst other things, Wille promoted the separate kitchen/living-room, a proper bathroom and provision for motorcycles, as well as the decent gardens that everyone could agree on.[28]

Alongside modernising the house's amenities and promoting the bourgeois dining-room, there were also attempts to improve the miners' taste in furniture. The IGB encouraged exhibitions of furniture appropriate for the smaller size of post-war housing. The employers too, particularly the 'Vereinigung der Freunde von Kunst und Kultur im Bergbau' did their bit to provide the miners with what they saw as a valid and integrative aesthetic.[29] One of its members, Heinrich Winkelmann, wrote of the need to assist the miners in aesthetic judgements about furnishing their house. He outlined what was wrong with the miners' choice of furniture:

> Die riesigen, schwellenden, Unruhe ausstrahlenden Küchenbufetts, die schweren protzigen Betten und Frisierkommoden, kurz all das was wir heute als 'Gelsenkirchener Barock' bezeichnen, ist in Wahrheit den inneren, geraden, einfachen Werten des Bergmanns fremd . . . Gerade weil wir mit der Frage der Wohnkultur zur persönlichsten Sphäre unserer Bergleute, ins Familienleben, in das Innenleben vorstossen, gerade darum ergibt sich hier für uns eine Aufgabe grundsätzlicher Bedeutung. Die Erziehung zu echtem Formgefühl, zu einem Gefühl für abgewogene Verhältnisse zwischen Raum und Einrichtung, die Hinwendung zu echten Formen

---

tion Law, but generally were not nominated in the mines until late 1952/3, because of the company restructuring going on.

27. IGBEA Handakten Rudi Quast, File 'M. Assistenten Tagungen (Alt)', Walter Wille to Heinrich Imig, 28.6.1954, appendix: 'Erfahrung mit der Mitbestimmung'.

28. Ibid.

29. IGB (ed.), *Jahrbuch 1953*, pp. 727ff; Heinrich Winkelmann, 'Heim und Herd und Sport und Spiel des Bergmanns', in Westdeutsche Wirtschafts-Monographie, Folge I, Steinkohle Ausgabe, April 1953, cited in 'Die Entwicklung des Bergarbeiterwohnungsbaus in Herne', no author, no date [1959] (available in Herne city archive).

und Farben sind Voraussetzungen für das Wachsen einer neuen Wohnkultur, die unserem innersten Wesen, unserer augenblicklichen Situation und unserem Bedürfnis nach Wahrhaftigkeit entspricht.[30]

Winkelmann expresses perfectly the Ruhr bourgeoisie's ambiguous approach to the miners. On the one hand, the image of the true and simple miner is very strong here. Winkelmann, like so many others involved in miners' housing, aspired to revive the spirit of the miner of yore, a man characterised by both *Standesbewusstsein* and modesty, who knew his place and had been uncorrupted by the *Vermassung* of modern times. On the other, there was the goal of creating a new *Wohnkultur*, of educating the miner to find balance and harmony in the post-war social order. Both goals were conservative in intent, but embodied different types of conservatism and different images of social integration. Whereas some employers and housing officials were clearly still immersed in the patriarchal relations of the nineteenth century, others sought to find a new type of integration, creating out of the miner a deproletarianised citizen. Often, as in this case, the two vocabularies coexisted unresolved, indicating a fair degree of uncertainty as to what the ideal post-war society should look like. Moreover, Winkelmann's statement contains not just uncertainty, but also a clear anxiety with respect to the kind of statement that the 'Gelsenkirchen Baroque' style was making. The robust, pompous showiness that characterised a lot of miners' furniture at that time was anathema to a nervous bourgeoisie anxious to restore restraint, modesty and propriety.[31]

The Joy of Home Ownership[32]

Alongside appropriate design, another strategy for enhancing housing's impact on workforce stability was promoting owner-occupied housing. As with many of the design proposals noted earlier, the aim was not just to give the miners what they

30. Ibid.; see also HStAD NW41, 747, Dr Hoernecke, Wiesbaden, Gedanken zur kulturellen Bergmannsbetreuung im Steinkohlenbergbau, 15.5.1952.
31. SoFoSt, 'Schlußbericht', pp. 35–6.
32. 'Freude am Eigentum', a section heading in Hibernia Konzern (ed.), *Sozialbericht 1956*, no place, 1957, p. 25.

wanted (or what the housing authorities felt they wanted) but to create the sort of environment that would, it was believed, bind them to their profession and cause them to grow roots in the locality.

Like most of the proposals mooted after 1945, the idea of giving workers the chance to become property-owners was not a new one. It had received a considerable boost in 1931 when the Brüning government had passed an emergency decree providing for the establishment of *Kleinsiedlungen*, owner-occupied houses for the unemployed with large vegetable gardens attached. Over the following years, the idea was extended to long-serving members of the workforce and a considerable number of *Kleinsiedlungen* were built in the Ruhr. By 1939, 7,500 owner-occupied homes had been built by the Treuhandstelle für Bergmannswohnstätten alone. Overall, though, owner-occupied homes remained a very small fraction of miners' housing.[33]

In the post-war period up to 1948 there were neither materials nor finance available for new building. Only at the end of 1949 did the Reconstruction Ministry feel able to make its first substantial contribution for the construction of owner-occupied homes for miners (DM500,000) and even this would pay for fewer than 100 homes.[34] Even if more money had been available from the Land, it is unlikely that more than a small minority of miners could have made use of it. A key problem that had limited the number of miners becoming *Kleinsiedler*, even before the specific problems of the wartime and post-war period arose, was that though the financial support from public funds was considerable, the owner-occupier still had to make a sizeable initial contribution himself. Many miners found the money impossible to raise. True, the required financial contribution could be commuted to labour, whereby the miner himself worked on the construction site, but this was an exhausting business, requiring the miner to follow his day's work at the mine with more toil on the building site. The higher building costs of the post-war period made it if anything even harder for

33. Deutscher Siedlerbund (ed.), *Die Kleinsiedlung und ihre Entwicklung. Ein Überblick über Sein und Werden der Kleinsiedlung und des Deutschen Siedlerbundes*, Hamburg, 1960; Treuhandstelle für Bergmannswohnstätten (ed.), *Dreißig Jahre Treuhandstelle für Bergmannswohnstätten*, Essen, no date [1949], p. 30.
34. HStAD 73, 47, WAM to IVB, 28.10.1948; BBA 8, 406, DKBL, circular no. IV-31 to mining companies and collieries, 26.6.1950.

the miners to pay their contribution, generally fixed at 20–25 per cent. A further financial disincentive to buy one's own home was that rents in the older mining properties were so very low. Once the miner had scraped the initial funds together, he would find himself with repayments more than twice as high as the typical rent in an older miners' estate. And of course there was the ever-present fear that an accident or loss of health might make it impossible to maintain the payments.[35]

In 1950 it seemed therefore as if *Eigenheim* and *Kleinsiedlung* would be little more than minor sidelines. Yet just four years later almost *half* the new houses built in the miners' housing programme were intended for owner-occupation. In a country where rented accommodation had traditionally dominated the urban housing market, and particularly the working-class housing market, this was a truly dramatic social innovation.[36] What had happened? One factor, of course, was that the volume of funds released by the new coal-mining levy made it easier for the state to increase grants to individual projects so as to reduce the burden on the miner. However, more decisive than the volume of funds was the energy with which the ECA and even more the federal parliament and government pursued the idea of owner-occupied housing. The ECA's idea was that it would provide a positive incentive to remain in mining and produce more coal. For their part, the German proponents went beyond the notion of a simple incentive, believing that owning a house would help the new miners put down roots in their local environment.

The federal government's hopes also involved a more far-reaching goal of social integration. Reviving one of the original ideas behind the *Kleinsiedlung*, the government argued that giving workers the chance to own property would enhance their self-esteem and their integration into society. The refugees, too, could be compensated for their losses and reconciled with their

35. WAM, 'Bestimmungen über die Förderung des Wohnungsneubaues (Kleinwohnungen und Kleinsiedlungen) im Lande Nordrhein-Westfalen (NBB)', *Ministerialblatt für das Land NRW (MBlNRW)*, vol. 4, no. 19, 1951, pp. 182–200; Knipping, 'Der Bergarbeiterwohnungsbau', pp. 3–4; Christoffel, 'Bergarbeiterwohnungsbau im rheinisch-westfälischen Steinkohlenbezirk', p. 344.
36. Ges.Verb. File 'Wohnungswesen 4 Bergarbeiterwohnungsbauprogramm 41 Programme. 1954–1961 Bezirksausschuß Sitzungen', minutes of the 12th Bezirksausschuß meeting, 16.12.1954.

new home. Paul Lücke, one of the housing experts in the Bundestag and later Housing Minister, argued that as well as protecting the occupants against future economic crises, home ownership 'garantiert die Bildung echter Persönlichkeitswerte, die allein der Vermassung, die uns aus dem Osten droht, Einhalt gebieten können'. Other voices chanted the same refrain.[37]

Because of the emphasis placed on the compensation and integration of refugees, they were the first group amongst the miners to benefit from the commitment to owner-occupied housing. The refugees received an interest-free loan (sometimes a straight subsidy) to cover the contribution to the house price which they would under normal circumstances have been expected to find from their own funds.[38] For miners as a whole, 1951 was the year in which the drive for owner-occupation really took off. When in October 1951 the Minister for the Marshall Plan set up a special committee to enhance productivity in coal-mining, he specifically mentioned the desirability of owner-occupation. A special subcommittee for housing was set up with federal, regional and industrial representatives. Over the following two years it was to concern itself extensively with making it easier to acquire a home. In the Miners' Housing Act, owner-occupied housing was given a clear priority over all other types of housing. The impact of this commitment was manifest in the financing provisions introduced by both the German and the ECA building programmes of 1951–2. Instead of the customary 20–25 per cent, the miners now had to find only 10 per cent of the house price in advance and even for this element the state was willing to offer interest-free loans. This was almost as good as the deal offered the refugees. Miners could now buy houses for little more than the cost of renting a new property (though rents for older houses were still considerably cheaper) and with

37. Paul Lücke, 'Die Funktion des Eigenheims in der Sozialordnung unserer Zeit', in *Die Funktion des Eigenheims in der Sozialordnung unserer Zeit. Vorträge und Referate des Dritten Deutschen Volksheimstättentages, Hannover 1951*, Bielefeld, 1951, pp. 57–71 at 59, 65.

38. 'Gesetz zur Milderung dringender sozialer Notstände [Soforthilfegesetz/ SHG] 8.8.1949', in *Gesetzblatt der Verwaltung des Vereinigten Wirtschaftsgebietes* no. 28, 1949, pp. 205–14, esp. 'Aufbauhilfe'; cf. SHG, §.44; WWA F35, 3554, DKBL, circular No. IV-1 to mining companies and collieries, 7.1.1950; HStAD NW10, 13, WAM IIIB6 to Regierungspräsidenten, 10.3.1951 and WAM, Erlaß, 'Bestimmungen über die Gewährung von Beihilfen als Ersatz für fehlendes Eigenkapital', 10.3.1951.

payments that accounted for under 20 per cent of gross income. 'Die neuen Bestimmungen', noted the DKBL, 'erleichtern . . . den Eigentumserwerb für den Bergmann in einer Weise, die bis vor kurzem kaum für möglich gehalten wurde. Bei gutem Willen kann der Bergmann fast risikolos bei einem verhältnismäßig nur geringen wertbeständigen Sparen zu einem Eigentum gelangen.'[39]

Though no one in the Ruhr was actually hostile to owner-occupied property, this sudden transformation met with a certain amount of scepticism. Many officials and housing society experts believed that few miners would respond. In any case, the 1952 building programme was mapped out before the new terms became known, so that it was dominated by rented property. The pressure from parliament and state to alter this emphasis showed just how important a measure the state believed it to be. Though the subcommittee for miners' housing had in December 1951 set an advertisement campaign in motion, this was not enough for the Parliamentary Committee for Housing and Reconstruction, which in June 1952 called for more intensive measures. This was more evidence that housing was seen as more than just an incentive. The parliamentarians were not content just to offer home ownership to those who expressed interest: they wanted actively to create that interest.[40]

In November the committee came to the Ruhr. At the centre of discussions was the question whether more could be done to promote owner-occupied homes. An SVR representative argued at a meeting with the committee that the achievement hitherto – almost 30 per cent of 1952 building being in the form of owner-occupied property – was considerable. But the deputies were not satisfied. They contended that most miners could be persuaded to buy their own property and stressed the importance of broadening property ownership as a bullwark against 'infiltration' from the other side of the Iron Curtain. As a result the NRW regional committee responsible for distributing funds raised by the miners' housing levy (*Bezirksausschuß*) decided to

39. WWA F29, 368/2, DKBL, circular no. IV-7 to mining companies and collieries, 4.2.1952, annex; Mark Roseman, 'New Miners in the Ruhr: Rebuilding the Workforce in the Ruhr Mines, 1945–1958', PhD dissertation, Warwick University, 1987.
40. MSA, '2. Fortschrittsbericht', p. 15; BAK B134, 1372, Unterausschuß III, 3rd report, 5.12.1951; 6th report, 3.7.1952.

commit 40 per cent of funds in 1953 to owner-occupied homes, a decision warmly received by the federal Housing Ministry. Mines' building proposals which envisaged more than 60 per cent of their building in the form of rented property were rejected.[41] Other voices, too, urged the transformation of the miners into a property-owning class. In a joint appeal distributed to all the mines, the Protestant and Catholic churches argued that 'Nur aus einer ethischen Haltung heraus und geschult in der Verantwortung um ein kleines Eigentum wird der Bergmann willig sein, die Aufgaben der sozialen Gemeinschaft in einem großen Industriebetrieb wie innerhalb des ganzen Volkes auf sich zu nehmen.'[42]

Incentive or Fetter?

The problem with using housing as a means of workforce integration was deciding what to do if the occupant left the company. On one view, the right to be a tenant was linked to the employment contract, which meant that unemployment was followed by eviction and, for those tenants still in employment, the employer could use the threat of eviction as a means of discipline. These were very high social costs. Alternatively, the tie between employment and housing was not enforced, which might well encourage the very behaviour it was supposed to prevent: would-be tenants or home-owners would work in the mines just long enough to obtain a dwelling and then leave.

The legislators of the Weimar Republic had already had a crack at this problem. In general terms they were hostile to company housing and by means of tax incentives and penalties encouraged employers to subsidise independent housing associations instead of building for themselves. On the other hand, the state wanted to ensure that the houses built with the considerable public funds flowing into the miners' housing

41. BAK B102, 33175, 'Kurzprotokoll über die Besichtigungsfahrt des Bundestagsausschusses für Wiederaufbau und Wohnungswesen in das Ruhrgebiet, 13/14.11.1952', 20.11.1952; B134, 3727, Unterausschuß III, 7th report, 28.10.1952.

42. WWA F29, 335, appendix to General Director, DKBL, circular no. IV-14 to mining companies, 8.3.1952; see also BBA 42, 65, 'Der Mensch im Bergbau. 1. Rundbrief aus der gemeinsamen Sozialarbeit der Konfessionen im Bergbau', no date.

programme would continue to be available to the mines. It therefore designed a compromise solution whereby housing built with the help of the levy was tied to the industry rather than to any particular mine, thus reducing the danger of employers abusing their power. A further restriction on the tie was that it lasted for only twenty years from the day the house was built. These restrictions applied only to houses built with the aid of the miners' levy. There was still a large stock of older company housing, and indeed of housing association properties funded by other means, whose tenancy agreements allowed employees leaving a mine to be evicted.[43]

Legislation and regulations in the early post-war period went further in weakening company ties. Though it was prepared to provide funds for repairs to existing company housing, NRW, for instance, gave no aid towards the construction of new company properties. The tax incentives provided by the 1949 tax law were largely denied to companies who did their own building. Most important of all was the First Federal Housing Law of 1950, which laid down that company housing could in future only receive public funds if the tie between employment contract and tenancy agreement dissolved once the tenant had been in company employment for more than five years. This was a considerable extension to previous legislation since it was phrased broadly enough to affect not only housing belonging to a particular company but also housing tied to an industry.[44]

It therefore looked in the post-war period as if general social–political considerations would be allowed to outweigh the economic desideratum of maintaining housing for the industry. However, in 1950–1 there was some intense lobbying by the DKBL and the Economics Ministry. The DKBL was critical of NRW's general financing regulations and fiercely critical of the

43. Josef F. Lang, 'Die geschichtliche und räumliche Entwicklung des Bergarbeiterwohnungsbaus im Ruhrgebiet', unpublished dissertation, Cologne University, 1952, pp. 86ff; Gesetz über Bergmannssiedlungen, 10.3.1930, in *Reichsgesetzblatt* 1930, I, p. 32 and *Reichsgesetzblatt* 1934, I, p. 354; Monika Sturm and Hartmut Hohmann, 'Der Bergarbeiterwohnungsbau im Ruhrgebiet nach 1945 unter dem Einfluß der wirtschaftlichen Entwicklung des Steinkohlenbergbaus', Diplomarbeit, Bielefeld University, 1977, pp. 78–9.
44. HStAD NW10, 92, WAM, 'Bestimmungen über die Förderung des Baus von Bergarbeiterwohnstätten', 24.3.1948; §.20, Erstes Wohnungsbaugesetz, 24.4.1950, *BGbl*, vol. 16, 1950, pp. 83–8; NBB, in *MBI-NRW*, vol. 4, no. 19, 12.3.1951, pp. 182–200.

five-year limit in the Federal Housing Law. Though unable to alter that law, it did enlist the support of federal Economics Ministry officials who put the industry's case forcefully to their colleagues in the Housing Ministry. Presumably because of the Economics Ministry's influence, the Miners' Housing Law of 1951, while maintaining the principle that housing could not be tied to a particular colliery, introduced a ferociously strict link between housing and mining employment which reversed not only the First Housing Law provisions but also Weimar legislation.[45] Whereas the *Bergmannssiedlungsgesetz* of 1930 had settled for a twenty-year tie, housing under the 1951 act remained 'permanently' tied to the industry, in other words until the loan from the mining levy funds had been fully repaid. A tenant leaving mining even after long service (though not someone retiring from mining) would be liable to eviction. The most invidious conditions applied to owner-occupied property. If, for example, a miner died and his son inherited the house before the loan had been paid off (a very likely event, since the loan took sixty-six years to pay), the son would be obliged to enter the mining industry or else lose his right to the house. Similarly, a miner's widow, though she herself could stay in the house, could lose the right to it if she married a non-miner. In addition, the loss of right to the house was initially intended to mean not just, as in NRW's other new housing legislation, having to pay the loan back faster and at a higher rate of interest than previously, but actually losing the house. The act laid down that houses were to be sold as *Reichsheimstätten* which meant that they could be bought back at a price unfavourable to the sellers if the stipulated conditions were not met.[46]

Even before the legislation was on the statute book, the housing authorities began a rearguard action to strengthen the occupants' rights. Together, the NRW Reconstruction Minister and the federal Housing Minister found a subtle way to alter the slant of the housing programme without any legislation, namely, by stipulating the conditions which agreements be-

45. See WWA F35, 3549, DKBL, circular no. Cj 48 to mining companies, 1.8.1950 and the DKBL's comments on the NBB in DKBL, circular no. IV-7 to mining companies and collieries, 4.2.1952, part II; BAK B134, 1365, BWoM 1334/4797/50, memo, 15.8.1950.
46. See the BAWBG, 23.10.1951 s.5 and HStAD NW9, 85, WAM, internal memo from Gruppe IB to IVC, 13.11.1951.

tween mortgagee and lenders had to contain. An example is given by miners who had taken out a loan to substitute for the 10 per cent initial contribution (*Eigenleistung*) they were normally expected to pay. Until this 10 per cent had been paid, the miners were technically not yet house-owners and could be evicted if they left the industry. In 1952, however, the DKBL was forced to accept a new model loan agreement which in such an eventuality restricted the employer's sanction to increasing the rate of repayments. This was more favourable to the mortgagee than even NRW's general housing regulations. In addition, the agreements ensured that housing was tied to the industry for no longer than twenty years.[47]

The most dramatic changes came in 1952–3. Under pressure from the Parliamentary Committee for Housing and Reconstruction, the mining productivity subcommittee for miners' housing looked into the reasons still inhibiting miners from becoming property-owners. As a result of the committee's deliberations a number of changes were now introduced. Amongst other provisions, the widow who remarried did not automatically lose her right to the house; adult children inheriting the house were also freed from the tie as long as at least part of it was sublet to a mining tenant. Finally, towards the end of 1953, a new set of loan conditions was imposed on the DKBL in which the grounds for terminating the loan did not include the occupant leaving the industry at all! The only grounds now listed were the normal technical reasons such as defaulting on payments and so forth. Exactly how this affected the DKBL's legal position is not clear, since the new wording of the model agreements was in direct contravention of the 1951 law. About a key decision in the following year, however, there was no doubt: when the Miners' Housing Act was renewed in 1954, the support given to owner-occupied properties became even more marked and the link between job contract and house was limited to ten years.[48]

In effect, two goals were in conflict. The priority of workforce

47. WWA F29, 367/1, DKBL, circular no. Cj 69 to mining companies and collieries, 5.9.1952 and annex; BAK B134, 1372, BAM II a1, memo, 14.5.1952.

48. BAK B134, 3727, 7th report of the Unterausschuß III, 28.10.1952; B134, 1365, 'Ergebnisprotokoll über die Sitzung vom 4. Februar . . .', no date [February 1953]; WWA F29, 367/1, DKBL, circular no. Cj 92 to mining companies and collieries, 19.11.1953, annex, esp. s.11 (1), (2); 'Schriftlicher Bericht des Ausschusses für Wiederaufbau und Wohnungswesen', esp. p. 3.

regeneration confronted the aspiration to create a broad property-owning working class. The housing authorities believed that the general social–political goals which owner-occupation was intended to fulfil would be fatally compromised if the property was burdened with the rigid and long-lasting conditions originally laid down in the Miners' Housing Act. Thus the *societal* integration strategy was progressively given greater priority than workforce regeneration. Of course, the two goals were not necessarily in conflict. There was the hope that by making the conditions for house ownership less irksome, the miners would voluntarily choose to stay in the industry – and this may even have been partially successful. The point was, however, that the drive to make home ownership easier was not *primarily* orientated to the interests of coal-mining, but to broader social–political goals.[49]

Housing and Wastage

Once the finance was sorted out, the early 1950s saw a truly massive building programme. By 1954, the waiting time for a house or apartment had at most mines dropped to less than a year. Of course, there were mines which by virtue of particularly heavy bomb damage and a poor financial position were still suffering from a severe shortage of family accommodation, but by and large the acute housing shortage present at the end of the previous decade had been solved. In 1955, most companies were in a position to offer all prospective miners an apartment within six months.[50]

What was the impact of all this building on the workforce? To what extent was it able to bring wastage under control? In 1949 it looked for a while as if the problem of workforce stability was about to be solved, with labour losses in that year lower than at any time since the end of the war.[51] Yet just four years later, mining's high labour demand was caused almost exclusively by

49. HStAD NW9, 85, WAM IVC to BWoM, 24.11.1951.
50. Ges.Verb. File 'Wohnungswesen 4 Bergarbeiterwohnungsbauprogramm 41 Programme 1954–1961 Bezirkssauschuß-Sitzungen', table 'Bergarbeiterwohnungsbau', Essen, 30.6.1956; Ges.Verb. File '300–301.1, Ausbildung von Neubergleuten', Hamborner Bergbau AG, 'Wegweiser' [1955].
51. *Glückauf*, vol. 85, nos. 49/50, 1949, pp. 911–13 at 913.

wastage. Unlike the labour movements of earlier eras, one colliery's loss was not another pit's gain: the key new feature of the post-1945 era was that the leavers were quitting the industry altogether. Thus, in 1953, when the UVR made an advance calculation of labour requirements for the following year it reckoned that in order to increase the workforce by 3,000 men, 61,000 recruits would be needed! At the end of 1953, it is true, the general downswing in economic activity temporarily reduced the flight from the mines, but in autumn 1954 wastage resumed its upward path and consistently outpaced the level of hirings.[52]

The costs of these losses were enormous. About DM1,000 spent on each man for recruitment and training went to waste. Productivity suffered, both because the number of inexperienced men in the mines was higher than it needed to be and because more experienced men were tied up supervising – albeit perfunctorily – the newcomers. Accidents increased, both because of the high proportion of newcomers and because the continual appearance of new gaps in the workforce forced deputies to keep transferring labour from one face and one set of working conditions to another. In addition, as will be seen, management was wasting its best chance to create a stable workforce. As time went on, the mines found themselves hiring new recruits who were less and less likely to stay.[53]

Wastage was also a key reason why selective recruitment was slow to have a really transformative effect on workforce age structure. Mining experts continually bemoaned the shortfall in the age range 25–40, generally regarded as the most productive group because of its combination of relative strength and experience.[54] As table 6.1 shows, from 1939 to 1948 this group fell as a share of the underground workforce by 50 per cent; and during

52. UVR calculation in OBADA I8007/520/55, ABB annual report 1954. The apparent anomaly that the underground workforce continued to grow despite the fact that underground recruitment was outpaced by wastage is explained by the fact that apprentices were being transferred underground having reached the age of 16. Apprentices were not counted as part of the hirings below ground because they were initially employed on the surface.
53. 'Der Pütt darf nicht Durchgangsstation bleiben!', *Industriekurier*, 25.11.1952; Max Oberschuir, 'Ein Beitrag zur Frage der Ausbildung des bergmännischen Nachwuchses', *Bergfreiheit*, vol. 22, 1957, pp. 437–445 at 438–9.
54. See Hans Heinrich Bischoff, 'Die Altersgliederung der Arbeiter im Steinkohlenbergbau', *Glückauf*, vol. 88, nos 41/2, 1952, pp. 1009–12.

Table 6.1 Age structure of underground workforce (cohorts as %)

Age cohort	1939	1946	1947	1948	1949	1950	1951	1953	1955	1957
16–24	11.3	15.4	19.5	22.4	26.2	29.4	31.0	33.2	32.2	31.7
25–39	56.1	29.5	29.9	30.7	29.9	29.5	29.7	32.0	34.6	37.6
40+	32.6	55.1	50.6	46.9	43.9	41.1	39.4	34.8	33.3	30.7

Source: Calculated from ZdKW, vol. 7, p. 38; vol. 16, p. 47; vol. 26, p. 47; vol 39, p. 50.

the 1940s and 1950s it grew only slowly because of the increasing difficulties in persuading young recruits to stay. Small wonder, then, that efficiency made only slow progress during the 1950s. When wastage first began to show serious signs of increase, in 1950–1, it did so at a time when funding for housing was still inadequate. It was thus taken as *prima facie* evidence of the need for more housing. The clamour for state funding reached fever pitch. Yet towards the end of 1952, a year after the miners' levy had been introduced, the federal Economics Ministry submitted a report to the miners' housing subcommittee (*Unterausschuß III*) which showed that the increased building rate had not had a measurable effect on wastage.[55] True, in 1953, when the time came to consider whether a renewal of the miners' housing levy was desirable, all the members of the subcommittee still believed that it was. It was noteworthy, however, that when the federal Housing Minister wrote to his colleague in the Economics Ministry for arguments that could be used in parliament to justify renewal, it was a rather uncertain reply that came back. After contending that housing was still important to reduce wastage and strengthen productivity, the Minister went on: 'Auch in diesem Punkte kann man skeptisch sein hinsichtlich des durch den Bergarbeiterwohnungsbau zu Erreichenden, aber das Argument dürfte zu verwenden sein.'[56] The chairman of the UVR's housing committee, Dubusc, noted that between 1949 and 1953 almost 50 per cent of the Klöckner miners had obtained new company housing. Yet productivity had not risen and, Dubusc contended, would probably not have

55. BAK B134, 3727, 7th report of Unterausschuß III, 28.10.1952; B134, 3727, 8th report of Unterausschuß III, 7.8.1953.
56. BAK B102, 33315, BWiM to BWoM, 26.7.1954.

fallen if there had been no new apartments. Somewhat surprisingly, given this judgement, it was his view that miners' housing was nevertheless probably worth it in the long run.[57] The evidence adduced by these experts and, indeed, by the wastage figures noted above, suggests that miners' housing was *not* worth it. Was the whole drive for miners' housing, then, based on an illusion?

One question must be whether the romantics had built houses that were actually unsuitable for the newcomers. No doubt a two- or three-storey building or a reasonably sized garden were acceptable to most, but could it really be assumed that the newcomers would want to live in the kitchen or to keep a pig or a goat? It should be remembered that where the stall for the animals was built directly on to the house it took up a fair amount of the ground floor space. In addition, many of the houses produced by the Treuhandstelle für Bergmannssiedlungen and other housing associations (at least until the early 1950s) balanced the cost of offering a fair-sized garden and keeping the number of storeys down by economising on the standard of amenities. What was the new miners' response to this? The available material is somewhat contradictory but writing in 1990s Britain with a general awareness of the architectural and social disasters created by modernisers in the 1950s and 1960s it is hard to resist the impression that the Ruhr did not really suffer from the conservatism of planners, designers and builders. The most general problem with German social housing from the 1950s was that to save time and expense it was often too small. This affected the miners too, but they were much better off than most. Above all, the newcomers were very aware of the cramped housing conditions existing for other population groups. Almost one-third of adult householders in NRW did not have an apartment to themselves. It was not surprising, therefore, that in a survey of reasons why men left the pits in 1954, discontent with housing conditions was virtually never raised.[58]

57. BAK B102, 33148, copy of memo concerning the meeting of Studienausschuß III des Beratenden Ausschusses 'Arbeiterwohnungsbau, Produktion, Produktivität' on 2.6.1954 in Luxembourg, 2.6.1954.
58. BAK B102, 33091, BWiM IIIA1 33079/54, memo, annex 8 and unauthored, undated, paper [probably by Ullrich, UVR], 'Bemerkungen zu der Sondererhebung zur Ermittlung der Abkehrgründe', p. 4; Edwin C. Abe and Alfons Echterhoff, *Das Vest – ein dynamischer Wirtschaftsraum*, Recklinghausen, 1955, p. 153; SoFoSt, 'Schlußbericht', pp. 13–14.

Why, then, was housing unable to prevent the high wastage of the 1950s? Many occupants of miners' housing could easily reach a steel mill from where they lived and it was indeed the mines of Essen, Bochum and Dortmund, situated near steelworks and other big industrial employers, which suffered some of the highest wastage levels. This competition in mining's back yard, coupled with the fact that evictions were now difficult to carry out (and that it was easier for home owners to quit the mines while retaining their house) reduced housing's ability to compel the occupants to remain in the workforce. There was evidence that quite a number of recruits came with the intention of obtaining a house and then leaving the mines. On the other hand, the extent of this phenomenon should not be exaggerated. Though the *number* of tenants in company houses no longer employed by the mines grew, the *proportion* of houses with such tenants fell steadily.[59]

A more important factor reducing the effectiveness of housing in controlling wastage was the fact that it came so late. By 1951–2 many mines had got themselves into a hiring–wastage cycle from which it was hard to extricate themselves. Forced in the post-1948 period to hire mobile young men because there was no family accommodation, the mines found in the early 1950s that they had increasingly little chance of choosing people likely to stay. Though the mines increasingly recognised the desirability of hiring married men who could be offered a home, their demand for labour was too large to allow more than a small proportion of it to be met by married men.[60] Because many of the people they hired in the 1950s were single and had expressed no intention to marry they would, at least in the short term, be unaffected by the housing programme. In 1952, for example, the IGB estimated that at the very outside 10,000 of the 36,000 or so occupants of the adult mining hostels might be interested in obtaining a house. A SoFoSt survey came to similar

59. WWA F29, 333/1, DKBL, circular no. IV-9 to mining companies, 12.2.1952, annex; StAM Regierung Arnsberg, 5.143, VRAD reports for May 1953 and March 1955.

60. BWiM memo and documents cited in note 58; Karl Heinrich Budde, 'Die Gründe und Auswirkungen des übermässig starken Belegschaftswechsels auf den Schachtanlagen des Ruhrgebiets in der Nachkriegszeit', unpublished dissertation, Herne, 1952, p. 40; StAM Arbeitsamt Dortmund, 46, ABB, circular 8/51, 13.7.1951.

conclusions, reinforced by housing allocation figures produced a year later which revealed that of 28,400 miners given
a house in that year, only 2,804 (about 10 per cent) had come
from the camps and a further 2,188 were new recruits. (The
rest were long-standing workers in unsatisfactory accommodation.) Yet it was precisely amongst the group of young
hostel occupants that wastage was at its highest. Thus there
was a sizeable proportion of wastage which housing could do
nothing to alleviate.[61]

The delay in developing a major housing initiative was exacerbated by the fact that the established workforce was frequently
allowed to come first on the housing list. With the exception of
some refugee housing and also the MSA programme, housing
allocation decisions were made within the collieries by management and works councils. The mines had to consider not only
the desirability of obtaining and integrating new labour but also
the rest of the workforce's 'moral economy', particularly the
attitudes of established miners, who were quick to believe that
newcomers were being overprivileged. It was only logical for
management to make sure that the established miners were kept
reasonably content. This tendency was strengthened by the fact
that, to avoid causing uproar through unpopular decisions,
management was keen to delegate a lot of the responsibility to
the works councils. The councillors generally tried hard to be
fair and were wont to say that decisions about housing were the
hardest they had to make, but it was only natural that they
should see to it that the established workforce was well looked
after. In the mine Shamrock 3/4, for example, 65 per cent of
housing recipients up to 1951 were from the established workforce and only 35 per cent were newcomers, despite the fact that
the latter made up 70 per cent of the workforce and presumably
an even higher proportion of those seeking housing. And Shamrock, it should be added, was a mine that approached its
newcomers with more understanding than most. The cost of
social peace, therefore, was that newcomers were slower to

<hr>

61. The IGB figure is in IGB (ed.), *Jahrbuch 1952*, pp. 440ff and IGBEA
Handakten Rudi Quast, File 'M.Assistenten Tagungen (Alt)', minutes of 3rd
meeting of the 'Herner Kreis', 24.6.1953; AZG File 'I 1 26 Zuweisung von
Arbeitskräften aus anderen Bezirken (Umschüler)', minutes of 2nd meeting of
Arbeitsgemeinschaft Arbeitsamt-Bergbau, 8.5.1953, p. 4; StAM Regierung Arns-
berg, 5.143, VRAD report, 20.1.1954.

Reshaping the Ruhr

Figure 6.1   Wastage and stability among Hibernia's new miners

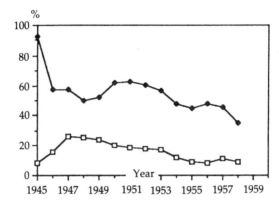

-□- Proportion of workforce accounted for by trainees hired in last 3 yrs
  (and still in pit)
-◆- Proportion of trainees hired over last 3 yrs who have not left pit

Source: Calculated from Hibernia Konzern (ed.), *Hibernia Sozialbericht
1958*, annex 4: 'Wechsel und Stand der Neubergleute
untertage'.

obtain housing than they might have been had purely productive criteria applied.[62]

All that having been said, there is ample evidence that without the rapid provision of reasonable quality housing, the mines
would have been far worse off than they were. Without housing, as the labour exchanges repeatedly testified, the mines
would have had difficulty in the 1950s in soliciting any long-
term (i.e. not seasonal) recruits at all. In addition, the colliery
workforces would probably have disintegrated. For, as detailed
figures from the Hibernia company reveal, whilst many newcomers did not stay in the mines, a sizeable minority did prove
highly stable additions to the colliery workforces.[63] This can be
established because of the different pattern shown by two sets
of statistics from Hibernia. One set of figures gives the proportion of men in the mines at any one time who had under three

62. BBA 35, 236, Belegschaftsversammlung Emscher Lippe, 23.5.1948; 35,
237, Belegschaftsversammlung Emscher Lippe, 21.5.1950; 32, 3055, minutes of
Belegschaftsausschuß Meeting, Shamrock 3/4, 3.10.1951.
63. See, e.g. StAM Arbeitsamt Dortmund, 11, AA Do to ABB, 25.11.1954;
Hibernia Konzern, *Sozialbericht* 1956 and 1958, annex 8. See also chapter 8.

216

Figure 6.2 Composition of underground workforce according to status when hired (mine Shamrock 1/2)

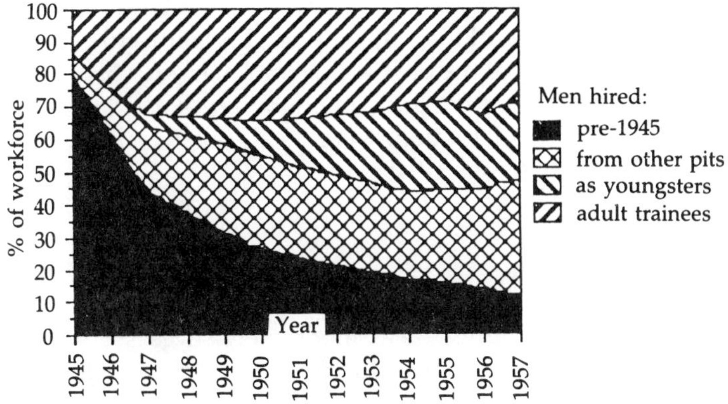

Men hired:
■ pre-1945
▨ from other pits
◩ as youngsters
▧ adult trainees

Source: Hibernia Konzern (ed.), *Hibernia Sozialbericht 1958*, p. 5.[65]

years' mining experience. As figure 6.1 shows, this proportion fell rapidly, despite the continued high levels of recruitment and a fairly stable overall workforce size. This was a clear sign that those recruited in the 1950s were not staying for long in the mines. As the lower curve on figure 6.1 makes clear, from 1949 onwards an ever smaller proportion of each year's new recruits were still there three years later. On the other hand, one of the Hibernia pits also kept a count of the total number of all present and former trainees. As figure 6.2 reveals, this was a fairly stable proportion of the workforce. This means that many of the earlier recruits must have actually remained in the mines throughout the 1950s.[64] It is unthinkable that the mines would have been able to maintain this core workforce had it not been for mining's lead over other industries (and general public housing programmes) in providing reasonable family accommodation.

These achievements were considerable, but clearly fell far short of the employers' hopes. Perhaps the most important and

64. See also Budde, 'Gründe und Auswirkungen', p. 60, table 30 and pp. 22–5, table 13.
65. The Shamrock figures are not entirely representative since its workforce barely grew in the period 1951–6, whereas the Ruhr labour force increased by more than 10 per cent over that period. In addition, the proportion of new miners is probably a little above the average.

217

obvious point about housing was that the expectations associated with it had been exaggerated from the start. Just as with
the apprenticeship programme, they had been based on a misunderstanding of workforce stability and a failure to recognise
the new challenges of the post-war labour market. The romantic
images of hearth, garden and simple miner, and the romantic
agrarian model of integration, were poor guides to the reality of
labour behaviour in post-1945 Germany.

Housing and Politics

If the housing programme was moderately successful at secur-
ing a core workforce for the industry, albeit one that fell short of
the numbers needed, was it also moderately successful at creating the integrated property-owning class? In numerical terms,
the results were substantial. Between 1950 and 1960, almost
50,000 owner-occupied properties were built and, in addition,
some housing companies, notably the Treuhandstelle, sold off
formerly rented property to their tenants. By 1957, some 10–15
per cent of the mining industry's employees must have been
owner-occupiers.[66]

But the really intensive drive to expand owner-occupation
was soon over. By 1955 it was coming up against a diminishing
number of prospective buyers. One problem, particularly in the
more heavily urbanised areas, was the shortage of suitable land;
the pressure on space made blocks of flats desirable and few
miners wanted to become owner of a flat. And of course the old
worries about invalidity and the ensuing payments burden
continued. In 1955 and 1956 the UVR and IGB both recognised
that they had got into a situation where if they built according to
the miners' wishes they would contravene the federal Housing
Minister's guidelines by creating too many apartments for rent.
In 1956 they avoided the problem by using regional funds to
build rented accommodation so that housing with the mining
levy funds produced the correct proportion of owner-occupied
property. In 1957 the Bezirksausschuß agreed that the owner-
occupied quota should not be taken too rigidly, and from 1956

---

66. UVR (ed.), *Jahresbericht 1958–1960*, table facing p. 94.

onwards the proportion of owner-occupied housing was indeed far lower than it had been previously.[67]

As in many other aspects of the mines' and the state's integration policy, both the hopes and the anxieties that lay behind these programmes were relatively short-lived. The voices warning against Eastern infiltration, or demanding the miner be given 'ein kleines Eigentum' were increasingly seldom heard. Whereas the 1954 renewal of the Miners' Housing Act had considerably strengthened the pro-ownership provisions, the 1957 law contained no further intensification. No doubt both the clear limits to the miners' willingness to become buyers and the general political stabilisation of the Republic combined to make owner-occupation an increasingly marginal issue.

The political impact of the housing itself is hard to gauge. It is, in fact, difficult to make *any* clear assessment of the miners', and particularly the new miners', political views, let alone to distinguish between home-owners and others. Recent work on the way in which the SPD attained hegemony in the Ruhr in the course of the 1950s has stressed the role of party patronage in creating large 'client groups' reasonably well disposed to the party.[68] One strand of this 'patronage' was the power of the SPD-dominated works councils in the allocation of scarce resources, above all housing. Certainly, many new miners obtained a house because they had a decent connection to the local union organisation and the works council. It is perfectly possible, therefore, that the impact of the building programme was to strengthen the hold of the SPD. This was probably not what the CDU-dominated Bundestag had had in mind!

---

67. Ges.Verb. File 'Wohnungswesen 4 . . . 1954–1961 Bezirksausschuß-Sitzungen', minutes of meetings, 16.12.1954 and 5.4.1957; table 'Bergarbeiterwohnungsbauprogramm 1956 (Vorschau)', no date; UVR to Schulz, IGB, 15.3.1956; memo on the meeting of the 'Kleiner Ausschuß' of the Bezirksausschuß, 9.4.1956; UVR (ed.), *Jahresbericht 1958–1960*, table facing p. 94.

68. Above all, Michael Zimmermann, '"Geh zu Hermann, der macht dat schon". Bergarbeiterinteressenvertretung im nördlichen Ruhrgebiet', in Lutz Niethammer (ed.), '*Hinterher merkt man, daß es richtig war, daß es schiefgegangen ist*'. *Nachkriegserfahrungen im Ruhrgebiet*, Berlin/Bonn, 1983, pp. 277–310.

7
Compulsive Talking and Constrained Silence: Propaganda in the Mining Hostels

The Hostel Occupants

The apprenticeship and the miner's house were the two main weapons in the employers' social–political armoury. However, there was one group of miners subject to a whole range of additional policies designed to encourage integration and to remould the workforce: the youngsters in the hostels. More than any other group, the boys from outside the Ruhr, separated from their parents, presented the employers with new responsibilities and new opportunities. As youths under the age of consent, they brought with them certain legal obligations of guardianship and protection for the employers. In addition to such statutory matters, a number of different state administrations let it be known that they expected the employers to look after their charges.

Because they lived in a mass and because most of them were young, unattached former refugees, many having lost not just their parents but also their homeland, the hostel occupants were seen as being particularly at risk from *Vermassung* and susceptible to radicalism. In guidelines produced by the Catholic church, for example, seminary students were advised to spend several months working and living in the hostels, 'um den modernen Massenmenschen kennenzulernen'.[1] At the same time, they represented an impressionable and captive audience who could be reached and fashioned not only in the workforce

---

1. BM A201, 47, Merkblatt für Theologen im Bergbau, no date; 'Vorschläge zum Bau und zur Führung von Berglehrlings- und Knappenheimen', *Mitteilungen der Kommission für soziale Aufgaben (KfSA)*, nos 1/2 (1952), p. 3.

and within the formal confines of the training programme but in their leisure hours as well.

Though later on there would be attempts to reach adult hostel inmates as well, initially all the employers' efforts were focused on the apprentices. In the pre-currency-reform period, when conditions in the adult camps were frequently appalling and colliery managers were doing little more than passively and resignedly watch the great mass of often unwilling labour flow through the mines, the apprentice hostels were generally in good order.[2] That this was not because of a general concern for the youngsters' welfare but in the interests of *Standesbildung* was made abundantly clear by the enormous discrepancy between the standard of apprentices' hostels, on the one hand, and the lack of provision for the admittedly smaller number of non-local young trainees (*Bergjungleute*), most of whom were housed with adult trainees in the camps. In 1947, both German and British authorities called repeatedly for young trainees to be segregated from their adult counterparts. Yet despite all the pressure the employers were extremely unwilling to do anything about the problem, indeed, even to acknowledge that it existed. Above all, they did not want to dilute the special atmosphere of the apprentice hostel or undermine the attempts to create a new elite by including other types of young labour.[3]

After the currency reform, conditions improved markedly in all the hostels, for apprentices and trainees alike. Yet even then the apprentice hostels continued to be particularly well appointed. In many there were no more than three beds to a room and the hostels were equipped with table-tennis rooms, small gymnasia, darkrooms, their own libraries and so on. Of course, the companies could recover some of their outlay by charging the apprentices for accommodation, but in fact the hostels were heavily subsidised, even more than their adult equivalents. In 1956, for example, the Hibernia company laid out DM1,355 per new miner in the hostels but DM1,786 for each apprentice.[4]

2. OBADA I6303/568/47, ABB to OBAD, 25.2.1947; I6301/969/47, ABB, circular to all colliery managements, 17.3.1947.

3. HStAD NW41, 746, Soz. Min. NRW IIIB/6 to colliery directors, 17.7.1947; NW41, 747, Soz. Min. III B/6, memo. 25.7.1948; NW41, 761, Soz. Min. IIIB/6, memo, 7.8.1948; OBADA I6303/1757/47, Elphick, 'Die Bedingungen junger Arbeiter in den Zechen', 15.1.1947; I6303/2572/47, minutes of meeting on 5.9.1947.

4. Hibernia Konzern (ed.), *Hibernia Sozialbericht 1956*, pp. 15, 20.

Integration or Segregation?

Until 1948, the employers' endeavours were dominated by the struggle to obtain even the most basic items of equipment. After the currency reform, however, they were able to think more creatively about the optimum type of hostel environment. Fairly early on, a central dilemma emerged, namely: integrate or segregate? On the one hand, the employers wanted the new-comers to put down roots in the Ruhr and become permanent members of the workforce. On the other hand, they did not want them to assume the worst habits of the existing workforce (see chapter 5). In addition, the controlled environment in the hostels represented a marvellous opportunity to transmit the 'right' values to a captive and impressionable 'audience'.

The dilemma was summed up perfectly in a paper presented to the Kommission für Soziale Aufgaben (KfSA: the welfare organisation run jointly by DKBL and IGB) by Klaus von Bismarck, director of the Sozialamt of the Protestant church in Westphalia. The paper contained his thoughts about the best way to build and run a hostel. On the one hand, noted the (generally progressive) churchman, it was an often-observed fact that the girls from the local community exerted an unhappy influence on apprentices. On the other hand, 'ist das Streben zu bejahen, die Jungen mit ihrer neuen sozialen Umwelt in Verbindung zu bringen, insbesondere unter dem Gesichtspunkt, daß ihre Seßhaftmachung und Verwurzelung nur dann für die Dauer möglich ist, wenn sie die Menschen ihrer neuen Heimat, ihre Lebensgewohnheiten, Sitten und Gebräuche kennen und schätzen lernen'.[5] What was the answer? On the whole segregation seems to have been emphasised at the expense of integration. This was in part because both state and church reinforced the mines' wishes with their own fears and ambitions. As Klaus von Bismarck makes clear, there was widespread anxiety about the negative impact of proximity to the adult community. Drunken new miners and promiscuous miners' daughters seem to have been the chief dangers facing the apprentices. Von Bismarck himself concluded that, in the final analysis, building a

---

5. HStAD NW41, 747, 'Zusammenstellungen des Sozialamtes der evangelischen Kirche in Westfalen über die in einigen Berglehrlingsheimen angefallenen Erfahrungen', no date [1951].

hostel near a miners' estate had more negative than positive consequences.

Bismarck's guidelines were very influential and were adopted largely unchanged as the KfSA's own. Most hostels were built a good distance away from the mining estates. At least one reason for the comprehensive provision of facilities in the hostels was the desire to keep the apprentices out of the wrong company.[6]

The Organic Village

Perhaps the most innovative experiment, and a sign of just how far the employers were prepared to go to create their new workforce, was the establishment of special youth villages to house the apprentices. In 1948, the Pestalozzi Association – an organisation dedicated to disseminating the educational ideas of the eighteenth-century Swiss educational theorist Pestalozzi – approached the Vereinigte Stahlwerke's housing associations to see whether they would consider building a Pestalozzi village in the Ruhr. Together, Heinrich Vormbrock, a leading figure in the housing associations, and Walter Forstmann, board member of the GBAG, persuaded the GBAG chairman to endorse an experiment with two Pestalozzi villages, one in Dinslaken-Lohberg, site of a mine belonging to the GBAG's Hamborn group, and the other in Bochum. The idea then caught on elsewhere and by 1956 there were thirty-three such villages with, in all, 5,500 places, equivalent to almost a third of all the accommodation provided for apprentices and *Knappen*.[7] Generally, the villages consisted of a series of large houses with big gardens in the manner of the *Kleinsiedlung*, each house occupied by a 'parent' family and six youngsters. Each village had its own leader and, in time, its own community centre. The village parents obtained their accommodation free plus a monthly payment from which to feed the youngsters. The village leader supervised the parents and watched over the youngsters.[8]

6. Hans-Georg Erzmoneit, 'Was tut der Ruhrbergbau für seinen Nachwuchs?', *Bergbau*, no. 7, 1956, pp. 168–75 at 173, caption to illustration 8; IG Bergbau Bezirk VI (ed.), *Jahresbericht 1954*, p. 24.
7. HStAD NW41, 764, Forstmann, 'Ausführung in der Aufsichtsratsitzung vom 21.11.1949'. Statistics calculated from Arbeitsgemeinschaft Heimstatthilfe im Lande NRW (ed.), *Verzeichnis der Jugendheimstätten in NRW*, NRW 1956.
8. Otto-Wilhelm Roelen, 'Die Bedeutung der Pestalozzidörfer für die Gewin-

The attractions of the village concept were manifold. Although the cost factor was probably not decisive, it was certainly significant that the villages cost the employers less than conventional hostels. The initial investment was lower because they qualified both for housing subsidies from the Reconstruction Ministry and for the more usual apprentice hostel funds. The Reconstruction Ministry funds were particularly important because they were given at a much more favourable rate of interest than some of the loans with which builders of normal apprentice hostels had to make do. The low or non-existent interest charges and the low staff costs made the Pestalozzi villages cheaper to run as well. In addition, the houses could in the future be used as normal housing.[9]

The real logic of the village concept was that it was seen as a way of overcoming the conflict between integration and segregation. The idea was to introduce the youngsters to the best of the mining community in a controlled and monitored environment. The parents would be carefully chosen so as to avoid contaminating the youngsters with the *Untugenden* of the mining community and to transmit the appropriate values and outlook. The villages themselves were carefully situated well away from the miners' estates, 'Schmuckkästchen inmitten einer grünen Landschaft' as Walter Forstmann put it.[10] Thus the dangers of the wrong sort of company would be avoided but at the same time so would the risks associated with communal living in a large hostel. The degree to which contact with the local community was sought tended to vary from village to village, depending on the outlook of the village leader.[11]

The resonance which the idea of the miners' village enjoyed and the way in which it was implemented reveal many of the myths about the true miner and about social integration which

---

nung eines bergbaulichen Nachwuchses', unpublished dissertation, Cologne University, 1956, *passim*.

9. Klinkert Papers, minutes of the first meeting of the JHStW PV, 31.7.1948; HStAD NW41, 764, minutes of meeting on 21 November 1950 in Essen with DKBL, 23.11.1950; Roelen, 'Die Bedeutung der Pestalozzidörfer', pp. 163–4.

10. Walter Forstmann, 'Die Erziehung zum Eigentumsgedanken', *Die Volksheimstätte. Monatszeitschrift des Deutschen Volksheimstättenwerks*, vol. 7, no. 5, pp. 1–5.

11. JHStW PV (ed.), *Pestalozzieltern im Pestalozzidorf*, Essen, 1952, cited in Roelen, 'Die Bedeutung der Pestalozzidörfer', pp. 25ff; Roelen, 'Die Bedeutung der Pestalozzidörfer', p. 72.

abounded in the mining industry. The houses were built on the *Kleinsiedler* pattern (see chapter 6) in part so that the youngsters could be 'rooted' by means of garden work. This drew on that romantic notion of a link between farmer and miner, between working the soil and working the coalface, that we have already encountered in the industry's approach to housing policy generally. Related to this was the idea that working in local soil would cause the newcomer to put down deep psychological roots in the community: 'Man will die jungen Bergleute gleich mit der Arbeit im Stall und Garten vertraut machen und besonders ihre Lust und Liebe zur Kleintierzucht und Gartenbewirtschaftung erwecken, damit sie einmal auf eigenen Kleinsiedlerstellen oder als Einlieger sich fest in der Nähe ihrer Schachtanlage verwurzeln können.'[12] Though there was talk of *Ausgleich*, of pleasant compensation for the work underground, it was evident that the garden work was far more than that, because it was actually a duty for the youngsters. When at a meeting of the village leaders it was suggested that the youngsters were not necessarily all that interested in gardening, the chairman of the Pestalozzi Association came down very strongly on the issue, reminding all present that the villages had been created specifically 'um der Jugend den Grund und Boden nahe zu bringen'.[13] The designation *Dorfälteste* rather than *Dorfleiter* for the village leaders indicated the desire to resurrect the notion of an intact, quasi-rural community.[14] Another virtue of the housing design in the eyes of the village founders was that the apprentices would feel encouraged to become owner-occupiers. 'Das Ziel ist dann endgültig erreicht,' wrote Walter Forstmann, 'wenn der Weg zur Familiengründung im eigenen Heim geebnet ist.'[15]

From a fairly early stage it became apparent that though wastage remained low amongst apprentices ensconced in either hostels or villages, it rose rapidly in the first months after the youngsters qualified as *Knappen*. The OBAD wrote in a 1950 report to the Economics Ministry that there was no point in building beautiful apprentice hostels if the 17- or 18-year-old youngster was then abandoned to his own devices and forced to

---

12. Forstmann, 'Ausführung in der Aufsichtsratssitzung vom 24.11.1949'.
13. Klinkert Papers, File 'Niederschriften der Arbeitstagungen und Vortragsveranstaltungen', minutes of meeting of village leaders, 10.12.1958.
14. 'Die Pestalozzidörfer des Bergbaus', *Bergfreiheit*, vol. 8, 1951, pp. 17–19.
15. Forstmann, 'Die Erziehung zum Eigentumsgedanken', p. 5.

take an expensive private room or live in the rougher climate of an adult hostel. As experience showed, wrote the OBAD, 'ist dieser Übergang der Augenblick, in dem sehr viele Knappen der unfreundlichen Wohn- und Lebensverhältnisse wegen dem Bergbau trotz eben erfolgreich abgeschlossener Lehre den Rücken kehren'.[16] One might have thought that the goal of integration into the local community would make it desirable to find suitable lodgings with a mining family – and many *Knappen* did indeed become subtenants in miners' housing – yet both employers and the state were reluctant to encourage this. There was the feeling that the householders would not exercise the right sort of influence and a fear that the values and attitudes being inculcated in the apprentice hostels would be dissipated. As a result, the employers pressed for funds to construct hostels for the *Knappen* as well. Evidently, at one point, there were plans to construct enough hostels to offer a place to every single graduate apprentice, though in the end financial shortages (and probably also the inclination of many *Knappen* themselves) led to the more modest achievement of something over 3,000 places in hostels designated specifically for *Knappen* and a further 1,600 in hostels for young miners in the 18–25 age range.[17]

Various other attempts were made to sustain the special environment and protect the former apprentices from the ostensibly negative characteristics of the mining community. In the Pestalozzi villages, the youngsters were not expected to leave after qualifying and there was the hope that they would go straight from the village to marriage and their own home without ever passing through the intermediate phase of full exposure to the mining community as single men. A number of mining companies encouraged apprentices and *Knappen* to become owner-occupiers straight away, once again ensuring a direct transition from the sheltered atmosphere of the hostel to

16. OBADA I6301/774/50, OBAD to VfW (*sic*), 13.3.1950, annex: 'Bericht über die bergmännische Nachwuchs- und Ausbildungslage im Oberbergamtsbezirk Dortmund'.

17. BAK B102, 33189, Hensel BWiM, memo, 9.10.1951; HStAD NW41, 747, Sozialamt der evangelischen Kirche, 'Vorschläge zum Bau und zur Führung von Knappenheimen', 15.10.1951; Roelen, 'Die Bedeutung der Pestalozzidörfer', p. 91; BAK B102, 33189, BWiM IIIA3 (Imhäuser) to Min. Dgt. Classen, 30.5.1951. For the figures see minutes of AAA meeting, 14.1.1959 and calculation from Arbeitsgemeinschaft Heimstatthilfe im Lande NRW (ed.), *Verzeichnis der Jugendheimstätten in NRW*.

the binding environment of their own hearth and plot of land. The Hibernia company went even further along this road and in 1956 completed an experimental housing estate for twenty-five young owner-occupiers nearby the youth village where they had formerly been accommodated. Youngsters who had saved for a house were rewarded with an extra loan from the company on top of the usual employer contribution. This was a particularly striking example of the desire to maintain a protected environment and help the youngsters to put down roots without ever immersing them in the life of the mining community.[18]

Supervision and Control in the Hostels

A natural consequence of the anxieties and hopes aroused by the young hostel occupants was that the employers were at pains to keep works councillors and unions well away from them. Here, however, the employers found themselves from the start in a difficult situation. Under Control Council legislation, there was no doubt that works councillors had a right to co-determine social and cultural policy. Particularly during the immediate post-war years, employers did not feel strong enough to prevent works councillors from nominating hostel wardens. In addition, the DKBL was unwilling to antagonise the unions openly on social questions. Indeed, under British pressure it formed in 1948 the KfSA, an organisation jointly run with the miners' union to provide better services for the newcomers.[19]

However, the churches stepped forward to offer a solution. It was no accident that it was a church organisation, in this case the Sozialamt, which made the definitive general statement on building hostels. For the church played a crucial role in the hostel programme, providing personnel and assisting the employers to protect their apprentices both from too much contact with the local community and from union and works council influence.

18. Roelen, 'Die Bedeutung der Pestalozzidörfer', p. 92; Hibernia Konzern, *Sozialberichte 1956*, pp. 23ff. and *1957*, p. 23.
19. Control Council Law no. 22, Works Council Law, reprinted in *Military Government Gazette for the British Zone*, vol. 9, 1946, pp. 197–9, esp. Article V (f); BM A101, 251, DKBL to Bischöfl. Gen.vikariat, 29.4.1948; WWA S22 (OMGUS) BICO BISEC 11/104-2/2, UK/US CCG, report to BICO for December 1948. See also below.

The Catholics seem to have become aware of the apprentice hostels' specific importance in 1947 as a result of a Social Ministry conference to look into welfare policy for young miners. One of those present was Theodor Fennemann, director of what at that time was the only Catholic hostel for miners in the Ruhr. Fennemann was both alarmed and excited by what he heard and sent a letter to the Archbishop of Cologne and the bishops of the other dioceses in the region. What was alarming for Fennemann was the generally anticlerical atmosphere, emanating mainly from the union but not openly opposed by any of the other bodies present at the conference. No one seemed to be envisaging including Christian teaching or religious supervision amongst the proposed welfare measures and it was evident that the church was not to be given any major role. If the projected figures for apprentice recruitment were realised, wrote Fennemann, the implications could be disastrous. Unless the church organisations did something soon, there would be a strongly anticlerical atmosphere in the apprentice hostels and this could well mean that in fifteen years' time the entire mining community was lost to the church. The good news for the church, however, was that both Social Ministry and Labour Administration were privately well disposed to the idea of hostels being run under church supervision. This was an opportunity the church could not afford to miss.[20]

This feeling that the apprentice hostels represented an opportunity to influence the character of the entire mining community was echoed by a number of church organisations over the following years. The Catholic Workers Movement, for example, approved an attempt to found a Catholic hostel in Westerholt with the argument that the local mine was '90 per cent red'[21] and that the hostel was the only chance to break this Marxist stronghold. The Caritas organisation and the Christliche Arbeiterjugend (CAJ) were increasingly active in promoting the establishment of Catholic hostels, while similar initiatives emanated from the Christlicher Verein junger Männer (CVJM) and the Innere Mission on the Protestant side. As the Caritas organisation argued in a pamphlet devoted to its new apprentice

20. BM A101, 251, T. Fennemann, Director St. Johannesstift der Salesianer to Kardinal Frings et al., 12.7.1947.
21. BM A101, 252, Winkelheide to Generalvikariat, 27.11.1948.

hostel in Bottrop, 'wer einen christlich ausgerichteten bergmännischen Nachwuchs hat, der hat später auch einen christlichen
Bergmannsstand'.[22] In 1950 the Arbeitsgemeinschaft katholische Heimstattbewegung für heimatlose Jugend im Lande NRW
was formed to co-ordinate these initiatives for the Catholic
side.[23]

The employers' response was initially extremely cautious. At
confidential meetings, influential employers gave the church to
understand that their initiatives were very welcome but only if
handled delicately enough. Nevertheless it did not take them
long to see that handing hostels over to the churches was the
best way to keep union and works councils at bay. From 1950
onwards, the DKBL felt confident enough actively to promote
the establishment of church-run hostels. An early step was to
establish a special camp at Adelheide, a former aerodrome,
where homeless youngsters not yet ready for an apprenticeship
could be prepared under church supervision. Even where mines
were not particularly disposed to involve the church, they were
urged by the DKBL to do so. 'Ich brauche Ihnen gegenüber nicht
zu betonen,' wrote the DKBL's Lorenz Höcker to the director of
the mine Emscher-Lippe, 'daß nach unserer Auffassung der
christliche Geist überall, insbesondere aber in den Heimen aus-
strahlen muß. Ist er doch letzlich die einzige Kraft gegenüber
dem nicht nur im Osten herrschenden Ungeist!'[24] As well as
protecting the youngsters from unions and works councils and
spreading a 'Christian spirit', whatever that was, the churches
saved the employers money, in some cases because they were
able to tap external sources of funding but more generally
because in 1953 the IGB managed to extend the industry's wage
norms to employees in colliery-run hostels. Church hostels were
not covered by the agreement and their employees cost considerably less.

In 1953, the director of Caritas in Bottrop had very interesting

22. BM A101, 253, 'Caritas Berglehrlingsheim Bottrop. Ein Beitrag zum
christlichen Nachwuchs des Bergmanns', [1949/1950].
23. BM A101, 252, paper, 'AG der kath. Heimstattbewegung in der Diözese
Münster', Duisburg, no date; BM A101, 253, paper, 'Die religiöse Situation und
die seelsorgliche Betreuung in den Wohnheimen und Lagern des Industriege-
biets', no date.
24. BBA 35, 267, Höcker to Premer, 3.6.1950. See also BM A101, 251, Julius
Angerhauen to Bischof Michael Keller, 9.4.1948 and DKBL to Bischöfl.Gen.vi-
kariat, 29.4.1948; Ges.Verb File '003 Adelheide', Sogemeier to Kost, 9.6.1949.

news for the Bishop of Münster. Dr Köker from Hibernia had arranged a meeting to inform the director of Hibernia's wish that control over its apprentice hostels be transferred to the church. Since Hibernia controlled some 20 per cent of all apprentices in the industry this could not but be of interest to the church. According to Dr Köker, Hibernia was having difficulty bringing up the youngsters in an appropriate way because the works council, unions and the youngsters themselves undermined the wardens' best intentions. At the same time the union was insisting that the company pay wardens according to the industry's wage rates. The question for Hibernia was how to get the hostels into church hands against the opposition of the powerful communist-led works council. Hibernia suggested that the church should 'pressure' the company into changing its hostel regime. 'Wir müssen uns darüber klar sein,' said Dr Köker, 'daß durch ein Klingelzeichen der Bischöfe von Münster und von Köln der gesamte Nachwuchs im Bergbau aus den katholischen Gegenden gesperrt werden könnte.'[25]

There is no denying that the employers enjoyed considerable success in enlisting church aid and that for a while the IGB was very much on the defensive. In 1951, it felt the situation serious enough to send a circular to all works councillors warning them of Caritas and Innere Mission efforts. Once the hostels were under church control, warned the IGB, union and works council lost the power to influence the youngsters. It attributed the employers' support for the church to a desire to undermine the union. A copy of the circular fell into the hands of Caritas which passed it on to the Bishop of Münster with the commentary that the letter 'kennzeichnet in seiner ganzen Schärfe die Situation, in der wir augenblicklich stehen'.[26] A quiet war developed, with church representatives wooing the employers, and union representatives trying to prevent the mines from putting their hostels in the churches' hands.[27]

The IGB suffered the disadvantage that a number of state

25. BM A101, 253, Caritas-Verband Bottrop to Bischöfl.Gen.vikariat, 23.7.1953; A101, 253, Gen.vikar to Caritasdirektor Dr Pelster, 24.7.1953; A101, 253, Caritas-Verband für die Stadt Bottrop to Bischöfl.Gen.vikariat, 23.7.1953.
26. BM A101, 252, B.v.Heyden to Gen.vikar, 3.8.1951.
27. IGBEA File 'Jugend', August Enderle to August Schmidt, 12.5.1949; IGB Abteilung Schulung und Bildung to Enderle, 1.6.1949; IGB Hauptverwaltung, circular no. 88/51 to works councils and social representatives, 23.7.1951.

agencies gave the churches a great deal of covert support. An official in the Labour Administration Mining Office informed the diocese of Münster that funds could be diverted to enable Catholic hostels to be built; another official in the same administration offered to segregate incoming apprentices on confessional lines to facilitate the founding of Catholic hostels. In October 1951, Hensel, one of the mining specialists in the Economics Ministry, sent a letter to the NRW Social Ministry's youth officer Willi Weber. In response to the IGB circular mentioned above, Hensel asked Weber if he could not get the religious organisations to show the absurdity of the union's accusations. In the same breath, however, he continued, 'Das christliche Element darf im Bergbau keinesfalls erstickt werden, besonders nicht bei der Bergbau-Jugend. Die letzte Bremse gegen die sowieso schon zu stark fortgschrittene Radikalisierung wäre auf diese Weise beseitigt.'[28]

In view of this official backing, it is not surprising that the churches made rapid headway. By the end of 1952, according to IGB calculations, some 108 apprentice and *Knappen* hostels had been completed. Of these thirty-three, or just under a third, had been removed from colliery control. Thirteen were in the hands of Caritas, fifteen run by the Innere Mission and five by other church organisations. A further thirty hostels were under construction, virtually half of which were church-controlled. The IGB calculated that by 1954 the church would be in charge of getting on for 40 per cent of young miners' hostels. Certainly, by 1956, of the 187 Ruhr hostels for apprentices and *Knappen*, only 119 were in the mines' hands, thirty-one being run by the Catholic organisation, thirty-three by Protestant groups and four by other independent organisations.[29]

However, the institutionalised rights provided by the new works council law of 1952 and in particular the extra rights of co-determination enshrined in the *Montanmitbestimmungsgesetz*

28. BAK B102, 33189, Hensel to Weber, 13.10.1951; BM A101, 252, Winkelheide to Gen.vikar, 27.11.1951; B.v.Heyden to Bischof Keller, 15.3.1951; IGBEA V3, IGB, two internal memos from Abteilung VII to Geschäftsführenden Vorstand, both dated 17.6.1952.

29. Figures calculated from DGBA Protokoll-Sammlung, IGB, Hauptverwaltung, Abteilung Jugend (ed.), *Geschäftsbericht 1950–1952*, [Bochum 1953], p. 87; IGBEA V6, IGB, memo concerning transfer of hostels to outside organisations (*Trägerverbände*), 10.5.1954; Arbeitsgemeinschaft Heimstatthilfe im Lande NRW (ed.), *Verzeichnis der Jugendheimstätten in NRW*.

of 1951 began to change the situation. The 1952 law, admittedly, did not give works councils the same power they had enjoyed under Control Council legislation. But, in the present case, this did not matter once the new labour directors (labour-appointed members of the executive) provided for by the Co-determination law of 1951 learned to extend their authority. As the labour directors began to take charge, most of the anti-union elements in company social policy disappeared. True, the labour directors' behaviour on the hostel question was to confound the expectations of the union: for, because of the lower costs, the labour directors were very often well disposed to the church hostels. They were keen not to have to pay the wardens according to the industry's general wage rates because not doing so left them with more money to spend on other aspects of social services! However, the fundamental point was that the labour directors were able to insist on agreements that ensured union and works council free access to the hostels. In the case of Hibernia, for example, the labour director and works council abandoned their opposition to church-run hostels once it appeared that a low-cost, pro-union solution was possible. The IGB was then able to drop its hard line against the church hostels, particularly since the church was feeling its way towards some sort of an arrangement. Thus, although in hostels covered by existing agreements the union sometimes continued to have problems of access, new agreements with the church caused less concern. From the employers' viewpoint, they therefore offered less protection from the union than before and were probably inspired more by the desire to save money than by anything else.[30]

The Adult Hostels, Welfare and Cultural Policy

Another way in which the employers could respond to and influence the hostel inmates was by providing suitable entertainment, cultural and leisure activities. Often this was done locally, on a hostel-by-hostel basis, but between 1948 and 1951 a number of Ruhr organisations were created to initiate and co-

30. IGB Bezirksleitung Essen (ed.), *Geschäftsbericht 1954/1955*, p. 117; IGB (ed.), *Jahrbuch 1956*, p. 252; IGBEA Handakten Rudi Quast, File 'Arbeitskreis-Arbeitsdirektoren 1952–1956', meeting of Arbeitskreis der Arbeitsdirektoren, Bezirk Recklinghausen, 30.9.1953; IGB, memo, as note 29.

ordinate policy in the mining hostels at a regional level. The value of these organisations for the historian is that they tend to be much better documented than the local initiatives. They also stimulated amongst the providers of the relevant services much more thorough, and often fascinating, discussions about what were the appropriate messages to transmit to the youngsters. However, before we can look at them more closely, we need briefly to consider the situation in the *adult* hostels. For it was the conditions there, rather than in the better equipped and provisioned apprentice hostels, which initially provided the stimulus to setting up a central welfare and cultural initiative.

As we know, the employers for a long time found it hard to get overly interested in the spiritual welfare of their adult hostel occupants.[31] As a result, a number of organisations began to concern themselves with the new miners' well-being and to put pressure on the employers to take their responsibilities more seriously. One of most influential was the welfare officer of the UK/USCCG, C. S. Hudson, who went so far as to spend a week in a new miners' camp incognito in order to discover what life there was like. Hudson concluded that by solving some of the new miners' difficulties and providing them with entertainment, wastage could be reduced and productivity increased. To this end, he suggested the creation of a joint employer–union organisation to look into new miners' welfare.[32]

At the same time both state and church were growing increasingly concerned about conditions in the camps. They were less worried about boosting coal production than about what they saw as the moral and political dangers of camp life. The NRW Social Ministry and labour administration were particularly worried about the lack of supervision and guidance being offered to the younger men, who were not being protected from alcoholism, sexual excess or possibly even political extremism. These anxieties were echoed by the churches. Many churchmen were unnerved by the 'eisige Kälte, die einem beim Betreten des Lagers entgegenschlägt',[33] as one priest put it, and felt there to

31. WWA S22 (OMGUS) BICO BISEC 11/104–2/2, US/UK CCG, report to BICO for October 1948.
32. HStAD NW42, 912, paper, 'Besuch der Gutehoffnungshütte, Oberhausen, 12.–19.Dezember 1948', no date; C. S. Hudson, 'Denkschrift über die Englandreise im Januar 1948', 19.1.1948; NW53, 492, Wheatley to Labour Minister, NRW, 3.1.1947 [*sic*: it should be 1948].
33. BM A101, 251, Pfarrer Tebroke to Dechant Niehues, Westerholt, 15.3.1947.

be a radical, anti-Christian spirit pervading the camps.[34]

The union, too, began to wake up at central level to the needs of the new miners. The IVB encouraged camp and hostel occupants to set up committees and appoint representatives. From the end of 1947 onwards, the union organised conferences where grievances could be articulated and suggestions for improvements to camp life or union activity put forward. Some union branches began to think about ways of offering entertainment and education to hostel inmates. In addition, towards the end of 1947 both SPD and KPD intensified their efforts to mobilise support from new labour. Partly under cover of union activity, partly alongside it, the battle for support in the works councils was probably fiercer in 1947 than in any subsequent year (see chapter 9).

All these groups helped to stimulate employer interest in providing entertainment, education and cultural welfare policies for the camps. The British were able to exert pressure directly, and it was largely due to Hudson's urgings that in spring 1948 the DKBL and IVB created the KfSA,[35] the primary function of which was to provide better services for the new miners. The state administration's ability to influence the employers was more indirect but no less effective, particularly when it came to the apprentices. The labour administration, for example, could and did deny young labour to those mines which failed to provide adequate supervision. In addition, as state funding for apprentice hostels came in prospect, the mines were at pains to demonstrate the pedagogical and other services they performed. Union activities, too, galvanised employers into action since they had no desire to leave the field open to works councils and the IGB, and certainly not to the SPD and KPD. Thus by the end of 1948, management was showing considerable interest in this area.[36]

34. IGBEA BR7, ABB to IVB, 28.4.1947; HStAD NW41, 746, Simons, 'Die Berglehrlingsheime in NRW', 14.7.1947; BM A101, 251, Diözesanverband Katholische Arbeiterbewegung (KAB) to Kapitularvikar, 26.2.1947.

35. Initially, 'Kommission für Bergmannswohlfahrt'. On its first meeting, see WWA S22 (ÖMGUS) CO HIST BR 3/404–1/7, UK/US CCG, report to BICO for March 1948.

36. Ges.Verb., File '"K"', vol. 2' [the distinction between vol. 1 and vol. 2 has been introduced by the author as a means to distinguish between two files with the same name], unsigned and undated paper, 'Vorgeschlagene Tagesordnung für die erste Siztung des Bergarbeiter-Fürsorge-Ausschusses'. See DKBL (ed.),

However, there were still obstacles hindering a more comprehensive welfare and cultural policy for the hostel occupants. The first was money. The mines were for a long period extremely hard pressed for funds. Not only the accounts but also the Coal Control Group spoke against extravagance in areas away from the immediate needs of production. When the DKBL tried to earmark a small amount of the coal price as a permanent levy to provide steady funding for welfare policies, the UK/USCCG refused. This made the mines reluctant to hire large numbers of additional personnel to offer services to the hostels. Secondly, there was, once again, the problem of ensuring that social and cultural programmes did not get hijacked by organised labour and in particular by radical or militant groups within the IGB and works councils.[37]

The question, therefore, was who should provide the hostels with entertainment. This time, the churches did not seem to be the answer. Though they gave some discreet encouragement to the churches, the employers were reluctant to allow them to hold meetings in company-owned hostels, because of the danger that this would give other political groups *carte blanche* to organise events there and would antagonise important groups within the IGB. The DKBL did manage, at first experimentally, then as a permanent fixture, to include religious instruction in the curriculum at the apprentice training schools, albeit at a cost of allowing the unions to hold some lectures too. But, sympathetic as it was, the DKBL did not want to take the risk of giving church organisations free access to mine-owned hostels. The non-communist element within the IGB leadership, too, was agreeable to a general prohibition on 'political' meetings (under which heading it included the church) because this would keep not only the church but also the KPD youth groups at bay.[38]

In place of the churches, the state stepped in to the breach, and at the beginning of 1949 negotiations between the DKBL

Die Berglehrlingsheime des Steinkohlenbergbaus; HStAD NW41, 747, Soz.Min. IIIB/6, memo, 25.7.1948.

37. WWA S22 (OMGUS) CO HIST BR 3/404–1/7, minutes of 18th meeting of UK/USCCG, 6.8.1948; interview with Siegfried Schroeder, 18.2.1984.

38. BM A101,252, Kath. Lagerwerk to Bishop of Münster, 10.6.1949; Ges. Verb., File '"K"', vol. 2', minutes of KfSA meeting, 16.11.1950. See also chapter 9.

and the Ministry for Education and Culture led to the creation of a Fachstelle für Bergarbeiterbetreuung, run by the regional association for adult education (Landesverband der Volkshochschulen). The Fachstelle was wound up in 1949 and replaced by the Revierarbeitsgemeinschaft für die kulturelle Bergarbeiterbetreuung (RAG), an organisation that persists till this day. Five field-workers were appointed to stimulate and co-ordinate cultural activities in the miners' hostels. The sums invested were not large, but the RAG in conjunction with local wardens and *Volkshochschulen* did organise a considerable number of events.[39]

Compulsive Talking

Once the employers had begun trying to influence their 'charges', there was no stopping them. Over the following years, virtually no entertainment or service was offered the miners that did not in some way carry a moral or political message. Even when in reality all that was being provided was a little entertainment, the employers and other German groups involved were simply unable to concede that that was all they were doing. There was a compulsion to find a higher purpose, a deeper mission to everything that was done.

This was one of the most striking differences between the British and American attempts to help in the new miners programme and the Germans' approach. The British proposals were usually very simple – to provide some sort of room or meeting-place with appropriate facilities and a little supervision so that the young miners could do what they wanted. If there was any 'higher' aim than providing entertainment, it was to give the youngsters a taste of democracy by letting them organise their own club.[40] A British investigation of mining trainees conducted in 1947, for instance, concluded that 'The trainees

39. HStAD NW17, 136, Landesverband der Volkshochschulen NRW, circular to members of the Landesverband, 10.1.1950; Egon Dietzel, 'Kulturelle Bergmannsbetreuung, eine Notwendigkeit. Gedanken zur kulturellen Bergmannsbetreuung der Volkshochschule Bochum', *Der Anschnitt*, vol. 6, no. 2, 1954, pp. 20–1.

40. OBADA I6303/1757/47, copy, Elphick, 'Die Bedingungen junger Arbeiter in den Zechen. 2RCD u. 3RCD Bereich', 15.1.1947.

should not be nursed and cosseted but induced to do things for themselves.'[41]

The German proposals of the time have a completely different tone. They are full of anxieties and hopes, of the dangers of doing nothing and the high moral ideals towards which the youngsters must be led by wise elders. A small indicative example came at a meeting of the KfSA's subcommittee for entertainment. It was suggested that films might be provided at some of the hostels because the new miners often had no going-out clothes and many hostels were some distance away from the cinema. Immediately, it was then proposed that only culturally valuable films should be shown so as to raise the intellectual and spiritual level of the miners. And a further justification for showing the films was found: it would keep the newcomers away from 'abwegigen Vergnügungsrummeln' in the local towns.[42]

This compulsion to have a mission, and the compulsion to guide rather than to let speak, seems to have been a fundamental characteristic of bourgeois culture in post-war Germany. On one level, it manifested the belief that the post-war era presented both considerable danger and a very real opportunity. The danger was primarily that radicalisation that might result if the youngsters were to get into the wrong hands.[43] The opportunity was, as the previous chapters have indicated, to restore both a stable workforce and a stable, ordered society. However, the almost compulsive moralising of the German policy-makers suggests there was also a deeper, hidden drive. The whole idea that the young or dispossessed needed guidance from their elders to lead them back to the values and behaviour of an ordered society seems in part to have been a way of suppressing the anxiety that it was precisely the older generation and the established classes who had been compromised by fascism, whose values had been called into question and who could no

41. PORO (ed.), *A Social Survey: The Mining Trainee 1947*, Bielefeld, 1948, p. 30.

42. Ges.Verb.File 'I.II', section 024, 3, minutes of 2nd meeting of Arbeitskreis II, 24.8.1948.

43. For fears of radicalism, see BM A101, 251, Diözesanverband KAB to Kapitularvikar, 26.2.1947; HStAD NW41, 747, Curt Bondy, 'Gedanken zur außerbetrieblichen Beeinflussung von Bergbaulehrlingen, Knappen und jungen Neubergleuten', Hamburg, November 1951.

longer provide convincing leadership for the young. An inner uncertainty was being turned outwards into a mission to rescue the 'uprooted' and transmit firm values (see also discussion in chapter 5). The employers, the churchmen and others were, it seems, struggling to make something *within themselves* strong. As the Bochum director of apprentice education, Dr Herwick, said in a talk about the moral and educational goals beyond the schools' narrower technical curriculum: 'Steins Worte waren unser Wegweiser: "Was wir an äußerem Ruhm verloren haben, müssen wir durch innere Werte wiedergewinnen". Unser Glaube stützte sich auf die Ewigkeitswerte der deutschen Seele, die nur verschüttet sein konnten, für die aber nach Goethes Wissen alle Länder und Meere zu klein sind, um ihren Reichtum zu fassen.'[44]

Conveying the True Ethos of the Miner

Turning to the actual practical work of providing services for the new miners, the first obvious feature is that a lot of energy was expended on trying to increase their pride and interest in mining. Both church and state recognised the priority of strengthening *Berufsstolz* through suitable lectures. There was a widespread hope that, if the right spiritual guidance were given, it would be possible to convey to the newcomers a specific mining mentality, as Jürgen Heuer wrote in his account of the Pestalozzi villages: 'Hier ist es erforderlich . . . ein Gefühl für die Mentalität des Bergmanns zu erwecken. Die Vermittlung eines echten Traditionsbewußtseins in Verbindung mit einem fundierten Berufsstolz und Standesbewußtsein, das das Ansehen des Bergmanns hochhält, ist hier eine der wesentlichen psychologischen Aufgaben, die vor allem den Pflegeeltern des Pestalozzidorfs obliegt.'[45] Or, as Curt Bondy put it, a new *Standesbewußtsein* was to be created through 'außerbetriebliche Beeinflussung'.[46]

44. Archive of the Westfälische Berggewerkschaftskasse (WBKA), photocopied extract from *Mitteilungen der WBK*, no. 3, 1950, Vortrag des Bezirksschuldirektors Herwick, 'Unsere Bergberufsschule als Erziehungsschule'.
45. Jürgen Heuer, 'Pestalozzidorf – Sozialleistung des Bergbaus. Aufbau und Probleme', in H. J. Seraphim (ed.), *Siedlungen und Wohnungen von heute*, Münster, 1952, p. 62.
46. HStAD NW41, 746, copy, Caritasverband Bottrop, Berglehrlingsheim

At a celebration to commemorate the 100th anniversary of the mining company Concordia, two short musical recitals were followed by three poems; first came the miner with long service behind him and then a new miner, who recited the following:

Die Werksgemeinschaft schließt mit unsichtbaren Bänden
Zusammen all, die sich hier zusammenfanden.
Sie webt um Lehrling, Knappen, Hauer, Veteranen
Und um uns Neubergleute, die von weither kamen,
Um Arbeit und auch Heimat hier zu finden
Und altem Stamm uns glücklich zu verbinden.[47]

An even more theatrical attempt to emphasise this continuity with the past and to celebrate the steadfastness of the miner was a ceremony at the Diergardt–Mevissen mine. The 250,000th newcomer to be found a job in the Ruhr was symbolically presented with the miner's tools by the oldest miner in the pit. The celebration was attended by the 50,000th newcomer, the 100,000th and so on as well as a mining family of grandfather, father, son and son-in-law, all of whom worked at the mine Hugo. And there were countless other attempts to cultivate a sense of tradition and the miners' mentality.[48]

Apart from communicating a sense of mining's inner worth and tradition, there were also various attempts to convey the notion that occupational loyalty was a sign of personal strength. *Der Förderturm*, for example, offered its readers an article of high moral tone, 'Wer besitzt Bildung'. It stressed that genuine personality was more important than any school-book education and lamented the absence of the harmoniously balanced personality, full of occupational ethos and integrity.[49] The view that occupational loyalty was the sign of a balanced personality, and could be inculcated as such, is also apparent in the criteria for

---

Erziehungsgrundsätze, Bottrop, 21.10.1948; Bondy, 'Gedanken zur außerbetrieblichen Beeinflussung'.

47. BBA 8, 191, 'Festfolge. Feierstunde der Concordia BAG Oberhausen Rhld', September 1950.

48. Außenstelle Bergbau (ed.), 'Sechs Jahre Außenstelle Bergbau des Landesarbeitantes NRW', unpublished MS, no place, no date [1952], p. 79; 'Von Art und Seele des Bergmanns', *Der Förderturm*, July 1948, and many other articles in subsequent issues; HStAD NW41, 747, Dr Hoernecke, Wiesbaden, 'Gedanken zur kulturellen Bergmannsbetreuung im Steinkohlenbergbau' (Gutachten für die KfSA), 15.5.1952.

49. 'Wer besitzt Bildung', *Der Förderturm*, June 1948.

choosing the village 'parents' laid down by the JhStW PV. The second in the list of criteria was 'Bodenständigkeit und Heimatverbundenheit',[50] the implication being that this could be transmitted to the youngsters by the force of the parents' personality.

Of course, not all the attempts to encourage integration were in this romantic historical mould. A glance through the RAG's standard lecture topics in 1953 shows a large number of more straightforward subjects: 'Was kann ich dazu beitragen, um in meinem Beruf zu bleiben und vorwärtszukommen'; 'Welche Bildungsmöglichkeiten und welches Verhalten erleichtern dem Neubergmann die Eingewöhnung in die neue Heimat'; and so on, though the programme was not without lectures on the history of mining and the mentality of the miner.[51]

Political Education: Between Angst and 'Neutrality'

There was a considerable amount of explicit political education. The general consensus was that the new miners should be educated to be good democrats. The stress, however, was on the duties and responsibilities of the citizen, rather than on his freedom or participation. As Herwick, the director of apprentice education, declared: 'Wir hoffen . . . Menschen zu formen, die sich später schämen in der Straßenbahn zu sagen: "Das ist demokratische Freiheit, jeder kann machen was er will".'[52] The emphasis on the dutiful democrat, rather than the active citizen, reflected that profound and often unarticulated uncertainty about the relationship between democracy and the organic society which we have already encountered. In keeping with the desire to return to some lost moral order, there was a strong emphasis on the need for a moral reawakening or a moral rearmament. There was also frequent stress on the need for European unity, on European integration as the ultimate aim of politics.[53]

50. JHStW PV (ed.), *Pestalozzieltern im Pestalozzidorf*, Essen, 1952, cited in Roelen, 'Die Bedeutung der Pestalozzidörfer', pp. 27ff.

51. Ges.Verb., File 'Unternehmensverband 662–668', Tätigkeitsbericht der RAG 1953.

52. Herwick, 'Unsere Bergberufsschule'.

53. HStAD NW17, 141, RAG, Bericht über die Tagung in Kronenburg,

In terms of the approach to the miners, the older generation's anxiety, natural authoritarianism and burning sense of mission all tended to preclude much practical democracy. Again there was a striking contrast between the British initiatives and those of their German counterparts. Consider the closing words of the British survey of trainees in 1947:

> Finally, there is presented here a golden opportunity to introduce democratic practices. The trainees should not be nursed and cosseted but induced to do things for themselves. It might be recommended to the trainees in each camp that they set up a social committee. A house committee is also indicated, to decide upon those day to day matters and questions of conduct and discipline which fall outside the general supervisory functions of the pit management or camp leader. Such a committee could also act as the representative voice of the trainees in dealing with the management of the pit or with outside bodies. A seat on the Works' Council should be reserved for a representative elected by this committee.[54]

In German hands, by contrast, instruction and moral education was often realised in a very authoritarian manner, particularly in relation to the young apprentices. There was a general feeling that the uprooted young needed to be brought up within a firm and a religious environment. They had been deprived too long of the 'strenge, richtungsweisende väterliche Hand'.[55] The hostel rules produced by Caritas in Bottrop reveal this particularly clearly. Beginning with the menacing greeting, 'Unser Heim soll Dein "Zuhause" sein. Du sollst Dich hier wohlfühlen,' it goes on to tell the youngster when to get up, how to wash and in what state the room must be left. No matter what the weather, the windows must be opened on awakening – 'Wir sind alle Freunde der frischen Morgenluft'. Only on two weekdays and Sundays did the youngsters have free use of their leisure time. (Needless to say, churchgoing was compulsory.) The youngsters were trained to sing grace in canon at mealtimes. But outside the hostels, even local-born youngsters experienced a

---

21–26.9.1953, Lecture by Sieburg, 'Staatsbürgerliche Willensbildung in der kulturellen Bergmannsbetreuung.'

54. PORO, *The Mining Trainee 1947*, p. 30.

55. Erwin Jochum, 'Das sexuelle Problem unserer heutigen Jugend und der Beitrag der Bergberufsschule zu seine Lösung', *Mitteilungen für die Bergberufsschulen*, vol. 6, 1954, p. 8.

new religious–authoritarian spirit in their schools. Indeed, it pervaded the way mining employers brought up their own children, as the memoirs of mining engineer Rudolf Wawersik make clear.[56]

Free discussions were difficult and often unrewarding because so many areas were taboo. This was partly because the employers were hemmed in by so many institutional and political constraints. In particular, the state-sponsored agencies involved were extremely concerned to appear politically and religiously neutral. Both *Volkshochschulen* and NRW ministries felt their work could not be effective if this neutrality was placed in jeopardy. Apart from the risk of alienating the union, it was believed that speakers would lose their credibility *vis-à-vis* the young hostel occupants and might even drive them to extremes. Thus lectures tended to concentrate on formal issues. As a speaker at a conference for hostel wardens said, a good topic was not 'socialism or capitalism' but 'the refugee and equal rights', 'I read a constitution', or 'what is politics and is it necessary'.[57] Religious questions, too, were evidently seen as dangerous if they dragged the lectures into any area that could be considered denominational. At a conference on cultural policy in 1953, the question was raised whether religious issues should be discussed. Yes, was the answer, and the fieldworkers must be in a position 'die oft sehr prekären Fragen zu beantworten'. Again, there was a strong sense of danger here if the tightrope of 'neutrality' was left.[58]

Apart from such public pressures to be 'neutral', there were the fundamental inner uncertainties that made any discussion dangerous. 'Wo ist seelisch im deutschen Volk das Geschehen der letzten 20 Jahre wirklich verarbeitet worden?' asked Oberkirchenrat Kloppenburg, in a lecture to mining educationalists whose refreshing openness contrasted strongly with so much

56. HStAD NW41, 746, Caritasverband Bottrop, Berglehrlingsheim Hausordnung, 21.10.1948; Hans Diether Baroth, *Aber es waren schöne Zeiten*, Cologne, 1978, p. 58; Rudolf Wawersik, *Ausbeute eines Bergmannslebens. Erinnerungen an den oberschlesischen, saarländischen und westfälischen Bergbau*, Essen, 1981, p. 131.
57. HStAD NW42, 912, Simons, report on a course for wardens of hostels for apprentices and young miners, 6–10.10.1947, 18.1.1948.
58. HStAD NW17, 136, Kultusministerium NRW IIE5, internal memo to Minister Teusch, 8.11.1950; NW17, 141, RAG, report on the conference in Kronenburg 21–26.9.1953, October 1953; BM A101, 252, B.v.Heyden to Bishop Keller, 15.3.1951.

that was said after the war.[59] 'Wie sollen wir,' continued the speaker, 'wenn wir selber in Hysterie geraten bei der Diskussion über diese Dinge, erwarten, daß eine Jugend gesund reagiert?'[60] If the Nazi era was mentioned at all, it was usually rushed through discussion under the euphemism of 'jüngste Vergangenheit'. This same inner uncertainty also made discussion of many contemporary issues very rigid. In a revealing phrase in his dissertation about the Pestalozzi villages, Roelen observed that religious groups had been set up in a number of villages where the youngsters could discuss religious issues and 'eliminate religious doubts'.[61] There was no room for doubt. This fear of admitting uncertainty or embarking on contentious issues gave a lot of the political and religious messages a rather sterile quality.

It should be noted, however, that, because of the formalistic approach to democracy, when democratic experiments *were* made, they were made on a thorough and institutional basis. For instance, when the CVJM set up special hostels known as 'Guilds' to help the young migrants who streamed in from the GDR in the mid-1950s find their feet, they contained special courts and parliaments to give the youngsters a taste of democracy. Some of the Pestalozzi villages had youth parliaments to allow the youngsters decide how to spend their leisure time. When the Ewald–König Ludwig mining company organised a skiing trip for its youngsters, they too formed their own parliament and shaped their time according to popular vote. And there were a number of other similar examples.[62]

'Man Benimmt Sich Wieder'

Because of the perceived danger of embarking on the central issues, a lot of the thrust of the educational programmes went into the secondary virtues. Indeed, the desire to teach proper

59. Kloppenburg, 'Jugend in Beruf und Freizeit', *Mitteilungen für die Bergberufsschulen der WBK 1957*, no. 15.
60. Ibid.
61. Roelen, 'Die Bedeutung der Pestalozzidörfer', p. 77.
62. 'Heimatlose haben wieder ein Zuhause', *Ruhr Nachrichten*, 7.1.1956; 'Im Gildenhaus gilt keine D-Mark', *WAZ*, 27.1.1956; Roelen, 'Die Bedeutung der Pestalozzidörfer', p. 89; 'Schi-Freizeit unserer Berglehrlinge in Willingen', *BAG Ewald-König Ludwig*, February/March 1950, pp. 15–18.

behaviour and inculcate a proper respect for authority was so strong that it often conflicted with the goal of integrating the newcomers into the local environment. The pressure to detach the hostels from the mining community, which we observed ·earlier in this chapter, is an obvious example of this.

No programme for cultural welfare was complete without a reference to reviving an 'aktive christliche Gesinnung',[63] to the 'erzieherischen und ethischen Werte des Christentums',[64] or the values of 'der auf christlicher Grundlage beruhenden abendländischen Kultur'.[65] Exactly what was meant by Christian values was never specified but the value on which greatest emphasis was placed was undoubtedly respect for authority. At the very top of the Pestalozzi Association's criteria for selecting village parents, for example, was a sense of duty and responsibility. 'Gegen Unbescheidenheit, Mangel an Ehrfurcht, Ablehnung jeglicher Autorität anzugehen, benutze ich jede Gelegenheit, jede Aussprache', reported one of the field-workers in cultural welfare.[66]

Controlling sexual behaviour was another priority and many hostels instituted dance classes as a way of regulating how young men and women came together. There was a discussion in 1953 about whether youngsters should be allowed to take their girlfriends on trips. Yes, was the answer, because the young miner then has 'einen gesunden Ehrgeiz, den anderen gegenüber mit diesem Mädel bestehen zu können; danach wird er sich seine Gefährtin aussuchen und wird sich selbst entsprechend benehmen. Das sind Dinge, die zu erreichen die kulturelle Bergmannsbetreuung als einen ihrer Programmpunkte betrachtet.'[67] Suitable lectures were also offered to influence the youths' choice of partners, on 'Gesunde und ungesunde Frauenschönheit', for example, which presumably warned the young

---

63. Klinkert Papers, File 'Niederschriften der Arbeitstagungen und Vortragsveranstaltungen', Vormbrock, 'Überblick über die bisherige Arbeit des Jugendheimstättenwerks und den Entwicklungsstand der Pestalozzidörfer', 7.10.1953.
64. BAK B102, 3306, Hensel to Ullrich, 23.10.1952.
65. Pestalozzidörfer des Bergbaus', p. 17; Roelen, 'Die Bedeutung der Pestalozzidörfer', p. 26.
66. HStAD NW17, 10, Erich Burrisch to Kultusmin., 2.12.1949, annex; JHStW PV (ed.), *Pestalozzieltern im Pestalozzidorf*, reproduced in Roelen, 'Die Bedeutung der Pestalozzidörfer', pp. 27ff.
67. HStAD NW17, 141, lecture from Fischer in report on the RAG conference at Kronenburg 21–26.9.1953.

miners against flashy girls wearing too much make-up. The hostel wardens were instructed how to help prevent premature sex and masturbation. General social behaviour too, needed improving, and fitting lectures with titles such as 'Man benimmt sich wieder' were given to meet this need.[68]

These 'secondary virtues' became the symbols of the struggle to preserve or revive a past moral order. Two examples will suffice to show the strength of the anxieties that were aroused here. In a lecture given in 1954, Erwin Jochum talked about the way in which the apprentice schools could help to shape apprentices' sexual behaviour. He described some of the shocking cases that had come to his attention, the worst being two young miners who, invited to spend the night at the house of a widow, slept with her two daughters after having drawn straws to see who slept with whom. Leaving aside the fact that the story in the form in which it is presented seems rather apocryphal, it is noteworthy that Jochum went on to say: 'Da öffnet sich ein Abgrund, der uns mit Ekel und Grauen erfüllen muß. Doch das ist die Situation unserer Tage . . . das ist das unheimlich glimmende Feuer unter der Oberfläche, das sich zu einer verheerenden Feuersbrunst ausweiten kann.'[69] Less apocalyptic, but no less striking was a paper delivered in the previous year at a conference for field-workers and other interested participants in cultural welfare policy. Without embarrassment, but with an emotion that comes through clearly in the text, Dozent Fischer had this to say about the cultural value of organised outings with young miners: 'Es wird so oft gesagt, daß die jungen Menschen keinen Sinn mehr für ethische Werte hätten. Diese Auffassung entspricht nicht ganz den Tatsachen. Es ist immer wieder ein Erlebnis, festzustellen, wie diese Menschen im Dom still und ruhig werden und sogar die Hände falten. Das allein könnte schon die Berechtigung der Betreuungsarbeit unterstreichen.'[70] There is a sort of shuddery feeling of pleasure here at that little physical gesture of bourgeois propriety. The decently held hands, though in reality indicating nothing more

---

68. Ibid.; Roelen, 'Die Bedeutung der Pestalozzidörffer', p. 84; HStAD NW42, 912, Simons, Bericht über den Lehrgang für Heimleiter von Berglehrlingen- und Ledigenheimen vom 6.10.1947, 18.1.1948.

69. Jochum, 'Das sexuelle Problem', esp. p. 10.

70. HStAD NW17, 141, lecture from Fischer in report on the RAG conference at Kronenburg 21–26.9.1953.

than that their owners were intimidated by the atmosphere of a large cathedral and uncertain as to how to behave, symbolise for the speaker an acceptance of proper values. The values themselves remain undefined. Such gestures – decent behaviour, respectful demeanour and so on – became the focal point of cultural policy, because of the difficulty in actually specifying what the deeper values might be.

Hostels and a Stable Workforce

What was the impact of all the effort expended on hostel design and management? How far did the industry's cultural and welfare policies affect the behaviour of the hostel residents? The employers' biggest disappointment was the failure to cultivate any noticeable increase in workforce stability from the group which, more than any other, had been the recipient of the most intensive efforts, namely, the apprentices. The experience of the company with the longest experience of Pestalozzi villages, the Hamborner Bergbau AG (formerly Gruppe Hamborn of the GBAG), is instructive. In 1955 its training and social services director reported that the village had made little difference to the number of former apprentices leaving the company and worse, leaving the industry. The Hibernia company had much the same to report a year or two later. No doubt some of the lectures and guidance offered to hostel occupants had their positive impact: a decision here to enter the mining school after a lecture on career opportunities in mining; an accident avoided there as a result of gaining some general background knowledge about mining techniques and so on. But, generally speaking, there was little sign that even the finest hostels or the most intensive welfare and cultural policy made much difference to the wastage levels amongst apprentices who had finished their training.[71]

As chapter 5 on the apprenticeship programme has already indicated, the employers' exaggerated expectations were based on a number of unrealistic myths about the nature and origins of workforce stability. One of these myths was the belief that job-changing was a sign of an unbalanced personality. Another

71. Ges.Verb. File 'Arbeitsausschuß', minutes of Arb.aus.f.A. meeting, 5.4.1955; Hibernia Konzern, *Sozialbericht 1957*, p. 24.

notion which enjoyed a tremendous significance in the Ruhr was that garden work and the rural setting would 'root' the young newcomers in the area. That this was not so was clear to many hostel wardens and village 'parents' who were often far more down-to-earth and realistic than the senior personnel involved in creating the institutions. In the Pestalozzi villages, for example, house parents and village leaders, recognising the meaninglessness of enforced garden work, were happy to let the youngsters concentrate on repairing their motorbikes rather than tilling the soil, much to the chagrin of the Pestalozzi Association's founders.[72]

There were other factors, too, which prevented the employers from getting their message across. One was shortage of personnel, for, while enormous resources were ploughed into providing the right physical environment, many of the hostels employed only a small number of staff. These were often not particularly well paid (indeed, the KfSA itself admitted to being rather shocked at the employment conditions it found in some hostels) and, as a result, often lacked the motivation or the qualifications to guide and instruct the youngsters very intensively.[73] A more central problem of hostel policy was that, where they were successful at getting the youngsters to make extensive use of their services and facilities in the hostels, employers actually inhibited the development of links with the locality. This, indeed, was often their aim. The desire to integrate was overriden (and thereby undermined) by the desire to segregate. Towards the young adults, too, the RAG field-workers seemed often far more concerned to transmit ideals than create good local contacts. It must be acknowledged, however, that even when the wardens or field-workers were favourably disposed towards the idea, it was difficult to cement links between hostel and neighbourhood. Local sports organisations often wanted only good talent and were not interested in offering a game to anyone who came along. Other groups had a specific religious or political affiliation, which made it difficult for the cultural workers to promote them. The result was that

72. Klinkert Papers, File 'Niederschriften der Arbeitstagungen und Vortrags-veranstaltungen', minutes of meeting of village leaders, 10.12.1958. It was noteworthy that in 1954 the village leaders insisted on their title being changed from the archaic *Dorfälteste* to *Dorfleiter*.
73. *Mitteilungen der KfSA* nos 1/2, 1951, p. 4.

the hostel environment, though in ideological terms often less detached from the outside world than the employers wanted, was in social terms rather isolated.[74]

There is, of course, no doubt that the provision of decently furbished hostels was essential during the 1940s and 1950s and there is equally no doubt that many of the former hostel occupants went on to be long-serving members of the workforce. The decision to build apprentice accommodation on a grand scale opened up sources of well-educated youngsters on whom the industry could not normally have drawn. Quite a number of these youngsters were to provide the deputies and lower management of the following decades. For these reasons, the hostel programme was far from being a total failure. It cannot even be asserted with certainty that the resources invested in the hostels or in the cultural and welfare programmes would have been better spent elsewhere.

It does seem likely, however, that if more money and energy had been expended on social integration – rather than on spiritually improving the newcomers or on recasting the workforce – more hostel occupants would have been won for the industry. To take one small example: partly because of convenience and partly because of moral fears, provision was seldom made for young miners, even young adults, to bring girlfriends back to the hostel. It was therefore often very difficult to develop intimate friendships with girls from the town. This was a small but significant barrier to integration which the mines should have been able to solve.[75]

The Political Impact of the Hostel Programme

Even if they failed to create a stable workforce, did the employers enjoy some success in transmitting the desired values to the young men in their charge? Part of the answer to this question will have to be deferred until we have considered the union's activities towards new labour (see chapter 9). Neverthe-

74. IGB, (ed.), *Jahrbuch 1952*, pp. 441–2, *Jahrbuch 1955*, p. 244 and IGBEA Handakten Rudi Quast, File 'M. Assistenten-Tagungen (alt)', 3rd meeting of Herner Kreis, 24.6.1953.

75. 'Jugend ohne innere Bindung' IV Industrieheime mit Komfort und ohne Seele', *Neue Zeitung*, 1952, no. 218, p. 5.

less some tentative conclusions can be advanced at this stage. As far as adult new miners were concerned, one problem limiting the effectiveness of cultural work in particular was that spending remained fairly limited. It is therefore unsurprising to discover from a 1952 survey that 60 per cent of new miners had not taken part in any of the Volkshochschule courses offered in the hostels. The reasons for this lack of funding are not hard to find. Mine managers, though they may have shared the values and aspirations embodied in the lectures and other cultural work, were often reluctant to spend money on matters that seemed so far removed from the needs of daily production. There were, however, large variations here between collieries. One problem common to all, which we have already encountered with respect to housing provision, was that they were nervous of investing too much in the outsiders for fear of alienating local men. The 'moral economy' of the established workforce (and, it should be said, of those newcomers who had found lodgings or housing locally) dampened any potential over-exuberance in the provision of services for hostel occupants.[76]

Apart from financial constraints, another serious problem was that for many hostel occupants, whether trainees or apprentices, the lectures and courses offered were often wide of their target, either because they were too intellectually demanding or because they were motivated by anxieties or concerns not shared by their audience. There were, it is true, those amongst the new miners who were very conscious of the break in their education caused by war and its aftermath and who responded enthusiastically to the educational opportunities offered. Courses on German, mathematics and other basic subjects found a small circle of enthusiastic participants. In general, however, the hostel occupants seem to have 'subverted' for their own purposes what was on offer, attending courses and events according to their entertainment value and ignoring those that seemed out merely to improve. Theatre and film evenings enjoyed good audiences, sporting events drew the best participation, while

76. Ges.Verb. File '"K"', vol. 2', minutes of KfSA meeting, 15.3.1951, esp. Köker's comments; Theodor Terhorst, 'Zehnjährige Zusammenarbeit im Dienste der Mitbestimmung beim Hamborner Bergbau', unpublished MS [Duisburg], 1963, p. 134; BM 201, 47, Sozialamt der ev. Kirche, 'Gedanken zur Volksbildungsarbeit im Steinkohlenbergbau', 20.9.1952.

lectures were often poorly attended unless bolstered by a good slide show or a sexy topic. Thus a report from a Lohberg hostel in April 1950 noted 195 participants for the film *Schüsse in Kabine 7* and 104 for a lecture on 'Young women of today and their problems', but only nineteen for 'The world of the unconscious'. The lecture 'Beautiful women in changing times' (with slides) overfilled the hall. In general, the greater the choice of entertainment in the locality, the worse attended were the cultural events in the hostels. As local services improved after the war and television became more widespread in the hostels, the field-workers found it ever more difficult to drum up an audience.[77] Apart from the attendance problem, one of the weaknesses of the lectures and of other attempts to influence the young miners was, as already noted, that a core message was often lacking. True, there was a clear 'yes' to democracy and a 'yes' to Europe, but in terms of practical politics or of moral and religious values there was often uncertainty and anxiety about what to communicate.

Much of the work was simply unnecessary, in that it was impelled or shaped by fears that were understandable but inappropriate. Gradually the realisation spread that neither the Ruhr in general nor the hostels in particular were hotbeds of radicalism. As a speaker at a conference on cultural policy noted in 1953, recent elections had revealed 'in welchem Ausmaß bereits dem Radikalismus und darüber hinaus dem Nihilismus abgesagt wurde'. Contemporary youth turned out not even to be particularly rebellious, despite possibly regarding the older generations and established institutions with something less than the reverence they would have liked.[78] Certain values were clearly shared by both the providers of cultural services and their recipients, so that the work here found a good resonance. Above all, there was a very moral approach to public and political life. Communal welfare was rated above individual

---

77. Ibid.; HStAD NW17, 236, Joachim Müller to Bundesministerium für Erziehung und Unterricht, 20.11.1949; NW17, 10, Stadt Dortmund Bildungswerk kulturelle Betreuung der Bergarbeiterlager to Kultusminister, 19.4.1950 and report on cultural events in Lohberg, April 1950.

78. HStAD NW17, 141, RAG conference at Kronenburg 21–26.9.1953, Sieburg speech; see P. Arnold Dannemann, 'Die Situation des Jugendlichen im Steinkohlenbergbau und unsere pädaogische Verpflichtung', in *Mitteilungen für die Bergberugsschulender WBK*, vol. 4, 1956, p. 4; Kloppenburg, 'Jugend in Beruf und Freizeit', p. 2.

good; youth parliaments in the hostels tended to be draconian in their sentences. Though the approach of the older generation was often felt to be oppressive, no one advocated 'doing your own thing'. Party politics was often condemned as self-seeking. As far as private morality was concerned, though sexual mores were undoubtedly changing, there was nevertheless a strong current within the younger generation affirming the need for self-discipline and decency.[79] The proffered values met with least response as soon as they became romantic. Many hostel wardens, lecturers and churchmen identified this lack of il-lusions on the part of younger men, sometimes wrongly diag-nosed as nihilism. Appeals to the 'German spirit', the invoking of a 'christliche Weltanschauung and so on, only served to repel the far more pragmatic and realistic younger generation.[80]

An End to Social Engineering

By the mid 1950s the mining employers were shedding many of the anxieties and hopes that had shaped hostel policy and given it such impetus. Cultural welfare policy began to run out of steam. Between 1953 and 1956, the committee supervising the RAG did not meet once. When it met again in 1956 it did so despite clear signs of the UVR's lack of interest. By then, the RAG field-workers were barely in evidence in many adult hos-tels, though the apprentices continued to enjoy their services for a while longer. A glance through the works newspapers reveals the collieries' declining commitment to cultural policy for hostel occupants. Whereas in 1950 the *Förderturm*, for example, gave a great deal of space to Christmas activities for the new miners, the January 1954 issue devoted only a small paragraph to the festivities and the January 1958 issue nothing at all. The churches too, lost both their sense of mission and their anxiety and gradually wound down their activities in the mines. A

79. HStAD NW17, 10, Burisch to Kultusmin, 2.12.1949, annex; Roelen, 'Die Bedeutung der Pestalozzidörfer', p. 89; more generally, see Theo Pirker, 'Die Jugend in der Struktur unserer Gesellschaft', in DGB Abteilung Jugend (ed.), *Protokoll der Arbeitstagung der Gewerkschaftsjugend 25–30.11.1951*, Düsseldorf, 1952, pp. 7–30 and Kloppenburg, 'Jugend in Beruf und Freizeit'.
80. Ges.Verb. File 'Unternehmensverband 662–668', RAG paper, 'Bergar-beiterbetreuung', no date [1951]; 'Der "Lager Mensch" – Symptom einer Ent-wicklung', *Neue Zeitung*, 7.8.1951; see also chapter 9.

number of institutions continued to tick over – indeed, some still exist – but more because of institutional inertia than for any other reason. The Katholisches Lagerwerk transferred its attentions to foreign exchanges for young people and indeed many of the mines' former villages were made available for general youth work, while others were turned into normal housing.[81]

Even the core of the regeneration project, the apprentice hostels and villages, lost their appeal. Apart from their failure to prevent wastage, they could do nothing about the marked decline in the size and quality of apprentice intake from 1955 onwards. By 1958, the mines felt that they were receiving only those youngsters whom the labour exchanges had difficulty disposing of elsewhere. According to one Pestalozzi village leader, 60 per cent of the incoming youngsters had a criminal record. It should therefore not surprise us that, for example, the executive of the Pestalozzi village association did not meet between October 1956 and March 1958 and that at the latter meeting only half the board were present. For a few more years apprentice hostels continued in operation, though in ever-diminishing numbers, until by 1960 or so the stream of apprentices from outside the Ruhr had virtually disappeared. The great experiment was over.[82]

81. Ges.Verb. File 'Unternehmensverband 662–668', Ullrich, memo, 18.4.1956; UVR to Kultusmin, 13.7.1956; Ottokar Mund (ed.), *25 Jahre Katholisches Lagerwerk e.V. Versuch einer zeitgeschichtlichen Übersicht*, Recklinghausen 1973; BAK B102, 33092, minutes of meeting of the Manpower and Training Committee, 2.5.1957.
82. Klinkert Papers, File 'Niederschriften der Arbeitstagungen und Vortrags-veranstaltungen', minutes of meeting of village leaders on 10.12.1958; UVR, *Jahresbericht 1958–1960*, p. 89 facing.

8
Of Work and Wastage

The Whys and Wherefores of Wastage

Why, despite all their efforts, were the mines losing so many men? During the 1950s this question gave rise to a great many hours of earnest deliberation in smoky committee rooms. To catch the secret of the mines' unattractiveness, fleets of interviewers trawled carefully prepared questionnaires across the Ruhr. In 1952, for example, the Marshall Plan coal production committee set up a special working party to look into the issue. In 1953, the DKBL's manpower and training committee had a go. A year later, to forestall a threatened public enquiry, the mines carried out another investigation. In 1955, the federal government would no longer be deflected and commissioned a study of its own, the result of which was a 250-page manuscript produced by the Institut für Sozialforschung, Frankfurt. In the 1960s another even more detailed study was commissioned by the EGKS and carried out by INFAS. The information that we have on mining is thus probably unrivalled by any other occupational group.[1]

Despite all this attention, firm conclusions proved hard to

1. BAK B102, 33091, minutes of AAA meeting, 19.10.1953; B119, 1519, LAA NRW, minutes of 2nd meeting of Bergbau-Ausschuß on 10.2.1954, 12.4.1954; Institut für Sozialforschung, 'Die subjektiven und objektiven Abkehrgründe bei sieben Zechen des westdeutschen Steinkohlenbergbaues in ihrer Auswirkung auf die Sicherung des Belegschaftsstandes unter Tage', unpublished MS, Frankfurt/Main, 1955; Ludwig von Friedeburg, 'Zur Fluktuation im Steinkohlenbergbau. Ergebnisse einer industriesoziologischen Untersuchung', *Bundesarbeitsblatt*, 1957, pp. 705–21; Rudolf Petz, 'Die subjektiven und objektiven Abkehrgründe im Kohlenbergbau. Bemerkungen zu der industriesoziologischen Untersuchung', in ibid., pp. 721–34; Rudolf Petz, 'Fluktuation im Steinkohlenbergbau! Was kann noch dagegen geschehen?', unpublished MS, Bonn, no date [1958]; Institut für angewandte Sozialwissenschaft (INFAS), 'Untersuchung über die Fluktuation der Arbeitskräfte im Steinkohlenbergbau. Ergebnisbericht', unpublished MS, Bad Godesberg, 1966.

reach. For one thing, results varied from pit to pit. Then, patterns of wastage were continually in flux, as social and economic conditions changed. Moreover, it was often impossible to determine the exact factors that had induced the men to leave. Many were not really sure themselves what had precipitated their departure. Not a few left without giving notice, and thus could not be asked why they were leaving. Another problem for the investigators lay in determining which groups showed most propensity to quit. The pits' records rarely provided the data required to make serious statistical correlations. So intractable was this problem that the Institut für Sozialforschung study took the bizarre step of showing the relative proportion of different groups amongst the leavers without giving the equivalent proportion of those groups among the workforce as a whole! It made little sense to say, as the study did, that refugees accounted for 10 per cent of one mine's wastage and 20 per cent in another pit, without measuring the respective proportions refugees made up of the workforces as a whole, and of recent intake.

Nevertheless, some conclusions can be drawn. It is worthwhile confirming at the outset that wastage was to an overwhelming extent voluntary. Losses due to natural causes or to dismissals made up only a small and indeed diminishing proportion.[2] As one would expect, the gradual improvement in job opportunities outside the mines encouraged many new miners to seek employment elsewhere. The iron and steel industry proved a particularly powerful draw on mining's recruits. Table 8.1 reveals that the real problem was not so much that early recruits drifted away as that new miners hired in the 1950s were far less likely to become permanent additions to the workforce than those taken on in the period 1947–51. Between 1947 and 1950, Hibernia laid on 13,230 adult trainees of whom 5,630 or 43 per cent were still there five years after having been hired. Between 1951 and 1954 the mines laid on 8,355 men, of whom 2,537 or only 30.37 per cent were still there at the end of their first five years. Results for the period 1954–6 were clearly shaping up to be far worse. Other Hibernia figures show that, as we know, from 1950 each year's intake of new labour was less likely

2. Ges.Verb., StdKW., table 'Aufteilung des Abganges nach Gründen – Arbeiter unter Tage. Ruhr'.

Table 8.1 Wastage amongst all new miners hired by Hibernia

Year	New miners hired	% leaving mines in year after being hired:					Remaining after 5 years	
		1st	2nd	3rd	4th	5th	No.	%.
1945	732	9.84[a]	30.87	6.56	3.69	2.46	341	46.58
1946	3,209	36.58	16.39	5.86	2.71	2.43	1,156	36.02
1947	5,227	27.87	19.23	6.18	4.23	2.60	2,085	39.89
1948	3,052	24.38	18.48	7.54	4.16	2.16	1,321	43.28
1949	2,430	19.38	17.45	8.35	3.50	2.06	1,197	49.26
1950	2,521	17.73	22.53	6.82	4.40	7.77	1,027	40.74
1951	2,554	22.44	23.10	9.87	7.64	3.60	852	33.36
1952	2,750	29.02	26.47	11.85	3.89	1.89	739	26.87
1953	2,749	31.32	25.14	7.78	2.33	1.46	879	31.98
1954	302	29.47	30.79	7.95	6.95	2.65	67	22.19
1955	1,292	27.32	31.27					
1956	2,105	42.91						
1957	2,330							
1958	1,121							

(a) Figure distorted by the fact that recruitment of new miners began only late in the year.

Source: Calculated from Hibernia Konzern (ed.), *Hibernia Sozialbericht 1956, 1958*, annex 8. 'New miners' means in this case adult men who came to Hibernia with no previous experience.

than its predecessors still to be there at the end of three years (see figure 6.2). Statistics from other mining companies tell a similar story.[3] This was a clear sign of changing perceptions of the job market. Men hired before 1952 were taken on at a time when there were only limited well-paid alternatives to mining. By the time alternative employment was available, the men had often got so used to mining or tied to the locality that a change no longer seemed attractive. This did not apply to those hired after 1952. When the initial crisis of mining employment came – a first accident, unpleasant treatment by a deputy, the cash shortage of the first weeks and so on – there was every incentive to quit the mine and take on another job.

3. OBADA I8010/2924/48, OBAD Lagebericht for 3rd quarter 1948; author's calculation from Hibernia figures in Hibernia Konzern (ed.), *Hibernia Sozialbericht 1956*, annex 8 and *1958*, annexes 4 and 8. Gneisenau figures tell a similar story; see Mark Roseman, 'New Miners in the Ruhr: Rebuilding the Workforce in the Ruhr Mines, 1945–1958', PhD dissertation, Warwick University, 1987, pp. 333–4.

Table 8.2 Age structure of mines' labour intake

Year	Proportion of recruits in following age categories (%):				
	–18	19–25	26–30	31–35	35+
1946–7	7	47	22	10	15
	17–20	21–25	26–30	31–35	35+

(Official age limit for recruits 25)

1948	36	35	15	7	7
1949	45	41	9	3	3
1950	42	44	8	3	3

(Official age limit for recruits 32)

1951	40	40	13	5	5
1952	37	37	15	8	3
1953	35	36	17	8	3
1954	41	33	16	7	4
1955	37	34	18	8	3
1956	38	35	17	6	4
1957	39	34	18	7	3

Source: Ges. Verb., Heisingen papers, Reception Camp log-book.

The other reason for new recruits' changing behaviour was rather different and revealed both the opportunity with which the mines were presented in the late 1940s and the difficulties they faced by the mid-1950s. In the 1940s and early 1950s the mines drew on the 'unwillingly mobile', men who by dint of circumstance were set in motion – be it as a result of expulsions, the effects of the currency reform or whatever. Increasingly, however, the intake 'normalised' to young, single men out to maximise their earnings for a few years before settling down to some reasonably convivial occupation. This shift is evident if we look at the new miners' age and occupational structure (see tables 8.2 and 8.3). In the pre-1948 period, when men up to 40 years of age were being taken on, a considerable proportion of new miners were not of the age at which men normally moved into mining. Almost 50 per cent were over 25. Amongst the expellees in the period 1945–8, the proportion of over-25s may have been higher than 60 per cent, with almost 40 per cent being over 30. In 1948–9, the average age fell dramatically as the result of management's determination to rejuvenate the workforce. Many of the 'unwillingly mobile' who would have been prepared to make a go of mining were now prevented from doing so. By the 1950s, the mines could not attract older married men even when they wished to.[4]

The shift can also be observed in occupational structure. According to SoFoSt records, between 15 per cent and 20 per cent of expellees taken on in the period 1945–8 had formerly been in white-collar, managerial or professional occupations or self-employed. This was an indication of the degree to which necessity rather than personal volition played a role in migration. Over the following three years, the proportion from these groups shrank to less than 5 per cent. In 1949, the first year for which we have detailed records from Essen–Heisingen, unskilled labour still made up a relatively low proportion of labour intake – less than 50 per cent. This soon changed, first as the result of a rapid influx of agricultural labour and later as unskilled industrial labour came to dominate the recruitment picture (see table 8.3).[5]

The point is not that skilled or white-collar workers were necessarily more likely to remain miners than unskilled. Indeed, none of these factors – age, marital status or occupation – was necessarily a sign that recruits would stay. What they all are, however, is indices of the degree to which dire necessity overcame the normal promptings of personal volition. If older men with a background in white-collar work flock to the mines, then this is a sign that one is dealing with mobility that was the product of necessity and not a personal wish. In the early years, the mines attracted men, above all expellees, for whom the personal and psychological barriers to mobility in general and to taking up mining work in particular were very large. They were the 'unwillingly mobile'. By the end of the period this was no longer the case.[6]

This latter point is reinforced when we note a further feature of the mines' recruitment in the mid-1950s, namely that new

4. Ges.Verb., Heisingen Papers, Reception Camp log book; Helmuth Croon and K. Utermann, *Zeche und Gemeinde. Untersuchungen über den Strukturwandel einer Zechengemeinde im nördlichen Ruhrgebiet*, Tübingen, 1958, p. 296. Percentages are author's calculation.

5. Ibid.

6. It was above all expellees who made up the 'unwilling mobile', a point confirmed by INFAS, 'Untersuchung über die Fluktutation', pp. 99ff.

Table 8.3 Former profession of new miners (%)[a]

Year	Unskilled labourer			Skilled worker			White-collar eng/ self-emp.	Others[b]
	Agric.	Indust.	Total	Eng./ bldg	Other	Total		
Expellee new miners hired by mine Emscher-Lippe								
1945–8	17	15	32			40	16	10
1948–51	36	29	65			25	4	5
All new miners hired by mine Shamrock 1/2								
1945–8	16	36	52			38	7	4
Miners in the mining reception camp, Heisingen								
1949	18	31	49	28	15	43	4	n.a.
1950	27	40	67	13	15	28	4	n.a.
1951	24	39	63	14	17	31	4	n.a.
1952	22	33	55	18	19	37	4	n.a.
1953	23	35	58	19	18	37	4	n.a.
1954	20	39	59	21	14	35	3	n.a.
1955	18	44	62	20	13	33	2	n.a.
1956	17	44	61	21	12	33	3	n.a.
1957	12	48	60	22	12	34	2	n.a.

(a) Percentages do not always add up to 100% due to rounding up.
(b) Professional soldiers, students etc.

Source: Percentages calculated from Croon and Utermann, *Zeche und Gemeinde*, p. 296 (Emscher-Lippe); Gerhard Ludwig, 'Der Wandel in der Zusammensetzung der Grubenbelegschaft seit dem Kriegsende und die hieraus auf einer Schachtanlage des Ruhrreviers gezogenen praktischen Folgerungen', *Glückauf*, vol. 85, 1949, pp. 625–36 (Shamrock 1/2); Ges. Verb., Heisingen Papers, log-book. Former miners (coal, ore or potash) and mining apprentices have been excluded in each case.[7]

men with no previous experience provided an ever smaller proportion of the industry's labour intake. For one thing, the mines were forced into poaching labour from one another. Movement from pit to pit increased substantially, averaging

7. These were excluded because there was no guarantee that they had *consistently* been included in the category of new miners.

35 per cent of total wastage in the period 1954–8. The other main reason was that the mines were increasingly hiring men who were oscillating between mining and other employment. Most collieries were now even prepared to accept miners who had previously left the industry in breach of contract. Thus, by the mid-1950s, the mines were caught up in a hiring and wastage cycle, poaching labour off one another and hiring men who were clearly not going to stay long in the mines.[8]

If there was one call which echoed unceasingly round the Ruhr area throughout the 1950s, it was for mining to stand at the top of the wages heirarchy. The frequency with which this refrain was to be heard suggested that all mining had to do was offer a few Marks a week more than the competition to solve its labour problems. This was both more and less than the truth. It was less than the truth because even when the mines' wages were higher than those in iron and steel – as in 1956–7 after the introduction of the Miners' Bonus Scheme – the collieries continued to lose more men than they hired. In 1957, though earnings in mining were well above those in iron and steel, wastage was more than 10 per cent higher than recruitment. And it was more than the truth, because – as the 1955 investigation discovered – most of those who left the mines moved to a job *where they earned less than they had in mining*. Not only that, but they rated their new pay *better* than they had the higher earnings in the pits. The point was that there was a trade-off between the negative characteristics of the work on the one hand and the wage and other inducements on the other.[9]

Lack of light, the unhealthy atmosphere, the deafening noise of a long coalface full of pneumatic picks, the exertion of working at the coal in a confined space, the danger of falling stone – these were all features of mining about which (given the existing technology) the employers could do little. Yet the striking fact is, as the 1955 study was able to ascertain by interviewing former mining employees, that poor treatment by lower management

8. AZG File 'I 1 28 Verteilung von Arbeitskräften', table 'über die Zu- und Abgänge an "Bergfremden" in der Zeit vom 1.9.1945–31.8.1947'; File 'I 1 3, Einstellung und Entlassung von Arbeitern, 1.10.1953–31.12.1963', Gruppe Gneisenau to director Stodt, 18.8.1955 and appendices; ABB annual report for 1955.
9. On the bonus scheme see chapter 4. On wastage, see table 4.6; UVR (ed.), *Jahresbericht 1955–1957*, p. 60 facing; Institut für Sozialforschung, 'Die subjektiven und objektiven Abkehrgründe', p. 208.

figured almost as frequently as working conditions in expla-
nations for quitting the industry. All other complaints, even
those about inadequate pay, were of subsidiary significance. In
other words, a substantial proportion of mining's wastage was
at least partially, sometimes even wholly, motivated by the
experience of mining's management. In 1952, when the Sozialforschungsstelle carried out a survey of new miners at the
Victor–Ickern mine, it included the question 'Wie kommen Sie
mit den Vorgesetzten aus?' The first respondent complained
that the deputy had refused to allow him holiday leave and he
had had to go to the manager to get it; the second could not
stand his present supervisor, a fact which influenced his whole
perception of working in the mines; and the third, a highly
intelligent and articulate character who made a good impression
on the interviewer, produced a scathing critique of the mining
deputies. Though some were reasonably positive, many more of
the thirty-odd interviews on record were in the same mould.[10]

As far as new labour was concerned there were four main
things wrong with management. First, few miners felt that they
had been properly inducted into the work or looked after during
their initial employment period. Certainly, the available accident statistics suggest strongly that the newcomers were not
being adequately prepared for mining work. In 1952, a greater
proportion of Hibernia new miners were involved in accidents
than in 1948. New miners in their first five years of employment
were four times more likely to be involved in accidents than
apprentices with equivalent mining experience. The Ruhr
wage-arbitrators (*Gedinge–Inspektoren*) reported many instances
where newcomers were being set to work in conditions which
completely outstretched their abilities, despite the availability of
experienced men working in easier conditions, and complained
repeatedly that the newcomers were not being given enough
training.[11] It was not surprising, then, that wastage was par-

10. SoFoStA File 'Neubergleute-Befragung. Untersuchung Vincke Lager' (Lager belonging to mining company Victor-Ickern). See also Institut für Sozialforschung, 'Die subjektiven und objektiven Abkehrgründe', p. 228. 'Hier hat der
Bergbau versagt', *Rheinische Zeitung*, 31.10.1950. Carl Jantke made a somewhat
more positive assessment in *Bergmann und Zeche. Die sozialen Arbeitsverhältnisse
einer Schachtanlage des nördlichen Ruhrgebiets in der Sicht der Bergleute*, Tübingen,
1959 (see part 2: 'Vorgesetzte unter Tage', *passim*), though even here one face
was as bad as anywhere in the Ruhr.
11. BAK B102, 21395, memo, 'New miners and invalidity problems', table 10,

ticularly high during that initial period. In 1948–9, when the labour market situation was highly unfavourable for job seekers even in NRW, losses in the first few weeks and months of employment were striking. The Concordia mine hired 807 men in 1948, of whom 260 were gone by the end of the year. Of those 260, forty two had moved to other mines, but the rest had left the industry. Twelve per cent of this wastage had taken place by the end of the first month of employment; 40 per cent by the end of the second; and 60 per cent by the end of three months.[12] By the early 1950s, the mines were losing up to 70 per cent of their trainees in the first five months.[13]

The newcomers' problems were not restricted to the period of induction itself. A second major cause of bitterness was that deputies tried to deceive the workforce in the contract wage calculations. Even after the calculation had been agreed, the deputies and overmen often made changes to the calculations – a problem so widespread that the Gedingekommission frequently called on employers to root it out. Thirdly, the arbitrariness and vindictiveness of officials who had taken some personal offence to a miner, was another recurrent complaint. The one-time new miner, later cultural director for the IGBE, Walter Köpping, a man well in excess of six foot, recalled being deliberately consigned to work in a low seam by a hostile deputy. Hans Dieter Baroth turned his back on the mines for good when, after failing to stand up when the overman approached, he found himself permanently consigned to one of the most unpleasant loading jobs at the pit bottom. Finally, the deputies' general tone and approach were frequently condemned. At a church convocation for the Siebenbürger Sachsen (see below) in 1955, for example, one of the men declared that he had left mining because of the 'rauhe Ton' there, while another had been on the point of resigning over the 'unflätige Schimpfworte' which the deputy had directed at him.[14]

---

new miner share of accidents; IGBEA T4, Dr Köker's lecture Jan 1953; IGBEA BR5, reports by the wage arbitrators for August, September and October 1948; Hibernia Konzern (ed.), *Sozialbericht 1958*, annex 14.

12. BBA 8, 384, Concordia, Circular from Direction 1, 15.2.1949, annex 1.

13. Calculated from Annex 8 in Hibernia Konzern (ed.), *Sozialbericht 1958*; see also Roseman, 'New Miners', p. 341.

14. AZG File 'I 1 13, Gedinge-Regelung, 1.1.45–31.12.1953', DKBL, circular to district representatives, 25.11.1948; Walter Köpping, 'Als Betriebsobmann auf

Perhaps the starkest condemnation of mining's managerial style was contained in 'Alarm im Bergbau', a young theology student's account of his experiences working in the mine, which found its way into the ministerial files.[15] The report begins by describing the typical new miner's entry into the pit. Our (Bavarian) newcomer finds himself entrusted with moving coal-tubs around at a staple shaft and cannot quite cope with the pace with which they are coming at him, particularly as one of the points is sticky:

> Mit seiner armseligen Grubenlampe steht der Neue im Scheinwerferlicht des Blitzers, der von der Brust des Rutschenbass's auf ihn herableuchtet. Im Scheinwerferlicht sieht der Rutschenbaß die Wagen neben den Schienen liegen und nun ist es vorbei. 'Sag mal', brüllt er los, 'lernst Du das hier denn überhaupt nicht, bist sicher auch nur hierher gekommen, weil sonst keiner etwas mit Dir anzufangen weiß. Hast sicher geglaubt, hier wäre Platz für so blöde Hunde wie Du einer bist. So etwas kann auch nur aus Bayern kommen!'[16]

Hardly has one foreman disappeared, then another surfaces and screams at the hapless *Bayer* for not having got enough coal-tubs together. The account is then interrupted and we rejoin the trainee some weeks later when he has begun to come to terms with the work. His problem now is that, though working in damp conditions, he is not given a chit for a rubber suit by the deputy. By the time the suit finally arrives, the poor recruit is already ill. It is enough to drive him from the mines for good.[17]

Leaving the fate of this particular individual, the report goes on to consider more general problems in the approach to the new miners. Apart from the personality of the deputies, the whole system is not geared up to taking the newcomers' needs seriously. The lack of preparation is overwhelming. The newcomers have to ask for protective clothing themselves and no one tells them that they should have it. Because output is

---

"Julia" 1947–1949', in Köpping (ed.), *Lebensberichte deutscher Bergarbeiter*, Oberhausen, 1984, p. 404; Baroth, *Aber es waren schöne Zeiten*, pp. 187ff; Ges.Verb. File 'SBZ Arb 130.0–130.25', confidential memo for Dr Ullrich, 31.8.1955.

15. BAK B102, 33091, BWiM, memo, Ref: III A – 10934/56, annex 5: 'Alarm im Bergbau'.

16. Ibid., p. 8.

17. Ibid., p. 11.

demanded from on high, the instructors, even when well-meaning, have no time to respond to the newcomers' difficulties. Packing, coal-getting, recovering props – all these jobs are demonstrated in a few minutes at the beginning of the shift and the new men then left to get on with it. And when the newcomer finally finds himself in the productive faces, 'kümmert sich erst recht keiner mehr um den Neuen'.[18]

Probably the most striking thing about this report was not its content, but the fact that at a meeting of the *employers'* manpower and training committee in 1956, no one present – as far as we can tell from the minutes – criticised the paper. No one even said that it was exaggerated. Instead there was a consensus that 'Alarm im Bergbau . . . ohne Zweifel für einen großen Teil der Zechen zutreffen [dürfte]'.[19] Of course, 'Alarm im Bergbau' and the many other exposés on similar lines were ideological statements as much as they were simple observations. They were born of an age that wanted to see pragmatic, co-operative solutions to the problems of industrial society. The notion that the antagonism between labour and capital could be solved by paying proper attention to the 'Mensch im Betrieb' was a classic 1950s theme. Phrases like, 'Mensch nicht Markennummer' tripped easily off enlightened tongues. But the point is that the new miners themselves, as the field surveys reveal, were influenced by this ideology. They had a sense of what was modern, *zeitgemäß*, and responded accordingly. Thus, even at its most 'ideological', 'Alarm im Bergbau' does convey the reality of the newcomers' perceptions.[20]

Management, Induction and Integration

For their part, many managers rejected the notion that anything was fundamentally wrong at work. Very often, for example, accidents were attributed to defects in the newcomers' character.

18. Ibid., p. 26.
19. BAK B102, 33091, AAA Meeting, 30.5.1956. See also Herbert Berger, 'Als Neuling im Pütt', in IGBE (ed.), *Bergleute erzählen. (Beiträge zur Geschichte der IGBE)*, Bochum, 1982, pp. 29–35.
20. See Carl Jantke cited in Manfred Fronz and Gerd Peter (eds), *Sozialwissenschaftliche Forschung im Steinkohlenbergbau*, vol. 2: *Der Steiger. Auszüge aus empirischen Untersuchungen 1950–1982*, Bochum, 1983, pp. 15–53 at 44; 'Hier hat der Bergbau versagt', *Rheinische Zeitung*, 31.10.1950.

There was something of a consensus among colliery managers that the 'charakterlichen Eigenschaften der Neubergleute . . . nicht sonderlich hoch zu bewerten sind'.[21] A Concordia memorandum attributed the high accident level to the new miners' 'mangelnde Arbeitsmoral' and complained that the newcomers 'sich nichts sagen lassen wollen. Wenn Sie kurze Zeit im Bergbau gearbeitet haben, kommen sie sich als alte Bergleute vor, glauben nach eigenem Ermessen handeln zu können und lehnen Ratschläge und Belehrungen von Kamaraden, aber auch Anordnungen von Vorgesetzten ab, oder lassen sie unbeachtet.'[22] No doubt there was something in this. Young men are more likely to take risks than older colleagues, newcomers less knowledgeable than long-established workers. But in truth the new miners could not be expected to behave in any other way when they were given so little proper training and expected to work independently almost from the beginning. The collieries' perfunctory approach to induction *encouraged* the notion that the trainee did not have all that much to learn.[23]

Similarly, there are many indications that managers saw wastage as evidence of the inadequacy of the recruits. After noting that the bulk of new recruits after 1945 left within a short period, a DKBL survey intended for public consumption could not refrain from adding the parenthetical comment, 'die Schwere der Arbeit hatte für alle halben Charaktere ihre wohltuende Schockwirkung getan'.[24] And at a meeting of mine directors in September 1949, almost all present complained about 'wenig oder gar keine Disziplin bei den Neubergleuten, die in großen Scharen wieder abwandern'.[25] Despite criticism from many outside groups, the employers were not prepared to give the newcomers the benefit of the doubt and test whether a better induction programme or more favourable conditions might produce better results. A good example of this was the demand for bridging loans that would help the newcomers from out of town

21. HStaD Kalkum BA Duisburg 181, copy of memo from Inspektion II to Direktion III (Gruppe Hamborn), 4.7.1949.
22. BBA 8, 352, memo from Arbeiterpersonalbüro, 12.7.1952.
23. Cf. 'Alarm im Bergbau'.
24. DKBL (ed.), *Ruhr Almanach. Vom Bergmann und Bergbau*, Cologne, 1950, p. 95.
25. BBA 8/448, memo about discussions between CCCG and mine directors of DKBL district Niederrhein, 19.9.1949. Discussions before arrival of CCCG representatives; see also 8, 352, memo from Arbeiterpersonalbüro, 12.7.1952.

deal with the first few weeks of employment. Often arriving with no funds, the newcomers had to wait ten days for their first payment and then found themselves confronted with hostel charges, deductions for work clothing and other expenses which reduced the first pay packets to a level on which it was hardly possible to live, a problem that was particularly acute for married men who were trying to support their families at the same time. In the early years after the currency reform, getting by on the wages paid for general labouring was hard enough anyway. The mines refused to offer subsidies, despite continual requests from the labour administration that they do so. Indeed, so little were they prepared to acknowledge the newcomers' genuine difficulties that an attempt by the Economics Ministry to get the labour administration to give some sort of bridging loan (i.e. at no cost to the employers) failed due to lack of mining support.[26]

How do we square management's approach and attitudes, as observed here, with the policies analysed in the previous chapters? The emphasis placed on the apprenticeship programme, for example, indicated that management took wastage extremely seriously. Similarly, the attention devoted to the housing and hostel environment manifested the employers' willingness to use generous and imaginative social engineering as a means of creating a stable workforce. Yet, *vor Ort*, we encounter what seems to be a quite different mentality – mean-spirited, counting the coal and ignoring the human costs – and a managerial philosophy of 'I shout therefore I am.' Was the point that there were two breeds of manager? As we will see shortly, there *were* clear differences within management, differences which emerged very clearly in debates about how to train and induct the adult newcomers, for instance. Yet the contrast between the adults' working experience, on the one hand, and the rhetoric and thrust of the collieries' social policy, on the other, was not primarily the outcome of a clash of philosophies. Nor should we see it as recalcitrant lower management thwarting the benign intentions of more enlightened men at the top (although there are overtones of this too). As 'Alarm im Bergbau' reveals, the

26. OBADA I8006/1792/51, WiM NRW to OBAD, 30.7.1951, annex: copy of minutes of 4th LAA NRW executive board meeting on 25.6.1951; 'Neubergleute verlassen das Revier', *Deutsche Woche*, Munich, 21.1.1951; BAK B102, 21395, BWiM III A 1, memo, 11.12.1952.

deputies were often simply passing on the pressures and treatment meted out to *them*. In fact, it was often one and the same colliery director who with one breath extolled the apprenticeship and with the next argued that 'eine Erziehung zur Disziplin, Arbeitseinsatz und Leistung' was more important for getting production out of the adult newcomers than formal skills training.[27] The combination of authoritarianism within the mine and a more generous paternalism outside was, in fact, mining's traditional 'package'. Indeed, in the past they had been seen as complementary, the stick and carrot that bound the workforce to the pits.

The persistence of this traditional package was, in three senses, testament to the employers' traditionalism. First, there was the simple point that the continuity of industrial social policy had only briefly been interrupted by the war. In many areas, such as housing policy or training, the mines simply resumed policies that had been suspended in wartime, ready to be brought out again after the cessation of hostilities. Secondly, both the employers' romanticism and their authoritarianism, though apparently contradictory, in fact often stemmed from the same underlying feeling, namely of being profoundly at odds with contemporary society and the existing workforce. The employers dreamed of giving new life to their (highly romanticised) image of the miner of times past; and hand in hand with this ideal went an extremely negative view of the existing workforce. On one side of the coin was the lofty project of rescuing the worker's genuine personality from the depredations of mass society: turn the coin over, however, and there was the assumption that many of those currently in the mines were 'halbe Charaktere', the mass, rootless men of a materialistic age.

Thirdly, there was a thorough distrust of modern managerial practices. The Mining School (the establishment where deputies and overmen received their training), for example, contained in its curriculum 'no provision for acquainting the students with modern management techniques or labour relations'.[28] An illuminating episode came at the end of the 1940s, when the Americans were trying to persuade German managements to

27. HStaD Kalkum Bergamt Duisburg 181, draft of a letter from Betriebsführervereinigung Hamborn-Oberhausen to OBAD (eventually sent 25.7.1949).
28. WWA S22 (OMGUS), Manpower 7/44–2/14, Shaw to Marshall, 22.10.1948.

adopt their TWI (Training Within Industry) programme. The programme's goal was to disseminate new techniques of man management and team leadership, particularly at shop-floor level, with the aim of enhancing morale and productivity. Many industries responded enthusiastically to the idea, but mining's response was lukewarm and little seems to have been undertaken.[29] True, one factor which made it hard for the mines to offer a more satisfactory induction programme was that they suffered from a shortage of training personnel. Even with their expanded number of classes, it would take the Mining Schools years to train all the deputies that the collieries needed. But the poor training represented deep-seated attitudes towards industrial relations and production. There was an almost total lack of awareness of pedagogical and human relations issues.[30]

Management Divided

Yet such traditional attitudes, though predominant, were not uniformly shared by all mining managers. Nothing illustrates this more clearly than the controversy generated by the OBAD's new training code in 1949. From autumn 1948, the OBAD had been involved in negotiations with employers and IGB about new training provisions for adult trainees. Quite apart from the interests of safety, the inspectorate was very conscious that the status of the profession could be enhanced only if all entrants were required to go through a more thorough training programme. As far as the existing regulations were concerned, their main weaknesses were, first and fundamentally, that the prescribed training was too short and covered too little of the miners' work; and secondly, the fact that training could take place anywhere in the mine and that the underground manager (rather than the training director) was responsible for carrying it out, meant that it was often purely notional.[31]

29. WWA S22 (OMGUS), Manpower 7/44–2/14, memo from Leo Werts; Manpower 7/51–1/3 GWJ Cole Chief, Manpower Gp, BICO, to J. Chairmen UKUSCCG; Snyder to Cole, 28.2.1949.
30. WBKA, WBK (ed.), 'Verwaltungsbericht 1.1.49–31.12.49'; BBA 55, 12200, no. 11, minutes of Bergausschuß meeting, 22.8.1950.
31. OBADA I6307/374/49, OBAD, memo concerning a meeting of the Oberbergamt on 25.10.1948; HStaD Kalkum Bergamt Duisburg 181, OBAD to

The new regulations, issued in May 1949, rectified these earlier weaknesses and for the first time since the war really bound the mines to certain clear and reasonable minimum standards. This was demonstrated by the great chorus of opposition with which the works managers greeted the new code. Its basic elements were that the new miner had to spend at least a month getting to know the environment as a general labourer underground, during which time he was to be supervised by experienced miners. Then he was to be trained for at least three months, at least two of them on a fixed time-rate. Special training faces were now compulsory for both the time-rate and the contract wage stages of training. The new miners were to be given a broad training covering all the face skills – coal-getting, packing and shifting the conveyors. Special attention was to be paid to the particularly dangerous job of packing and recovering props. During the two months on time-rates there should be no more than four miners to each experienced hewer, a ratio which could be increased to six during the training in contract wage.[32] Perhaps the most significant provision – certainly the most controversial – was that the training director was now fully responsible for the whole training period and answerable directly to the managing director (i.e. not to the underground or works manager). Both training director and works council were to be involved in drawing up a list of newcomers and making sure they received the proper training.[33]

Even though it enjoyed union backing, the OBAD would probably not have been able to push this code through against colliery opposition had it not been for the support given by influential circles within the DKBL. For the DKBL's manpower and training committee (AAA), there was much here to be welcomed. The committee had long believed that the changed conditions of 1948 provided employers with the opportunity to improve the training and induction of new labour. In its earliest versions of Plan A, the DKBL stressed the need for the 'assimilation [sic] and a planful [sic] training of the non-miners'.[34] The

Betriebsführer-Vereinigung Hamborn-Oberhausen, 15.8.1949; OBADA I6307/ 450/49, IVB to OBAD, 10.2.1949;

32. OBADA I6307/1316/49, Bestimmungen über Anlernung und Einsatz von Neubergleuten im Steinkohlenbergbau.

33. Ibid.

34. The fate of the DKBL's translator is not known! See WWA S22 (OMGUS),

very large number of accidents involving new miners provided further economic and social grounds to induct the newcomers more carefully. Many of the OBAD's suggestions in fact derived from proposals which the DKBL had submitted in December 1948.[35]

The real opposition to the code came from the collieries' works managers. In district meetings of the DKBL, in the Verband Oberer Bergbeamten (VOB) and in specially convened committees, the colliery managers vented their spleen. The new code, they argued, 'soll unter allen Umständen zu Fall gebracht werden'.[36] The tone adopted was unusual enough to make it clear that something fundamental was at stake. The regulations contradicted some of the managers' most cherished assumptions. It was surely an indication of the mines' management style and their attitude to new labour that in defending the emphasis on discipline they made no distinction between the wartime experiences with conscript labour and the approach to the adult trainees of the post-war period: 'Die Erfahrungen der letzten 10 Jahre, die an den Grubenbeamten durch die Überweisung der verschiedenartigsten Arbeitskräfte einmalige Anforderungen stellten, haben gezeigt daß die Menschenführung ebenso wesentlich bei der Erziehung zum Bergmann ist wie die praktische Unterweisung.'[37] Because they put their trust in the heavy hand rather than the training session, managers objected to the costs the OBAD rulings would incur. This applied particularly to the compulsory training faces.[38]

Apart from committing the mines to what they saw as an expensive and overindulgent training programme, the OBAD had also assaulted another cherished notion, namely that the *Betriebsführer* had complete freedom to dispose of labour as he wished. The OBAD was heavily criticised for the responsibility

BICO ERPSOC 11/95–2/3–4, DKBL document, Plan A, Essen 20.2.1948.

35. OBADA I6307/1918/49, OBAD to BA Recklinghausen 1, 29.4.1949; I6307/1720/49, minutes of meeting in dining-room of Mine Friedrich-Heinrich, 11.7.1949; I6307/374/49, OBAD to DKBL and IGB, 14.2.1949, annex memo concerning AAA meeting on 1.12.1948. See, though, DKBL criticisms in Ges.Verb. File 'Arbeitsausschuß 1948–1958', Arb.aus.f.A meetings, 12.4.1949, 21.7.1949.

36. BBA 10, 594, report on meeting of DKBL Bochum District, 18.6.1949.

37. Ibid. See also BBA 10, 594, report on meeting of DKBL Bochum District, 18.6.1949; Roseman, 'New Miners', pp. 304–5.

38. HStAD Kalkum BA Duisburg 181, OBAD to Betriebsführer-Vereinigung Hamborn-Oberhausen, 15.8.1949.

it gave the training director. Decisions about the length of training necessary and whether adequate supervision was being provided should, it was argued, be left with the works manager. Part of what was at stake here was the desire to maintain complete flexibility so that the short-term needs of coal production would always have priority. But it was also a question of prestige. It was seen as an unacceptable infringement of the works manager's status that he should have to inform training directors of new miners taken on by the mine. The training director should inform himself. The works council should also not be involved as this represented an equally unacceptable extension of its prerogatives.[39]

The AAA's largely favourable stance on the one hand and the works managers' condemnation on the other revealed the existence of two schools of thought within mining. Mining's long-established authoritarian style with its sink-or-swim approach to new labour continued to dominate at the level of overseers and underground and works managers. They had nothing but contempt for a softer, more safety-conscious approach and condemned the 'nebensächlicher Unterausschuß' of the DKBL which, without consulting the 'mit der Kohlenförderung betrauten Kreise', had had the temerity to agree to the OBAD's proposals.[40] On the other hand, a new breed of training and manpower manager, including amongst others such as the Hibernia training director Dr Köker, the Gruppe Hamborn training director Senft and even more his successor, Dr Steffen, were looking for a different approach with greater emphasis on qualification and better man-management. For their part, they condemned the VOB's failure to listen to the training directors and to respond only to the wishes of works managers. The DKBL's top manpower expert, Dr Ullrich, continued to argue that the regulations were basically acceptable and at a conference of training directors in June 1949 the new code was praised for its clarity and simplicity in contrast with the old regula-

39. HStAD Kalkum Bergamt Duisburg 181, draft of a letter from Betriebsführervereinigung Hamborn-Oberhausen to OBAD (eventually sent 25.7.1949); memo from Inspektion II (Gruppe Hamborn), 4.7.1949; StAM BA Bottrop A18, 176, Arenberg to BA Bottrop, 15.10.1949; OBADA I6307/1720/49, minutes of meeting in dining-room of Zeche Friedrich-Heinrich, 11.7.1949.
40. BBA 10, 594, minutes of meeting of Bochum district of DKBL, 18.6.1949.

tions.[41] Often, both viewpoints existed within the same management. Thus at the same time as Senft from the Gruppe Hamborn was one of the strongest supporters of the new code, it was a Gruppe Hamborn director, Schloms, who was one of its most militant opponents.[42] In the neighbouring mining company Diergardt-Mevissen, the training director found himself permanently at odds with the works managers.[43]

Because of DKBL and IGB backing, the OBAD was able to ride out the storm and adopt a much tougher tone towards its opponents than it was wont to do. The regulations remained in force. Within the collieries, however, it was clear that the training directors and other members of what might be called the progressive wing would have difficulties asserting themselves in the face of the established management style. In practice, the newcomers continued to receive a very cursory preparation for their work. True, they were now obliged to spend at least one month as general labourers underground. However, many spent the month or two of general labouring without any proper supervision at all, with the result that they were exposed to accidents and learned very little. True, the mines were now obliged to train the young men in special training faces, but in fact these were often run suspiciously like their productive counterparts.[44] In effect, the new miners were learning the bare minimum necessary to enable them to mine coal. The face, where the trainees were most heavily concentrated, approached 1938 productivity levels far faster than other parts of the mine. By 1952, coal-getting (*Gewinnung*) in the Hibernia company, for example, was more efficient than it had been in 1938. Trainees who stayed in mining were therefore not depressing productivity (although the high wastage and the resulting large number of trainees in training at any one time continued to be a negative factor). But they were a danger to themselves and to

41. Ges.Verb. File 'Arbeitsausschuß', minutes of Arb.aus.f.A meeting 18.11.1949; minutes of meeting in dining-room of Zeche Friedrich-Heinrich, 11.7.1949; OBADA I2107/3231/49, minutes of a meeting with directors of local inspectorates, 6.10.1949; BBA 10, 594, Mine Friedrich der Große to Bergassessor Lange, 28.6.1949.
42. He was the chairman of the outspoken Betriebsführervereinigung Hamborn-Oberhausen.
43. HStAD Kalkum BA Duisburg 181, BA Duisburg Verfügung 417/272, 16.8.1951 concerning training of new miners in Diergardt-Mevissen company.
44. 'Alarm im Bergbau'.

others and were ill equipped to cope with problems, interruptions or other unexpected eventualities.[45]

The Struggle for Labour

Wastage thus remained higher than it could have been. Initially, however, though the costs in terms of hiring and training replacements and in terms of lower productivity were considerable, the supply of willing labour was sufficient to make good workforce losses. This changed for the first time in 1952 when some mines reported serious difficulties in recruiting during the summer months. Seasonal losses to agriculture and the building trades were traditionally high in the late spring and early summer period and these were now being compounded by the steel mills' labour demands and a general increase in NRW employment opportunities.[46] By summer 1953, most mines were finding losses hard to replace. For the first time they began to encounter serious competition outside NRW. In part this was because the NRW iron and steel industry itself was recruiting in the mines' hunting grounds, but it also reflected the increase in economic activity in hitherto depressed regions.[47]

Apart from the gradual growth of alternative employment opportunities, one other brake on labour supply was the sealing of the GDR's borders in 1952. Prior to that date a fair number of GDR migrants had crossed the borders illegally and made their own way to the pits. From 1952 onwards this became impossible. Refugees and migrants wishing to enter the Federal Republic had to be transported there by train or plane from Berlin. All now went through the procedure laid down by the *Notaufnahmegesetz* of 1950, by which they were assessed for refugee status and its attendant privileges (priority social housing and so forth). Migrants who failed to obtain refugee status spent long periods in the so-called *Stammlager* in Berlin, until by obtaining

45. BAK B102, 4363, lecture from Dr. Köker given to members of the Arbeitsausschuß, 19.1.1953.
46. In 1953, the total cost of recruitment campaigns was around DM1.5 million. Ges.Verb. File 'Arbeitsausschuß', Arb.aus.f.A meeting, 17.5.1954; ABB, annual report for 1954.
47. OBADA I8007/2142/55, ABB quarterly report, 1.4.–30.6.1955; I8007/2932/55, ABB report 1.7–30.9.1955.

employment or some other means, they gained the right to remain in the Federal Republic (though not to the special aid for refugees).[48] These new conditions reduced the number of GDR citizens coming to the Ruhr mines. Those who had attained refugee status often felt secure enough to wait for a better offer, while those without it had difficulty getting into the FRG. In 1950, refugees amounted to 17,694, or almost 70 per cent of all new miners coming through the Heisingen reception camp; but by 1953, despite the growing numbers entering the FRG via Berlin, this had fallen to 12,840 or 31 per cent.[49]

For technical and financial reasons, mechanisation was making only slow progress in the Ruhr. Up until 1956, for example, coal-cutting had been fully mechanised in under 5 per cent of all faces.[50] There were thus strict limits on the degree to which the mines could save on labour through increased use of capital. As a result, the mines were forced to begin thinking more seriously about labour problems within the mines. After years of labour administration pressure, the employers finally acknowledged that many newcomers and particularly married men found the initial period of employment financially very difficult. By 1953, most mines had agreed to suspend charges for the first months' board and lodgings and, after a year's employment at the same mine, to waive them altogether. Despite rising costs, hostel charges barely increased. Some mines even introduced additional subsidies for younger miners.[51]

In addition, two areas of working life received particular attention. One was the newcomer's first few weeks. It had long been well known that wastage at this point was particularly high. A number of mines responded to this by appointing advisers to help the newcomers adjust and to deal with any problems arising. The HBAG, one of the companies where co-determination first made a real impact on the quality of labour and social policy, set up a special unit to co-ordinate all questions relating to newcomers, the EOA (Einsatz orstfremder

48. *BGBl* 1950, 36, pp. 367ff., Gesetz über die Notaufnahmen von Deutschen in das Bundesgebiet, 22.8.1950; ABB annual report 1955.
49. Ges.Verb., Heisingen Papers, Heisingen annual reports and File 'Statistik', compilation of refugee statistics.
50. UVR, *Zahlen zur Betriebsstatistik. Zeitvergleich 1956 bis 1969. Ruhrrevier, Bundesgebiet*, no place, no date, p. 30.
51. OBADA I8007/520/55, ABB annual report 1954.

Arbeitskräfte). It ensured that there was a personal continuity, whereby the individual involved in recruiting a new miner also accompanied the newcomer on his first day at the mine and maintained contact during the first few weeks at work. The other aspect of working experience to receive some amelioration was the progression of the qualified apprentice, now *Knappe*, into normal productive labour.[52]

And yet, at least until 1955, the main problem of working life – the character of management and human relations – seemed to be so intractable that little was undertaken to change it. True, a number of leading figures in the industry began in the early 1950s to promote new ways of approaching the problem of the *Mensch im Betrieb*, as they put it. But the impact of these initiatives was very limited. There were a number of reasons for this, some which we will return to in the conclusion. One major reason was that those figures in the industry who were most aware of the need for a new style of human relations – labour directors, training personnel, manpower experts and so on – were not or not yet in a position to assert themselves against the colliery managers.[53]

It was no accident that the two areas given special attention were both problems of transition into the production process. It was easier in such cases for training personnel and manpower specialists to wrest some control from the works manager than it was on the issue of the factory 'climate' in general.

Another area outside the actual production process where the collieries' personnel directors felt freer to innovate was recruitment. Instead of relying on the labour exchanges to turn up likely labour, the mines began to carry out recruitment campaigns across the length and breadth of Germany. In 1954, the bulk of labour obtained from outside the Ruhr came by this

52. Theodor Terhorst, 'Zehnjährige Zusammenarbeit am Dienste der Mitbestimmung beim Hamborner Bergbau', unpublished MS [Duisburg, 1963]; Ges. Verb. File '300–301.1 Ausbildung von Neubergleuten', copy, 'Merkblatt für die Werbung von Neubergleuten', Hamborn 20.12.1954. See also chapter 5.
53. A lot of this, of course, is invisible to the outsider. Dr Steffen, the former deputy to the HBAG's labour director and one of the industry's leading training experts, described in an interview the battle between Terhorst, the labour director, and the Betriebsführer. Interviews 1.12.1982 and 24.5.1983. On the human relations initiatives, see Heinrich Kost, 'Die Tätigkeit der Deutschen Kohlenbergbauleitung. Schlußbericht', in *Glückauf*, vol. 90, nos 3/4, 1954, pp. 89–106, esp pp. 104ff.

means. The approach became increasingly professional, and campaigns were carefully co-ordinated with all the relevant administrations in advance.[54] Works councillors and sometimes former new miners now accompanied the campaigns to provide convincing accounts of mining life. A major change came in 1955, when the UVR decided to replace 'du' with 'Sie' in its campaign propaganda. This was probably the first time that existing or potential miners had ever been addressed as 'Sie' by Ruhr mining employers. An ABB circular in October 1955 offered a sample of the sort of invitation issued prior to a local recruiting event. Beginning with a 'Sehr geehrter Herr!', the invitation contained amongst other things the suggestion, 'Bringen Sie doch Ihre Ehefrau oder Ihre Braut mit,' a tone and indeed an idea that would have been inconceivable in 1950. By 1955, however, it had become standard to suggest to recruits that they bring their wives or fiancées along to the information evenings. In many cases, the potential miner and his partner had a face-to-face chat with mines' representatives and local labour administration officials. In effect, senior employers' representatives were introducing here the sort of personal relations approach they failed to institute within the works themselves.[55]

Despite all this ingenuity, the labour supply from the provinces began to dry up; and so the mines began to look for a new hinterland where expectations were lower and opportunities more restricted than in the FRG. At least initially, the mines seemed also to have hoped that they might encounter that older, simpler and more loyal mentality whose passing in the Federal Republic they so bemoaned. Certainly such expectations were apparent in the campaign to recruit 'Siebenbürger Sachsen' from Austria and the employers devoted considerable ingenuity and energy to obtaining and integrating these men. A whole series of campaigns followed, designed to draw labour from the pockets of ethnic Germans dotted around Europe. Other groups from Austria, German-speaking communities in the Italian Tirol, former German POWs who had remained in France and many more were recruited by the mines.[56]

54. OBADA I8007/520/55, ABB annual report 1954.
55. Ibid.; StAM Arbeitsamt Dortmund 46, ABB, circular no. 6/55 to labour exchanges, 26.10.1955; Ges.Verb. File 'Arbeitsausschuß', 'Merkbatt für die Werbung von Neubergleuten', Hamborn, 20.12.1954.
56. Ges.Verb. File 'SBZ Arb 130.0–130.25', copy of memo from Dr Niehues,

All this effort was not enough to secure the mines a plentiful supply of labour. When the crisis came in 1955, and even the most intensive campaigning proved unable to mobilise the labour required, the mines had to think again. By now, there were really only two options. Either the wages and incentives offered to the miner could be improved so substantially as to create a stable workforce (that would depend on governmental help); or a more modest package could be offered and the mines progressively shift to using foreign labour. Many collieries recognised that the available sources within the Federal Republic were drying up, but the problem was that no one really wanted to bring in foreign workers. The unions were hostile, fearing a source of cheap labour that would be hard to unionise, create a permanent division within the labour force, keep wages down and endanger mine safety. All groups felt that admitting foreigners would undermine the attempts to improve the industry's status. The employers believed Italians and other Mediterranean groups to be unproductive workers, inclined to sully their hostels and politically as well as productively unreliable. The OBAD feared the implications for mines' safety, while the federal ministries were anxious about the political implications of admitting large numbers of foreigners. After all, there was still considerable unemployment within Germany and in addition there were many ethnic German groups in Austria and elsewhere, trying vainly to gain admittance to the Federal Republic.[57]

Nevertheless, during the summer of 1955, the mines began seriously to consider recruiting foreigners and the press was full of speculation on the subject. For a while, the threat was forestalled by a package of support measures from the state. However, even the Miners' Bonus Scheme, introduced in 1956, could not prevent wastage from outpacing recruitment. As a result, 1957 saw foreign recruitment, in the form of 1,679 Italians and

---

12.5.1952, annex; notes of a meeting in the Auswärtiges Amt, 22.8.1952; Hibernia to DKBL, 17.10.1952; Ullrich, memo, 17.9.1952; memo, 9.2.1953; Roseman, 'New Miners', pp. 349ff.

57. Terhorst, 'Zehnjährige Zusammenarbeit', chapter 'Werbung von Erwachsenen', *passim*; OBADA I8006/2262/55, IGB to OBAD, 17.8.1955; on the political fears see Ges.Verb. File 'Arbeitsausschuß', meeting of UVR Training Subcommittee, 31.8.1955; OBADA I8006/3534/54, UVR to OBAD, 21.12.1954 and annex President of BAVAV to UVR, 25.11.1954 and BAM to UVR, 9.12. 1954.

Table 8.4 Labour intake, 1955–68

Year	Workforce size, 1 January	Underground intake[a]
1955	300,308	43,834
1956	300,166	53,233
1957	308,162	51,602
1958	312,185	28,316
1959	296,080	7,867
1960	260,523	14,661
1961	238,288	14,700
1962	224,231	10,742
1963	207,336	11,777
1964	195,840	10,055
1965	188,719	7,098
1966	174,374	4,906
1967	148,061	2,017
1968	124,391	4,693

(a) Excluding movement from pit to pit.

Source: Ges. Verb., StdKW, table 'Belegschaftswechsel – Arbeiter Untertage. Ruhr'.

also 272 Hungarian refugees, make its first major breakthrough in the mines: 8.6 per cent of the Heisingen intake now consisted of foreigners.[58]

The End of an Era

It is hard to say what the industry would have done had the coal crisis not begun in spring 1958. Probably the employers would have begun to import foreign labour on a large scale, for most of their fears in respect of hot-blooded, workshy southerners rapidly proved groundless. The Italians were no more inclined to wastage than their German counterparts. And indeed the mines did bring in a considerable number of foreigners over the following years. By 1960, for example, 60 per cent of workers taken on from outside the Ruhr were foreigners. But the 1960 intake of

58. Ges.Verb., Heisingen Papers, Heisingen annual report 1957; Heisingen Papers, miscellaneous statistics, table 'Herkunftsgebiete 1946/7–1965'.

outsiders' most striking feature was not its composition but its size – just 5,648 miners or less than 20 per cent of the 1957 figure. This was clear proof of the dramatic change in coal's fortunes that had taken place over the last three years.[59]

59. BAK B102, 33092, AAA meeting, 20.9.1956; INFAS, 'Untersuchung über die Fluktuation', p. 90; Ges.Verb., Heisingen Papers, miscellaneous statistics, table 'Herkunftsgebiete 1946/7–1965'; Ges.Verb., Heisingen Papers, annual report for 1960.

9
Mining's New Relations: New Labour, the Labour Movement and Labour Relations, 1945–1958

For any one familiar with the British coal industry or the Ruhr in the 1920s, the previous chapters may well offer something of a puzzle. Why in the course of this book has there been so little confrontation between capital and labour? Readers with a knowledge of practices in some of the more backward American mining regions may indeed be wondering when the shooting is going to start! Granted, there may be no reason to assume that the gun thugs of Harlon County should surface in Wanne-Eickel, but surely one would expect, given the fundamental issues raised by the hiring, training and integration of hundreds of thousands of new recruits, that there would be major conflicts between employers and union?

One possibility is that the union was so weak that it could not really oppose the employers. Another is that it was so conservative or co-operative that it shared management's goals. Or, if we take Stephen Lukes's third definition of power, was the real truth that labour had so *much* power that the employers had never really even thought to do anything which was not in labour's interest, so that union opposition was simply unnecessary?[1] It is time to look more closely at the relationship between new labour and the labour movement and at the newcomers' impact on labour relations in the mining industry.

Confusion, Coercion and Constraint, 1945–6

Until 1947, the newcomers had little impact on labour relations, despite the very substantial number of men being brought to the

1. Stephen Lukes, *Power: A Radical View*, London, 1974.

mines. At central level, this was because there *were* no labour relations. Military government authorised the formation of union groups only on a pit-by-pit basis and it was not until December 1946 that the IVB came into being as a single zonal organisation.[2] Moreover, the military government did not regard its decisions as bargaining propositions. Its policies were backed up, ultimately, by military force, reluctant though the British authorities were to use coercion. And if it was hard for the fragmented union movement to bargain with the British, it was even harder for them to make any headway on wage issues: miners' wages were set by four-power decision in Berlin, far removed from miners' influence.[3]

At the local level of day-to-day decision-making in the mines, labour representatives, above all the works councils, did enjoy considerable influence. Yet here, too, the continuing influx of large numbers of new recruits barely affected labour relations, primarily because the councils' power was not derived from the muscle, militancy or solidarity of the workforce. Instead it rested on two peculiar characteristics of the post-war era. First, there was a considerable community of interest between management and labour. Many normal sources of conflict did not obtain because the collieries had little to no control over resources and were not under pressure to make a profit or cut costs. Employers and works councils were united by their opposition to military government policy, particularly to the high levels of coal exports and to labour conscription. Both were involved as equal partners in illegal bartering operations, whereby coal was traded for foods and other commodities.[4]

Not that there was any love lost between the two sides. But

2. Astrid Föllmer-Edling, 'Die Politik des IVB in Ruhrgebiet 1945–1948. Die Anstrengungen um die Erhöhung der Kohlenförderung im Ruhrbergbau', unpublished dissertation, Bochum University, 1977, pp. 14ff; Hartmut Pietsch, *Militärregierung, Bürokratie und Sozialismus. Zur Entwicklung des politischen Systems in den Städten des Ruhrgebiets 1945–1948*, Duisburg, 1978, pp. 96ff.
3. Pietsch, *Militärregierung*, pp. 96, 102ff.
4. See Michael Zimmermann, *Schachtanlage und Zechenkolonie. Leben, Arbeit und Politik in einer Arbeitersiedlung 1880–1980*, Essen, 1987, p. 213; Lutz Niethammer, 'Privat-Wirtschaft. Erinnerungsfragmente einer anderen Umerziehung', in Niethammer (ed.), '*Hinterher merkt man, daß es richtig war, daß es schiefgegangen ist*'. *Nachkriegserfahrungen im Ruhrgebiet*, Berlin/Bonn, 1983, pp. 17–107, esp. pp. 69–73; IGBE Bezirk Ruhr-Nord, Recklinghausen (ed.), *Jahre die wir nicht vergessen 1945–1950. Recklinghäuser Bergbau-Gewerkschaftler erinnern sich*, Recklinghausen no date [1980], pp. 109ff.

when it came to conflict, the works councils were in a strong position to assert their wishes. Military government's support for the employers was far from absolute. The NGCC did not want to be seen as hostile to the workers. In addition, the British were committed to denazification and this placed officials permanently under threat. Another source of management insecurity was that the confiscation of German mining assets in December 1945 appeared to portend socialisation. Properly exploited, these circumstances could give a confident and militant works council considerable leverage within the mines. In some mines, councillors were able to influence even senior management appointments.[5] The recruitment of large numbers of new miners could make little difference to this situation. There was no question of the newcomers or the potential recruits at the colliery gates acting as a 'reserve army'. If the influx of new miners affected the power of organised labour at all during this period, it was only in that the IVB was able to use the levels of labour wastage as a vital card in its arguments for giving the miners more incentives.[6]

All this is not to say that the new recruits did not present labour representatives with particular challenges; simply that they had little bearing on labour's position *vis-à-vis* management or military government. The biggest source of conflict between new labour and established workforce was the allocation of scarce resources. Many of the new miners were refugees, quite a number of whom arrived with their families – and very little else. They often lacked the most basic essentials, as well as that most scarce of all commodities, a decent place to live. Almost all the newcomers lacked proper work clothing. At the same time, many established miners had been bombed out, lost many of their household goods and were wearing work clothing that was little better than rags. As a result, distribution conflicts arose between the established and new 'claimants' which mirrored what was happening all over Germany as established communities were forced to absorb refugee families.

5. Willi Braukmann, former works councillor in the pit 'Nordstern', in IGBE, *Jahre die wir nicht vergessen*, p. 100; BBA 32, 740, minutes of directors' meeting, 8.8.1947; 32,882, memo 'Betrifft: Ernährungsverhältnisse', 23.5.1947; and see chapter 2 above.
6. Braukmann, in *Jahre die wir nicht vergessen*, p. 100; Otto Wagner, 'Eine Menge zu Sagen', in ibid., pp. 149–52 at 150; Karl Biermann, 'Die Unterschrift des Angestelltenvertreters', in ibid., pp. 153–5.

In the mines, as elsewhere, both newcomers and locals felt that the other side was being privileged at their expense. Locals believed that official guidelines gave refugees and new miners generally too much priority. Works councils and employers worked secretly to counteract military government directives and redress the balance. For their part, the newcomers often felt it was they who were being disadvantaged. Undoubtedly, therefore, this period saw the emergence of tensions which could potentially have created abiding division in the work-force.[7] However, two factors very much mitigated the effect of such divisions and helped to ensure that conflicts between new and established miners, or between refugees and locals, were far more limited in the Ruhr than in other West German communities. For all the similarity with other communities, the crucial difference here was that those newcomers who stayed and worked in the mines were, by entering the community of work, able to legitimate their claim to key resources. Those who were willing and able to work could usually find a 'backer,' be it colleagues, the local works council, union officials or management, who endorsed their right to resources and helped them jump the queue.[8] Elsewhere in Germany, by contrast, refugees were foisted on communities that had little or no gainful employment for them and thus found it hard to legitimate their claims. The second, related, point is that most of those outsiders who were disgruntled left. Since housing rights were increasingly tightly linked to employment in the Ruhr, there was little chance for a large body of claimants on local resources to build up who were not in some way integrated by work.[9]

Incentives and the IVB, 1946–8

Many of the features characterising the pre-incentives period continued to apply in varying degrees until 1948. In the course

7. BBA 30, 267, memo from the office for new labour (*Einsatz ortsfremder Arbeitskräfte*), Oberhausen, 9.9.1946; 10, 507, minutes of works council meetings with management on 29.10.1946, 1.11.1946 and 20.4.1948 (*Gesamtbetriebsrat*); *Hochlarmarker Lesebuch. Kohle war nicht alles. 100 Jahre Ruhrgebietsgeschichte*, Oberhausen, 1981, pp. 213ff.

8. Interviews with Hermann Kuhn, June–July 1982, Josef Laslop, 9.5.1984, Alfons Nowak, 2.7.1985.

9. HStAD NW9,55, WBSR to Oberstadtdirektoren, 1.2.1947; Falk Wiesemann,

of 1947, however, the IVB grew increasingly worried about new labour. Apart from the simple numbers involved, there were several factors that gave the IVB particular cause for concern. The first was that the union had good reason to be anxious about the organisational and political reliability of the newcomers. Above all, the thousands of outsiders to the Ruhr, perched in their hostels and with few contacts amongst the other workers, appeared to the union to create a potential division in the workforce which employers would be able to exploit. Trade union organisation was lower in the hostels than among any other group of miners. According to one survey in 1948, barely more than 50 per cent of hostel occupants were unionised. Many union functionaries commented on the newcomers' ignorance of the purpose and value of trade unions.[10]

The IVB's concern over divisions in the workforce and new labour's political unreliability was fuelled by the introduction of the Care Packet scheme in 1947. Initially, the IVB wanted to reject the scheme as too divisive because, by contrast with the Points System, it excluded many categories of worker, including all surface workers. However, the union leadership was uncertain about the degree of solidarity which the underground workers, particularly the newcomers, would show with their colleagues on the surface, and feared that if it rejected the programme out of hand, a good part of the underground workforce would go ahead and participate anyway. Thus it did not try to organise any opposition (though it did manage to amend the terms of later Care Packet actions) but resolved to do all it could to strengthen workforce solidarity.[11] There were other worries too. Several cases of newcomers found smoking underground graphically illustrated the way undisciplined, ill-informed recruits threatened the workforce's well-being. In some cases, too, newcomers' absenteeism and underproduction were affecting group earnings and thus the pay of their established colleagues.[12]

Flüchtlingspolitik in Nordrhein-Westfalen', in Wolfgang Benz (ed.), *Die Vertreibung der Deutschen aus dem Osten. Ursachen, Ereignisse,* Folgen, Frankfurt/Main, 1985, pp. 173–82.

10. IGB district reports for 1947 and 1948 from districts I, IV and V; IGBEA BR4, H. Gutermuth, Works Councils Division report for 1948, no date.

11. Föllmer-Edling, 'Politik des IVB', pp. 73ff.

12. Ibid, p. 80; BBA 32, 882, report on meeting of production committee deputy chairmen, 25.6.1947; see also chapter 2.

The union's response to these concerns was to initiate a more energetic campaign to integrate new miners. A special officer post was created to respond to the newcomers' needs, particularly those living in the camps. A series of instructions to take the newcomers more seriously were sent to local branch secretaries. The union press was full of similar exhortations. The IVB encouraged the hostels to elect representatives and organised a first conference of the *Lagersprecher* at the end of 1947.[13] So concerned was the union to prevent the emergence of a permanent split in the workforce that it refused to sanction punitive action against misbehaving newcomers. For example, despite the extreme dangers associated with smoking underground (an offence committed almost exclusively by new miners), unions and works councillors were reluctant to endorse a hard line. It was not until the beginning of 1948 that the OBAD instituted body searches for smoking materials at the pit head, and even then the IVB and a number of works councils opposed them. Instead the union emphasised education and persuasion as the way to change the young trainees' behaviour.[14]

Alongside this overt campaign to cement ties between new miners and established workforce went another, more covert war as social democrat and communist groups within the union vied with each other to win the newcomers' support. The politically divided IVB leadership could not openly acknowledge this struggle, committed as it was to the maintenance of a unified, party-politically neutral organisation. Power was still fairly evenly balanced between communists and social democrats, the latter being slightly stronger at the very top, while the communists' dominance was particularly marked at the level of local leaders. So no one wanted to be seen openly rocking the boat of union unity. Under the surface, however, the 1947 elections were politically the most hard fought of all the postwar contests in the mines.[15]

13. Interview with Siegfried Schroeder, 18.2.1984; IVB (ed.), *Jahrbuch 1947*, section 'Neubergleute'; see also IVB district reports detailed in note 10; numerous articles in the IVB journal *Die Bergbau Industrie*, 1948–9.
14. BBA 32, 882, report on meeting of production committee deputy chairmen, 25.6.1947; Fölllmer-Edling, 'Die Politik des IVB', p. 80; OBADA I5200/3119/47, GMSO, circular, 25.11.1947; I5200/255/48, OBAD, circular, 31.1.1948; I5200/376/48, OBAD, circular, 14.2.1948; I5200/255/48, various BA responses to the above.
15. Ulrich Borsdorf, 'Speck oder Sozialisierung. Produktionssteigerungskam-

The SPD, alarmed by the KPD's success in the 1946 works council elections, was the pacemaker here. It saw the works council elections in mining as having national and indeed international significance, and threw considerable resources at the 1947 campaign.[16] Once it began to pay close attention to the political conditions in the mines, it became very aware of the opportunities and challenges presented by the new miners. On the one hand, there was the electoral potential of the many thousands of refugees and expellees flooding into the mines, many of whose first- or second-hand experiences at the hands of the Red Army had strengthened their anti-communism. On the other, the SPD was very conscious of the vital significance of winning over young newcomers to the industry with as yet no established political affiliation: 'Die heutigen Belegschaften. . (enthalten) zum großen Teil junge Leute, die weder mit der Gewerkschaft noch mit der Partei Kontakt hätten. Diese jungen Menschen zu erfassen. ., ist das Gebot des Tages.'[17] Using simple slogans like 'Rußland oder Weltkapitalismus – Nein. Das Ruhrgebiet, Kohle und Eisen dem schaffenden Volk – SPD', the SPD made considerable headway amongst the newcomers, particularly the refugees.[18]

The communists had recognised from 1946 both the importance of winning over young miners, particularly those from outside the mining community, and the fact that this would not be an easy task. The refugees were acknowledged to be a particularly hostile group. The KPD therefore worked actively during 1947–8 period to mobilise new miners in works council elections. Behind the language of party political neutrality, reports from communist-dominated district leaderships of the IVB make clear that the party hoped to get new miners as

pagnen im Ruhrbergbau 1945–1947', in Hans Mommsen and Ulrich Borsdorf (eds), *Gluckauf Komeraden! Die Bergarbeiter und ihre Organisationen in Deutschland*, Cologne, 1979, *passim*; Pietsch, *Militärregierung*, pp. 276ff.

16. Comments of Erich Meier in ASD-FESt WW68, Protokoll der Ruhrbergbau-Konferenz am 31.8.1047 in Bochum, no date; Michael Clarke, 'Die Gewerkschaftspolitik der KPD 1945–1951, dargestellt am Beispiel des IVB/IGB im Ruhrgebiet', unpublished dissertation, Bochum University, 1982, p. 56.

17. ASD-FESt WW68, Protokoll der Ruhrbergbau-Konferenz am 31.8.1047 in Bochum, no date.

18. ASD-FESt N25, vol. 1946–8, SPD Bezirk Westliches Westfalen, Bericht über die Betriebsrätewahlen im Bergbau, Dortmund 10.11.1947; Clarke, 'Die Gewerkschaftspolitik der KPD', p. 56.

communist candidates for the works councils and thereby to draw a bigger following amongst their fellow newcomers. Pit newsletters were produced, highlighting the new miners' problems and promising action. Yet, as the KPD itself acknowledged, it made little headway among much of the industry's new intake. If the new miners had an impact on labour relations in this period, then, it was above all to help weaken the power of the radical element within the working-class movement. Certainly, by 1950 the KPD's influence in the IG Bergbau was very much on the wane, though the party continued to enjoy good representation in the works councils until its banning in 1956.[19]

It is a point worth making that even if war had *not* left gaping holes in the workforce and such recruitment as took place in the post-war era had been of modest proportions and composed largely of local youngsters, the established parties would *still* have faced the challenge of a younger generation whose political affiliation was an unknown quality. Nazi terror and war had disrupted communication across the generations and had broken the political continuity. Indeed, this breach in political and social continuity applied to the older generation as well. Many local men had gone through powerful new experiences in the fascist era. Former communists, for example, had seen a war on the eastern front that, whether deservedly or no, shattered many of their hopes of the Soviet Union. In other words, even without new labour, political and group identities were in a state of flux, and it was undoubtedly the communists who were most negatively affected by this, though it is possible that the church and community ties which had sustained the Catholic vote in the past had also been weakened. New labour was thus just one more agent in the fermenting political brew of the Ruhr.[20]

19. Ernst Schmidt Papers, File 1900, doc. 1946–44, Resolutionsentwurf der KPD im Ruhrgebiet, no date [end of 1946]; File Hermes II 1948, 'Programmgestaltung' (report for the IVB district V annual conference, 1948), no date; Clarke, 'Gewerkschaftspolitik der KPD', pp. 58ff.
20. On new experiences and changing political values in the Ruhr, see IGBE, *Jahre die wir nicht vergessen*, p. 256; Lutz Niethammer, 'Heimat und Front. Versuch, zehn Kriegserinnerungen aus der Arbeiterklasse des Ruhrgebietes zu verstehen', in Niethammer (ed.), *'Die Jahre weiß man nicht, wo man die heute hinsetzen soll'. Faschismuserfahren im Ruhrgebiet*, Berlin/Bonn, 1983, pp. 163–232, esp. pp. 226ff; Karl Rohe, *Vom Revier zum Ruhrgebiet. Wahlen, Parteien, politische Kultur*, Essen, 1986. See also below.

Hard Currency, Slack Labour Market: 1948–53

The year 1948, as we have seen, saw very considerable changes
to the framework within which workforce rebuilding took place.
Colliery managers were largely freed from the twin anxieties of
future socialisation and the denazification panel. The miners
thereby lost at least some of the special leverage they had
enjoyed by virtue of the immediate post-war situation. The
introduction of a hard currency restored the function and value
of collective bargaining, both at the regional level, where pay
norms were set, and at the face, where, for the contract workers,
the actual earnings were negotiated. The mines' new financial
priorities led them to cut demand for labour just at a time when
unemployment was rising. Labour supply now far exceeded
demand. In addition, the employers, looking to their costs,
began to think more urgently about rejuvenating the workforce
by mass redundancies of older workers.[21]

The IGB[22] observed these changes with growing alarm and
became progressively more hostile to continued recruitment of
adult labour.[23] In June, an American investigating team commented that 'it is reliably reported and quite apparent that
considerable resentment is felt against the "outsiders". . . There
is a very real fear of the possible future competition for jobs by
those who can remember former periods of unemployment and
low wages.'[24] Unionists feared that employers would exploit the
situation to mount a general assault on the union. The minutes
of a workforce meeting at the mine 'General Blumenthal' in July
1948 record the following comments from the local IGB branch
chairman: 'In nächster Zeit seien Entlassungen zu erwarten. Die
Zechenleitungen ließen sich von Gesichtspunkten wie produk-
tive und unproduktive Arbeiten leiten, doch der wahre Grund
sei, neue Kameraden hineinzuschleusen nicht um die Leistung
zu steigen, sondern, da es noch ungeschulte Gewerkschaftler

21. OBADA I8010/2924/48, report for 3rd quarter 1948.
22. The IVB changed its name to Industrie-Gewerkschaft Bergbau at the end
of 1948.
23. 'Stellungnahme des Vorstandes des IVBergbau zur Anwerbung von
Neubergleuten', *Die Bergbau-Industrie*, vol. 1, no. 7, 1948, p. 1.
24. WWA S22 (OMGUS), BICO BISEC 11/104–1/39, Special Intelligence Report, 'Some German Views of the Political, Economic and Sociological Aspects of
Ruhr Coal Mining', 19.6.1948.

sind, die Bergarbeiterschaft auseinander zu bringen.'[25] By 1949, with the future market for coal temporarily very uncertain, the union had come out openly against large-scale recruitment. To deter adult recruits and create the climate for a change in recruitment policy, the IGB organised a press conference in February proclaiming that the day of mass recruitment was over and to warn of imminent changes in the energy market.[26]

The union's concern was a response not only to the potential threat of redundancies, but also to the behaviour of many newcomers now that hard currency could be earned in the pits. Many were working at a pace and with a disregard for safety that revealed both their inexperience and the fact that they were not intending to stay in the industry for long. Union officials and works councillors continually complained about infringements of safety regulations and about the *Gedinge Kaputtmacher* from the mining hostels. Moreover, the unions continued to find hostel inmates hard to organise in the union, partly because of the high wastage rate and partly because of their lack of understanding of the union movement.[27]

Much of this anxiety reflected the fact that, once normal market conditions and labour relations had been re-established, the miners were a group particularly vulnerable to the impact of new labour. First there was the question of safety. More than almost any other working group, their lives depended on the common maintenance of certain safety standards. Secondly, there were no formal skill barriers. Within a few weeks, any new recruit could be doing the same work as his more experienced colleagues. Thus the earnings, status and job security of the established workforce was far more easily affected by new recruitment than in industries where unskilled labour could be marginalised and the union could protect the privileges of core occupational groups. Finally, the existence at the faces of the group contract wage, in which the earnings of up to fifty men

25. Zimmermann Papers, File 'Betriebsratsprotokollen 1948–1951', minutes of the workforce meeting of 18.7.1948.
26. 'Weitere 200,000 Bergleute notwendig?', *Die Bergbau-Industrie*, vol. 1, no. 9, 1948, p. 6; 'Bergarbeiter-Werbung überflüssig', *Wiesbadener Kurier*, 10.2.1949; 'Gestern zu wenig – übermorgen vielleicht zu viel Kohle', *Rhein-Ruhr Zeitung*, 11.2.1949.
27. Eberhard Kadow, 'Jugendwohnheime und Jugendheimleiter', *Bergbau und Wirtschaft*, vol. 5, no. 4, 1952, pp. 88–90; DGBA, File 'IG Bergbau. Monatsberichte der IG Bergbau 1949', reports for April, May and June.

were dependent on their joint output, meant that even small groups of newcomers could upset the rhythms and norms of working life and the earnings of their colleagues.

Because the union was unable to influence the collieries' recruitment policy directly, it tried to find indirect means to restrict entry to the workforce. One was to make the adult trainees' pay package seem less attractive. In 1949, when the IGB called for negotiations to restructure trainees' pay, top IGB officials made it quite plain that their aim was to reduce the number of job-seekers in the mines and thus protect older miners from what would be a permanent threat of losing their jobs.[28] When it came to the negotiating table, however, the union, as we saw in chapter 5, proved unable to make any fundamental changes to the wage incentives offered to new trainees. In the first place, it wanted to integrate existing new labour and could not afford to leave it unprotected. Secondly, any wage ruling affecting new labour was also likely to impinge on the workforce as a whole. The absence of a skill barrier meant that it was impossible to discriminate against the newcomers.[29]

The union therefore sought another means of limiting newcomers' access and it saw this in control of training. First, it called for a much longer training period for the adult trainees. This would be a powerful means to deter potential recruits or at least to reduce the pace at which they gained access to the workforce. It would in effect create a skill barrier, protecting the established workforce from the reserve army beyond the pit gates. Accordingly the IGB wrote to the OBAD in February suggesting that, before being allowed to train at the face, all newcomers should spend an entire year in the mines as general labourers! Here, too, the IGB was unable to assert its wishes, though it found much to welcome in the OBAD's new training code.[30] In addition, the union joined the employers in calling for

28. See references in note 26 and 'IG Bergbau fordert Stabilisierung der Löhne', *Westfälische Rundschau*, 10.2.1949.
29. AZG File '"61" [=I1 61], Bezahlung der Neubergleute bzw Umschüler', undated memo concerning meeting of Tarifausschuß on 11.3.1949. See Roseman, 'New Miners in the Ruhr: Rebuilding the Workforce in the Ruhr Mines, 1945–1958', PHD dissertation, Warwick University, 1987, pp. 316–7.
30. OBADA I6307, 450, 49, IGB Abt. Angestellte to OBAD, 10.2.1949; I6307/1918/49, OBAD to BA Recklinghausen, 29.4.1949; I6307/1720/49, minutes of meeting in Mine Friedrich Heinrich, 11.7.1949.

replacement of adult trainees by expanded apprentice recruit-ment. Indeed, from 1947 onwards it had, as we know, been one of the most enthusiastic supporters of the apprenticeship scheme. From the IGB's point of view, the lengthy training would not only serve as a filter and a brake on recruitment, but would eradicate many of the other problems to which adult new labour gave rise. The union hoped that the young apprentices would be persuaded to stay in the industry and would also become committed members of the union.

Yet all these measures were unable to prevent adult recruit-ment from continuing at a high level or to shield the miners from the reality that between 1948 and 1951/2 there was a surplus of job applicants over jobs available. To what extent, then, did the employers try to exploit this situation and how far did the newcomers undermine the position of established labour? There is no doubt that the period from 1948 until the early 1950s did see the employers go on the offensive. As early as February 1948, the union began to complain that the managers were 'zunehmend aggressiv in ihrem Vorgehen gegen Arbeiter'.[31] In wage bargaining at the face, management took a firmer stand and gradually forced through tougher contracts. In terms of collective wage bargaining at the regional level, it is undoubt-edly significant that there was no wage increase between sum-mer 1948 and the beginning of 1950.[32]

Alongside the tougher wage policy, the works councils' powers were steadily reduced after 1948 and management communica-tions reveal a progressively more self-confident and aggressive tone. The example of the Friedrich Heinrich mine is instructive. In 1947, the heyday of the works councils, the colliery director went as far as publicly stating the view, to the workforce, that the production committees were a transitional experiment on the road to socialisation.[33] By 1949, however, the works council was so far reduced in influence as to send the following sorry little request to the management: 'Im Interesse einer weiteren

31. DGBA File 'Industrieverband Bergbau 1946–1948. Tätigkeitsberichte', monthly report for February 1948.
32. BBA 10, 594, DKBL Bezirk Bochum to Bergwerksleiter, 26.6.1948; IVB, Bezirk Bochum, circular 6/48, Bochum 3.7.1948; 35, 237, union meeting at mine Emscher Lippe, 3.4.1949.
33. BBA 10, 507, minutes of works council meeting with management, 31.1.1947.

guten Zusammenarbeit möchten wir die Verwaltung bitten, uns nicht allzu schulmeisterlich behandeln zu wollen.'[34] Thus a new wind was blowing through the collieries and clearly the labour surplus had something to do with this (though, as we have noted, there were plenty of other factors strengthening management's hand, not least the end of denazification, the partial withdrawal of Allied influence and the power to the deputies' elbows provided by the restoration of a stable currency).

These remarks on the post-1948 period have concentrated on the impact of the reserve army at the pit gates. But the behaviour of new miners *after they were hired* also sometimes deleteriously affected the workforce's position or bolstered management's power. After all, especially in the early years after the currency reform, the new intake was in social terms extraordinarily heterogeneous. Different groups with very different aspirations and needs were thrown alongside each other. It would have been surprising if the workforce's cohesion and solidarity had not in some way been affected by this. Another feature of the new miners which engendered conflicts and divisions was that many of them came to the mines intending to stay only for a few years. Their behaviour at work was therefore often different from that of the established men and sometimes played into management's hands. Moreover, many of those newcomers recruited from outside the Ruhr lacked any tie to the community, a fact which made it hard for unions or the established workforce to transmit the norms of working life. Finally, a key problem of the post-war period was the missing middle generation. The great gap between the large number of established men in their forties and the large number of newcomers in their twenties meant that there was at times a particularly sharp conflict between the aspirations of the established men and the behaviour of the newcomers.

In the years immediately following the currency reform some new miners were accused of willingness to accept whatever treatment the deputies cared to hand out to them. A sociological investigation into pit life in 1950 found that the small group of individuals who claimed to be completely indifferent to the way management dealt with them were, without exception, new miners. Older expellees, in particular, were often anxious not to

34. BBA 10, 507, works council to management, 19.4.1949.

lose their jobs and consequently kept their heads down.[35] A more frequent complaint was that the new miners were trying to maximise their earnings irrespective of the cost. This had a number of damaging effects. First, it led many newcomers to reject the group contract wage because that would have meant sharing their earnings with slower workers. Such men thus helped management bring in individual piece-rates against the wishes of many established workers.[36] Secondly, the newcomers' behaviour often triggered the so-called wage scissors effect: higher output led to renegotiation of the piece- or contract-rate by management so that, in future, earning the same wage would require more effort.[37] In addition, the other workers on the face came under pressure to fit in with the higher pace of work or to leave the face for lower-paid work elsewhere in the pit. Older men in particular faced an agonizing choice between taxing their health by working harder or accepting loss of earnings for the sake of easier work.[38] In other pits, however, the newcomers were condemned for being *Drückeberger*, that is, for not working hard enough. Here, too, the effect was to undermine group solidarity and the group contract system. 'Meistens entsteht aus dem Kameradschaftsgedinge erst das Einmangedinge,' complained a 37-year-old *Hauer* in an interview in the early 1950's, 'weil von den Neuen sich viele auf die faule Haut legen.'[39] And the works manager confirmed the complaint.[40]

The fact that such contradictory complaints existed does not mean that they were false. Rather, they remind us of the presence of different groups within the general group of new labour. On the one hand, there were those who had good reason to want to maximise their earnings. Young family men, who had come to the mines for a short period only, had no interest in

35. Carl Jantke, *Bergmann und Zeche. Die sozialen Arbeitsverhältnisse einer Schachtanlage des nördlichen Ruhrgebiets in der Sicht der Bergleute*, Tübingen, 1953, p. 57.
36. Helmut Hohmann, 'Lagerleben und Einzelgedinge', in IGBE Bezirk Ruhr-Nord (ed.), *Jahre die wir nicht vergessen 1945–1950. Recklinghäuser Bergbauwerkschaftler erinnern sich*, Recklingshausen, 1980, p. 169.
37. Ibid., p. 170.
38. On the resentment of many older men, see Bernd Parisius, 'Arbeiter zwischen Resignation und Integration. Auf den Spuren der Soziologie der 50er Jahre', in Niethammer, *'Hinterher merkt man'*, pp. 107–48, esp. pp. 126–7, 129.
39. Jantke, *Bergmann und Zeche*, p. 45.
40. Ibid, p. 40.

supporting older colleagues or in finding effort norms that would not damage their health over the years. The expellees and refugees, in particular, had lost everything and were now hell-bent on building up a home. On the other hand, as in the pre-currency-reform period, there continued to be a youthful element among the newcomers determined to do as little work as possible, which naturally aroused resentment. Usually bachelors, and often living in hostels, they had relatively low living costs and no great interest in maximising their earnings. Often not particularly worried about losing their jobs, they were relatively unconcerned by either collegial pressure or admonitions from the deputy. The specifically new feature was not that the youngsters were inclined to lark about or disregard their elders (no doubt young miners had always been so inclined), but that, since many did not come from within the mining community and lived in hostels, they were particularly immune to the strictures of parents or older colleagues.[41]

However, the negative impact of new labour should not be exaggerated. First, the removal of the one-man contract, though speeded on its way by new miners, had really been a foregone conclusion since the introduction of long-wall mining in the 1920s (see chapter 5). This is amusingly, though unwittingly, demonstrated by Carl Jantke's study, *Bergmann und Zeche*. Jantke provides some powerful evidence demonstrating the link between new labour's behaviour and the advance of the one-man contract, yet evidently had not realised (or chose not to acknowledge) that in the mine he was studying, Emscher-Lippe, the one-man contract had actually already become the dominant form before the war. The collective contract had merely been temporarily revived in the post-war era and its disappearance again was therefore no great surprise. Secondly, and this is a point to which we must now turn, the degree to which the employers were able to exploit the newcomers' behaviour – or, indeed, labour supply conditions generally – was actually both limited and short-lived.[42]

41. Hohmann, 'Lagerleben und Einzelgedinge', p. 169; Jantke, *Bergmann und Zeche*, p. 45; Rudolf Schmitz, 'Das Gedinge, seine Bedeutung und seine Wirkung auf die zwischenmenschlichen Beziehungen im Ruhrkohlenbergbau', unpublished dissertation, Münster University, 1952, pp. 160ff.
42. Jankte, *Bergmann und Zeche*, p. 1; Schmitz, 'Gedinge', pp. 160ff. BBA 35, 236, minutes of workforce meeting, 15.8.1948, comments by Saffin; 35, 237,

New Labour and the Limits to Employer Power

Whilst the *Bergassessoren* did undoubtedly regain lost ground in the years after 1948, an observer familiar with the Ruhr of the 1920s would probably be struck not by management's new aggressiveness but rather by the opposite, by what management did *not* try to do. In 1924, as in 1948, the post-war phase of economic and political uncertainty and high demand for labour was replaced by unemployment, rationalisation and renewed confidence on the part of employers. But in the post-1924 period, Ruhr employers moved with increasing vehemence against the union with mass sackings, lock-outs and so on. Compared with this, the reaction after 1948 was tame indeed. There was no frontal assault on the union; the framework for collective bargaining was never repudiated either formally or verbally; sackings were used as a means of discipline to only a limited extent.[43]

Consider the issue of mass redundancies, a matter about which the IVB had had grave anxieties for a long time. This was, if you like, the sharp edge of workforce regeneration. There was the political threat that employers would use new labour to push out unwanted elements; and there was the purely economic threat that large numbers of older workers would be dismissed or forced into early retirement to make way for younger men. In 1923–4, some Ruhr pits had sacked their entire workforces, and had then rehired only those who were seen as productive and politically reliable. Between 1922 and 1924, the Ruhr labour force had fallen by 100,000 and over the following four years, rationalisation had reduced it by a further 50,000.[44]

In summer 1948 there were some signs that this might happen again. Many employers began to draw up plans for compulsory retirement of large numbers of older miners. The pressure to do so came not only from the balance sheet but also from the UK/USCCG, which urged the collieries to cut back on unproductive elements in the workforce. Moreover, the employers may

---

minutes of first workforce meeting in 1949, comments by works councillor Brandt; minutes of union meeting, 3.4.1949, comments by Brandt.

43. For employers' behaviour 1923–4, see Rudolf Tschirbs, *Tarifpolitik im Ruhrbergbau 1918–1933*, Berlin/New York, 1986, pp. 190ff.

44. Ibid., pp. 190ff, 252.

well have felt that a display of readiness to engage in mass
sackings would make the remaining members of the established
workforce more compliant and efficient. The question was
whether the unions would be able to do anything about this, or
whether the reserve army of willing labour had undermined
union power. There was little doubt that few miners wanted to
take retirement. Though wages increased in June 1948, *Knappschaft* payments did not, so that pensions stood in no relation to
earnings.[45] The interesting thing is that mass sackings did not
take place. One reason was that the pits' labour demand continued to run at a relatively high level so that they could not
afford to shed too much labour. This in turn was the result of a
number of different factors. Unlike the 1920s, demand for coal
remained relatively strong for most of the period. Secondly,
financial and technical problems hindered mechanisation so that
the industry could not rationalise at the same pace as after 1924.
Thirdly, the high level of wastage meant replacements continued to be required.

However, differences in the level of labour demand alone will
not explain the contrasts in management's behaviour. There is
little doubt that, left to their own devices, the employers in 1948
would have liked to embark on a more radical programme of
redundancies. What restrained them was, first, the fact that
labour exchange approval continued to be required for redundancies and the labour administration remained conscious of its
responsibilities towards the labour force; and secondly, the
DKBL itself proved willing to compromise with the IGB on the
issue. A special committee was set up by the ABB, IGB and
DKBL to consider how the employers should react to the
changed labour market situation since the currency reform. The
committee agreed that mass redundancies should not be undertaken. In cases where they seemed necessary, the committee
had to be involved. The ABB advised all labour exchanges in
mining areas of their powers to prevent mass redundancies.[46]

45. Außenstelle Bergbau (ed.) 'Sechs Jahre Außenstelle Bergbau des Landesarbeitamtes NRW', unpublished MS, no place, no date [1952], p. 71; BBA 35,
51, minutes of meeting of DKBL Bochum District, 29.4.1948; Willy Siebert, 'Der
Umschichtungsprozeß der Belegschaften im westdeutschen Steinkohlenbergbau', unpublished dissertation, Münster University, 1953, pp. 120ff.
46. 'Sechs Jahre Aussenstelle Bergbau', pp. 72–3; BBA 35, 51, minutes
of meeting of DKBL Bochum District, 29.4.1948; 55, 12200, no. 11, minutes of
meeting on 24.2.1950.

Table 9.1 Losses due to ill health and old age[a]

Year	Below ground	All workers[47]
1947	2,698	n.g.
1948	3,388	6,166
1949	4,559	8,156
1950	6,857	12,224
1951	4,971	8,675
1952	5,298	9,329
1953	5,987	10,715
1954	6,514	11,922
1955	3,614	7,134
1956	3,088	6,250
1957	4,139	7,715

(a) Figures until 1954 include deaths at work, which averaged about 1,000 a year.

Source: Ges.Verb., StdKW, table 'Aufteilung des Abganges nach Gründen – Arbeiter insgesamt. Ruhr', and parallel table for workers underground.

As a result the number of redundancies remained within limits. Admittedly, it is hard to identify exactly how many workers were affected. The mines' statistics listing those retired from the mines for reasons of old age or ill health (see table 9.1) were probably not comprehensive, but do at least indicate that the post-currency-reform period was not characterised by exceptional redundancies. Only 1950 was well above the average for the following period (largely because modest improvements in *Knappschaft* payments in mid-1949 made both miners and employers more willing to consider retirement). Other statistics, too, support the idea that redundancies moved within normal bounds.[48] Thus workforce rejuvenation was prevented from being an explosive issue, the employers accepting that it would take place more slowly than direct cost and productivity con-

47. Few underground miners were made redundant directly. Normally, as they got older, they were transferred to less demanding and lower-paid jobs above ground. This had a knock-on effect, forcing other older miners above ground into full retirement.

48. 'Sechs Jahre Außenstelle Bergbau', p. 92; BBA 55, 12200, no. 11, minutes of Bergausschuß meeting, 27.1.1950. For additional evidence, see Roseman, 'New Miners', pp. 321–2.

siderations made desirable.[49] This is not to say that the labour supply situation had *no* influence on the union's position. The fact is, however, that the IGB was in general terms not radically affected by the labour market.

Why were the employers willing to compromise on the issue? At central level a key reason for this was that both the state and the employers had good reasons for courting the IGB, reasons that were barely affected by the labour market situation. The state, in the form of the labour administration and the NRW regional ministries, proved in many different circumstances to be very concerned to win the support of organised labour. Relations between the NRW government and the DKBL, which Karl Arnold and his colleagues seem to have regarded as a state within a state, usurping powers rightly belonging to regional government, were poor. When they took these disputes to Frankfurt, later to Bonn, the NRW ministries wanted to know they had the union's support. Since the Cabinet was in a number of areas more socially minded than the employers, there was a natural basis for agreement, despite the fact that the Cabinet was largely Christian Democrat, while the union was dominated by the SPD. The federal government, too, was anxious not to antagonise the IGB – particularly during 1950–1, when Adenauer was involved in discussions over the Schuman plan, and a closed front between state, employers and IGB was seen as essential if the FRG was to get the terms it wanted.[50]

The DKBL had equally good reasons not to drive the IGB into open opposition. For a start, there were union nominees within the DKBL itself who had some influence on the organisation's policies. Far more important, however, was the importance of maintaining a closed front towards the Allies. The DKBL was in a different position to colliery managers. The managers, growing more secure in their positions by the day, were prepared to

49. A fact which helps explain the slow progress of productivity away from the core area of contract wage employment. See Hibernia's productivity figures, in Hibernia Konzern (ed.), *Hibernia Sozialbericht 1958*, annex 14.

50. HStAD NW53, 643, WAM to NRW Minister-Präsident, 14.7.1948; Minister-Präsident to Bishop, NRW Regional Commissioner, 24.7.1958; Landrat Ernst to Arnold, 18.8.1948; NW73, 47, WAM to IVB, 28.10.1948; NW10, 83, WAM III B 5 305, memo, 3.4.1951; Norbert Ranft, *Vom Objekt zum Subjekt. Montanmitbestimmung, Sozialklima und Strukturwandel im Bergbau seit 1945*, Cologne, 1988, p. 43; G. Müller-List, 'Adenauer, Unternehmer und Gewerkschaften. Zur Einigung über die Montanmitbestimmung 1950/1', *VfZ* vol. 35, no. 2, 1985, pp. 288–309.

take an aggressive line against labour. The DKBL leadership, on the other hand, though sympathising with the managers, needed IGB support if it was to block Allied proposals for a reorganisation of the mining industry. From the middle of 1949, the IGB was closely involved in the formulation of alternative German proposals. Finally, there was also the threat that the federal government would (as it eventually did in the 1951 co-determination law) impose a new industrial relations structure on the industry. During 1949 and 1950, leading employers worked hard to forestall this by means of some voluntary code agreed with the unions.[51] In other words, at the local level, outside agencies, above all the Allies, ceased to represent a threat; at higher levels, the employers and the federal government still needed union co-operation to have a strong hand in negotiations.[52]

This repeatedly produced a discrepancy between management actions at lower levels, where the new conditions after 1948 produced tougher rhetoric and policies, and behaviour at the top, where there was much more awareness of the need for compromise. The wage negotiations after the currency reform are a case in point. The wage agreement of June 1948 provided for a stronger orientation towards 'normal' levels of output and removal of the special concession of the post-war era. Yet when some employers responded by calling for wage contracts to take 1938 output as their basis with no regard at all for the continuing special problems, they were undoubtedly going beyond what the DKBL's negotiators had envisaged. Senior DKBL officials declared themselves 'betroffen über die Ungeschicktheit mit der mit dem Jahre 1938 als "normales Jahr" für die Gedingesetzung operiert wurde'. The result, here as elsewhere, was that pit managers were held in check by the caution of senior figures in the industry.[53]

51. Werner Abelshauser, *Der Ruhrkohlenbergbau seit 1945. Wiederaufbau, Krise, Anpassung*. Munich, 1984, pp. 52ff.; Heinrich Kost, 'Die Tätigkeit der Deutschen Kohlenbergbauleitung. Schlaßbericht', *Glückauf*, vol. 90, nos. 3/4, 1954, pp. 89–106.
52. A fact clearly demonstrated in the government's decision to support codetermination in iron and steel. See Abelshauser, *Ruhrkohlenbergbau*, p. 61.
53. BBA 10, 594, report on a meeting of the DKBL, Bochum district, with the CCCG and DKBL leaders, 8.9.1949; BBA 35, 51, minutes of meeting of the mines in the Bochum district of the DKBL on 5.7.1948, Emscher-Lippe 7.7.1948.

The 'Unreserved' Army

One other factor preventing the employers from exploiting the new recruits to weaken the labour force as a whole was the resourcefulness and independence of the recruits themselves. For the new miners proved able and willing to defend their rights. Contemporaries may have complained about the compliant expellee; but they were just as likely to point out the contrary tendency amongst the younger expellees, namely, that they stood up to the deputies and management with a resolution and an effectiveness that had been lacking in the community. An investigation of the contract wage in the post-war period discovered that not infrequently it was new miners who through their self-confidence and ability to put across their point of view became the spokesmen of the entire face.[54]

Where did that confidence come from? The newcomers' standards were different. As outsiders they were less accustomed to the tone current within mining. Not a few new miners and, in particular, many expellees came from non-working-class backgrounds. According to SoFoSt records, getting on for a fifth of expellees taken on in 1945–8 had formerly been in white-collar, managerial or professional occupations or self-employed and they were used to a quite different approach to human relations. Their unwillingness to put up with the rough, patriarchal treatment of the mining industry was shared by the not inconsiderable number of new men who had held positions of responsibility and authority in the army.[55]

Far more important than their willingness to stand up and fight, however, was the newcomers' readiness to leave. As young and often single men they were less tied to the mines

54. See Walter Köpping, 'Als Betriebsobmann auf "Julia" 1947–1949', in Köpping (ed.), *Lebensberichte deutscher Bergarbeiter*, Oberhausen, 1984, pp. 404–7. Günther Eckerland, 'Lagersprecher', in ibid., pp. 407–10; Schmitz, 'Gedinge', pp. 158–9. Hans Walter, a senior wage arbitrator, drew attention to the fact that young, inexperienced newcomers frequently became face spokesmen in his article 'Zehn Jahre Gedingeschlichtung im westdeutschen Steinkohlenbergbau', *Glückauf*, vol. 94, nos 43/4, 1958, pp. 1537–46.

55. Jantke, *Bergmann und Zeche*, cited in Manfred Fronz Gerd Peter (eds), *Sozialwissenschaftliche Forschung im Steinkohlenbergbau*, vol. 2: *Der Steiger. Auszüge aus empirischen Untersuchungen 1950–1982*, Bochum, 1983, pp. 22ff. Calculation of social background from Helmuth Croon and K. Utermann, *Zeche und Gemeinde. Untersuchungen über den Strukturwandel einer Zechengemeinde im nördlichen Ruhrgebiet*, Tübingen, 1958, p. 296. Interview with Walther Köpping on 16.8.1983.

than the established workforce and, for the reasons outlined above, were often less willing to put up with the conditions in mining. At no point in the post-currency-reform period do they seem to have shown any great anxiety about obtaining employment elsewhere. This is a reminder that, although much higher elsewhere, unemployment never went above 5 per cent in NRW.[56] In addition, many newcomers probably drew strength from the sort of wartime and post-war experiences described by Lutz Niethammer. Many had made the most incredible odysseys, first as retreating soldiers, then as discharged soldiers or ex-POWs trudging hundreds, sometimes thousands, of miles till they found their families, then further great treks with or without the family westwards in search of work. No doubt there were plenty who now hankered after stability; indeed, it is hard otherwise to see why so many stayed in the mines; but they were, by and large, not frightened of moving.[57]

The Romantic Partners

The absence of conflict between capital and labour over workforce rebuilding was not just a sign of the constraints on employers' power. It also reflected the fact that union representatives and works councillors proved extremely willing to work cooperatively with the employers on even the most difficult of issues. On involuntary retirement and redundancies, for example, the IGB generally took a balanced view. Typical of union attitudes were the comments by Böing, works councillor and union branch chairman at the mine Emscher-Lippe: 'Wir müssen uns mit der Tatsache abfinden, daß wenn wir unter Tage einstellen, dann muß ein anderer Platz machen . . . Wenn ich Betriebsrat sein will, muß ich auch zu diesen Dingen Stellung nehmen, die unabwendbar sind und wenn sie auch unangenehm sind. Wenn wir uns aus der kritischen Situation, die augenblicklich besteht, herausziehen wollen, dann brauchen wir keinen Betriebsrat.'[58] Bolstered by the complex 'quadripartite' network of interdepen-

56. Calculated from *Statistisches Jahrbuch für die Bundesrepublik Deutschland*, 1955, pp. 114–15.
57. Niethammer, 'Heimat und Front', *passim*.
58. E.g. BBA 35, 237, minutes of union meeting at mine Emscher Lippe, 3.4.1949. Comments of branch chairman Böing.

dency amongst employers, state, Allies and labour, the IGB played an important co-operative role in almost every area of new labour policy. Even after the Allies' influence had effectively been removed, established institutional patterns within and outside the mining companies, and the ever-tightening labour market, ensured that labour's influence continued.

Consider, for instance, the recruitment of new labour. Works councillors played an increasingly important part in recruitment campaigns. The IGB was decisive in obtaining favourable treatment for the mines from the federal labour administration. After all, the Bundesanstalt für Arbeitsvermittlung und Arbeitslosenversicherung (BAVAV, the head of the German labour administration, created in 1952), though a public body, was jointly run by the state, the employers and the unions. Enlisting the IGB's support was vital when the employers wished to get the BAVAV to reduce its charges for recruiting and transporting new miners.

Housing was another area where, as shown in chapter 6, the union possessed considerable expertise and influence. It sat on the district housing committees created by the 1951 housing law and also in the separate bodies responsible for allocating the ECA houses. At a lower level, the works councils were very important in assigning priority ratings to the applicants in the colliery housing lists. Once the new *Arbeitsdirektoren* were in office, they too tended to see miners' housing as an ideal area in which to exert their influence, since it was one where good results could be readily shown.[59]

One key fact which made it easier for the union to work alongside the employers was that, because the state ultimately held the purse-strings, pay bargaining was often less a matter of fighting it out within the industry than of jointly prevailing on the federal government to provide the industry with additional resources. True, there were some bitter wrangles between the UVR and the IGB, as in the 1953 dispute over a shorter working week. But pay negotiations increasingly tended to take the form of both sides agreeing that the miner should stand at the top of the pay scale but that at present the industry could not afford to fulfil this demand, and then driving down to Bonn to persuade the Economics Minister to increase the coal price.

59. On labour directors and housing, see IGB (ed.), *Jahrbuch 1953*, p. 153.

Another perhaps more striking reason for the IGB's ability to co-operate with the employers was that it shared many of their fundamental aims and views. Perhaps most important, no one was keener than the IGB to raise the miner's status and self-esteem. Both sides shared the aspiration of reviving a lost mining tradition (see chapter 5). The union's leaders, just like their counterparts on the other side of the labour–capital divide, wanted to restore a vanished social order in which the *Bergmannsstand* would once again enjoy its rightful place. In his study of the IGB, Hans Eckbert Treu has shown that senior union leaders had a vision of the organic 'ständische Gesellschaft' as strong as that of any mining manager.[60] In housing policy, for example, we find the IGB too working with images of the solid, settled, dependable and simple miner, though perhaps without some of the most patronisingly docile elements contained in the employers' vision. We find the union strongly endorsing the idea of owner-occupied housing and many of its leaders sharing the more political hopes and fears of their bourgeois counterparts. When the Bundestag deputy Frau Dr Bröckelschen came to the Ruhr to advocate more owner-occupied housing, she had no qualms about declaring that housing could act as a bulwark against Eastern infiltration, even though union representatives were present. She knew she was among friends.[61] Writing in the union journal *Bergbau und Wirtschaft* in 1953, labour director Triem criticised the employers for having too long neglected the 'Eigentums- und Entproletarisierungsfrage'.[62] And like the parliamentarians, the IGB saw eminent dangers in big estates full of rented accommodation.[63]

60. See chapter 5; also Hans-Eckbert Treu, *Stabilität und Wandel in der organisatorischen Entwicklung der Industriegewerkschaft Bergbau und Energie*, Frankfurt, 1979, pp. 105–6; 'Der "Lager Mensch" – Symptom einer Entwicklung', *Neue Zeitung*, 7.8.1951.
61. BAK B102, 33175, 'Kurzprotokoll üer die Besichtigungsfahrt des Bundestagsausschusses', 20.11.1952.
62. J. Triem, 'Wohn- und Lebensstil unserer Bergleute', *Bergbau und Wirtschaft*, 1953, no. 6, pp. 98–100.
63. DGBA, File 'IG Bergbau (1949–1966)', IGB Hauptverwaltung to DGB Vorstand, 21.3.1953. BAK B134, 3727, 6th report of Unterausschuß III; IGB (ed.), *Jahrbuch 1952*, p. 429.

Organisation without Mobilisation: The IGB and New Labour

Of course, the IGB still had its own interests, in opposition to those of the employers. Naturally enough, it continued to expend considerable energy on ensuring that all new recruits became union members. In keeping with its general style, however, the IGB leadership had no ambitions to mobilise the new miners for action or to develop out of the young, single men an activist potential. The only exception to this rule came from the communist element within the union, which maintained hopes of exploiting the hostel occupants' special grievances to create a militant core in the workforce. In 1951 the party set up a special committee, the *Ausschuß zur Wahrung der Interessen der Jung- und Neubergleute*, which campaigned on issues such as recent rises in the price of board and lodging. The party tried hard to persuade the young miners of the link between US imperialist ambitions, German remilitarisation and the conditions in which they were living. At an all-German miners' conference in 1952, new miners were supposed to play a major role. By the end of 1952, however, the KPD's hopes seem to have evaporated.[64]

By contrast, the increasingly dominant social democrat and Christian democrat leaders in the IGB expected a far more passive, disciplined role from union members.[65] Senior IGB figures often took a rather authoritarian approach towards the young miners. In 1946, for example, a discussion took place between DGB leaders, IVB president August Schmidt and military government representatives. A British official pointed out the discrepancy between the military government law which allowed all employees to vote in works council elections, and the DGB ruling which restricted this right to the over-18s. Hans Böckler for the DGB said 'er würde 10 mal lieber zum Arbeitsgericht gehen, als nur einem einzigen Jugendlichen unter 18 Jahren das Recht zugestehen, einen Betriebsrat zu wählen, oder selbst gewählt zu werden'. When Foulds, the British officer,

---

64. Ernst Schmidt Papers, *Unser Weg, Monatsschrift für aktuelle Fragen der Arbeiterbewegung*, ed. KPD Executive, Düsseldorf, issues for October 1951, March 1952, May 1952; ASD-FESt N171, vol. 1952–7, unsigned, undated [1952] KPD circular 'An alle Mitglieder des Initiativekomitees!', p. 4; unsigned, undated [1951–2] KPD circular from the 'Ausschuß zur Wahrung der Interessen der Jung- und Neubergleute'; Clarke, 'Die Gewerkschaftspolitik der KPD', pp. 58ff.
65. Treu, *Stabilität und Wandel*, pp. 69ff.

pointed out that this was not likely to educate the youngsters to
be good democrats and that the same held true for the DGB's
minimum age of 24 for a works councillor, August Schmidt's
response was to say that 24 was too low for the mining industry!
In Schmidt's view a minimum age of 28–30 was more suitable.
On the other hand, however, the IGB was responsible for
setting up elected committees in the hostels.[66]

Though it resisted mobilising the young newcomers and was
slow to give younger members a taste of power, the IGB leadership was very interested in transmitting to them what it saw as
the right values, both through its own courses for interested
participants and by playing a role in the cultural activities for the
hostels. In 1953, for example, the IGB spent DM 250,000 on
summer youth camps alone. In terms of the values offered, we
find the IGB increasingly occupying much of the same ground
as its bourgeois counterparts, and indeed, the union generally
praised the VHS work.[67] Both sides shared, for example, a
commitment to party political neutrality. This was, after all, the
keystone of the new post-war unity within the labour movement, even if it concealed an increasingly comprehensive assault on communist unionists. A report on the union's annual
youth conference in 1953, for example, noted: 'Hierbei hatten
die Delegierten Gelegenheit, zu beweisen, daß parteipolitische
oder weltanschauliche Gefahrenquellen durch sie nicht akut
sind.'[68] Given that the report arose from a session in which the
delegates were discussing 'youth and the democratic state', it
must have taken considerable ingenuity to avoid being 'party
political' or expressing a *'Weltanschauung'*![69]

Another point of common ground was the model of democracy being propagated. Like the employers, the IGB gave priority
to educating young people to be aware of their duties, before
giving them a taste of democracy. At the union's first post-war
youth conference, Walter Maibaum, the IGB's youth secretary,
said that the goal was 'pflichtbewußte junge Menschen zu

66. Ernst Schmidt Papers, File '1900', doc. 1946–10, 'Kurzer Bericht über eine
Sitzung mit Vertretern der Militärregierung in Düsseldorf', 4.9.1946.
67. IGB Bezirk IV (ed.), *Jahresbericht 1950*, p. 14; IGB (ed.), *Jahresbericht 1953*,
p. 289. Initially, perhaps under KPD influence, some districts were more critical
of the VHS work.
68. IGB, *Jahrbuch 1953*, p. 293.
69. See also comments by Helmuth Schorr, DGB, in HStAD NW42, 912, Dr
Simons, Bericht über den Lehrgang für Heimleiter, 18.1.1948.

erziehen' who would be the citizens of tomorrow and convinced democrats. Theo Pirker has argued convincingly that older unionists had no understanding for the aspirations of the younger generation and 'eine ganz bestimmte Vorstellung der sozialen Ordnung . . . eine Vorstellung dessen, was gehörig ist und nicht gehörig ist'.[70]

IGB figures also saw in Germany's recent experience, particularly the upheavals of the post-war period, the dangers of *Vermassung*. They too talked of rescuing the youngsters' personalities from this *Vermassung* and from nihilism. Astonishingly, given the recent past, the union felt obliged to defend itself against the employers' charge that, as a mass organisation, it was contributing to *Vermassung*.[71]

On morality and culture, the older generation of union officials had much in common with the employers and state representatives. Union officials, like employers, felt that young miners needed to learn good manners for the sake of the status of the profession. Unionists talked of leading youngsters towards the true values of Western culture, while rejecting the modern excesses of American civilisation. 'Wenn man sich anderswo so nackt wie eben möglich auszieht, so braucht das durchaus nicht unesere Lebensart zu werden.'[72] In 1953 the IGB paper *Bergbau und Wirtschaft* actually published an article about the *Ruhrfestspiele* with the title 'Mensch und deformierte Kunst'.[73]

Having said that, the local IGB and DGB youth organisations did offer a number of young miners a chance to learn a much more direct and participatory democracy. Many youngsters who

70. DGBA Protokoll-Sammlung, IGB Hauptverwaltung (ed.), *Protokoll des 1.Verbandsjugendtags Bochum 1950, Sept 22–24*, Bochum 1950, comments of Maibaum and Bartoniczek, pp. 15, 31ff.; IGB Hauptverwaltung Abt. Jugend (ed.), *Geschäftsbericht 1950–1952*, pp. 54ff.; Theo Pirker, 'Die Jugend in der Struktur unserer Gesellschaft', in DGB, Abteilung Jugend (ed.), *Protokoll der Arbeitstagung der Gewerkschaftsjugend 25–30.11.1951*, Düsseldorf, 1952, pp. 10–19.

71. Johann Platte, 'Die Nachwuchsfrage im Kohlenbergbau', *Arbeitsblatt für die britische Zone*, vol. 2, no. 11, 1948, pp. 399–400; IGB Hauptverwaltung (ed.), *Protokoll des 1.Verbandsjugendtags*, esp. pp. 15, 31ff.; Treu, *Stabilität und Wandel*, pp. 105–6.

72. Helmut Schorr, 'Wege und Ziele der Gewerkschaftsjugend', talk reprinted in IGB Hauptverwaltung (ed.), *Protokoll des 1. Verbandsjugendtags*, pp. 88ff. at 97.

73. H. W. Peupelmann, 'Mensch und deformierte Kunst. Ein offenes Wort an die Künstler', *Bergbau und Wirtschaft*, vol. 5, no. 13, 1952, pp. 331–2; Kadow's remarks in IGBEA Handakten Rudi Quast, File 'M. Assistenten-Tagungen (alt)', 3rd meeting of Herner Kreis, 24.6.1953.

found the lack of democracy in normal union meetings and congresses stifling enjoyed a far freer atmosphere in the youth section. Younger union officials tended to be more informal, allowing youngsters to address them with the 'du' form, for example, or incurring employer suspicions by allowing young apprentices to drive with them on the way to union weekends and camping trips.[74]

The biggest difference between the union and the rest of the workers in the cultural welfare field was that the IGB was hostile to any attempts to segregate the newcomers from the rest of the workforce. It grew increasingly critical of such things as separate sport or other activities for hostel occupants which prevented the inmates from seeking more links with the local community. There is little doubt that the union's own efforts were concentrated far more on building bridges between newcomers and locals than creating a new ethos in the hostels.[75]

Union Activity and its Impact

How successful was the IGB at integrating and influencing new labour? Despite the problems of obtaining access to some of the church-run apprentice hostels, the IGB found little difficulty in unionising the apprentices, more than 90 per cent of whom were union members. Some branches even claimed 100 per cent youth membership. As far as adult new labour was concerned, the unions found that the lower levels of recruitment and wastage in 1948–9 made it easier for them to unionise new recruits than hitherto. In Bochum, for example, though the union continued to complain of difficulties with young adult trainees, unionisation levels in the hostels rose from 35 per cent at the beginning of 1949 to 78 per cent a year later. By 1951, the figures were in the 90s.[76]

74. Hans Dieter Baroth, *Aber es waren schöne Zeiten*, Cologne, 1978, p. 177; IGB (ed.), *Jahrbuch 1953*, p. 286; Treu, *Stabilität und Wandel*, pp. 111–12; Zimmermann Papers, interview with Heinrich Klever, 15.7.1980.

75. IGBE Presse-Archiv, File 'Arbeitskräfte für den Bergbau. Neubergleute bis 1952', IGB, Referat Neubergleute, circular 133/49, 21.1.1949; IGB (ed.), *Jahrbuch 1952*, p. 442; IGBEA Handakten Rudi Quast, File 'M. Assistenten-Tagungen (alt)', minutes of 3rd meeting of Herner Kreis, 24.6.1953.

76. IGB Bezirk IV Bochum, *Jahresberichte*, 1949, report of Bochum branch (Geschäftsstelle); 1950, p. 28; 1951, p. 27; 1952, pp. 16–18.

Problems developed in 1953, in part because of the high wastage levels and the fact that the industry was now recruiting men who had no intention of staying in mining. An even more serious cause of declining membership was the employers' decision in 1953 to stop collecting union dues. The IGB was forced to go out and confront its members with the weekly unpleasant duty of coughing up their contribution. As a result, between 1953 and 1955 membership levels fell for the industry as a whole by 14 per cent. The drop among new miners was more dramatic and some branches were reporting organisation levels among hostel occupants down to around 40 per cent.[77] There is little evidence, however, that falling rolls seriously threatened the IGB's organisational integrity or its ability to use strike action as a weapon. In the vote at the end of 1952 on potential industrial action over the introduction of the seven-and-a-half-hour day, the IGB achieved extremely high (over 90 per cent) votes in favour of strike action. In what was virtually the only mining strike since the currency reform, the so-called 'Reusch strike' of 1955, the response was also very good. Even substantial numbers of apprentices took part.[78]

On the question of what the newcomers actually thought of the IGB, the evidence is, as Bernd Parisius observes in his recent oral history study of coal and steel workers, somewhat contra-dictory. Carl Jantke, in the SoFoSt survey *Bergmann und Zeche*, contrasted the older miners' close ties to the IGB with the new recruits' more critical attitude. Jantke explicitly stressed that the difference in attitude was associated less with age than with years of experience in mining. Other studies and surveys, how-ever, do not really confirm these results. The responses to another SoFoSt survey, this time of miners in a hostel at the Victor Ickern pit in Castrop Rauxel, reveal a generally favourable attitude to the union amongst the new miners. The IGB itself commissioned a survey of members' attitudes towards the end of the 1950s. This EMNID investigation identified that virtually all the miners, even non-union-members, believed the IGB was doing a valuable job, and it found no marked differences be-tween long-established and new or between young and old

77. Treu, *Stabilität und Wandel*, p. 58 and table 5; annual report of Bezirk V for 1954–5, p. 53; annual report of Bezirk VI for 1951/2, p. 31 and 1953, pp. 24–5.
78. IGB, *Jahrbuch 1952*, p. 208 and Ges. Verb. File 'Arbeitsausschuß 1948–1958', minutes of Arb.aus.f.A meeting 3.2.1955.

miners. In general, the union does not seem to have faced any special problem in winning the new miners' allegiance.[79]

Certainly, the union offered many outsiders and newcomers the chance of upward mobility within its own ranks. The union's reports show that a great many of those attending the training courses for functionaries or moving up through the ranks were outsiders of one sort or another. This is not surprising, given the high educational levels of many of the adult trainees coming into the Ruhr in the late 1940s or of the young apprentices in the hostels in the 1950s. Many of the union's most promising youth officials, for instance, were graduates of the apprentice hostels.[80]

On the other hand, the union faced stiff competition from the employers, who were also keen to grab promising young men and persuade them to train for managerial positions. A sample investigation of microfiche records of the Mining School pupils during the 1950s revealed that some 50 per cent of all the pupils came from non-mining backgrounds. Hans Alker, the former deputy president of the IGB, told the present author in an interview that in the late 1940s and early 1950s there was a scramble between the IGB and the employers to get the best people before the other side got to them. Alker himself had nearly fallen prey to entreaties to enter the Mining School. Thus both union and employers were open to bright newcomers with ambitions to rise up through the ranks. By the 1980s, when the research for this study was carried out, senior levels of both industry and union were full of men who had come as outsiders to the Ruhr in the 1940s and 1950s.[81]

79. Jantke, *Bergmann und Zeche*, pp. 141ff., 154; Parisius, 'Arbeiter zwischen Resignation und Integration', pp. 132–140; unpublished EMNID survey conducted in April 1958, in the library of the IGBE, Bochum.

80. IGB, *Jahrbuch 1953*, pp. 291–3.

81. Using microfiche records belonging to the WBK, the author analysed a sample of some 200 randomly selected graduates of the mining school. The sample was restricted to those who began studying in the school between 1945 and 1960. The results showed that only 50 per cent of the school entrants came from the Ruhr, with just over one-third coming from the territory of the GDR or the lost Eastern territories. Similarly, less than one-third were sons of miners, while over 40 per cent came from white-collar, professional, civil-service or other middle-class backgrounds. On the attempts by the two sides to snatch up likely lads, interview with Hans Alker, May 1984. A rough head-count of the number of former new miners now at the top of the IGB was made on the basis of the potted biographies in Martin Martiny and Hans-Jürgen Schneider (eds), *Deutsche Energiepolitik seit 1945*, Cologne, 1981 and further information kindly provided by Norbert Ranft and Hans Alker IGBE.

Turning to the wider political values of the newcomers, we find that it is virtually impossible to say whether the new miners had a specific political profile, different from the rest of the workforce. The only clear statement we can make is, as already noted, that they helped tip the balance against the KPD. On the other hand, it is worth restating an admittedly rather speculative point made in chapter 6 on housing. In housing as in many other areas of social policy, labour representatives were from the start of the Occupation closely involved in the allocation and distribution of scarce resources. The IGB's heavy administrative and managerial input into housing was, in fact, increasingly typical of the way large areas of industrial and urban social policy were carried out in the Ruhr. All levels of Ruhr politics and administration were permeated to an ever-greater degree by a dense, interconnected network of union and Social Democratic Party officials. Michael Zimmermann has written persuasively of the 'Stadtteil Ayatollahs', the countless local figures who might well combine the offices, say, of works councillor, IGB branch chairman, *Knappschaft* official, SPD town councillor and so on. For many newcomers to the Ruhr, particularly those who chose to make the Ruhr their home, it was the patronage or backing of these individuals that enabled them to get a home or obtain other important resources. This power of patronage was undoubtedly a powerful source of strength for the social democrats and contributed greatly to their growing hegemony within the Ruhr.[82]

Yet for all these signs of organisational and ideological integration, the IGB leadership was undoubtedly just as deeply disappointed by the outcome of workforce regeneration as the employers were. Though the high wastage levels gave the IGB ever more convincing arguments in pay negotiations with the employers, the union would much rather have seen a stable workforce and a situation where all recruitment came via the apprentices, so that mining really could present itself as a skilled profession. The IGB fought bitterly against the use of foreign labour, partly because of the dangers to workforce unity but also because it was clear that it would be the death knell of any

82. Michael Zimmermann, '"Geh zu Hermann, der macht dat schon". Bergarbeiterinteressenvertretung im nördlichen Ruhrgebiet', in Niethammer, '*Hinterher merkt man*', pp. 277–310.

attempt positively to transform public perceptions of coal mining. However, the inevitable came. As the first planeloads of Italian workers were flown into the Ruhr, the union's last hopes flew out.

In its educational and ideological work, and in relation to its younger members, the union leadership also faced the disappointment of encountering a more pragmatic generation that did not share many of its enthusiasms. This was less because many of the newcomers came from outside the Ruhr than because of the different experiences and outlook of the younger generation generally. When older unionists talked of the harmonic ideal of social partnership, invoked the pathos of the labour movement or conjured up the image of the miner of bygone times, they could be as sure as their bourgeois counterparts of losing their younger audience.[83] Ultimately, neither the bourgeoisie nor the union got quite the following it wanted, but nor were the worst fears of either confirmed. As a result both union and employers had to come to terms with a generation that did not fit into conventional categories and, worst of all, with a generation that would not stay.

83. Pirker, 'Jugend', pp. 25–7.

Conclusion

Resourcing the Ruhr

In the years between the end of hostilities and the currency reform the greatest possible priority was given to increasing coal production and specifically to rebuilding the colliery work-forces. Despite this enormous commitment, it proved extraordinarily difficult to harness labour effectively. Why? Could the occupying powers have been expected to do better? And would a German government have been more effective?

It was in 1945–6 that the failure to retain labour, or to get it to work effectively, was at its most dramatic. The fact that in January 1946 the pits produced only 41 per cent of their pre-war output was disturbing. That eight months later they were actually bringing less coal to the surface than in January was astonishing. The problem was simple: there was no incentive to work in the mines. In an age of empty shops, the miner's wage was worthless. Special allocations of consumer goods were not forthcoming. The miner's ration fell sharply. To compensate, the British tried to coerce men into the pits, yet in such a half-hearted way that they neither deterred the unhappy conscripts from fleeing nor prevented the productivity of the established men from falling disastrously.

Why were real incentives, or real force, not forthcoming? No government in Germany would have found it easy to provide the miners with extra foodstuffs or to make enough coal available for the production of incentives and pit supplies. Coal and grain, after all, were the elusive masters of European recovery. Shortages of these commodities, the basic energy sources for machine and man respectively, formed the dramatic and frightening backcloth against which any reconstruction strategy had to be developed. Britain faced in addition enormous commitments overseas. It was in the unenviable position of a bankrupt imperial power, presiding over an empire that in both

political and economic terms had been profoundly affected by
the war. Even without the claims of occupied Germany, Britain's resources were overstretched. As well as being mortgaged
to the hilt, it had little coal or grain to spare for its friends, let
alone its former enemies.

These facts necessarily constrained progress in the immediate
post-war period and Britain could do nothing about them.
Perhaps America, with its potentially enormous grain surplus,
could have been expected to provide more food for Europe. A
more efficient grain export programme before spring 1948,
when large-scale imports finally did begin, might have done
much to restore labour's motivation and efficiency.[1] Britain,
however, was powerless.

Because resources were so scarce, coal output could be increased only if some group somewhere made enormous sacrifices. Either the Ruhr labour force would have to be kept
behind barbed wire and worked at gunpoint, or German civilians elsewhere held down to near-starvation rations so that the
miners could enjoy a decent meal; or the French would have to
be forced to wait for the Ruhr coal they so desperately needed.
Understandably, no one volunteered to carry the burden. The
French did not see why they should suffer just to improve the
German miners' standard of living. The Germans had little
desire to harness themselves to the cart of a largely export-
orientated coal drive.

This created a most unenviable dilemma that would have
confronted any occupying power in the Ruhr. Lacking the
ruthlessness of the French or the resources of the Americans,
the British found themselves singularly handicapped. No occupying power seems to have been more nervous. Britain did
not feel morally justified in asking forbearance of the French,
nor diplomatically strong enough to risk antagonising them.
That left the Germans to carry the costs. But the problem here
was that the sacrifices demanded by coal were completely out of
line with Britain's overall approach to reconstruction. Partly for
financial reasons, partly out of general conviction, Britain
favoured a small staff, a non-coercive presence, considerable
delegation of authority and a general policy of not applying

1. John E. Farquharson, *The Western Allies and the Politics of Food: Agrarian
Management in Post-war Germany*, Leamington Spa/New York, pp. 98ff.

measures that would require a police state to enforce them. Military government was thus not prepared to risk the public disorder which might well result if it starved the general population to feed the miners. It therefore decided to manage without incentives. But when it then tried to 'direct' labour to the pits, it lacked the machinery, the legitimacy and the ruthlessness to enforce Nazi-style labour controls.

It would be a brave historian, however, who could confidently assert that the British should have depressed civilian rations further or told the French to expect no more coal. The conclusion on the early period must therefore be that Britain's problems were not due to incompetence, but that because of its specific constellation of interests, ties and anxieties, Britain retarded recovery in a way that other occupying powers and certainly a German government would not have done.

To break out of that constellation, the British were forced to rethink their entire approach to the Occupation of Germany and their relationship with the Allies. Britain opted for closer dependence on the US and, in return, gained material and moral support from the Americans. Thus it won the limited freedom of manoeuvre that was all that was necessary to make a breakthrough in the Ruhr. The importance of that breakthrough should not be understated and the winter of 1946–7 was undoubtedly a turning point with regard to the coal supply. Nevertheless, the coal programme continued to operate with enormous inefficiency.

In part this was unavoidable. With the possible exception of temporary wartime innovations, the fixed-price controlled economy has yet to be invented which is not characterised by withdrawal of labour and goods from normal channels, a lively black market and poor incentives to productivity and efficiency. A controlled economy is synonymous with wastage. And in the period 1945–7 there was no alternative to such a system. At least until the end of 1947, restoring a free market was out of the question. Shortages were so acute, communications so disrupted and the need to impose economic preferences alien to the Germans themselves (above all support for liberated nations) so obvious that central allocation of resources was inevitable.

Having said that, the unresponsiveness of officials and managers and the failure to tap and divert key resources went far beyond the inherent weaknesses of the controlled economy. To an extent this was because there continued to be a contradiction between the military government's (increasingly) indirect rule and the fact that key Anglo-American policies were not supported by the Germans. Above all, the belief that Germany should contribute to the reconstruction of the liberated European countries met with little sympathy within Germany. The British could hardly expect the Germans to give their full backing to a production drive which denied the normal consumer any coal at all and exported considerable amounts to France. Nevertheless, it is difficult to see what the British or Americans could have done about this. Denying their Allies support was as unthinkable as halting the process of devolution within Germany. The occupying powers were therefore not being incompetent, but they were responsible for inefficiency.

Two further forces contrived to weaken the economic administration in Germany. As we know from Werner Plumpe's work, conservative bureaucrats and industrialists co-operated in preventing, at local and regional level, the establishment of an effective administration. Of possibly even more crucial importance was the fact that at central bizonal level the Länder's particularism, backed by the US, hindered the creation of powerful bizonal bureaucracies. Neither the Verwaltung für Ernährung, Landwirtschaft und Forsten nor the Verwaltung für Wirtschaft was in a position to make the Bavarians hand over their grain or their timber.

Ultimately, the Americans' commitment to free enterprise played a key role in preventing the controlled economy from working more effectively. Apart from the weakness of the Frankfurt bureaucracies, there was the fact that, from 1947 onwards, a currency reform was hanging in the air, thus undermining confidence in present values and encouraging a wait-and-see attitude. Had the British been able to influence bipartite policy more effectively the bizonal administration might have enjoyed a little more muscle.

Does the experience of mining suggest that the occupying powers hindered economic reconstruction? For the period 1945–6, undoubtedly so. Thereafter, there is no doubt that a lot of the inefficiency with which the economy operated was due to their presence and influence. In addition, the continued high volume of underpriced coal exports cost the Germans dearly.

On a more general plane, there were many other Allied measures such as partition, denazification and dismantling which, however justified some or most of them were, had a very deleterious impact on economic recovery.

On the other hand, the Allies' sense of responsibility for their subject populations meant that considerable and critically needed food resources were imported. Both in general terms and for the coal drive in particular these were of great value. Even more important was the way the Allied presence eased very painful decisions about the transfer of resources. The concentration on the miners of scanty food supplies and stocks of consumer goods, for example, was an essential but deeply distressing measure. Would a German government have carried it out? Probably it would have had to, but at significant political costs. To impose such a decision on the population would very likely have involved a German government in assuming dictatorial powers and this would certainly have made a later transition to democracy very difficult.

What redounded to Germany's advantage was the fact that the Allied presence was not obtrusive enough to arouse open opposition but was sufficiently evident to provide a scapegoat for the German authorities. True, this resulted in considerable inefficiency but at least it allowed decisions to be made without creating bitter conflicts within German society. Painful measures of the post-war period such as the Points System or that other landmark of resource redistribution, the currency reform, were seen ultimately as Allied policies. German politicians and thus German democracy were able to emerge with their hands clean. Seen in these terms, as the unfortunate by-product of a system which helped steer Germany towards democracy, the inefficiency of the coal drive does not seem so serious.

In many respects, the currency reform of June 1948, and the other economic and institutional changes associated with it, transformed the mines' situation. The dynamic Deutschmark stubbed out the 'cigarette economy' of the immediate post-war years. Now everything was to be had – for a price. Now, too, the old problems of authority and legitimacy disappeared. The *Bergassessoren* were back in the saddle. The Allies speedily withdrew to the lofty pinnacles of the Combined Coal Group and their respective High Commissions. Labour found that the magic words which had once turned tough managers into timorous mice, 'denazification' and 'socialisation', had lost their spell. And for the workforce, there were no longer points to be earned for attendance. There was only hard currency for hard graft.

Plus ça change, plus c'est la même chose. Though more cost-effective, workforce regeneration was ultimately not much more successful in the post-1948 era. Once again the government failed to find the resources necessary for the task – only now the real need was for more cash to help stabilise the workforce. Erhard had not thought through (or was loath to respond to) the consequences of holding down the coal price to avoid inflation. As a result the industry faced recurrent financial problems. In the early years it was house-building that suffered, while in the mid-1950s the mines could not afford to pay competitive wages.

The pre- and post-currency-reform eras were thus united by a failure to regenerate the workforce effectively. Both the British and the *Bergassessoren* experienced immense difficulties in achieving quite limited results. The Allies' target was to be producing 400,000 tons a day by the end of 1948, yet the high levels of wastage and the low levels of efficiency with which the men were working meant that actual output fell far short of this. After 1948, the employers' priority was to create a stable and productive workforce and this they singularly failed to do. Not only was wastage substantial but, largely because of it, productivity remained well below pre-war levels for much of the period.

Common to both eras was the enormous challenge presented by mining's peculiar conditions. In the first place, regenerating the workforce (and reconstructing the industry generally) required resources on a scale that the governments of the day were understandably reluctant to supply. In 1945–6, the potential costs were primarily political: providing the incentives that the mines needed might lead either to unrest in Germany or to outrage in France. In 1948–50, the costs (or, at any rate, the costs as the government perceived them) were primarily economic. Erhard feared that if he increased the coal price inflation would result, while to raise taxation would undermine public confidence in the economy and retard growth elsewhere.

Why did successive administrations find it so hard to deal with coal? The reasons were very similar in both periods. In the first place, both before and after 1948, the foreign consumers of

German coal were unwilling to pay a market price for it. That meant that an unfair burden had to fall on the German economy. Secondly, both the British and the federal government were trying to treat the mining industry in a way out of line with their general reconstruction policy. For the British, coal was the only German resource which they needed so badly that they were not prepared to follow the path of least resistance. In almost all other spheres of production they were willing to accept lower output, if doing so avoided major difficulties. For Erhard and the German administration, no other major industry was seen as presenting the same threat to price stability as coal. Thus, only coal was subject to such stringent price controls. Ultimately the point was that coal had a unique significance to the economy, was therefore treated specially and thus generated problems all of its own.

Eventually, the British and the German governments provided at least some of the resources required. The periods 1946–7 and 1951–2 mark the two turning-points here. What did the delay in responding to mining's needs say about the two administrations? Both had proved a little inflexible, the British out of understandable anxieties about diplomatic isolation and civil unrest, the German government out of a perhaps slightly less justified fear of inflation. Common to both, also, was uncertainty about the degree of help that would be forthcoming from the United States. The British were unsure how much grain and how much diplomatic support they could expect, while Erhard had probably expected that Marshall Aid would fill the gap in mining's funding. It is not surprising to find, therefore, that in both cases it was the US which brought about the change in policy. But this was not just because of the Americans' economic clout. The Americans proved particularly flexible in their response to changing economic conditions. Arriving as the punishers of evil Germany, they rapidly recognised the need for a rapid recovery fuelled by an incentive-led mining industry. Then, enthusiastic defenders of the free market though they were, they nevertheless had no qualms about vigorously advocating a *dirigiste* capital transfer policy to benefit bottleneck sectors of the economy.

Apart from the fact that mining made unique demands on the public purse, the other fundamental feature common to both the pre- and post-currency reform periods was that mining suffered

from two key handicaps that made productive labour integration particularly difficult. In the first place, the work was
very unattractive. The physical conditions were unpleasant and
taxing, the dangers associated with the work considerable and
the prospect of almost certain ill health in old age most uninvit-
ing. These conditions bedevilled attempts to hold on to new
labour throughout the period under review. Secondly, the conditions under which coal was produced made it difficult for
management to create a positive and yet productive relationship
with the workforce. Much of the time the men worked with little
direct supervision. Managerial control was necessary, however,
because safety demanded it and because, even in semi-
mechanised long-wall mining, the tempo of production was
regulated by machines to a far lesser extent than in many other
industries. Another problem was that the vagaries of geological
conditions made it impossible to establish universal norms of
output and efficiency. Piece-rates had continually to be renegotiated, an exercise which was as much a test of power as an
objective assessment of face conditions. So, during the deputy's
rounds and in the monthly contract-wage negotiations, management had somehow to assert itself and achieve a good level of
output.

Management's authority over the production process was
therefore fragile and there was always a danger of losing control. That, indeed, was the problem in 1945–8 when, because of
their political principles and their fear of unrest, the British were
unable to come down firmly on management's side. At the same
time, there was inherent in the nature of coal production the
opposite danger, namely, that in struggling to maintain control
management would ultimately adopt an approach so unyielding
and authoritarian as to drive new recruits from the pit. That was
the scourge of the post-1948 era.

Could management have been expected to do any better at
stabilising the workforce after 1948? Or did the limited resources
available and the poor working conditions associated with
semi-mechanised mining preclude results any better than those
achieved? Most other European countries were experiencing
similar difficulties. Belgium, for instance, had employed foreign
labour since 1951. Did this not suggest that Germany could hope
for little better? It may be, of course, that failure in those
countries was not inevitable either – that the employers in

Belgium or France also lacked the vision to respond to post-war conditions. However, the central point is that the presence of millions of refugees, expellees and other uprooted groups presented the Germans with an opportunity not existing anywhere else in Europe. Uniquely, the Ruhr mines were offered the chance to integrate a vast group of youngsters and adults, many of them unwillingly mobile and seeking a secure profession. The comparative argument is therefore not compelling. It *is* true that once the German government had failed to fund the housing programme in the early years, mining's chances of profiting from this special opportunity were significantly reduced. Yet in explaining the failure to create a stable workforce we cannot confine our examination to the constraints of geology, technology or economics. The employers themselves rightly recognised that money alone was not the key to success, yet the formula that would hold labour in the mines eluded them to the end.

Reshaping the Ruhr

To understand management's choice of style and strategy we have to trawl our net wider – through the murkier, richer seas of culture and ideology. Indeed, it is the influence of ideology, rather than the dictates of economics, which is historically the most interesting feature to emerge from the reports, letters and journal articles associated with rebuilding the Ruhr workforce during the late 1940s and early 1950s. For one thing, there is the sheer quantity of moral and political statements on the subject. Beyond prosaic questions of productive integration, an astonishing amount of ink was devoted to the task of shaping the newcomers' mentality. In industrial journals normally more concerned with the merits of the latest coal-plough, the reader prepared to plough through the coal will find grand proposals for reshaping the workforce. From the pens of regional labour administration officials flowed poetic broadsides about creating a new juvenile elite among the miners. No matter where you look – at employers, union, state or church – the Ruhr resounded with romantic, right-wing rhetoric.

To note this rhetoric and ideology, to take it seriously and to analyse it, is not to make the mistake of assuming that the hard-headed *Bergassessoren* were in the first instance ideologues or combatants in the class war and only secondarily business-men in pursuit of financial rewards. The bottom line for the employers was hard coal and hard currency. Often the speech-ifying and the cultural policy was just a smokescreen, designed to conceal the quiet dictatorship of the balance-sheet, or to impart a moral tone to the fact that thousands of young refugees were being sent down the mines because there was no other employment for them. Ringing phrases of high-minded purpose were the standard patter with which coal companies teased cash out of social services, housing departments and refugee ministries.

Yet it was more than just rhetoric. The industry put its money where its mouth was. There were, of course, limits to how much the collieries would fork out where there was no obvious econ-omic return. The high-minded endorsements of the Pestalozzi village, for example, concealed the fact that, for the employers, the village was a far cheaper investment than the apprentice hostel. Yet, here and elsewhere, the investment in labour and social policy remained considerable. Moreover, the policies which Ruhr mining managers pursued were quite different from those envisaged by the British mining engineers initially in-volved in the Ruhr. The way the Ruhr employers defined their ideal labour force, the wider ideological and political goals they allowed to trickle into that definition and the strategies they developed to achieve their ends all revealed underlying social perceptions, myths and hopes as much as they did any objective economic interests. How else are we to explain, for example, the emphasis placed on the apprenticeship and the colliery house, or the hopes they raised? How else do we understand manage-ment's inability to acknowledge the link between poor labour relations and high wastage?

One of the most noteworthy aspects of the employers' think-ing is the broad scope of their aspirations. To achieve workforce stability, the policy-makers hoped to make fundamental changes in the perceptions, values and behaviour of the miners, in particular of the newcomers among their ranks. Pick up a paper on miners' housing, for instance, and you are likely to find a blueprint for social and psychological engineering on a generous scale. Moreover, the aspirations did not stop at work-force stability. Far-reaching moral and political goals were never far from view. Thus, in Ruhr planner's rhetoric, the four walls, roof and generous garden of the miner's house reappear as an aladdin's lamp out of which could be conjured the spirit of miners past, as an agent of deproletarianisation or as a bulwark against communism. Similarly, the hidden battle, almost *Kulturkampf*, between churches (and behind them, the employers) and unions over control of and access to young miners' hostels, was surely evidence of the political stakes involved. And alongside the hopes for the future were continual references to the dangers of the present, to the threats of collectivism, nihilism and radicalisation which only the right sort of integration could keep at bay.

Many of these aspirations would not have enjoyed such prominence had it not been for the influence of the state. That influence was particularly important when it came to transcending the narrower goal of workforce stability and channelling resources and administrative energy towards broader ideological aims. After all, for the various ministries and departments involved, the goal of increasing coal output was but one of many reasons prompting intervention or assistance. The moral and political goal of offering young refugees suitable employment was at least as significant. Many officials did indeed feel unhappy about sending young refugees down the mines; but that only intensified their desire to give recruitment and training programme a moral aspect. And there were other ambitions, too, many of them deriving from the state's sense of responsibility for the youngsters in the mines or its desire to transform the miners, that archetypal proletarian group, into settled citizens. The public administrations, in turn, forced the employers to take seriously issues which they might otherwise have ignored. Many of the welfare measures adopted, for example the Pestalozzi villages, owed their rapid introduction to state financial help. By setting priorities and offering financial inducements, the state, if you like, made it financially and economically rational for employers to espouse moral and political aims.

Yet one should not see the employers simply as responding to state pressure on such matters. The *Bergassessoren, Beamten* and *Bischöfe* had in common deep anxieties about the threat to the fragile post-war order posed both by the newly uprooted and dispossessed – the expellees, refugees and homeless youth – and by the historically disadvantaged – the working class. At an even deeper level, they also shared a suppressed unease about their role in the Nazi era. These anxieties produced a powerful sense of mission, an urgent need to influence and 'improve' the young miners.

What is striking is the degree to which the reshapers of the Ruhr were looking nostalgically backwards, rather than boldly into the future. Few of the blueprints for change were trying to create a brave new world. On the contrary, most of them involved returning to a vision of past society. The ideal world as described was overwhelmingly pre-industrial. The ideal miner, rooted in the land, mystically absorbed in the battle with underground natural forces, secure in his social position, modest and loyal, belonged to the nineteenth century. The romantic images of the miner's house and garden, of the symmetry between miner and farmer, and of the rustic house's power to root the newcomer in local soil, were all similarly bucolic. Countless statements testify to the appeal of the organic, hierarchic society. The counterpart to these visions was a highly articulated, strongly critical attitude to the modern age. Germany's present condition was held up as proof positive of mass society's spiritual shortcomings. The gap between the reality of the workforce's behaviour and the managers' ideal was similarly attributed to the loss of an intact organic social order. Indeed, not just managers, but civil servants and priests attributed job-changing to the unstable personality and this in turn to the havoc wreaked by mass society on the individual psyche. The task was to reverse the process of *Vermassung*. The efforts to revive a sense of 'Christian values' (which remained undefined) or a love for authentic German culture against the depredations of Hollywood and Glen Miller point to the same fervent desire to restore and communicate something intact, healthy, 'organic' and ordered from Germany's past.

It is worth noting that though some of the anxieties which had given rise to this restorative impulse were new to the post-1945 era, the impulse itself was not. Of course, an exact comparison between the policies before and after 1945 is not possible, since workforce rebuilding as such was not a feature of the 1920s or 1930s. In Weimar, the initial expansion after the war was soon followed, for economic and technical reasons, by a rapid contraction of the workforce. In the Third Reich, once the industry had dragged itself out of the slump it found that new labour was not to be had for love or money. That realisation, indeed, had provided a lot of the impetus for the policies of the post-war era. Yet if we look more generally at the mines' labour and social policy in the Weimar Republic and the Third Reich, we find a great many of the same romantic, pre-industrial images, the same attempt to re-create the 'organic' hierarchy within industrial society. In many ways, the policy-makers' rhetoric and ambitions after 1945 can be seen as the last flowering of a long conservative tradition, spiced with new anxieties born of Nazism's collapse.

Yet in other respects the mines' approach to labour integration after 1945 diverged significantly from that of earlier years. At a purely ideological level, this can be seen in a new ambivalence and uncertainty which vitiated the attempt to convey a specific message to the newcomers. The yearning to recover something from the past, though strong, was not the only motif in the approach to labour integration. Two contradictory images existed alongside each other, unresolved. On the one hand, there was the notion of returning to the organic society and straightforward worker of the past, of shoring up the simple working man against the anomie of modern times. Yet, on the other hand, most elements of the Ruhr bourgeoisie were now resigned to the necessity of the democratic system. Many participants in social and cultural policy, particularly state officials, introduced the goal of creating the democratic citizen, of educating the worker in bourgeois values. Thus the organic collided with the democratic. And when it came actually to communicating with the young newcomers in the Ruhr, there was an additional reason for mumbling the message: the bourgeoisie's own buried unease and self-doubt, that 'unheimlich glimmende Feuer unter der Oberfläche', which threatened to overturn the whole threadbare restoration of ordered society. Indeed, the most appropriate epitaph on the 1950s may well be that despite all the noise and fine speeches, it was the silence on central issues that was deafening.

The lack of clear ideological punch, the fuzziness at the centre, is particularly apparent in the employers' relationship to the labour movement. Here, the ideological uncertainties were reinforced by a far more powerful set of pressures. The need to maintain a closed front *vis-à-vis* the Allies forced both employers and the federal government to co-operate closely with the

Conclusion

unions. The NRW ministries had their own strong reasons for ensuring that the IGB had an influential place in policy discussions. For a start, there were close ties between the Christian democrat elements in government and union. But perhaps more important was that the NRW government resented some of the incursions the DKBL was making into areas which it saw as its own responsibility. To the NRW ministers in Düsseldorf, it was clear that these matters could be resolved successfully in Bonn only if the IGB was behind them. And even in Bonn, delicate negotiations over the Schuman plan inclined the government to try and keep the IGB happy.

Thus, from an early stage, despite all the ideology, the points were set to carry industrial relations down a co-operative track. Even while harking back to the loyal miner of yore, the employers were forced to co-operate with the IGB. Even as they romantically invoked the *ständische Gesellschaft*, the colliery directors were sitting down in countless committees with their union counterparts. Yes, the employers had tried to enlist church aid to keep organised labour away from the apprentices: but this was a covert affair, very cautiously entered into, and soon undermined by the arrival of the labour directors. The mass influx of new workers was never exploited as a means of undermining the union movement. The propaganda in the hostels never contained open attacks on the IGB. It was committee work and consensus rather than confrontation.

Admittedly, the IGB made it easy. No one was keener to eradicate radical influence than the social and Christian democrats in the union headquarters in Bochum. Social partnership and harmonious co-operation were not just management shibboleths but fervently held ideals on the labour side. There was nothing the union leadership liked better than sitting down and finding mutually acceptable managerial solutions. On workforce rebuilding itself there was much to agree on. Both sides were interested in creating a stable workforce. Both were concerned to keep out foreign labour. Both sought special support from the state. Above all, the IGB was at least as attracted as the employers to the notion of reviving the miners' lost status.

In the final analysis, then, the approach to workforce rebuilding, and the ideological ambitions which shaped it, were complex and contradictory. There was no clear vision of the new society or the new workforce, but a confusing amalgam of

324

romantic yearnings for a mythical past, resigned acceptance of the democratic system and pragmatic adaptation to the power realities of the post-war situation. The restorative elements in the employers' ideology were indeed striking, but the co-operative, unaggressive approach to workforce regeneration was evidence that the years after 1945 were marked not just by restoration but also by new beginnings.

The one big qualification to this argument, however, lies in the management of the production process. Here, entrenched managerial attitudes and values ensured that little had changed for fifty years or more. The leverage enjoyed by the Allies, the state or the unions was insufficient to force through a new style. Yet, as countless studies showed, the management of production was a decisive factor in increasing wastage in the mines. The point was that the employers were dealing with a new workforce, whose standards and assumptions differed from those with which they were familiar. The main factor strengthening new labour's hand and raising its expectations was the ever-tighter labour market which offered ample opportunity to leave the industry. But the newcomers also brought with them considerable personal resources. Many had come through testing wartime experiences. They had had enough shouting in the army barracks and would not put up with the deputy's invective. In the early years, a significant minority of new miners came from skilled manual or white-collar backgrounds. They, too, rebelled against the 'rauh aber herzlich' tone so common in the industry.

Could the industry have adapted? It was sometimes argued that the production conditions existing in the 1950s precluded more modern styles of management. In its analysis of wastage, the Institut für Sozialforschung concluded: 'Es spricht vieles dafür, daß die Autoritätsstruktur im Bergbau, das Verhältnis zwischen Vorgesetzten und Untergebenen, insbesondere die im Vergleich zum Industriemeister weitergehenden Machtbefugnisse der Steiger, mit den spezifischen Arbeitsbedingungen unter Tage zusammenhängt.'[2] Yet in reality, this was being overgenerous to the industry. The only sense in which one

2. Institut für Sozialforschung, 'Die subjektiven und objektiven Abkehrgründe bei sieben Zechen des westdeutschen Steinkohlenbergbaues in ihrer Auswirkung auf die Sicherung des Belegschaftstandes unter Tage', unpublished MS, Frankfurt/Main, 1955, p. 228.

could see production conditions as being *the* decisive cause of management style and technique in mining was that, in those industries which in the nineteenth century had shared mining's style of management, technical changes had in the meantime undermined this naked authoritarianism and produced a new approach. The enormous increase of management control and technical co-ordination in the factory environment had produced a different, less authoritarian style and had transformed lower management's role from that of subaltern to that of intermediary and conciliator. To this extent, it was mining's inability to attain factory production's levels of control and co-ordination that was ultimately decisive for the maintenance of '*Grubenmilitarismus*'.[3]

This did *not* mean – and this is where the Institut für Sozialforschung was wrong – that many aspects of management could not be changed, if there was a will to do so. It meant only that technical development had not of itself created the impetus for change. Yet during the 1940s and 1950s there was little interest shown in creating a new type of management. There was grave distrust of modern methods. The experts in the manpower and training committee who took 'Alarm im Bergbau' so seriously were really at odds with the main tenor of opinion in the industry. The debate about training policy revealed all too clearly the gulf between the training experts on the one hand and the *Betriebsführer* on the other.

Change did come to the industry – but much later, in the 1960s and 1970s, as the labour directors' influence grew, the pace of technological change quickened and the industry came to terms with the contraction in coal demand. The present author was able personally to experience a very different type of management when on a visit in the Friedrich Heinrich mine in 1984. As our small party of visitors neared the coalface, the overman was approached by a group of miners who were having a problem with the influx of water. What was striking for someone with a knowledge of labour relations in the 1950s was the nature of the relationship here. There was, on the part of the men, no deference, except for the deference to expertise; and on

---

3. Ludwig von Friedeburg, *Soziologie des Betriebsklimas. Studien zur Deutung empirischer Untersuchungen in industriellen Großbetrieben*, Frankfurt/Main, 1962, pp. 106–26.

the part of the overman, no side or terseness or ordering about, but a consultative and confident approach to the problem. It was a small indication of the way recession, technological change and government intervention had turned the mining industry upside down since the early 1960s. In the era of the new miners, however, mining's authoritarian past was, at the level of day-to-day production, far more evident than its co-determined future.

Bibliography

1. PRIMARY SOURCES

1.1. Archival Sources

Archiv der Sozialen Demokratie, Friedrich-Ebert-Stiftung, Bonn (ASD-FESt)

WW 68	Schriftwechsel Unterbezirk Dortmund
N25	Newspaper clippings archive: Betriebsräte
N171	Newspaper clippings archive: Bergarbeiter

Works archive of the Zeche Gneisenau (AZG)[1]

'I 1 26,	Zuweisung von Arbeitskräften 1945–56'[2] (3 files) [F79, 985]
'I 1 3,	Einstellung und Entlassung von Arbeitern, 1953–63' [F79, 948]
'I 1 13,	Gedinge-Regelung 1.1.45–53' [F79, 968]
'I 4 1,	Betriebsrat Gneisenau 1945–55' [probably F79, 1089]
'I 4 2	Betriebsratssitzungen mit der Verwaltung 1956–59' [F79, 1090]
'"61"	Bezahlung der Neubergleute bzw. Umschüler' [missing, presumed destroyed]

Bundesarchiv, Koblenz (BAK)

Z1	Länderrat
Z2	Zonenbeirat
Z4	Länderrat des VWG
Z13	Direktorialkanzlei des Verwaltungsrats des VWG
Z40	Zentralamt für Arbeit

1. The archive has since been transferred to the WWA. The new WWA classmark is given in brackets.
2. To facilitate identification in archives where there was no clear list of shelf numbers, the exact description on the file cover is given here (in quotation marks).

328

OMGUS BICO (Coal Control Group) 17/8186–17/8190

B102	Bundeswirtschaftsministerium
B119	Bundesanstalt für Arbeitsvermittlung und Arbeitslosenversicherung
B134	Bundesministerium für Wohnungsbau
B149	Bundesarbeitsministerium

Bergbau-Archiv, Bochum (BBA)

5	Zollern/Germania
8	Concordia
10	Friedrich d. Grosse
15	RWKS
30	BAG Neue Hoffnung
32	Hibernia
35	Emscher-Lippe
38	Walsum
42	Diergardt-Mevissen
55	GBAG

Bistumsarchiv, Münster (BM)

A101, 251	Katholisches Lagerwerk
A101, 252	Katholische Heimstattbewegung
A101, 253	Katholische Heimstattbewegung
A201, 47	RAG (Sammlung Tenhumberg)

Private collection of Mr Henry Collins (Collins Papers)

Folder of papers from the Washington conference, August–September 1947 (Washington papers)

Archive of the Deutscher Gewerkschaftsbund (DGBA)

'Verschiedene Protokollen ab 1945'
'IG Bergbau (1949–1966)'
'Ruhrproblem: Pressemeldungen'
'Industrieverband Bergbau 1946–1948. Tätigkeitsbericht'
'IG Bergbau britische Zone. Vorschläge neuer Besoldungsordnung . . .
    Tätigkeitsbericht 1947–1949'
'IG Bergbau Monatsberichte der IG Bergbau 1949'
'Gewerkschaftliches Zonensekretariat Brit Zone 1 1946'
'Gewerkschaftliches Zonensekretariat Brit Zone 2 1946'
'Gewerkschaftliches Zonensekretariat Brit Zone 1947 1'
Protokollsammlung

Bibliography

Private archive of Dr Ernst Schmidt, Essen (Ernst Schmidt papers)

1900   Chronologische Sammlung
19–250   Dokumentation Hermes
Bestand Jarrek
Issues of KPD monthly journal *Unser Weg*, 1951–4

Archive of the Gesamtverband des deutschen Steinkohlenbergbaus, Essen (Ges.Verb.)

a. Papers of Abteilung 1:
'Rundschreiben Werbung 1946–1949'
'Rundschreiben Ausbildung 1946–1950'
'Rundschreiben Ausbildung 1956–1963'
'Arbeitsausschuß 1948–1958'
'Niederschriften Arbeitsausschuß 1956–1967'
'Niederschriften Arbeitseinsatz- und Ausbildungsausschuß 1957–1967'
'"K"' (Kommission für soziale Aufgaben – two files)
'"I/II"' (Arbeitskreis I/II of KfSA)
'"III/IV"' (Arbeitskreis III/IV of KfSA)
'UVR 662–668 (Revierarbeitsgemeinschaft)'
'III.2–III.2.7 Berglehrlinge'
'300–301.1 Ausbildung von Neubergleuten'
'413.6–413.6.3 Ausbildungspersonen. Bezirkliche Zusammenkünfte'
'003 Adelheide'
'Arb. 130.0–130.25 SBZ Flüchtlinge'
'Arb. 130.30–132.15 SBZ Flüchtlinge'
'Arb. 132.2–132.6 SBZ Flüchtlinge'
'Arb. 133.00–134.0 SBZ Flüchtlinge'
'210.0/2–214.1 Jugendwohnheime'
'215.0–215.4 Jugendwohnheime'
'240.0–242.0 Jugendpläne ab 1954'
'250–267 Arbeitsgemeinschaft Heimstatthilfe'
'122.300 Bildungswesen, Hauerausbildung' (two files)
b. Papers of Housing Department
'Wohnungswesen Ausschuß 9 Wohnung und Siedlung'
'4 Bergarbeiterwohnungsbauprogramm 41 Programme – Bezirksausschuß-Sitzungen 1951–1953'
'4 Bergarbeiterwohnungsbauprogramm 41 Programme – Bezirksausschuß-Sitzungen 1954–1961'
c. Papers of former mines' reception camp Heisingen (Ges.Verb., Heisingen papers)
Logbook of the camp
Annual reports of the camp
Loose statistical papers

d. Unpublished statistical materials of the Statistik der Kohlenwirtschaft, e.V. (Ges.Verb., StdKW)
Tables showing wastage, intake and causes of labour loss

Hauptstaatsarchiv, Düsseldorf (HStaD)

NW9, 10, 73, 81, 87, 109 Wiederaufbauministerium
NW17 Kultusministerium
NW41, 42, 45, 62, 63, 67, 200 Arbeits- u. Sozialministerium
NW53, 179 Staatskanzlei

Hauptstaatsarchiv, Düsseldorf, Zweigstelle Kalkum (HStaD Kalkum)

Bergamt Duisburg
Bergamt Dinslaken

Archive of the Industriegewerkschaft Bergbau und Energie, Bochum (IGBEA)

Annual reports of IGB and IGB districts
V1, V2, V3, V6 Vorstandsakten
'Werbung'
'Rundschreiben der Verwaltung' (3 vols, 1950–1953)
BR 3, 5, 7, 9 Betriebsratsabteilung
Div 1, 2 Mat. Heinrich Weeke
T4
W14, W22.1, W22.2, W22.3
'Jugend'
Handakten Rudi Quast
Pressearchiv

Private papers from Jugendheimstättenwerk Pestalozzi-Vereinigung eV, in possession of Herr Klinkert, Gelsenkirchen (Klinkert Papers)

Loose paper – Minutes of 1st meeting of JhstW PV
'Niederschriften der Arbeitstagungen und Vortragsveranstaltungen'
'Sammlung Vorstandssitzungen ab 1956'

Archive of the Landesoberbergamt, Dortmund (OBADA)

I 1002, 1003 Erlasse
I 2023, 2100, 2107 Bergbehörden
I 3050, 3062, 3063, 3850, 3873, 3874 Grubensicherheit, Gesundheitsschutz

Bibliography

I 5200, 5203, 5207, 5208 Bestrafung
I 6000, 6300, 118.10, 6301, 6303, 6305, 6307, 6308 Ausbildung
I 7301 Zulagen
I 8000 Bergwirtschaft
I 8005, 8006, 8007 Arbeitseinsatz
I 8010 Lageberichte
I 9101 DKBL

Parlamentsarchiv, Bonn (PA)

1 Zonenbeirat
2 Wirtschaftsrat

Public Records Office, Kew (PRO)

FO 371 Foreign Office: General Correspondence
FO 942 Economic and Industrial Planning Staff
FO 943 Control Office: Economic
FO 1005 Records Library
FO 1013 North Rhine-Westphalia
FO 1028 Coal Control
FO 1030 HQ SHAEF, Special Echelon and Military Government HQ
FO 1039 Economic Divisions

Archive of the Sozialforschungsstelle, Dortmund (SoFoStA)

'Datteln II. Verleihbares Material'
'Dr Jantke Sozialausschüsse der evgl. Kirche 4.11.51 12'
Dr Jantke Sozialausschüsse der evgl. Kirche 4.11.51 11'
'Dattelner Neubergleute-Befragung'
'Untersuchung Vincke Lager'

Staatsarchiv, Münster (StAM)

Arbeitsamt – Ahlen, Bochum, Bottrop, Dortmund, Gelsenkirchen
Bergamt – Bochum 1 (A12), Bottrop (A18), Castrop Rauxel (A7), Dort-
   mund (A4), Gelsenkirchen (A11), Herne (A8)
Regierung Arnsberg – Wohnbauförderung B401 3.2, B411
Regierung Münster – Wohnbauförderung B220/2, B219/220

Archive of the Westfälische Berggewerkschaftskasse, Bochum (WBKA)

Microfiche records of pupils of the Bergschule
Verwaltungsberichte
Mitteilungen für die Bergberufschulen

332

'Statistische Erfassung der bergmännischen Berufs- und Fachschulen',
vols 1–4

Westfälisches Wirtschaftsarchiv, Dortmund (WWA)

F26 Concordia
F29 Alte Haase
F35 Arenberg
S 22 (OMGUS)
   AG 1945–9;
   BICO ERP SEC 11/90–11/101
   BICO BISEC 11/101–11/109
   BICO PABR 11/121–11/122
   BICO BECG/PABR 11/132–11/135
   BICO JSEC 11/138–11/139
   BICO LIB BR 11/140–11/149
   BICO 17/8192–17/8208
   CO HIST BR 3/404–3/410
   COS 3/176–3/177
   Manpower 7/43–7/51, 17/257–17/258
   ODI 7/25–7/27

Private papers of Michael Zimmermann, Essen (Zimmermann Papers)

Records from the mine General Blumenthal, including Works Council
Minutes 1948–51

1.2. Interviews and Conversations

Interviews/conversations conducted by the author

Hermann Kuhn (former new miner), several conversations, June 1982
Walther Köpping (former new miner and IGBE executive member for
culture and education), August 1982
Dr Heinz Steffen (former personnel director, HBAG), December 1982,
May 1983
Clemens Kreienhorst (former communist head of Hibernia works coun-
cil), August 1983
Siegfried Schroeder (former IGB official responsible for new miners),
February 1984
Professor Helmut Croon (former researcher of the Sozialforschungs-
stelle Dortmund), April 1984
Hans Alker (former new miner and at time of interview deputy presi-
dent of the IGBE), May 1984
Josef Laslop (former new miner and expellee), May 1984

Henry Collins CBE (former head of NGCC, later NCB production director), June 1984

Alfons Nowak (former new miner), July 1985

Hubert Sommerfeld (former new miner and at time of interview still a miner), July 1985

Interview transcripts made available by

a. The LUSIR group, Fernuniversität Hagen (interviews with former new miners Hans-Georg Stasiewsky, Paul Scheffler, Rudolf Sass, Stefan Puhr, Anton Kessner, Konrad Boronski; interview with Josef Hermes);

b. Michael Zimmermann, Alte Synagoge, Essen (interview with Heinrich Kleve)

1.3. Unpublished Manuscripts

Außenstelle Bergbau (ed.), 'Sechs Jahre Aussenstelle Bergbau des Landesarbeitsamtes NRW', unpublished MS, no place, no date [1952]

Bonkowski, Heinfried, 'Im Kohlenpott und anderswo . . . Erinnerungen und Gedanken eines Kumpels', unpublished MS, Lünen-Horstmar, 1981

Institut für angewandte Sozialwissenschaft, 'Untersuchung über die Fluktuation der Arbeitskräfte im Steinkohlenbergbau. Ergebnisbericht', unpublished MS, Bad Godesberg, 1966

Institut für Sozialforschung, 'Die subjektiven und objektiven Abkehrgründe bei sieben Zechen des westdeutschen Steinkohlenbergbaues in ihrer Auswirkung auf die Sicherung des Belegschaftsstandes unter Tage', unpublished MS, Frankfurt/Main 1955

Köpping, Walter, 'Welches Verhältnis hat der gelernte bzw. der ungelernte Bergmann zu seinem Beruf? Eine soziologisch-empirische Untersuchung', unpublished MS, no place, 1952

Petz, Rudolf, 'Fluktuation im Steinkohlenbergbau! Was kann noch dagegen geschehen? Empfehlungen zu den Ergebnissen einer industriesoziologischen Untersuchung des Instituts für Sozialforschung . . . nach Erörterung im Ausschuß für sozialpolitische Fragen im Kohlenbergbau, zusammengestellt von dem Vorsitzer dieses Ausschusses Ministerialdirektor Dr Rudolf Petz im Bundesministerium für Arbeit und Sozialordnung', unpublished MS, Bonn, no date [1958]

Sozialforschungsstelle Dortmund (SoFoSt) (ed.), 'Soziologische Erhebung zum Bergarbeiterwohnungsbauprogramm. Schlußbericht', unpublished MS, Dortmund, 1952

—— (ed.), 'Die Aufnahme der Sowjetzonenflüchtlinge in Westdeutschland. Bericht der Sozialforschungsstelle an der Universität Münster in Dortmund über ihre Erhebung in den Wohnlagern einer Grossstadt des Ruhrgebiets (Mai/Juni 1953)', unpublished MS, Dortmund, 1953

Terhorst, Theodor, 'Zehnjährige Zusammenarbeit am Dienste der Mitbestimmung beim Hamborner Bergbau', unpublished MS, no place, no date [Duisburg 1963]

1.4. Printed Sources

Akten zur Vorgeschichte der BRD (ed. Weisz et al.), vols 4, 5, Munich 1983, 1981

Arbeitsgemeinschaft Heimstatthilfe im Lande NRW (ed.), *Verzeichnis der Jugendheimstätten in NRW*, Düsseldorf, 1956

Berger, Herbert, *Der Pütt hat mich ausgespuckt. Ein Ruhrkumpel erzählt aus seinem Leben*, Oberhausen, 1981

Booms, Hans (ed.), *Die Kabinettsprotokolle der Bundesregierung. 1949ff*, Boppard am Rhein, 1984

Breder, Paul, *Geschichten vor Ort. Erinnerungen eines Bergmanns*, Essen, 1979

Brose, Hanns W., *Die Nachwuchsnot im deutschen Bergbau*, Frankfurt, 1945

——, 'Eine Gemeinschaftswerbung zur Gewinnung von Nachwuchs für den Bergbau', repr. from *Die Werbung*, July 1950

Collins, H. E., 'Progress in Rebuilding the Coal-mining Industry in Western Germany', *Transactions of the Institution of Mining Engineers*, vol. 107, no. 8, 1947–8

——, *Mining Memories and Musings: The Autobiography of a Mining Engineer*, London, 1985

Deutscher Gewerkschaftsbund Abteilung Jugend (ed.), *Protokoll der Arbeitstagung der Gewerkschaftsjugend 25.–30.11.1951*, Düsseldorf, 1952

Deutsche Kohlenbergbauleitung (DKBL) (later Statistik der Kohlenwirtschaft eV) (ed.), *Zahlen der Kohlenwirtschaft*, Essen 1946–

—— (ed.), *Entwicklung des Kohlenbergbaus in den Vereinigten Zonen (Plan A)*, Essen, 1948

—— (ed.), *Ruhr-Almanach. Vom Bergmann und Bergbau*, Cologne, 1950

—— (ed.), *Überblick über den Umfang, die bisherige Abwicklung und die weitere Durchführung des Bergarbeiterwohnungsbaues*, Essen, 1950

—— (ed.), *Für den Bergbau ein Eigenheim*, Essen, 1952

—— (ed.), *Bedarf an Bergarbeiterwohnungen bis Ende 1954*, Essen, 1953

Deutscher Siedlerbund (ed.), *Die Kleinsiedlung und ihre Entwicklung. Ein Überblick über Sein und Werden der Kleinsiedlung und des Deutschen Siedlerbundes*, Hamburg, 1960

Die Funktion des Eigenheims in der Sozialordnung unserer Zeit. Vorträge und Referate des Dritten Deutschen Volksheimstättentages, Hannover 1951, Bielefeld, 1951

Bibliography

Dreißig Jahre Treuhandstelle für Bergmannswohnstätten, Essen, no date [1949]

Europäische Gemeinschaft für Kohle und Stahl, Gemeinsame Versammlung (ed.), *Bericht im Namen des Unterausschusses über die Möglichkeit einer Finanzierungshilfe durch die Hohe Behörde für den Arbeiterwohnungsbau*, Document 19, June 1956

——, Hohe Behörde (ed.), *Entwicklung der Löhne und die Lohnpolitik in den Industrien der Gemeinschaft 1945–1956*, Luxemburg, 1960

Falk, L. and Blümich, W. (eds), *Einkommenssteuergesetz. Kommentar*, Munich, 1982

Forstmann, Walter, 'Die Erziehung zum Eigentumsgedanken', *Die Volksheimstätte. Monatszeitschrift des Deutschen Volksheimstättenwerks*, vol. 7, no. 5, 1955, pp. 1–5

Franz, Fritz, *Ich war ein Bergmannskind. Eine Zeitgeschichte aus dem Kohlenpott*, Duisburg-Neumühl, 1981

Handbuch des Landtags NRW, Düsseldorf, 1951–

Hibernia Konzern (ed.), *Hibernia Sozialbericht 1956[–]*, no place, 1957–

Industriegewerkschaft Bergbau (IGB) (ed.), *Jahrbuch 1948/1949[–]*, Bochum, 1949–

IGB Bezirk I (ed.), *Geschäftsbericht für das Jahr 1948[–]*, Oberhausen, 1949– [and annual reports of Bezirke IV, V, VI]

IGB Hauptverwaltung (ed.), *Protokoll des 1.Verbandsjugendtags Bochum 1950, Sept. 22–24*, Bochum, 1950

IGB, Hauptverwaltung, Abteilung Jugend (ed.), *Geschäftsbericht 1950–1952*, Bochum, 1953

IGBE (ed.), *Bergleute erzählen. (Beiträge zur Geschichte der IGBE)*, Bochum, 1982

IGBE Bezirk Ruhr Nord, Recklinghausen (ed.), *Jahre die wir nicht vergessen 1945–1950 Recklinghäuser Bergbaugewerkschaftler erinnern sich*, Recklinghausen, 1980

Industrieverband Bergbau (ed.), *Jahrbuch 1947*, Bochum, no date [1948]

Kommission für soziale Aufgaben (ed.), *Mitteilungen der Kommission für soziale Aufgaben*, Essen, 1948–

Köpping, Walter (ed.), *100 Jahre Bergarbeiterdichtung*, Oberhausen, 1982

—— (ed.), *Lebensberichte deutscher Bergarbeiter*, Oberhausen, 1984

Landesamt für Datenverarbeitung und Statistik NRW (ed.), *Beiträge zur Statistik des Landes NRW*, Düsseldorf 1949–

Martiny, Martin, and Schneider, Hans-Jürgen (eds), *Deutsche Energiepolitik seit 1945*, Cologne, 1981

Minister für Wirtschaft und Verkehr des Landes NRW, *Jahresbericht der Bergbehörden des Landes NRW für das Jahre 1952[–]*, Düsseldorf, 1953–

Ministerial-Blatt Nordrhein-Westfalens 1948[–], Düsseldorf, 1948–

Oberbergamt Dortmund (ed.), *Bericht über das Bergwesen im Obergbergamtsbezirk Dortmund für das Jahr 1952[–]*, Dortmund, 1953–

Public Opinion Research Organisation, Political Division (ed.), *The*

Bibliography

Ruhr Miner and his Family 1947: A Social Survey, Bielefeld, 1948
—— (ed.), *A Social Survey: The Mining Trainee 1947*, Bielefeld, 1948
Statistisches Bundesamt (ed.), *Statistisches Jahrbuch für die BRD 1953*[–], Wiesbaden, 1954–
Taschenbuch für Verwaltungsbeamte 1950–1951[–] *Behördennachweis und Personenverzeichnis*, Berlin, Detmold, Cologne, Munich, 1952–
Unternehmensverband Ruhrbergbau (ed.), *Jahresbericht 1953–1954*[–], Essen, 1954–
Verweyen, Heribert, *Erfassung und Abgrenzung der für die bergmännische Ausbildung der Jugendlichen bei der Hamborner AG entstehenden Kosten*, Essen, 1955
Wawersik, Rudolf, *Ausbeute eines Bergmannslebens. Erinnerungen an den oberschlesischen, saarländischen und westfälischen Bergbau*, Essen, 1981
Westfälische Berggewerkschaftskasse zu Bochum (ed.), *Verwaltungsbericht für die Zeit 1.1.47 bis 31.12.48*[–], Bochum 1948–

1.5. Systematically Evaluated Periodicals

Arbeitsblatt für die britische Zone
Arbeit und Sozialpolitik
BAG Ewald-König Ludwig (later given the name *Ewald Kohle*), works newspaper of the Bergbau AG Ewald-König Ludwig
Die Bergbau-Industrie
Bergbau-Rundschau
Bergbau und Wirtschaft
Bergfreiheit
Bundesarbeitsblatt
Der Förderturm (works newspaper of the GBAG's Gruppe Hamborn, later Hamborner Bergbau AG)
Glückauf
Die Grubenlampe (works newspaper of the mines Hannover and Hannibal)
Mitteilungen der WBK

2. SECONDARY SOURCES

Abe, Edwin C. and Echterhoff, Alfons, *Das Vest – ein dynamischer Wirtschaftsraum. Die sozialwirtschaftliche Entwicklung und Struktur des Vestes Recklinghausen und seine wohnungs- und siedlungswirtschaftliche Problematik*, Recklinghausen, 1955
Abelshauser, Werner, *Wirtschaft in Westdeutschland 1945–1948. Rekonstruktion und Wachstumsbedingungen in der amerikanischen und britischen Zone*, Stuttgart, 1975
——, 'Probleme des Wiederaufbaus der westdeutschen Wirtschaft 1945–1953', in Heinrich August Winkler (ed.), *Politische Weichenstel-*

337

lungen im Nachkriegsdeutschland 1945–1953, Göttingen, 1979, pp. 208–53

——, 'Ansätze "korporativer Marktwirtschaft" in der Korea-Krise der frühen fünfziger Jahre. Ein Briefwechsel zwischen dem Hohen Kommissar John McCloy und Bundeskanzler Konrad Adenauer', *VfZ*, vol. 30, no. 4, 1982, pp. 715–56

——, Wirtschaftsgeschichte der Bundesrepublik Deutschland 1945–1980, Frankfurt, 1983

——, *Der Ruhrkohlenbergbau seit 1945. Wiederaufbau, Krise, Anpassung*, Munich, 1984

——, 'Kohle und Marktwirtschaft. Ludwig Erhards Konflikt mit dem Unternehmensverband Ruhrbergbau am Vorabend der Kohlenkrise', *VfZ*, vol. 33, no. 3, 1985, pp. 489–546

——, 'Schopenhauer's Gesetz und die Währungsreform', *VfZ*, vol. 33, no. 1, 1985, pp. 214–18.

Ackermann, Volker, 'Integration: Begriff, Leitbilder, Probleme', in Bade, *Neue Heimat*, pp. 14–36

Adamsen, Heiner R., *Investitionshilfe für die Ruhr. Wiederaufbau, Verbände und soziale Marktwirtschaft 1948–1952*, Wuppertal, 1981

Autorenkollektiv (Ernst-Ulrich Huster, Gerhard Kraiker et al.), *Determinanten der westdeutschen Restauration 1945–1949*, Frankfurt/Main, 1972

Bade, Klaus J. (ed.), *Neue Heimat im Westen. Vertriebene, Flüchtlinge, Aussiedler*, Münster, 1990

Bahl, Volker, *Staatliche Politik am Beispiel der Kohle*, Frankfurt, 1977

Bahne, Siegfried, 'Die KPD im Ruhrgebiet in der Weimarer Republik', in Reulecke, *Arbeiterbewegung*, pp. 315–54

Balfour, Michael, *Four Power Control in Germany and Austria 1945–1946*, New York, 1956

Bandemer, Jens Diether von and Ilgen, August Peter, *Probleme des Steinkohlenbergbaus. Die Arbeiter- und Förderverlagerung in den Revieren der Borinage und Ruhr*, Tübingen, 1963

Baroth, Hans Dieter, *Aber es waren schöne Zeiten*, Cologne, 1978

——, *Streuselkuchen in Ickern*, Cologne, 1980

Bauer, Franz J., 'Aufnahme und Eingliederung der Flüchtlinge und Vertriebenen. Das Beispiel Bayern 1945–1950, in Benz, *Die Vertreibung der Deutschen aus dem Osten*, pp. 158–72

——, *Deutsche Familien nach dem Kriege*, Darmstadt, 1954

Baumert, Gerhard, *Jugend der Nachkriegszeit. Lebensverhältnisse und Reaktionsweisen*, Darmstadt, 1952

Becker, Josef, Stammen, Theo and Waldmann, Peter (eds), *Vorgeschichte der BRD. Zwischen Kapitulation und Grundgesetz*, Munich, 1979

Bednarz, Homar, 'Die Fluktuation im Ruhrbergbau und die Versuche zu ihrer Bekämpfung', Diplom-Arbeit, Cologne University, 1957/8

Benz, Wolfgang, 'Wirtschaftspolitik zwischen Demontage und Währungsreform', in Institut für Zeitgeschichte (ed.), *Westdeutschlands Weg zur*

Bundesrepublik 1945–1949, Munich, 1976, pp. 69–89

—— (ed.), *Die Vertreibung der Deutschen aus dem Osten. Ursachen, Ereignisse, Folgen*, Frankfurt/Main, 1985

Berg, Werner, *Wirtschaft und Gesellschaft in Deutschland und Großbritannien im Übergang zum 'organisierten Kapitalismus'. Unternehmer, Angestellte, Arbeiter und Staat im Steinkohlenbergbau des Ruhrgebietes und von Südwales 1850–1914*, Berlin, 1984

Berghahn, Volker R., *The Americanisation of West German Industry 1945–1973*, Leamington Spa/New York, 1986

Bethlehem, Siegfried, *Heimatvertreibung, DDR-Flucht, Gastarbeiterzuwanderung: Wanderungsströme und Wanderungspolitik in der BRD*, Stuttgart, 1982

Blei, Anton, 'Die Kriminalität der Jungbergleute der Ruhrmetropole Essen nach dem Zusammenbruch (1945–1951)', Staatsexamensarbeit, Bonn University, 1953

Böll, Heinrich and Chargesheimer, K., *Im Ruhrgebiet*, Cologne/Berlin, 1958

Bollermann, Hans, 'Die Kriminalität der Ruhrbergleute 1945–1955', dissertation, Bonn University, 1961

Borsdorf, Ulrich, 'Der Weg zur Einheitsgewerkschaft', in Reulecke, *Arbeiterbewegung*, pp. 385–414

——, 'Speck oder Sozialisierung. Produktionssteigerungskampagnen im Ruhrbergbau 1945–1947', in Mommsen and Borsdorf, *Glückauf Kameraden!*, pp. 345–66

——, and Hemmer, Hans O. (eds), *Gewerkschaftliche Politik. Reform aus Solidarität. Zum 60. Geburtstag von H. O. Vetter*, Cologne, 1977

Brecht, Julius, 'Die gemeinnützigen Wohnungsunternehmen in einer marktwirtschaftlichen Wohnversorgung', in *Deutsche Siedlungs- und Wohnpolitik*, pp. 151–75

Brehpohl, Wilhelm, *Industrievolk im Wandel von der agraren zur industriellen Daseinsform dargestellt am Ruhrgebiet*, Tübingen, 1957

Brozio, Norbert, *Gewerkschaftlicher Wiederaufbau im nördlichen Ruhrgebiet 1945–1947*, Münster, 1980

Brüggemeier, Franz-Josef, *Leben vor Ort. Ruhrbergleute und Ruhrbergbau 1889–1919*, Munich, 1983

Brunn, G. (ed.), *Nordrhein-Westfalen und seine Anfänge nach 1945/1946*, Essen, 1986

Buchheim, Christoph, 'Die Währungsreform 1948 in Westdeutschland', *VfZ*, vol. 36, no. 2, 1988, pp. 189–231

——, *Die Wiedereingliederung Westdeutschlands in die Weltwirtschaft 1945–1958*, Munich, 1990

Buchholz, Ernst W., 'Der Bergarbeiterwohnungsbau als planerische und sozialpolitische Aufgabe', *Soziale Welt*, vol. 4, no. 1, 1952, pp. 38–50

Budde, Karl Heinrich, 'Die Gründe und die Auswirkungen des

übermässig starken Belegschaftswechsels auf den Schachtanlagen des Ruhrgebiets in der Nachkriegszeit', Staatsexamensarbeit, Herne, April 1952

Carlin, Wendy, 'Economic Reconstruction in Western Germany, 1945–55: The Displacement of "Vegetative Control"', in Turner, *Reconstruction in Post-war Germany*, pp. 37–66

Clarke, Michael, 'Die Gewerkschaftspolitik der KPD 1945–1951, dargestellt am Beispiel des IVB/IGB im Ruhrgebiet', Staatsexamensarbeit, Bochum University, 1982

Corsten, Hermann, *Bibliographie des Ruhrgebiets*, vols 2 and 3, Düsseldorf, 1955–1962

Crew, David, F., *Town in the Ruhr: A Social History of Bochum 1860–1914*, New York, 1979

Croon, Helmuth and Utermann K., *Zeche und Gemeinde. Untersuchungen über den Strukturwandel einer Zechengemeinde im nördlichen Ruhrgebiet*, Tübingen, 1958

Daberkow, Manfred, 'Die Seßhaftmachung der vom westdeutschen Steinkohlenbergbau aus bergfremden Gebieten angeworbenen Berglehrlinge', Examensarbeit, Sozialschule Gelsenkirchen, 1955

Deighton, Anne, *The Impossible Peace: Britain, the Division of Germany and the Origins of the Cold War*, Oxford, 1990

Dennis, N., Henriques, F. and Slaughter, C., *Coal is Our Life: An Analysis of a Yorkshire Mining Community*, London, 1956

Deutsche Siedlungs- und Wohnungspolitik. Gegenwartsproblematik und Zukunftsaspekte. Festschrift zum 25 jährigen Bestehen des Institutes für Siedlungs- und Wohnungswesen an der Westfälischen Wilhelmsuniversität, Cologne, 1956

Ebsworth, Raymond, *Restoring Democracy in Germany: The British Contribution*, New York, 1960

Farquharson, John E., *The Western Allies and the Politics of Food: Agrarian Management in Post-war Germany*, Leamington Spa/New York, 1985

Faulenbach, Bernd, 'Die Herren an der Ruhr. Zum Typos des Unternehmers in der Schwerindustrie', in Niethammer et al., *'Die Menschen machen ihre Geschichte nicht aus freien Stücken'*, pp. 76–85

Föllmer-Edling, Astrid, 'Die Politik des Industrieverbands Bergbau im Ruhrgebiet 1945–1948. Die Anstrengungen um die Erhöhung der Kohlenförderung im Ruhrbergbau', Staatsexamensarbeit, Ruhruniversität Bochum, 1977

Foschepoth, Josef, 'Zur deutschen Reaktion auf Niederlage und Besatzung', in Ludolf Herbst (ed.), *Westdeutschland 1945–1955*, Munich, 1986, pp. 151–66.

Friedeburg, Ludwig von, 'Zur Fluktuation im Steinkohlenbergbau. Ergebnisse einer industriesoziologischen Untersuchung des Instituts für Sozialforschung über die Gründe der Fluktuationsdifferenzen bei sechs Zechen im Ruhrgebiet', *Bundesarbeitsblatt*, 1957, pp. 705–21

Fronz, Manfred and Peter Gerd, (eds), *Sozialwissenschaftliche Forschung im Steinkohlenbergbau*, vol. 2: *Der Steiger. Auszüge aus empirischen Untersuchungen 1950–1982*, Bochum, 1983

Gebhardt, Gerhard, *Ruhrbergbau, Geschichte, Aufbau und Verflechtung seiner Gesellschaften und Organisationen*, Essen,1957

Geiger, Till, 'British Policy on the Allocations, the Distribution and the Prices of Ruhr Coal Exports 1945–1947', MSc dissertation, London School of Economics, 1987

Gillingham, John, 'Die Ruhrbergleute und Hitlers Krieg', in Mommsen und Borsdorf, *Glückauf Kameraden!*, pp. 325–43

——, *Industry and Politics in the Third Reich: Ruhr Coal, Hitler and Europe*, London, 1985

Gimbel, John, *Amerikanische Besatzungspolitik in Deutschland 1945–1949*, Frankfurt, 1971

Graml, Hermann, 'Die Alliierten in Deutschland', in Institut für Zeitgeschichte (ed.), *Westdeutschlands Weg zur Bundesrepublik 1945–1949*, Munich, 1976, pp. 25–52

Grebing, Helga, *The History of the German Labour Movement*, London, 1969

Grube, Frank and Richter, Gerhard, *Die Schwarzmarktzeit. Deutschland zwischen 1945 und 1948*, Hamburg, 1979

Grün, Max von der, *Irrlicht und Feuer*, Rheinbek, 1967

Grundmann, Ingrid, 'Erfahrungen Essener Neubergleute. Untersuchungen zur Problematik Vertriebener im Ruhrgebiet nach dem Zweiten Weltkrieg', Staatsexamensarbeit, Essen University, 1981

Hartmann, Heinz, *Authority and Organisation in German Management*, Princeton, NJ, 1959

Haumann, Heiko (ed.), *Arbeiteralltag in Stadt und Land – Neue Wege der Geschichtsschreibung*, Argument Sonderband 94, Berlin, 1982

Heinrichsbauer, A., *Industrielle Siedlung im Ruhrgebiet in Vergangenheit, Gegenwart und Zukunft*, Essen, 1936

——, *Der Ruhrbergbau in Vergangenheit, Gegenwart und Zukunft*, Essen, 1948

Heinze, Joachim, 'Die Änderung der Bevölkerungsstruktur der Stadt Duisburg seit der Flüchtlingswanderung von 1945', *Duisburger Forschungen*, vol. 4, 1967, pp. 108–43

Herbert, Ulrich, *Fremdarbeiter. Politik und Praxis des 'Ausländer-Einsatzes' in der Kriegswirtschaft des Dritten Reiches*, Berlin/Bonn, 1985

Herchenroeder, Karl H., *Neue Männer an der Ruhr*, Düsseldorf, 1958

Heuer, Jürgen, 'Pestalozzidorf – Sozialleistung des Bergbaus. Aufbau und Probleme', in Seraphim, *Siedlungen und Wohnungen von heute*, pp. 54–72

Hickey, Stephen, *Workers in Imperial Germany: The Miners of the Ruhr*, Oxford, 1985

Hochlarmarker Lesebuch. Kohle war nicht alles: 100 Jahre Ruhrgebietsgeschichte, Oberhausen, 1981

Hockerts, Hans Günther, *Sozialpolitische Entscheidungen im Nachkriegsdeutschland. Alliierte und deutsche Sozialversicherungspolitik 1945 bis 1957*, Stuttgart, 1980

Hoff, Hans Viktor von, *Die Entwicklung der wirtschaftlichen und Bevölkerungsstruktur in Herne 1950–1970*, Frankfurt/Main, 1974

Holup, Gerhard, 'Die Deckung des Arbeitskräftebedarfs im Steinkohlenbergbau des Ruhrgebiets', Diplom-Arbeit, Cologne University, 1953

Horstmann, Theo, 'Die Angst vor dem finanziellen Kollaps. Banken- und Kreditpolitik in der britischen Zone zwischen 1945 und 1948', in Petzina and Euchner, *Wirtschaftspolitik im britischen Besatzungsgebiet*, pp. 215–34

Husmann, Heinrich, 'Lebensformen und ihr Wandel beim Arbeiter in Hamborn', *Rheinisch-Westfälische Zeitschrift für Volkskunde*, vol. 4, nos 1/2, pp. 1–39

Hüttenberger, Peter, *Nordrheinwestfalen und die Entstehung seiner Demokratie*, Sieburg, 1973

Institut für Sozialforschung (ed.), *Betriebsklima, eine industriesoziologische Untersuchung in Mannesmann Bereich*, Frankfurt, 1955

Ipsen, Günther (ed.), *Daseinsformen der Großstadt. Typische Formen sozialer Existenz in Stadtmitte, Vorstadt und Gürtel der industriellen Großstadt*, Tübingen, 1959

Jantke, Carl, *Bergmann und Zeche. Die sozialen Arbeitsverhältnisse einer Schachtanlage des nördlichen Ruhrgebiets in der Sicht der Bergleute*, Tübingen, 1953

Jüres, E. A. and Kesting, H., *Die Reaktion von Hüttenarbeitern auf technische Neuerungen*, Dortmund, 1957

Kerr, Clark, 'Collective Bargaining in Post-war Germany', *Industrial and Labour Relations Review*, vol. 5, no. 3, 1952, pp. 323–42

Klages, Helmut, *Der Nachbarschaftsgedanke und die nachbarliche Wirklichkeit in der Grossstadt*, Cologne-Opladen, 1958

Kleinert, Uwe, *Flüchtlinge und Wirtschaft in Nordrhein-Westfalen 1945–1961. Arbeitsmarkt–Gewerbe–Staat*, Düsseldorf, 1988

——, 'Die Flüchtlinge als Arbeitskräfte – zur Eingliederung der Flüchtlinge in Nordrhein-Westfalen nach 1945', in Bade, *Neue Heimat*, pp. 37–60.

Klemm, Bernd and Trittel, Günter, 'Vor dem "Wirtschaftswunder": Durchbruch zum Wachstum oder Lähmungskrise? Eine Auseinandersetzung mit Werner Abelshausers Interpretation der Wirtschaftsentwicklung 1945–1948', *VfZ*, vol. 35, no. 4, 1987, pp. 571–624

Kleßmann, Christoph and Friedemann, Peter, *Streiks und Hungermärsche im Ruhrgebiet 1946–1948*, Frankfurt, 1977

——, *Polnische Bergarbeiter im Ruhrgebiet 1870–1945. Soziale Integration und nationale Subkultur einer Minderheit in der deutschen Industriegesellschaft*, Göttingen, 1978

——, 'Betriebsräte und Gewerkschaftspolitik in Deutschland 1945–52', in Winkler, *Politische Weichenstellungen im Nachkriegsdeutschland 1945–1953*, pp. 44–73

——, 'Betriebsgruppen und Einheitsgewerkschaft. Zur betrieblichen Arbeit der politischen Parteien in der Frühphase der westdeutschen Arbeiterbewegung 1945–1952'. *VfZ*, vol. 31, no. 2, 1983, pp. 272–307

Kocka, Jürgen, '1945: Neubeginn oder Restauration?', in Carola Stern and Heinrich August Winkler (eds), *Wendepunkte deutscher Geschichte 1848–1945*, Frankfurt, 1979, pp. 141–68

Konze, Heinz, *Entwicklung des Steinkohlenbergbaues im Ruhrgebiet 1957–1974*, Essen, 1975

Kramer, Klaus-Dietrich, *Die Erziehung zum Bergmannsberuf. Wie wirkt sich die Erziehung im Pestalozzidorf im Vergleich zur Erziehung im Berglehrlingsheimund im Elternhaus auf die Arbeit der Bergberufsschule und die Erziehung zum Bergmannsberuf aus?*, Bochum, 1955

Kühr, Herbert, 'Die katholische Arbeiterbewegung im Ruhrgebiet nach 1945', in Rohe and Kühr, *Politik und Gesellschaft im Ruhrgebiet*, pp. 74–92

Kundel, Heinz, *Der technische Fortschritt im Steinkohlenbergbau, dargestellt an der Entwicklung der maschinellen Kohlengewinnung*, Essen, 1966

Lang, Josef F., 'Die geschichtliche und räumliche Entwicklung des Bergarbeiterwohnungsbaus im Ruhrgebiet', dissertation, Cologne University, 1952

Lange-Kothe, Irmgard, 'Eine Bergmannssiedlung und ihre Bewohner', *Der Anschnitt*, vol. 10, no. 1, pp. 12–15

Lemberg, Eugen and Edding, Friedrich (eds), *Die Vertriebenen in Westdeutschland. Ihre Eingliederung und ihr Einfluß auf Gesellschaft, Wirtschaft, Politik und Geistesleben*, vols. 1–3, Kiel, 1959

Lübcke, Otto, *Die Subventionierung des Wohnungsbaues insbes. seit 1945*, Münster, 1951

Mai, Günther, '"Warum steht der deutsche Arbeiter zu Hitler?" Zur Rolle der Deutschen Arbeitsfront im Herrschaftssystem des Dritten Reiches', *Geschichte und Gesellschaft*, vol. 12, no. 2, 1986, pp. 212–34

Maier, Charles S., 'The Two Post-war Eras and the Conditions for Stability in 20th century Western Europe', *American Historical Review*, vol. 86, no. 2, 1981, pp. 327–52

Mannschatz, Gerhard and Seider, J., *Zum Kampf der KPD im Ruhrgebiet für die Einigung der Arbeiterklasse und die Entmachtung der Monopolherren 1945–1947*, Berlin (GDR), 1962

Marchwitza, Hans, *Die Kumiaks*, 2nd edn Berlin/Weimar, 1975

Marciniak, Friedhelm, *Wahlverhalten in Nordrheinwestfalen 1948–1970. Eine statistisch-ökologische Analyse*, Cologne, 1978

Marshall, Barbara, 'German Attitudes to British Military Government 1945–1947', *Journal of Contemporary History*, vol. 15, no. 4, 1980, pp. 655–84

Martiny, Martin, 'Arbeiterbewegung an Rhein und Ruhr vom Scheitern der Räte- und Sozialisierungsbewegung bis zum Ende der letzten

parlamentarischen Regierung der Weimarer Republik (1920–1930)',
in Reulecke, *Arbeiterbewegung*, pp. 241–74

Mausolff, Anneliese, *Gewerkschaft und Betriebsrat im Urteil der Arbeitnehmer*, Darmstadt, 1952

Merritt, Anna J. and Merritt, Richard L., *Public Opinion in Occupied Germany: The OMGUS Surveys 1945–1949*, London, 1970

Mielke, Siegfried, 'Der Wiederaufbau der Gewerkschaften: Legenden und Wirklichkeit', in Winkler, *Politische Weichenstellungen im Nachkriegsdeutschland 1945–1953*, pp. 74–88

Milert, Werner, 'Die verschenkte Kontrolle. Bestimmungsgründe der britischen Kohlenpolitik im Ruhrbergbau 1945–1947', in Petzina and Euchner, *Wirtschaftspolitik im britischen Besatzungsgebiet 1945–1949*, pp. 105–20

Milward, Alan, *The Reconstruction of Western Europe 1945–1951*, London, 1984

Mommsen, Hans, 'Die Bergarbeiterbewegung an der Ruhr 1918–1933', in Reulecke, *Arbeiterbewegung*, pp. 275–314

——, 'Staatliche Sozialpolitik und gewerkschaftliche Strategie in der Weimarer Republik', in Borsdorf and Hemmer, *Gewerkschaftliche Politik*, pp. 61–80

—— (ed.), *Arbeiterbewegung und industrieller Wandel: Studien zu gewerkschaftlichen Organisationsproblemen im Reich und an der Ruhr*, Wuppertal, 1980

—— and Borsdorf, Ulrich (eds), *Glückauf Kameraden! Die Bergarbeiter und ihre Organisationen in Deutschland*, Cologne, 1979

Müller-List, Gabriele, 'Die Entstehung der Montanmitbestimmung', in Walter Först (ed.), *Zwischen Ruhrkontrolle und Mitbestimmung*, Cologne, 1982, pp. 121–44

Mund, Ottokar, *25 Jahre katholisches Lagerwerk e. V. Versuch einer zeitgeschichtlichen Übersicht*, Recklinghausen, 1973

Munton, M., 'Training Young Miners in the Ruhr', *Colliery Engineer*, vol. 33, 1956, pp. 294–8

Neuloh, Otto, *Der neue Betriebsstil*, Tübingen, 1960

Neumann, Walter, *Die Gewerkschaften im Ruhrgebiet. Voraussetzungen, Entwicklung und Wirksamkeit*, Cologne, 1951

Niethammer, Lutz 'Strukturreform und Wachstumspakt. Westeuropäische Bedingungen der einheitsgewerkschaftlichen Bewegung nach dem Zusammenbruch des Faschismus', in Vetter, *Vom Sozialistengesetz zur Mitbestimmung*, pp. 303–358

——, 'Rekonstruktion und Desintegration. Zum Verständnis der deutschen Arbeiterbewegung zwischen Krieg und kaltem Krieg', in Winkler, *Politische Weichenstellungen im Nachkriegsdeutschland 1945–1953*, pp. 26–43

——, *Umständliche Erläuterung der seelischen Störung eines Communalbaumeisters in Preußensgrößtem Industriedorf oder: die Unfähigkeit zur Stadtentwicklung*, Frankfurt, 1979

—— (ed.), *Wohnen im Wandel. Beiträge zur Geschichte des Alltags in der Bürgerlichen Gesellschaft*, Wuppertal, 1979

—— (ed.), *'Die Jahre weiß man nicht, wo man die heute hinsetzen soll'. Faschismuserfahrungen im Ruhrgebiet*, Berlin/Bonn, 1983

—— (ed.), *'Hinterher merkt man, daß es richtig war, daß es schiefgegangen ist'. Nachkriegserfahrungen im Ruhrgebiet*, Berlin/Bonn, 1983

——, and Peter Brandt (eds), *Arbeiterinitiative 1945. Antifaschistische Ausschüsse und Reorganisation der Arbeiterbewegung in Deutschland*, Wuppertal, 1976

—— et al. (eds), *'Die Menschen machen ihre Geschichte nicht aus freien Stücken, aber sie machen sie selbst'*, Berlin/Bonn, 1985

Oppen, Dietrich von, *Familien in ihrer Umwelt. Äußere Bedingungen von Familien im Prozeß der industriellen Verstädterung einer Zechengemeinde*, Cologne/Opladen, 1958

——, 'Soziale Mobilität und Stabilität in einer Stadt des Ruhrgebiets', *Zeitschrift für die gesamte Staatswissenschaft*, vol. 112, 1956, pp. 685–719

Oswald, H., 'Ergebnisse der deutschen Gemeindesoziologie nach 1950', *Archiv für Kommunalwissenschaften*, vol. 5, 1966, pp. 93–111

Petz, Rudolf, 'Die subjektiven und objektiven Abkehrgrunde im Kohlenbergbau. Bemerkungen zu der industriesoziologischen Untersuchung', *Bundesarbeitsblatt*, 1957, pp. 721–34

Petzina, Dietmar, 'Wirtschaftliche Entwicklung und sozialer Wandel in der Stadtregion Dortmund im 20.Jahrhundert', in G. Luntowski and N. Reimann (eds), *Dortmund. 1100 Jahre Stadtgeschichte*, Dortmund, 1982, pp. 297–312

—— and Euchner, Walter (eds), *Wirtschaftspolitik im britischen Besatzungsgebiet 1945–1949*, Düsseldorf, 1984

Peukert, Detlev, 'Zur Regionalgeschichtsschreibung der Arbeiterbewegung', *Das Argument*, vol. 20, no. 110, 1978, pp. 546–65

——, *Die KPD im Widerstand. Verfolgung und Untergrundarbeit an Rhein und Ruhr 1933 bis 1945*, Wuppertal, 1980

——, 'Kolonie und Zeche. Arbeiterradikalismus, Widerständigkeit und Anpassung der Bergarbeiter zwischen Faschismus und Wirtschaftswunder', *Sozialwissenschaftliche Informationen für Unterricht und Studium*, vol. 9, 1980, pp. 24–30

——, 'Arbeiteralltag – Mode oder Methode?', in Haumann, *Arbeiteralltag in Stadt und Land*, pp. 8–39

—— and Reulecke, Jürgen (eds), *Die Reihen fast geschlossen. Beiträge zur Geschichte des Alltags unterm Nationalsozialismus*, Wuppertal, 1981

Pfeil, Elisabeth, *Die Wohnwünsche der Bergarbeiter. Soziologische Erhebung, Deutung und Kritik der Wohnvorstellungen eines Berufes*, Tübingen, 1954

—— and Buchholz, Ernst Wolfgang, *Eingliederungschancen und Eingliederungserfolge: Regionalstatistische Analysen der Erwerbslosigkeit. Berufsstellung und Behausung der Vertriebenen*, Bad Godesberg, 1958

Pfläging, Kurt, *Die Wiege des Ruhrkohlenbergbaus. Die Geschichte der Zechen im südlichen Ruhrgebiet*, Essen, 1978

Pietsch, Hartmut, *Militärregierung, Bürokratie und Sozialismus. Zur Entwicklung des politischen Systems in den Städten des Ruhrgebiets 1945–1948*, Duisburg, 1978

Pingel, Falk, '''Die Russen am Rhein?'' Zur Wende der britischen Besatzungspolitik im Frühjahr 1946', *VfZ*, vol. 30, no. 1, 1982, pp. 98–116

——, 'Der aufhaltsame Aufschwung. Die Wirtschaftsplanung für die britische Zone im Rahmen der außenpolitischen Interessen der Besatzungsmacht', in Petzina and Euchner, *Wirtschaftspolitik im britischen Besatzungsgebiet 1945–1949*, pp. 41–64

Pirker, Theo, 'Die Jugend in der Struktur unserer Gesellschaft', in DGB, Abteilung Jugend (ed.), *Protokoll der Arbeitstagung der Gewerkschaftsjugend 25.–30.11.1951*, Düsseldorf, 1952, pp. 7–30

——, *Die blinde Macht. Die Gewerkschaftsbewegung in Westdeutschland*, vols 1 and 2, Munich, 1960

——, Braun, S. and Lutz, B., *Arbeiter, Management, Mitbestimmung, eine industriesoziologische Untersuchung der Struktur, der Organisation und des Verhaltens der Arbeiterbelegschaft in Werken der deutschen Eisen- und Stahlindustrie, für die das Mitbestimmungsgesetz gilt*, Stuttgart/Düsseldorf, 1955

Plato, Alexander von, 'Nachkriegssieger. Sozialdemokratische Betriebsräte im Ruhrgebiet – Eine lebensgeschichtliche Untersuchung', in Niethammer, *'Hinterher merkt man, daß es richtig war, daß es schiefgegangen ist'*, pp. 311–59

——, 'Fremde Heimat. Zur Integration von Flüchtlingen und Einheimischen in die Neue Zeit', in Lutz Niethammer and Alexander von Plato (eds), *'Wir kriegen jetzt andere Zeiten'. Auf der Suche nach der Erfahrung des Volkes in nachfaschistischen Ländern*, Berlin, 1985, pp. 172–219.

Plumpe, Werner, 'Auf dem Weg in die Marktwirtschaft: Organisierte Industrieinteressen, Wirtschaftsverwaltung und Besatzungsmacht in Nordrhein-Westfalen 1945–1947', in Brunn, *Nordrhein-Westfalen und seine Anfänge nach 1945/1946*, pp. 67–84

——, *'Vom Plan zum Markt.' Wirtschaftsverwaltung und Unternehmerverbände in der britischen Zone*, Düsseldorf, 1987

Popitz, H., Bahrdt, H. P., Jüres, E. A. and Kesting, H., *Das Gesellschaftsbild des Arbeiters*, Tübingen, 1961

Poth, Fritz, *Die Entwicklung der Löhne im Steinkohlenbergbau, in der eisenschaffenden Industrie und im Baugewerbe seit 1924*, Cologne, 1950

Pounds, N. J. G., *The Ruhr: A Study in Historical and Economic Geography*, London, 1952

Ranft, Norbert, *Vom Objekt zum Subjekt. Montanmitbestimmung, Sozialklima und Strukturwandel im Bergbau seit 1945*, Cologne, 1988

Reding, Josef, *Der Mensch im Revier*, Recklinghausen, 1967

Reich, Nathan, *Labour Relations in Republican Germany*, New York, 1938
Reichling, Gerhard, *Die Heimatvertriebenen im Spiegel der Statistik*, Berlin, 1958
Reiners, Leo, *Herne 1945–1950. Fünf Jahre Wiederaufbau*, Herne, 1950
Reulecke, Jürgen (ed.), *Arbeiterbewegung an Rhein und Ruhr. Beiträge zur Geschichte der Arbeiterbewegung in Rheinland-Westfalen*, Wuppertal, 1974
—— and Weber, Wolfhard (eds), *Fabrik Familie Feierabend. Beiträge zur Sozialgeschichte des Alltags im Industriezeitalter*, Wuppertal, 1978
Ritschl, Albert, 'Die Währungsreform von 1948 und der Wiederaufstieg der deutschen Wirtschaft', *VfZ*, vol. 33, 1985, pp. 136–65
Roden, Günter von, *Geschichte der Stadt Duisburg*, Duisburg, 1974
Roelen, Otto-Wilhelm, 'Die Bedeutung der Pestalozzidörfer für die Gewinnung eines bergbaulichen Nachwuchses', dissertation, Cologne University, 1956
Rohe, Karl, 'Vom alten Revier zum heutigen Ruhrgebiet. Die Entwicklung einer regionalen Politischen Gesellschaft im Spiegel der Wahlen', in Rohe and Kühr, *Politik und Gesellschaft im Ruhrgebiet*, pp. 21–73
——, *Vom Revier zum Ruhrgebiet. Wahlen, Parteien, politische Kultur*, Essen, 1986
——, 'Vom sozialdemokratischen Armenhaus zur Wagenburg der SPD. Politischer Strukturwandel in einer Industrieregion nach dem Zweiten Weltkrieg', *Geschichte und Gesellschaft*, vol. 13, 1987, pp. 508–34
—— and Kühr, Herbert (eds), *Politik und Gesellschaft im Ruhrgebiet. Beiträge zur regionalen Politik-Forschung*, Königstein, 1979
Rohlfing, Marga, *Lohn und Lebenshaltung*, Dortmund, 1947
Roseman, Mark, 'New Miners in the Ruhr: Rebuilding the Workforce in the Ruhr Mines, 1945–1958', PhD dissertation, Centre for the Study of Social History, Warwick University, 1987
——, 'The Uncontrolled Economy: Ruhr Coal Production 1945–8', in Turner, *Reconstruction in Post-war Germany*, pp. 93–124
——, 'The Organic Society and the "Massenmenschen": Integrating Young Labour in the Ruhr Mines, 1945–58', *German History*, vol. 8, no. 2, 1990, pp. 163–94
——, 'Political Allegiance and Social Change: The Case of Workers in the Ruhr', in John Gaffney and Eva Kolinsky (eds), *Political Culture in France and West Germany*, London, 1991
Rudolph, Fritz, 'Wie steht der Arbeiter zu Betrieb, Arbeit und Gewerkschaft?', *Neue Gesellschaft*, vol. 3, no. 6, 1956, pp. 411–41
Runge, Erika, *Bottroper Protokolle*, Frankfurt, 1968
Sänger, Heinz, 'Flüchtlinge und Vertriebene. Ein Beitrag zum Flüchtlingsproblem dargestellt am Beispiel der Stadt Witten an der Ruhr für die Zeit von 1945 bis 1955', dissertation, Mannheim University, 1971
Schädel, Gudrun, 'Die KPD in Nordrhein-Westfalen 1945–1956', dissertation, Bochum University, 1973

Bibliography

Schäfer, Hans Dieter, *Das gespaltene Bewußtsein. Über die Lebenswirklichkeit in Deutschland 1933–1945*, Munich, 1981

Scharf, Claus und Schröder, Hans-Jürgen (eds), *Die Deutschlandpolitik Grossbritanniens und die britische Zone 1945–1949*, Wiesbaden, 1979

Schelsky, Helmut, *Die skeptische Generation. Eine Soziologie der deutschen Jugend*, Düsseldorf/Cologne, 1963

——, *Auf der Suche nach Wirklichkeit*, Düsseldorf/Cologne, 1964

——, *Wandlungen der deutschen Familie in der Gegenwart*, 5th edn, Stuttgart, 1981

Schmidt, Eberhard, *Die verhinderte Neuordnung*, Frankfurt, 1970

Schmidt, Uwe and Fichter, T., *Der erzwungene Kapitalismus*, Berlin, 1971

Schmitz, Rudolf, 'Das Gedinge, seine Bedeutung und seine Wirkung auf die zwischenmenschlichen Beziehungen im Ruhrkohlenbergbau', dissertation, Münster University, 1952

Schrumpf, Emil, 'Gewerkschaftsbildung und -politik im Bergbau', dissertation, Münster University, 1958

Schulze, Rainer, Brelie-Lewin, Doris von der and Grebing, Helga (eds), *Flüchtlinge und Vertriebene in der westdeutschen Nachkriegsgeschichte. Bilanzierung der Forschung und Perspektiven für die künftige Forschungsarbeit*, Hildesheim, 1987

Schuster, D., *Die deutschen Gewerkschaften seit 1945*, 4th edn, Berlin, 1973

Schwarz, Hans-Peter, *Die Ära Adenauer: Gründerjahre der Republik 1949–1957*, Stuttgart, 1981

Seraphim, H. J. (ed.), *Siedlungen und Wohnungen von heute*, Münster, 1952

Siebert, Willy, 'Der Umschichtungsprozess der Belegschaften im westdeutschen Steinkohlenbergbau', dissertation, Münster University, 1953

Stahlberg, Gertrud, *Die Vertriebenen in Nordrhein-Westfalen*, Berlin, 1957

Steinberg, Heinz Günter, *Sozialräumliche Entwicklung und Gliederung des Ruhrgebiets*, Bad Godesberg, 1967

Steinbock-Fermor, Alexander, *Meine Erlebnisse als Bergarbeiter*, Stuttgart, 1928

Steininger, Rolf, 'England und die deutsche Gewerkschaftsbewegung 1945/1946', *Archiv für Sozialgeschichte*, vol. 18, 1978, pp. 41–118

——, 'Die Rhein–Ruhr Frage im Kontext britischer Deutschlandpolitik 1945–6', in Winkler, *Politische Weichenstellungen im Nachkriegsdeutschland 1945–1953*, pp. 111–66

——, 'Westdeutschland ein "Bollwerk gegen den Kommunismus"? Grossbritannien und die deutsche Frage im Frühjahr 1946', *Militärgeschichtliche Mitteilungen*, vol. 35, no. 2, 1985, pp. 163–207

Streit, Christian, *Keine Kameraden. Die Wehrmacht und die sowjetischen Kriegsgefangenen 1941–1945*, Stuttgart, 1978

Sturm, Monika and Hohmann, Hartmut, 'Der Bergarbeiterwohnungsbau im Ruhrgebiet nach 1945 unter dem Einfluß der wirtschaftlichen

Entwicklung des Steinkohlenbergbaus', Diplomarbeit, Bielefeld University, 1977

Teleaak, Heinrich, 'Das Nachwuchsproblem im Steinkohlenbergbau der Montan-Union', dissertation, Cologne University, 1954

Tenfelde, Klaus, *Sozialgeschichte der Bergarbeiterschaft an der Ruhr im 19.Jahrhundert*, 2nd edn, Bonn, 1981

Thies, Jochen, 'What is Going On in Germany? Britische Militärverwaltung in Deutschland 1945–1946', in Scharf and Schröder, *Die Deutschlandpolitik Großbritanniens und die britische Zone 1945–1949*, pp. 29–50

Tosstorff, Heinz, *Der Bergarbeiterwohnungsbau. Ein Kurz-Kommentar über die Gesetze zur Förderung des Bergarbeiterwohnungsbaus im Kohlenbergbau*, Essen, 1952

Treu, Hans-Eckbert, *Stabilität und Wandel in der organisatorischen Entwicklung der Industriegewerschaft Bergbau und Energie*, Frankfurt, 1979

Trischler, Helmuth, *Steiger im deutschen Bergbau. Zur Sozialgeschichte der technischen Angestellten 1815–1945*, Munich, 1988

Tschirbs, Rudolf, *Tarifpolitik im Ruhrbergbau 1918–1933*, Berlin/New York, 1986

Turner, Ian (ed.), *Reconstruction in Post-war Germany: British Occupation Policy and the Western Zones 1945–1955*, Oxford, 1989

——, '"Being beastly to the Germans?" British Policy on Direct Imports of German Goods from the British Zone of Occupation to the UK 1946–1948', *Journal of European Economic History*, forthcoming

Utermann, Kurt, *Freizeitprobleme bei der männlichen Jugend einer Zechengemeinde*, Cologne/Opladen, 1957

Vetter, H. O. (ed.), *Vom Sozialistengesetz zur Mitbestimmung. Zum 100. Geburtstag von Hans Böckler*, Cologne, 1975

Wald, Renate, *Industriearbeiter privat. Eine Studie über private Lebensformen und persönliche Interessen*, Stuttgart, 1966

Waldmann, Peter, 'Die Eingliederung der Vertriebenen in die westdeutsche Gesellschaft', in Becker et al., *Vorgeschichte der BRD*, pp. 163–92

Watt, Donald C., 'Hauptprobleme der britischen Deutschlandpolitik 1945–1949', in Scharf and Schröder, *Die Deutschlandpolitik Grossbritanniens und die britische Zone 1945–1949*, pp. 15–28

Wehling, Eberhard, 'Die Zusammenarbeit der Sozialpartner während des Bestehens der DKBL auf sozial- und wirtschaftspolitischem Gebiet', Staatsexamen, Herne, 1958

Wehrmann, Heinz-Helmut, *Hamborn, eine wirtschaftsgeographische Untersuchung*, Krefeld, 1960

Weisbrod, Bernd, 'Economic Power and Political Stability Reconsidered: Heavy Industry in Weimar Germany', *Social History*, vol. 4, no. 2, 1979, pp. 241–65

Werner, Wolfgang, *'Bleib Übrig'. Deutsche Arbeiter in der nationalsozialistischen Kriegswirtschaft*, Düsseldorf, 1983

Bibliography

Wiel, Paul, *Wirtschaftsgeschichte des Ruhrgebiets*, Essen, 1970

Wiesemann, Falk, 'Flüchtlingspolitik in Nordrhein-Westfalen', in Benz, *Die Vertreibung der Deutschen aus dem Osten*, pp. 173–82

—— and Kleinert, Uwe, 'Flüchtlinge und wirtschaftlicher Wiederaufbau in der britischen Besatzungszone', in Petzina and Euchner, *Wirtschaftspolitik im britischen Besatzungsgebiet 1945–1949*, pp. 297–326

Winkler, Heinrich August (ed.), *Politische Weichenstellungen in Nachkriegsdeutschland 1945–1953*, Göttingen, 1979

Wirth, Dieter, 'Die Familie in der Nachkriegszeit. Desorganisation oder Stabilisation', in Becker et al., *Vorgeschichte der BRD*, pp. 193–216

Wisotzky, Klaus, 'Der Ruhrbergbau am Vorabend des 2. Weltkrieges. Vorgeschichte, Entstehung und Auswirkung der "Verordnung zur Erhöhung der Förderleistung und des Leistungslohnes im Bergbau vom 2. März 1939"', *VfZ* vol. 30, no. 3, 1982, pp. 418–61

——, *Der Ruhrbergbau im Dritten Reich. Studien zur Sozialpolitik im Ruhrbergbau und zum sozialen Verhalten der Bergleute in den Jahren 1933 bis 1939*, Düsseldorf, 1983

Zahn, Erich, 'Der Wohnungsbau im Ruhrgebiet nach 1945', in H. Wanderleb (ed.), *Eigenheime für den Bergmann*, Bonn, 1954, pp. 14–16

Zimmermann, Michael, '"Ein schwer zu bearbeitendes Pflaster": der Bergarbeiterort Hochlarmark unter dem Nationalsozialismus', in Peukert and Reulecke, *Die Reihen fast geschlossen*, pp. 65–84

——, 'Ausbruchshoffnungen. Junge Bergleute in den dreißiger Jahren', in Niethammer, *"Die Jahre weiß man nicht, wo man die heute hinsetzen soll"*, pp. 97–132

——, '"Geh zu Hermann, der macht dat schon". Bergarbeiterinteressenvertretung im nördlichen Ruhrgebiet', in Niethammer, *"Die Jahre weiß man nicht, wo man die heute hinsetzen soll"*, pp. 277–310

——, '"Betriebsgemeinschaft" – der unterdrückte Konflikt. Aus den Protokollen des Vertrauensrats der Zeche "Friedrich der Große"', in Niethammer et al., *"Die Menschen machen ihre Geschichte nicht aus freien Stücken, aber sie machen sie selbst"*, pp. 171–4

——, *Schachtanlage und Zechenkolonie. Leben, Arbeit und Politik in einer Arbeitersiedlung 1880–1980*, Essen, 1987

Zwickhofer, Iris, 'Das Problem der Vertreibung in der Nachkriegszeit 1945–1950 unter besonderer Berücksichtigung der Integration Zwangsausgewiesener in Herne und Wanne-Eickel', Staatsexamensarbeit, Bochum University, 1981

Index

Aachen coalfield, 98
Abelshauser, Werner, 6, 7, 137
Abs, Herman, J., 142
absenteeism, 25
accidents
  see mine safety
Adamsen, Heiner, R., 8, 137
Adelheide youth camp, 229
Adenauer, Konrad, 43, 180, 297
Agatz, Willy, 76
age structure, 1
  see workforce
Alarm im Bergbau, 262–3, 265–6, 326
Alker, Hans, 308
Allied Control Authority, Berlin,
  53–4
Allies, 1, 8, 66, 297–8
  coal policy, 2, 23, 87, 280
  labour movement and, 13
apprentice hostels, 166, 171, 220–32,
  246–52
  design, 222–7
  see also churches
apprentices, 18, 166–90
  recruitment, 155, 167, 183, 185
  wages, 167, 186–7
apprenticeship
  political function, 177–9
  pre-war origins, 164–6
  productivity and, 168
  quality of training, 168–70, 185–6
  status and, 169–73
  union endorsement, 181–2
  workforce stability and, 174, 185–6
Arbeitsgemeinschaft katholische
  Heimstattbewegung, 229
Arbeitsgruppe Kohle
  see German coal working party
Arnhold, Carl, 164
Arnold, Karl, 297
Arnsberg, 31, 37, 111

Ausschuß zur Wahrung der
  Interessen der Jung- und
  Neubergleute, 303
Außenstelle Bergbau des
  Landesarbeitsamtes NRW
  (ABB), 171–3, 295

Baroth, Hans Diether, 170, 185, 261
Bate, Phillip, 99
Bavaria, policy towards Ruhr, 104,
  115–16, 120, 123
Bax, Karl, 174
Belgian mines, 318
Beratungsstelle für Arbeit, Siedlungs-
  und Wohnungswesen, 96
Bergämter, 83
Bergassessoren
  see management
Bergbau und Wirtschaft, 302, 305
Berghahn, Volker, 10
Bergmannssiedlungsgesetz, 206–8,
  207n43
Bergschule
  see Mining School
Berlin, 272–3
Bevan boys, 43
Bevin, Ernest, 2, 48, 101
Bipartite Board
  see Bipartite Control Office
Bipartite coal committee (COCOM),
  85
Bipartite Control Office (BICO), 84–5,
  117, 133–4
Bipartite Economic Control Group
  (BECG), 105, 108
  Standing Committee on Ruhr
    Miners' Housing, 112, 117, 119
  Working Party on Miners'
    Housing, 105, 108, 113
Bipartite Economic Panel, 102, 105
Bishop of Münster, 230

351

restoration thesis, 13, 16
Reusch strike, 307
Revierarbeitsgemeinschaft für die
  kulturelle Bergarbeitbetreuung
  (RAG), 236, 251
Ritchie, Colonel, 41
Robertson, Sir Brian, 52, 55, 60, 67,
  69, 85
Roelen, Otto-Wilhelm, 243
Rostow, W. W., 58
Ruhr Coal Control, 24
Ruhr Housing Office (RHO), 97, 99
Ruhr occupation, 1923, 35
Russian coal, 157

Schmidt, August, 75, 303–4
Schumacher Report, 134–5
Schuman Plan, 297, 324
SHAEF, 23
Shamrock mine, 215, 217
Siebenbürger Sachsen, 261, 275
Siedlungsverband Ruhrkohlenbezirk
  (SVR), 95, 103, 110, 142, 147
silicosis, 165
Social Democratic Party (SPD), 13,
  219, 284–6, 297, 303, 309
social market economy, 8
Social Ministry, NRW, 228, 233–4
social partnership, 298, 300–2, 310,
  324
socialisation of mining industry, 39,
  41, 76, 81, 85–6, 290
Sogemeier, Martin, 139
Sonderausschuß zur Behandlung von
  Fragen der Kohlenförderung, 133
southern Länder
  see US Zone
Soviet Union, 5, 56
Soviet Zone of Occupation, 68
Sozialamt of the Protestant church in
  Westphalia, 222, 227
Sozialforschungsstelle Dortmund
  (SoFoSt), 183, 185, 214, 257, 260,
  299, 307
Stadtteil Ayatollahs, 309
State Department, 53
status of mining, 165–6, 183–9, 302
Steffen, Heinz, 270
Steiger
  see pit deputies
Street, Sir Arthur, 52
Streuselkuchen in Ickern, 170
strikes, 14, 15, 74, 307
student revolt, 13

subcommittee on miners' housing (of
  Marshall Plan coal productivity
  committee), 204, 205, 209, 212
Suez crisis, 157
sunday shifts, 76
supervisory board, 15
surface workers, 78
Szymczak, M. S., 103

tax incentives, 6, 207
Taylorism, 164
trades unions, 59, 64
trainees, adult, 18, 82–3, 254–65,
  272–7
  behaviour at work, 283–4, 291–3,
    299–300
  conflicts with established
    workforce, 215–16, 281–2, 288–9
  deployment within mine, 42, 72,
    89, 260, 271
  social background, 256–7, 291
  unionisation, 283, 306–8
  see also training, wages
trainees, juvenile, 18
training, adult, 42, 267–72
  adult safety and, 42, 260, 271–2,
    288
training directors, 174, 268–70, 274,
  326
Training Within Industry (TWI), 267
transportation, 101, 109
Treu, Hans Eckbert, 302
Treuhandstelle für
  Bergmannswohnstätten, 193,
  196–7, 202, 213, 218
Triem, J., 302
Turner, Ian, 4, 56
Turner, Sir Mark, 62

UK/US Coal Control Group, 86, 88,
  92, 130, 133, 233, 235, 294
  creation, 85
Ullrich, Dr (DKBL later UVR), 150,
  270
United States
  approach towards Germany, 110,
    117–18, 122–3
  policy towards Ruhr coal, 54, 55,
    63
Unternehmensverband Ruhrbergbau
  (UVR), 155–7, 251
  housing committee, 212
upward mobility, 308
US coal, 157

Index